TiM

Rethinking ADHD
From Brain to Culture

Edited by

Sami Timimi
and
Jonathan Leo

First published 2009 by
PALGRAVE MACMILLAN

Palgrave Macmillan in the UK is an imprint of Macmillan Publishers Limited,
registered in England, company number 785998, of 4 Crinan Street,
London N1.

Palgrave Macmillan in the US is a division of St Martin's Press LLC,
175 Fifth Avenue, New York, NY 10010.

Palgrave Macmillan is the global academic imprint of the above companies
and has companies and representatives throughout the world.

Palgrave® and Macmillan® are registered trademarks in the United States,
the United Kingdom, Europe and other countries.

ISBN-13: 978–0–230–50712–8
ISBN-10: 0–230–50712–3

This book is printed on paper suitable for recycling and made from fully
managed and sustained forest sources. Logging, pulping and manufacturing
processes are expected to conform to the environmental regulations of the
country of origin.

A catalogue record for this book is available from the British Library.

A catalog record for this book is available from the Library of Congress.

Contents

v

List of Figures and Tables

Figures

Tables

Notes on the Contributors

Louba Benassaya works as a Graduate Student Researcher at the UCLA Center for Healthier Children, Families, and Communities. Her research interests include maternal and child health, mental health, and racial and socioeconomic disparities in health. As an undergraduate at UCLA, she won the Sociology department's Leo Kuper award for her honours thesis on media representations of youth violence.

David Cohen is a researcher and Professor of Social Work at Florida International University, Miami, USA. He is currently designing a publicly funded, evidence-based critical curriculum on psychotropic drugs for non-medical professionals in child welfare. He has authored or co-authored more than 100 publications, and received the Elliot Freidson Award for Outstanding Publication in Medical Sociology from the American Sociological Association in 2003. Most recently, with Gwynedd Lloyd and Joan Stead, he edited *Critical New Perspectives on ADHD* (winner of the 2006 NASEN/Times Educational Supplement Prize for best academic book). As a licensed clinical social worker, David Cohen works with adults and children and is frequently consulted by individuals and families who wish to wean themselves off psychiatric drugs.

Lydia Furman is Associate Professor of Paediatrics at Case Western Reserve University School of Medicine and an attending physician at Rainbow Babies and Children's Hospital (RBC), Cleveland, OH. In the RBC Paediatric Practice she teaches paediatric resident physicians and provides direct care to an inner-city urban population. Her other interests include breastfeeding of term and preterm infants. Her interest in ADHD stems from the work of her father, Robert A. Furman, MD, who was a pioneer in evaluation of the ADHD literature and of the influence pharmaceutical manufacturers exert on diagnosis and treatment in biological psychiatry, including ADHD. Several of his contributions are cited in the references.

Nicky Hart is Professor of Sociology at the University of California Los Angeles where she teaches sociological theory and the sociology of health and medicine. She served as Research Fellow to the UK Government Inequalities in Health Working Group and drafted the conceptual and theoretical chapters of the *Black Report* (1980). She has published books and articles on divorce, health inequalities, gender and class politics, procreative health in historical demography, the sociology of health and medicine, ADHD and the sociology of food and eating. She has just finished a comparative study of *Women's Health in the Welfare Regimes of Western Europe.*

Thom Hartmann is live daily from noon to 3pm Eastern Time in New York, Los Angeles, San Francisco, Detroit, Seattle, Denver, Portland, Phoenix, Santa Fe, San Diego, Pittsburgh, Memphis, Grand Rapids, and on over fifty other stations nationwide including Chicago, Washington DC, Santa Barbara, Minneapolis, and on XM and Sirius Satellite radio. He is a four-time Project Censored-award-winning, *New York Times* best-selling author. Thom is the author of eight books on ADHD, and the creator of the 'Hunter in a Farmer's World' metaphor and of the Shadow Coaching programme for helping people whose lives are touched by ADHD achieve success.

Shannon Hughes received her MSW in Policy and Administration from Florida State University. She is currently a doctoral student in the School of Social Welfare at Florida International University. Her work focuses on examining outcomes in psychotropic drug research and practice.

Grace Jackson is a board-certified psychiatrist who earned her Medical Degree from the University of Colorado Health Sciences Center in 1996, then completed her internship and residency in the US Navy. A clinician, lecturer, and forensic consultant, Dr Jackson has served as an expert witness for the Law Project for Psychiatric Rights – a non-profit organization based in Anchorage, Alaska. Her first book *Rethinking Psychiatric Drugs: A Guide for Informed Consent* underscores the urgent need to protect the rights of consumers and clinicians who wish to participate in drug-free care.

David Jacobs is part of a group private practice in La Jolla, California, that specializes in outpatient addiction treatment (Pyrysys Psychology Group, Inc.). For many years, as a clinician and scholar, he has critically scrutinized and written about biopsychiatry and psychopharmacotherapy. No one can object to the identification of genuine somatic diseases or to drug treatment where the benefits and costs are disinterestedly investigated and candidly disclosed. He believes and writes about how this is far from the case in contemporary American psychiatry.

Jay Joseph is a licensed psychologist practising in the San Francisco Bay Area. Since 1998, he has published many articles in peer-reviewed journals focusing on genetic theories in psychiatry and psychology. He is an assessing editor of the *Journal of Mind and Behavior*. His first book, *The Gene Illusion: Genetic Research in Psychiatry and Psychology under the Microscope*, was published in 2003 in the United Kingdom by PCCS Books, followed by a 2004 North American edition published by Algora. His latest book, published in 2006 by Algora, is entitled *The Missing Gene: Psychiatry, Heredity, and the Fruitless Search for Genes*. For more information on his books and articles, please see <www.jayjoseph.net>.

Jon Jureidini, Child Psychiatrist, is Head of the Department of Psychological Medicine, Women's and Children's Hospital, Adelaide, where he is also on the patient care ethics committee. He is Senior Research Fellow, Department of Philosophy, Flinders University and is Clinical Associate Professor in the disciplines of Psychiatry and Paediatrics, University of Adelaide. He is the Chair of Healthy Skepticism (<www.healthyskepticism. org>). He has many publications in which he has addressed issues as diverse as immigration detention, parenting, prescribing for children, narrative, dissociation and consciousness, placebo analgesia, child abuse, and rehabilitation of adolescents with unexplained symptoms.

Brian Kean has over 30 years' experience in teaching and has held a variety of teaching and consultancy positions in special education and is qualified to practice in all areas of special education in Australia. He is currently Senior Lecturer at Southern Cross University. Brian is a member of the Board of Directors of the International Center for the Study of Psychiatry and Psychology (ICSPP) and is also a member of the Editorial and Advisory Committee for the ICSPP journal. Brian has recently completed a doctoral study focusing on the social impact resulting from the use of the ADHD diagnosis in Australia and the United States.

xiiNOTES ON THE CONTRIBUTORS

Jeffrey Lacasse is Assistant Professor in the Department of Social Work at Arizona State University, where he teaches courses in statistics, social policy, and group treatment to undergraduates. His research agenda focuses on the application of critical thinking within psychiatric social work. He has co-authored articles on clinical practice with children, direct-to-consumer advertising of antidepressants, and mental health education in social work. He has received multiple awards for both teaching and research.

Jonathan Leo is Associate Professor of Neuroanatomy at Lincoln Memorial University, USA. He has published numerous articles about the biological theories of mental health, covering topics such as the genetic basis of schizophrenia, the serotonin theory of depression, the paediatric trials of selective serotonin reuptake inhibitors, and ADHD. His articles have been published in *Society*, *Skeptic*, and the *Journal of Mind and Behavior*. He is the past Editor-in-Chief of *Ethical Human Psychology and Psychiatry*. His most recent article, co-authored with Jeff Lacasse, was about the disconnect between the scientific literature and the popular advertisements regarding serotonin and depression. The paper was published in the *Public Library of Science (PLoS)* and was subsequently covered by numerous media outlets including *WebMD*, *Nature*, *Forbes*, *The Scientist*, and the *Wall Street Journal*.

Begum Maitra is a Consultant Child and Adolescent Psychiatrist and Jungian analyst. Dr Maitra's early training in India triggered an abiding interest in the role of culture in mental health. This has grown and developed over the 20 years that she has worked in multicultural inner London, to influence her work on assessing risks to children, as well as her research and writing. She co-edited *Critical Voices in Child and Adolescent Mental Health* (2006) with Dr Sami Timimi.

Chris Mercogliano has been a teacher at the Albany Free School for 35 years and an administrator for the past 20. He is the author or co-author of six books and lives with his wife in downtown Albany, NY. His forthcoming book is *In Defense of Childhood: Protecting Kids' Inner Wildness* (Beacon Press).

Craig Newnes is a dad, gardener and Director of Psychological Therapies for Shropshire County PCT in the UK. He completed his clinical psychology training in 1981 and later trained at the Institute of Group Analysis and with the Boston Psychoanalytic Institute. He is editor of the *Journal of Critical Psychology, Counselling and Psychotherapy* and commissioning editor for the Critical Division of PCCS Books. His latest book is *Making and Breaking Children's Lives*. Until 2006 he was editor of *Clinical Psychology Forum*, the house journal of the British Psychological Society's Division of Clinical Psychology and Past-Chair of the BPS Psychotherapy Section.

Basant K. Puri is a specialist in imaging and psychiatry at Hammersmith Hospital, London, and is head of the Lipid Neuroscience Group at the Imaging Sciences Department, Imperial College London, and the MRC Clinical Sciences Centre. He has played a key pioneering role in the therapeutic use of long-chain polyunsaturated fatty acids in ADHD. He has published numerous articles and many books, including *Attention Deficit Hyperactivity Disorder: A Natural Way to Treat ADHD* published in 2005.

Simon Sobo is in private practice in Northwestern Connecticut. He has been published in the *Yale Review*, the *Psychoanalytic Study of the Child*, *Psychiatric Times*, as well as numerous self-published internet articles, including the original version of this article. He succeeded Scott Peck MD as Chief of Psychiatry at New Milford Hospital. His first book *The Fear of Death* was published in 1999. *After Lisa*, his just-completed novel based on a true story, depicts a horrifying scourge that has descended on patient care in Health Maintenance Organizations (HMOs) in America.

Sami Timimi is Consultant Child and Adolescent Psychiatrist in the National Health Service in Lincolnshire and a visiting professor at Lincoln University in the UK. He writes from a critical psychiatry perspective on topics relating to child and adolescent mental health and has published articles on many topics including eating disorders, psychotherapy, behavioural disorders and cross-cultural psychiatry. He has authored three books: *Pathological Child Psychiatry and the Medicalization of Childhood*, published in 2002; *Naughty Boys: Anti-Social Behaviour, ADHD and the Role of Culture*, published in 2005; and *Mis-Understanding ADHD: The Complete Guide for Parents to Alternatives to Drugs*, published in 2007, and he has co-edited (with Begum Maitra) *Critical Voices in Child and Adolescent Mental Health*, published in 2006, and (with Carl Cohen) *Liberatory Psychiatry: Philosophy, Politics and Mental Health*, published in 2008.

Acknowledgements

Jonathan Leo would like to thank several colleagues with whom he has worked over the years, including David Cohen, Jeffrey Lacasse, Joanna Moncrieff, Sami Timimi, and Jay Joseph – they have all been inspirational. It is a pleasure to work with such gifted thinkers. Like most teachers, he owes a debt of gratitude to those students who ask the difficult questions. He would especially like to thank his children, Phoebe, Noah, and Ingrid, for their inspiration and patience. Most importantly, his biggest thanks go to his fantastic and amazing wife Susan for her guidance, advice and friendship – and for listening to him go on and on about the latest revelations in the press.

Sami Timimi would like to thank his wonderful wife, Kitty, and three children, Michelle, Lewis and Zoe, for their love, patience, support, and for teaching him so much. Thanks to all the rest of his family and friends who 'have been there' when he has gone through difficult times. Thanks to all the colleagues with whom he corresponds and carries out academic endeavours who have helped him learn so much, in particular (and in no particular order) everyone in the critical psychiatry network, Begum Maitra, Jonathan Leo, Carl Cohen, David Cohen, Barry Duncan, Brad Lewis, Kenneth Thompson, Ann Miller, Brian McCabe, Neil Gardner, Joanna Moncrieff, Phil Thomas, Pat Bracken, Duncan Double, Eia Asen, Bob Johnston, Jacky Scott-Coombes, Katy Brown, and Mandy Brown.

It has been our distinct pleasure to meet and in many cases collaborate with professionals who have taken a more critical view of much of the current literature on attention-deficit hyperactivity disorder (ADHD). It is an even greater pleasure to have the opportunity to provide a voice for their critiques. We sincerely thank all of the chapter authors for their time and efforts.

Introduction

Sami Timimi and Jonathan Leo

Something strange has been happening to children in many Western societies in the past couple of decades. The diagnosis of attention deficit hyperactivity disorder (ADHD) has reached epidemic proportions, particularly amongst boys in North America. The diagnosis is usually made by a child psychiatrist or paediatrician with advocates of the diagnosis claiming that children who present with what the diagnoser considers to be overactivity, poor concentration and impulsivity are suffering from a medical condition which needs treatment with medication, mainly in the form of stimulants such as Ritalin™, whose chemical properties are similar to the street drugs speed and cocaine. ADHD has become firmly established in many local cultures, particularly in North America, Australasia, and Northern Europe, with economically and politically powerful groups (such as drug companies, doctors, psychologists and teachers) having had a major, but often unacknowledged impact on local communities' conceptions about the nature of childhood. A new category of childhood has emerged – that of the ADHD child.

A brief history of ADHD

Overactivity, poor concentration and impulsivity in children were first conceptualized as medical phenomena in the early years of the last century. The first recorded medical interest in children with poor attention and hyperactivity dates back to when a paediatrician, Frederick Still, described a group of children who showed what he felt was an abnormal incapacity for sustained attention, restlessness and fidgetiness, and went on to argue that these children had deficiencies in volitional inhibition, but he offered no treatment other than good discipline (Still, 1902).

1

Hyperactivity and poor attention in children then came to be viewed as linked when the diagnosis of minimal brain damage (MBD) was coined. The idea of MBD had originally gained favour following epidemics of encephalitis in the first decades of the twentieth century. Post-encephalitic children often presented with restlessness, personality changes and learning difficulties. Then, in the 1930s, came a chance discovery that psycho-stimulant medication could reduce the restlessness, hyperactivity and behavioural problems that some of these children presented with (Bradley, 1937). Bradley believed that this calming effect he observed was likely to apply to anyone who took low-dose stimulants, not just the hyperactive kids he was treating.

During the next few decades there were few doctors who showed much interest in this or saw such childhood behaviours as areas of legitimate concern for medicine. A few speculated that children who presented as hyperactive might have organic lesions in the brain that were the cause of their hyperactivity. Strauss's writing in the 1940s (e.g. Strauss and Lehtinen, 1947) is one such example. His suggestion was that hyperactivity, in the absence of a family history of sub-normality, should be considered as sufficient evidence for a diagnosis of brain damage, believing that the damage was too minimal to be easily found.

By the 1960s, however, the term MBD was losing favour as evidence for underlying organic lesions in children who displayed poor attention and overactivity was not being found. Instead, with the growing interest in behaviourally defined syndromes, the goal posts were about to be moved and a behaviourally defined syndrome articulated. Despite the abandonment of the minimal brain damage hypothesis, the assumption that this syndrome does indeed have a specific and discoverable physical cause, related to some sort of brain dysfunction, survived in the new definition. Yet, studies have shown that demonstrable minimal brain damage due to a variety of causes predisposes a child to the development of a wide range of psychiatric diagnoses as opposed to a particular type, such as ADHD (e.g. Schmidt *et al.*, 1987). Rutter (1982) concluded that the available evidence shows that overactivity is not a sign of brain damage and that brain damage does not usually lead to overactivity. We are not aware of any subsequent data that contradicts this conclusion.

In the mid 1960s the North American-based Diagnostic Statistical Manual (DSM), second edition (DSM-II) coined the label 'Hyperkinetic reaction of childhood', to replace the diagnosis of MBD

(American Psychiatric Association, 1966). Over the following three decades this new behaviourally defined condition rose from a matter of peripheral interest in child psychiatric practice and research in North America to a place of central prominence.

DSM-II was replaced in the early 1980s by the third edition (DSM-III, American Psychiatric Association, 1980). The disorder was now termed Attention Deficit Disorder (ADD). This could be diagnosed with or without hyperactivity and was defined using three dimensions (three separate lists of symptoms), one for attention deficits, one for impulsivity and one for hyperactivity. The three-dimensional approach was abandoned in the late 1980s when DSM-III was revised (and became DSM-III-R, American Psychiatric Association, 1987), in favour of combining all the symptoms into one list (one dimension). The new term for the disorder was Attention Deficit Hyperactivity Disorder (ADHD), with attention, hyperactivity and impulsiveness now assumed to be part of one disorder with no distinctions. When the fourth edition of DSM (DSM-IV, American Psychiatric Association, 1994), reconsidered the diagnosis the criteria were again changed, this time in favour of a two-dimensional model with attention deficit being one sub-category and hyperactivity-impulsivity the other. According to DSM-IV, the diagnosis 'ADHD not otherwise specified' should be made if there are prominent symptoms of inattention or hyperactivity-impulsivity that do not meet the full ADHD criteria. If we were to interpret this concretely (as doctors often do) it suggests that, as of DSM-IV, nearly all children (particularly boys) at some time in their lives could meet one of the definitions and warrant a diagnosis of ADHD.

The modern champion of the ADHD diagnosis and one of the strongest advocates for a brain dysfunction model and the use of drugs to 'treat' these children is Professor Russell Barkley. Barkley's (1981) book *Hyperactive Children: A Handbook for Diagnosis and Treatment* received widespread attention from both the public and professional communities. From there Barkley's campaign quickly caught the interest of the pharmaceutical industry and soon an avalanche of research to find more support for the disease theory and drug treatment ensued. This new partnership between the commercial interests of the pharmaceutical industry, the personal interests of individual researchers, and the professional interests of medical sub-specialities such as child psychiatry and paediatrics, has subsequently shaped the academic debate and clinical practice, leading it, in our opinion, away from scientific accuracy and towards an ideological position that has led the mass use of stimulants on children (primarily boys) to control their behaviour and improve their school grades.

ADHD today

The formal technical definition for ADHD can be found in the *The Diagnostic Statistical Manual (DSM)* now in its 4th edition (American Psychiatric Association, 1994). This defines ADHD as:

(A) Either (1) or (2):
(1) Six (or more) of the following symptoms of *inattention* have persisted for at least six months to a degree that is maladaptive and inconsistent with developmental level:

Inattention
- often fails to give close attention to details or makes careless mistakes in schoolwork, work, or other activities
- often has difficulty sustaining attention in tasks or play activities
- often does not seem to listen when spoken to directly
- often does not follow through on instructions and fails to finish schoolwork, chores, or duties in the workplace (not due to oppositional behaviour or failure to understand instructions)
- often has difficulty organizing tasks and activities
- often avoids, dislikes, or is reluctant to engage in tasks that require sustained mental effort (such as schoolwork or homework)
- often loses things necessary for tasks or activities (e.g., toys, school assignments, pencils, books, or tools)
- is often easily distracted by extraneous stimuli
- is often forgetful in daily activities.

(2) Six (or more) of the following symptoms of *hyperactivity-impulsivity* have persisted for at least six months to a degree that is maladaptive and inconsistent with developmental level:

Hyperactivity
- often fidgets with hands or feet or squirms in seat
- often leaves seat in classroom or in other situations in which remaining seated is expected
- often runs about or climbs excessively in situations in which it is inappropriate (in adolescents or adults, may be limited to subjective feelings of restlessness)

- often has difficulty playing or engaging in leisure activities quietly
- is often 'on the go' or often acts as if 'driven by a motor'
- often talks excessively.

Impulsivity
- often blurts out answers before questions have been completed
- often has difficulty awaiting turn
- often interrupts or intrudes on others (e.g., butts into conversations or games).

(B) Some hyperactive-impulsive or inattentive symptoms that caused impairment were present before age 7 years.

(C) Some impairment from the symptoms is present in two or more settings (e.g., at school [or work] and at home).

(D) There must be clear evidence of clinically significant impairment in social, academic, or occupational functioning.

(E) The symptoms do not occur exclusively during the course of a pervasive developmental disorder, schizophrenia, or other psychotic disorder and are not better accounted for by another mental disorder (e.g., mood disorder, anxiety disorder, dissociative disorder, or personality disorder).

Those with a critical eye would have spotted that words such as 'often', 'seems', 'difficulties', 'reluctant', 'easily', 'quietly', and 'excessively' that are used to 'define' ADHD symptoms are hard to define. For example the word 'often' appears in every one of the above 'symptoms', but what does it mean? Does it mean that the child does those behaviours at least once a day or at least once a minute?

These lists of behaviours that are used to define ADHD appear in questionnaires that are then usually given to parents and teachers. These questionnaires are the closest we get to having a 'test' for ADHD. These questionnaires can only rate a particular adult's perception of a particular child at a particular moment in time and in a particular setting. In other words they are measures of the *subjective* perception of the adult filling in the rating scale. What they cannot be is an *objective* factual piece of 'hard data' that measures something intrinsic to the child.

Hyperactivity, impulsivity and poor concentration are behaviours that occur on a continuum. All children, particularly boys, will present with such behaviour in some settings at some point. They are not behaviours that would be interpreted as abnormal whenever they occur. Without any medical tests to establish which individual has a physical problem causing these behaviour problems, defining the cut-off between normal and ADHD is arrived at by an arbitrary decision. Those who have argued that ADHD does not exist as a real disorder often start by pointing this out. Because of this uncertainty about definition it is hardly surprising that epidemiological studies have produced very different prevalence rates for ADHD ranging from about 0.5 per cent of school-age children to 26 per cent of school-age children (see Timimi, 2006).

Although this obvious problem with definition confronts you before you even start examining the scientific literature, it has not stopped, perhaps even encouraged (due to the criteria being so open to interpretive variation), increasing popularity of the diagnosis with a concurrent increase in the use of stimulants in the young. National consumption of Ritalin™ in the United States more than doubled between 1981 and 1992. Prescriptions of Ritalin™ have continued to increase in the 1990s, with over 11 million prescriptions of Ritalin™ written in 1996 in the United States. The amount of psychiatric medication prescribed to children in the United States increased nearly three-fold between 1987 and 1996, with over 6 per cent of boys between the ages of 6 and 14 taking stimulants by 1996. One study in Virginia in 1999 found that in two school districts, 17 per cent of white boys at primary school were diagnosed with ADHD and taking stimulants. There has also been a large increase in prescriptions of stimulants to preschoolers (see Timimi, 2005). In the UK prescriptions for stimulants have increased from about 6,000 in 1994 to over 450,000 by 2004, a staggering 7,000+ per cent rise in one decade (Department of Health, 2005).

Possible reasons for this dramatic change in medical practice in such a short space of time are explored further in this book. However, an important contribution to this trend comes from the way ADHD is currently portrayed in mainstream academic and other public institutions. A good example comes from the ADHD advocacy group – Children and Adults with Attention Deficit Hyperactivity Disorder (CHADD) – a large American-based 'parent support group'. CHADD engages in lobbying and claims to provide science-based, evidence-based information about ADHD to parents and the public. Critics point out that CHADD's basic function appears to have become that of promoting stimulant medications manufactured by its corporate donors. For example, pharmaceutical companies donated a total of $674,000 in the fiscal year 2002–2003 (Hearn, 2004). CHADD's website has this to say about ADHD:

Attention-deficit/hyperactivity disorder (AD/HD) is a condition affecting children and adults that is characterized by problems with attention, impulsivity, and overactivity. It affects between 3 and 7 percent of schoolage children, and between 2 and 4 percent of adults... The body of scientific literature documenting the reality of this condition is immense. (see <http://www.help4adhd.org/en/about/what>)

And:

Although precise causes have not yet been identified, there is little question that heredity makes the largest contribution to the expression of the disorder in the population.
In instances where heredity does not seem to be a factor, difficulties during pregnancy, prenatal exposure to alcohol and tobacco, premature delivery, significantly low birth weight, excessively high body lead levels, and postnatal injury to the prefrontal regions of the brain have all been found to contribute to the risk for AD/HD to varying degrees.
Research does not support the popularly held views that AD/HD arises from excessive sugar intake, food additives, excessive viewing of television, poor child management by parents, or social and environmental factors such as poverty or family chaos (see http://www.help4adhd.org/en/about/causes).

Those views are concordant with a vocal section of the medical community who appear to have appointed themselves as representative of 'mainstream' thinking. A good example of their beliefs and the style with which they prounounce their essentially ideological stance can be found in the article 'International consensus statement on ADHD' (Barkley *et al.*, 2002):

Numerous studies of twins demonstrate that family environment makes no significant separate contribution to these traits. This evidence, coupled with countless studies on the harm posed by the disorder and hundreds of studies on the effectiveness of medication, buttresses the need in many, though by no means all, cases for management of the disorder with multiple therapies…To publish stories that ADHD is a fictitious disorder or merely a conflict between today's Huckleberry Finns and their caregivers is tantamount to declaring the earth flat, the laws of gravity debatable, and the periodic table in chemistry a fraud. ADHD should be depicted in the media as realistically and accurately as it is depicted in science – as a valid disorder having varied and substantial adverse impact on those who may suffer from it through no fault of their own or their parents and teachers. (Barkley *et al.*, 2002; 89–90)

More recently evidence is emerging that the diagnosis of ADHD has opened the door to stimulants being used for an age-old indication – that of perceived performance enhancement. For instance, 'Results of a survey of physicians suggest that parents often request a "behavioral drug," such as Ritalin™, with the goal of enhancing their child's academic performance rather than treating an illness' (Gale, 2006). Despite this headline's apparent surprise at this practice, the prescribing of stimulants to improve academic performance is fully sanctioned by a leading ADHD researcher. According to Joseph Biederman, 'If a child is brilliant but is doing OK in school, that child may need treatment, which would result in performing brilliantly in school' (Gale, 2006).

A case study in the journal *Pediatrics* provides an interesting example of the forces at work in the diagnosis of an individual child with ADHD in the current academic and clinical climate. In 1999, the editors elicited commentaries from several prominent physicians about the case of a teenage boy who had been taking Ritalin™ for several years. The editors saw the boy's scenario as an interesting case, worthy of commentary from a group of prominent child psychiatrists. Ironically they unintentionally provided a much more interesting case study. From a sociological point of view the subject of the case was not the boy, but, instead, was the doctors and the editors. The case provides an excellent example of: (1) how a major determination in the diagnosis of ADHD is adult satisfaction, (2) how the medical community fully supports the use of stimulant medication as a performance-enhancing drug, (3) how the same mindset that approves of using one psychotropic drug easily leads to the use of multiple medications, and (4) how the mainstream medical journals have given little attention to the ethical implications of controlling and altering children to meet the demands of our contemporary educational/cultural system:

The 15-year-old boy announced to his parents and his paediatrician that he wanted to stop taking his medication: 'I don't need it...I'm fine...I don't see why I should take it.' He purposefully did not take the medication for a few weeks and he said he could not tell the difference...However, his parents observed that his test results, when off the medication, were below his standard scores...They also noted that he was more distractible and less attentive when doing his homework during that time. (Cohen *et al.*, 2002)

As stated by the physicians, the most important variable in determining whether this boy should keep taking his medication was the parental satisfaction with the medication, and the subsequent commentaries all focused on how to persuade the boy to continue taking his medication. The boy's wishes were not something to be listened to, but rather something to be managed. One of the commentators even suggested that the boy's reluctance to keep taking his Ritalin™ suggested this was a sign that he needed another medication. Thus the boy, who wants come off his one medication, would instead get two. None of the commentators in the *Pediatrics* article contemplated that the boy's wishes might be legitimate, but more importantly, as a sign of how one-sided the issue has become, the editors did not give space to a single commentator who questioned the ethics of giving a medication to improve grades.

What most of the current ADHD 'experts' are reluctant to acknowledge to the general public is that, no matter what area of their research one chooses, whether it is genetics, neuroimaging, or chemical imbalances, the more studies they publish, the further away the goal of finding a biological marker to help with diagnosing children with ADHD seems to become. To account for an increasing list of disparate results, their answer has been to develop ever more complicated theories about the biological basis of ADHD, but these theories can obscure only for so long a simpler possibility – that there may be no biological marker for ADHD.

This book therefore is an attempt at providing an antidote to the one-sided mainstream literature referred to above. In the past couple of decades an increasing number of authors have written about ADHD from a more critical perspective. These critiques have ranged from questioning the existence of the disorder and the way it is currently conceptualized in mainstream medicine to the safety and efficacy of popular drug treatment regimes for ADHD. Each of these critical authors has focused on their own particular area of interest be this culture, genetics, the influence of drug company marketing, the effects of medication, particular treatment regimes, and so on. This book brings something new and of great importance for the critical literature on ADHD. In this book we bring together a variety of critical perspectives, with each contribution dealing with a particular issue from culture to genetics and from drug companies to nutrition. The contributing authors are well known internationally and include senior and experienced clinicians, academics, and best-selling authors. Although many of the chapter themes overlap, we have divided the book into four sections to highlight the differing focus of different contributions.

Part One: ADHD and the Medical Model

In Chapter 1, Lydia Furman summarizes all the problems with efforts to pinpoint a biological deficit in children diagnosed with ADHD. The research, whether it is anatomical imaging, functional imaging, genetics, or neuropsychological research, reveals that there is no clear evidence for a discrete disease. As Furman documents, the current discourse coming from professional organizations overstates the evidence base for ADHD. In spite of this lack of evidence, the convergence of societal and financial pressures has given rise to the ADHD industry.

In Chapter 2, Jay Joseph challenges long-held beliefs about the role of genetics in a DSM-IV condition. For anyone who has been sceptical about the supposed genetic basis of ADHD or the oft-heard promises that discoveries of ADHD genes are right around the corner, Joseph's chapter is a must read. According to the genetic researchers, the hunt for ADHD genes is justified because of the twin and adoption studies but, as Joseph shows, these studies are fundamentally flawed and a careful examination of the twin and adoption studies shows why the search for genes has been unsuccessful. In 2000, Joseph made the bald statement that a gene or genes for ADHD will not be discovered because they do not exist. Seven years later he has yet to be proven wrong.

In Chapter 3, Jonathan Leo and David Cohen critically appraise neuroimaging studies in ADHD. Carefully analysing the published results from ADHD neuroimaging that are frequently used to support the notion cerebral pathology underlies the ADHD, they note that the variable of prior medication exposure must be carefully considered in studies used to support this claim. Their analysis reveals, however, that investigators have been prone to treat the variable of prior psychotropic drug use with less objectivity than its importance requires and have thus failed to show a consistent and distinct difference between children diagnosed with ADHD and controls. As a result an ADHD neuroimaging 'paradox' is emerging: as brain imaging technology becomes more sophisticated, as more imaging studies are published and more regions of the brain added to an ever-expanding list of potential problem areas with little reproducibility between studies, and as theories of ADHD become more and more speculative, then the likelihood of using imaging as a practical diagnostic tool becomes smaller and smaller. While some would say that this is a sign that researchers are becoming more sophisticated, the other possibility is that they simply do not want to acknowledge the obvious – that there is no biological marker in the brain for ADHD.

Part Two: ADHD and Culture

In Chapter 4, Sami Timimi sets out to explore the question: 'Why has there been a dramatic increase in diagnosis of ADHD and prescription of stimulant medication for this in the past few decades in most Western countries?' Shedding light on this question is crucial given the absence of good evidence to support the contention that ADHD is a physical condition. Timimi first addresses the question of what environmental factors may have resulted in a real increase in ADHD-type behaviours in children and then discusses the contribution of our changing understanding of childhood, child rearing and education and thus the changes in the way we think about, classify, and deal with children's behaviour. Finally he discusses the related question of why these dynamics of medicalization are occurring in the way that they are, at this point in time.

In Chapter 5, Craig Newnes critiques the role his profession has played in supporting the medical model discourse of ADHD. He notes that the profession of clinical psychology has become adept at jumping on bandwagons of a variety of practices as they become fashionable and develop potential for paying salaries. From psychometric assessment and psychotherapy to cognitive therapy and consultancy, the profession has embraced different practices while claiming a scientific basis for its new positions of power. He cautions that the enthusiasm with which clinical psychology has seen a potential role in the ADHD explosion gives cause for concern that, as a scientific discipline, clinical psychology has 'gone off the rails', but notes that 'islands' of constructive criticism and alternative conceptualizations still have solid support.

In Chapter 6 Brian Kean provides an overview of the history of ADHD in the United States, and an in-depth examination of its emergence in Australia, which was the first country outside of North America to make significant use of the diagnosis and subsequent drug treatment. As Kean points out, in the early 1990s the use of stimulant treatment in Australia was practically unheard of, but by 2003 there were reports of 7.5 per cent of 6–17-year-olds in Australia being diagnosed with ADHD. Kean looks at the forces and organizations responsible for this rise in ADHD diagnosis and medication.

In Chapter 7 Sami Timimi and Begum Maitra demonstrate the global to and fro movement of ideas about childhood behaviours, whether or not these are considered problematic, by whom, how responsibility is attributed, and the relationships between public and professional systems of attribution. They suggest that 'culture' is central to these systems of exchange. These global movements of people and ideas offer an opportunity to reconsider the basic premises of our professional beliefs about children and the construct of ADHD. To do this they examine some of the macro-dynamics of globalization, its relevance to psychiatry more generally, and then ADHD specifically. They argue that such an approach to the problematic concept of ADHD can help produce a greater diversity in our understanding and hopefully result in a more sophisticated approach to the way we deal with what is essentially a loose collection of qualitatively normal behaviours found in most children at some time in their lives.

In Chapter 8, Nick Hart and Louba Benassaya examine the different discourses of ADHD in Britain and the United States. ADHD research in the United States focuses on 'biology' and is confined to medical aspects. In contrast to the United States, in Britain there are much more data available to examine the ADHD phenomenon in a framework of social epidemiology. Instead of just biological explanations, these data show that the diagnosis of ADHD is dependent on environmental forces. Factors such as social class, health inequality, stressful life events, race, and parents' education all play a role in who gets diagnosed and is treated with medication. Unfortunately, there is little chance of doing this type of analysis in America as the overwhelming emphasis, coming from institutions such as the National Institute of Mental Health, is on searching for deficits within children's brains.

Part Three: ADHD Drug Therapies

In Chapter 9, Grace Jackson reviews the evidence on the effects of stimulants on the growing body and brain and concludes with some passion that 40 years' evidence has shown that stimulants are a prevalent source of developmental toxicity: disrupting the formation of cartilage, myelin (white matter), and neurons (grey matter); altering endocrine functions; disturbing the sleep cycle; and destroying the brain's capacity to respond to future experiences with healthy rewiring and new growth. She also concludes that there is no evidence that these drugs reverse or normalize alleged delays in maturation, but may, in fact, preclude or postpone the development of self-control, abstract thought, and other forms of higher cognition.

In Chapter 10, Jonathan Leo and Jeffrey Lacasse document the unfounded claims made in consumer advertisements of ADHD medications. They illustrate how the advertising claims that are made are controversial from a scientific standpoint, and at best, most of them should be explained as tentative hypotheses, not as they are presented – as well-established facts. The degree to which this advertising is shaping the public's perceptions of the issues should not be underestimated. The full impact that the consumer advertisements have had on the diagnosis and treatment of ADHD requires further study, but the lack of well-balanced, scientifically based information on ADHD in these consumer advertisements is troubling. They hypothesize that they are very effective at having their intended effect: guiding patients to the doctor and even guiding the subsequent conversation with the doctor. The net effect on the public, and the children who end up taking ADHD medications, they conclude, is likely to be negative.

In Chapter 11 David Cohen, Shannon Hughes, and David Jacobs explore the extent to which new critical awareness, as well as parallel regulatory requirements, may have impacted on the initial clinical trials of Strattera™ (atomoxetine), a drug manufactured by Eli Lilly and Company and approved for marketing by the United States Food and Drug Administration (FDA) for the treatment of ADHD in children and adults in November 2002. They find extensive discrepancies between published and non-published versions of clinical trial data, and problems with business-as-usual ways of evaluating psychoactive drugs for human consumption, resulting in likely preventible harm occurring to those prescribed this drug. They conclude that the clinical trials leave the clinician completely unprepared for the reality of the complex and unpredictable effects of psychoactive drugs such as Strattera™.

In Chapter 12, Basant Puri first reviews the drawbacks associated with conventional pharmacotherapy for ADHD and then reviews the evidence for the safety and efficacy of various nutritional interventions. He concludes that while there are many adverse side-effects from conventional pharmacotherapy for ADHD, there appears to be good evidence in support of the alternative use of fatty acids and of removing artificial colourings from the diet. Based on the evidence detailed in his chapter, Puri believes that an ideal treatment would be to remove all artificial colourings and other additives from the diet, in combination with supplementation with ultra-pure eicosapentaenoic acid (EPA) and evening primrose oil with no docosahexaenoic acid (DHA) present.

Part Four: Alternative paradigms for ADHD

In Chapter 13, Jon Jureidini argues that although 'ADHD' may represent a conceptual advance on 'hyperactivity' and 'minimal brain dysfunction' by formulating behaviour problems in terms of deficits of attention and other executive functions, it still suffers from being an overly reductionist concept to the point of being a 'description masquerading as an explanation'. Brain and mind functioning is more complex than the current ADHD conceptualization would have us believe. In his chapter he shows how the concept of 'self-regulation' helps to make better sense of children's behaviour problems. He argues that the behaviourally disturbed child is compromised in their capacity to use imagination to perform what Jureidini calls 'mind magic' that is needed to deal with their predicament, so that she or he signals their need for outside help in self-regulation through displays of affect, and/or seemingly dysfunctional behaviours.

In the semi-autobiographical Chapter 14, Simon Sobo provides a quasi-anthropological study of childhood in a Jewish community of 1950s Queens in New York. Drawing on memories of his childhood there, Sobo concludes that it has always been known that it is difficult to get children to do what you want them to do rather than what they want to do. He suggests that the symptoms of ADHD describe children when they cannot connect to imposed expectations. Sobo then argues that as culture changed from one in which moral concerns were at the centre of experience, to a more pleasure-oriented, stimulus-bound existence it becomes easier to get bored and distracted when work rather than fun is the agenda, and thus expression of ADHD behaviours has become more common.

In Chapter 15, Chris Mercogliano using the proverbial 'canary in the coal mine' analogy, compares childhood in modern America today with its quite recent past and suggests that labels such as ADHD are the new millennium's canaries in the coal mine highlighting that something has gone wrong with America's modern beliefs about and practices with children. He proposes that children attracting labels such as ADHD are not 'sick', as the medical establishment would have us believe; rather they are exhibiting signs of distress and unmet core needs. Mercogliano argues that what he calls their 'inner wildness' is being stifled. He believes that the right response to their 'signals' is not to classify and drug them, but to help them reclaim this 'inner wildness', and restore childhood to a place in which kids can grow slowly, and if need be, fitfully into a more 'authentic' self.

In Chapter 16, Thom Hartmann makes a passionate case for getting beyond seeing ADHD as 'pathology' and finding positives and strengths within the ADHD-labelled person. He argues that ADHD is best viewed as lying on a continuum of behaviour rather than as a discrete biological 'malfunction' of the brain. The focus on ADHD as a 'brain pathology' that needs correcting, else it causes all manner of poor outcomes, adversely affects the growing child's sense of themselves and their value to society. Hartmann believes that it is time for us to set aside these stories of sickness and villainy. It is time for us to look at the structure and nature of our schools. It is time for us to tell the rogue elements within the research community who seek to stigmatize our children with the 'no hope, no value' label of ADHD that we are not interested in our children being the villains in their dramas any more. Science does not support the absolute pathology model, common sense doesn't support it, and certainly any sincere hope for therapeutic outcomes and healthy children does not support it. For Hartmann it is time to look at ADHD in a new light, where strengths and abilities are noticed and self-esteem is protected in a world where all children are valued for their unique gifts.

References

American and Psychiatric Association (1966). *Diagnostic Statistical Manual of Mental Disorders, Second Edition (DSM-II)*. Washington, DC: APA.

American and Psychiatric Association (1980). *Diagnostic Statistical Manual of Mental Disorders, Third Edition (DSM-III)*. Washington, DC: APA.

American Psychiatric Association (1987). *Diagnostic and Statistical Manual of Mental Disorders, Third Edition Revised (DSM-III-R)*. Washington, DC: APA.

American Psychiatric Association (1994). *Diagnostic and Statistical Manual of Mental Disorders, Fourth Edition (DSM-IV)*. Washington, DC: APA.

Barkley, R. A. (1981) *Hyperactive Children: A Handbook for Diagnosis and Treatment*. New York: Guilford Press.

Barkley, R. A. *et al.* (2002) International consensus statement on ADHD, *Clinical Child and Family Psychology Review* 5, 89–111.

Bradley, C. (1937) The behaviour of children receiving Benzedrine, *American Journal of Psychiatry* 94, 577–85.

Cohen, D., Leo, J. L., Stanton, T., Smith, D., McCreedy, K., Laing, M. S., *et al.* (2002) A boy who stops taking stimulants for ADHD: Commentaries on a Pediatrics case study, *Ethical Human Sciences and Services* 4, 189–209.

Department of Health (2005) *Prescription Cost Analysis England 2004*. Department of Health, NHSE, available at <http://www.dh.gov.uk/PublicationsAnd Statistics/Publications/PublicationsStatistics/PublicationsStatisticsArticle/fs/en? CONTENT_ID=4107504&chk=nsvFE0>.

Gale, K. (2006) Ritalin requests often deemed innapropriate. See <http://www.medscape.com/viewarticle/544602?src=mp> (accessed 27 September 2007).

Hearn, K. (2004) Here kiddie, kiddie, available at <http://alternet.org/drugreporter/20594/> (accessed 15 June 2005).

Rutter, M. (1982) Syndromes attributed to minimal brain dysfunction in childhood., *American Journal of Psychiatry* 139, 21–33.

Schmidt, M. H., Esser, G., Allehoff, W., Geisel, B., Laught, M. and Woerner, W. (1987) Evaluating the significance of minimal brain dysfunction – results of an epidemiological study, *Journal of Child Psychology and Psychiatry* 28, 803–21.

Still, G. F. (1902) Some abnormal psychiatric conditions in children. *Lancet*, 1008–12, 1077–82, 1163–8.

Strauss, A. and Lehtinen, L. (1947) *Psychopathology and Education of the Brain Injured Child*. New York: Grune and Stratton.

Timimi, S. (2005) *Naughty Boys: Anti-Social Behaviour, ADHD and the Role of Culture*. Basingstoke: Palgrave Macmillan.
Timimi, S. (2006) The politics of Attention Deficit Hyperactivity Disorder, in S. Timimi and B. Maitra (eds), *Critical Voices in Child and Adolescent Mental Health*. London: Free Association Books.

Part I

ADHD and the Medical Model

Chapter 1

ADHD: What Do We Really Know?

Lydia Furman

Attention Deficit/ Hyperactivity Disorder (ADHD) has become the most frequently diagnosed behavioural condition among school-age children. Of children aged 2–17 years, 6.8 per cent have been diagnosed with ADHD, and 3.8 per cent receive ADHD medications (National Survey of Children's Health, 2003). This figure is conservative, with subgroups at higher rates: 9.3 per cent of 12–year-old boys in the United States receive ADHD medication (ibid.). The rate of diagnosis of ADHD among adults is rising, with the number of prescriptions for ADHD medications on a similar trajectory (Kessler *et al.*, 2006). Physicians write about 2 million ADHD medication prescriptions per month for children and about 1 million per month for adults (Mosholder and Pamer, 2006).

A growing number of thoughtful therapists and physicians, asked to streamline diagnosis of ADHD and promptly begin stimulant medication, are beginning to have concerns: (1) The diagnosis of ADHD is built on a checklist of subjective symptoms – there is no objective diagnostic test and no identified cause for the condition. This is problematic. (2) Children with ADHD symptoms may have educational or emotional difficulties – how do these fit into the diagnostic box of ADHD? This is also problematic. (3) Which medication is best for any one child, and if ADHD is a 'lifelong condition' what does one explain to parent and child about medication use? Do children grow out of or into ADHD? There are no easy questions and no easy answers.

Diagnostic criteria are the first stumbling block. Physicians are trained to use symptoms to *formulate* a differential diagnosis, not *as* a diagnosis. The symptoms of ADHD are 'impulsivity, hyperactivity and inattentiveness', with a behaviour checklist defining the diagnosis in the Diagnostic and Statistic Manual of Mental Disorders (DSM-IV, 1994). Other equally common paediatric symptoms however, such as cough and fever, do not similarly lead directly to a diagnosis, but rather to an evaluation (Furman, 2005). Cough, for example, may be a symptom of a benign and self-limited respiratory infection, pneumonia or sinusitis, a foreign body in the airway, asthma, a nervous habit, or less commonly, cystic fibrosis or even malignancy. A full history and physical exam, additional laboratory studies or radiographs, and often follow-up visits, are required to assess the problem. Most would doubt the competence of a physician who checklisted cough extent and duration (does it adversely affect functioning in two settings?) and then began codeine treatment. This Schedule 2 medication suppresses the symptom (cough) but obviously would not be curative for most causes of cough, and could seriously and adversely delay diagnosis and appropriate therapy for other causes. Symptoms are critical diagnostic clues in paediatric medicine, and the exception from this approach granted to ADHD is difficult to explain.

Below, I will review potential causes of ADHD, methods of diagnosis, and issues with stimulant treatment.

What is the cause of ADHD?

Does ADHD actually have a cause? Do the behavioural manifestations that describe ADHD derive from one basic biologic mechanism, like the protean symptoms of systemic lupus erythematosis result from autoimmunity? A major barrier to acceptance of ADHD as a disease state is that its cause is unknown, and there is no biomarker. A variety of theories have been espoused regarding the symptoms of inattention, impulsivity and hyperactivity, which are considered diagnostic of ADHD. These include: (1) attention is part of a learning disturbance that is one of eight 'neurodevelopmental constructs' which need to be viewed as a totality; (2) the symptoms represent an expression of temperament in childhood; or (3) a variation in normal behaviour, particularly for boys who are much more frequently diagnosed with ADHD; or (4) evidence of differential rates of developmental and brain maturation among children; or (5) are an artefact of rigid or unhelpful expectations by parents and educators in today's society (Carey, 2002; Coles, 1987; El-Sayed *et al.*, 1999, 2003; Levine, 2006; Mattes, 1980; McGuiness, 1989; Rydelius, 1994; Sandberg, 1996; Taylor, 1995).

More recent research has focused on 'dopamine dysregulation' theories as a cause of ADHD. Research can be divided into two broad areas: (1) the biological, including genetic and neuroanatomical, and (2) the neuropsychological.

Biological research appears to be driven entirely by the mechanisms of the ADHD drugs, methylphenidate and amphetamine salts, and recently atomoxitine, and is relentless in its pursuit of this hypothesis.

Catecholamine dysfunction

Pliszka states: 'Stimulants, a principal treatment for [ADHD], act on the norepinephrine (NE) and dopamine (DA) systems; this has led to a long-standing hypothesis of catecholamine dysfunction in ADHD' (Pliszka, 2005, p. 1385). Thus research has proceeded from medication mechanism to hypothesis. An American Academy of Paediatrics (AAP) educational brochure about ADHD for teenagers states that 'research shows [my italics] that ADHD is a medical condition caused by small changes in how the brain works... related to 2 chemicals in your brain called dopamine and norepinephrine' (American Academy of Pediatrics, 2005, p. 2). In fact, research over three decades does not show this, and the data are both confusing and incomplete.

The two drugs used most frequently to treat ADHD, methyphenidate and amphetamines, principally target the dopamine transporter (DAT), interfering with dopamine transport and indirectly activating both dopamine receptors and norepinephrine receptors (Madras et al., 2005). Atomoxitine, a selective norepinephrine reuptake inhibitor, has more recently been used in the treatment of ADHD. However, 'the relative contributions of dopamine and norepinephrine to ADHD pathophysiology and therapeutic response are obfuscated by the capacity of the NET [norepinephrine transporter] to clear dopamine as well as norepinephrine' (Madras et al., 2005, p. 1397). Work seeking to clarify the relationship of dopamine and norepinephrine to ADHD is difficult to interpret. For example, a recent study examined urinary norepinephrine and dopamine excretion in children aged 6–12 diagnosed with ADHD during a 'Test of Variables of Attention (TOVA)' (Llorente et al., 2006). Individual TOVA indexes showed a significant correlation with urinary excretion of norepinephrine but not dopamine. Neither a control group nor a control activity was studied. Does urinary neurotransmitter excretion provide a clinically relevant marker for a child's test performance? Any conclusions are complicated by methodologic issues including study design, and the report thus neither supports nor refutes an etiologic role for dopamine and norepinephrine in ADHD.

The data on adults with ADHD are conflicting with regard to dopamine transporter (DAT) binding levels, and whether this body of work applies to children is not known. Rat and primate models are used to examine the role of neurotransmitters in attentional behaviours, although the applicability of this research to human behaviours is not clear, since the 'models represent *elements* [my italics] of the behavioural units observed in subjects with ADHD clinically' and cannot include affective or cognitive influences (Oades *et al.*, 2005, p. 122; Viggiano *et al.*, 2004). Literature search identified one study, unhandicapped by use of adult subjects, pre-treated subjects, lack of controls, or subjects and controls with comorbidities, which provides evidence for a dopamine hypothesis. Cheon *et al.* examined the distribution of dopamine transporter density in the basal ganglia of nine drug-naïve children aged 6–12 years diagnosed with ADHD and compared them to six healthy controls (Cheon *et al.*, 2003). They reported a significantly increased level of DAT binding in the basal ganglia of the ADHD subjects as compared to the controls; however, binding did not correlate with ADHD symptom severity scores. The authors note that their sample size is small and further study is needed regarding this association and the 'dopamine dysregulation' theory. Observed differences may be developmental or maturational, and exploration of this possibility would require longitudinal data.

It may be relatively simplistic to expect that abnormal amounts of a single, or even two, neurotransmitters will explain the variety and spectrum of behaviours described clinically as ADHD. There is concern among 'non-believers' that research is being designed to provide a rationale for stimulant use rather than to explore disease mechanisms, and that the science of neurobiology is not yet ready to correlate human behaviours with specific levels of brain neurotransmitters or receptors. Despite a high level of interest in the mechanisms of action of ADHD drugs, there is not yet a sufficient body of evidence to conclude that ADHD is 'caused' by dopamine or norepinephrine abnormalities in the brain.

Anatomical neuroimaging

With the increasing availability of neuroimaging modalities, research has also been directed towards finding a neuroanatomic locus for ADHD. Seidman *et al.* present a comprehensive comparison of work using quantitative regions of interest (ROI) MRI, and conclude that 'the brain [in ADHD] is altered in a more widespread manner than previously hypothesized', specifically that 'a relatively consistent picture emerges' of decreases in brain volume in the dorsolateral prefrontal cortex, the caudate, the pallidum, the corpus callosum and the cerebellum (Seidman *et al.*, 2005, p. 1263). The authors acknowledge that studies have failed to control for potentially critical confounders known to affect brain imaging results, including prior or current medication use, gender, pre- and perinatal complications, and comorbidities such as depression, and that almost all studies in children have been underpowered, many using sample sizes of twenty or fewer. In addition, studies have used 'control' populations that may not be appropriate, including children with other pathologies, and have used a cross-sectional rather than longitudinal approach, despite evidence that brain maturation and myelination change over time.

Direct review of the studies thus reinforces Volkow's view: 'it should be noted that the imaging studies are still not definitive because of the discrepancies in the findings' (Volkow *et al.*, 2005, p. 1413). For example, of the five studies that examined total cerebellar volume, four are listed as showing an association of ADHD with decreased volume, while three do not. Three of the five studies have the same first author, suggesting the need for replication of results by other researchers. Specifically, Castellanos *et al.* (2001) and Durston *et al.* (2004) found a decrease in volume on the right but not on the left of the cerebellum in ADHD subjects, while Castellanos *et al.* (1996) and Castellanos *et al.* (2002) in separate studies reported decreased total cerebellar volume in ADHD subjects, and a third group (Hill *et al.*, 2003) found no volume difference between ADHD subjects and controls. Thus the naïve reader may not agree that this is a 'relatively consistent picture'. Review of the data for other brain regions shows similarly conflicting results. Given the limited number of studies, their small size, and the lack of replication, it is not scientifically reasonable to draw conclusions about the relationship between ADHD and individual regions of the brain. Further, the relationship of structural neuroanatomy to function, behaviour and cognition has not yet been elucidated. While optimistic researchers may continue to seek a 'eureka' anatomical finding for ADHD with the use of newer techniques such as MRI microanalysis of regions of interest, at this time there is no credible or consistent evidence for one or more neuroanatomic loci in ADHD.

Functional neuroimaging

Bush and colleagues have reviewed data on functional neuroimaging in ADHD, and conclude that 'convergent data' implicate the frontal-strial regions in the pathophysiology of ADHD (Bush and Seidman, 2005). Both study design and scientific concerns render this conclusion faulty. Most of the studies reviewed have design flaws, and use small populations with either no controls or a problematic control group. Of the 13 single photon emission computerized tomography (SPECT) studies reviewed, only two were described as 'diagnostically clean' or 'well designed': one of these used no controls and the other used a control group in which most subjects had a headache diagnosis. Both studies were authored by the same group, and documented changes in regional cerebral blood flow in the resting state with methylphenidate administration; while demonstrating medication effect, such studies do not provide etiologic information (Kim *et al.* 2001, 2002). The positron emission tomography (PET) studies used adults and adolescents, rather than child subjects, and will not be discussed here. These older methods, SPECT and PET, require intravenous injection and exposure to radiation, which has become increasingly unacceptable given the availability of functional MRI studies. Nine functional MRI studies are reviewed, of which four include child subjects; the largest sample size is eleven ADHD subjects and the largest control group includes seven subjects.

Although taxing, careful review of the methods and results is informative. For example, Vaidya *et al.* report a finding of 'differences between children with Attention Deficit Hyperactivity Disorder (ADHD) and healthy controls in their frontal-striatal function and its modulation by methylphenidate during response inhibition' (Vaidya *et al.*, 1998, p. 14494). This study has been widely quoted. Ten males with ADHD and six healthy controls matched for age, gender and IQ were studied. The ADHD subjects had been treated with methylphenidate for 1–3 years prior to study. A validated response inhibition task was performed by each ADHD subject and each control subject both on and off methylphenidate (MPH). ADHD subjects had just 36 hours off their regular medication prior to the 'off MPH' performance, and were given their regular dose (range 7.5–30 mg) for the 'on MPH' trial. Control subjects received 10 mg of methylphenidate for their 'on MPH' trial; thus ADHD subjects may have received up to three times as much medication as the control subjects with whom they were being compared. In addition, there was no placebo control or blinding. Overall, ADHD subjects made more errors than control subjects in all tasks, both before and after medication, but both groups improved with medication on at least part of the test. Methylphenidate increased frontal activation in both ADHD and control groups similarly. Medication effect on striatal activation differed by type of test (stimulus vs. response controlled), by group (control vs. ADHD), and by on or off medication. To quote:

MPH increased striatal activation in ADHD subjects ($t = 2.7$, $P = 0.01$) but decreased striatal activation in control subjects ($t = 2.1$, $P = 0.04$). Further, without MPH, striatal activation was greater in control than ADHD subjects ($t = 2.5$, $P = 0.01$), but with MPH, striatal activation tended to be greater in ADHD than control subjects ($t = 1.6$, $P = 0.06$). Frontal activation increased with MPH in both groups ($F(1, 14 = 7.0)$). No other effects were significant.

These results apply to the stimulus-controlled task only, not to the response-controlled task, in which medication did not affect activation in either group.

The most significant caveat to interpretation of this convoluted and confusing data set is that the ADHD subjects were not drug naïve, and it is possible that the 'atypical striatal response to methylphenidate' is due to chronic treatment, not an underlying condition (Cohen and Leo, 2004). Functional MRI requires the subject to remain physically still to avoid motion artefact; the authors note that their subjects are not typical of children with ADHD, due to their high IQs and lack of hyperactivity, enabling them to sit still and attend to the neurocognitive task provided. Vaidya *et al.* (1998, p. 14494) conclude that: 'These results suggest that ADHD is characterized by atypical frontal-striatal function and that methylphenidate affects striatal activation differently in ADHD than in healthy children.' A conclusion more compatible with the data might be: 'Children in this study given the diagnosis of ADHD who have been treated with methylphenidate for 1–3 years show different patterns of striatal activation with and without methylphenidate than untreated children. Generalizability is limited by sample size, sample characteristics and chronic medication use in the treatment group.' Furthermore, while functional MRI can show an association between regional cerebral blood flow and performance of specific tasks, this does not prove causation.

Genetic causes
The search for a biologic etiology for ADHD has also spawned a
large literature on the potential genetic causes of ADHD. The search
has been driven by the appearance of 'heritability' of ADHD from
twin and family studies. Two approaches have been used: the genome
scan, which surveys all genes unselectively, and the candidate genome
approach, which has focused on genes related to the mechanism
of action of the ADHD drugs, specifically the dopamine and norepinephrine transporter and receptor genes. Genome-wide scans have
not identified any regions that are consistently implicated. In retrospect, researchers contend that this is not surprising, since ADHD is so
'phenotypically variable'. There is little if any evidence for a relationship of ADHD to the norepinephrine transporter gene (NET1) even in
analysis using case and control pools that previously yielded positive
results (Xu *et al.*, 2005). In other analyses family- and case-based methods have yielded divergent results regarding NET1 and dopamine D1
receptor (DRD1), weakening any presumed association (Bobb *et al.*,
2005). Data regarding the dopamine transporter gene (DAT) are divergent and conflicting, with both positive (Barr *et al.*, 2001; Chen *et al.*,
2003; Cook *et al.*, 1995; Waldman *et al.*, 1998) and negative studies
(Maher *et al.*, 2002; Muglia *et al.*, 2002; Payton *et al.*, 2001; Smith
et al., 2003; Todd *et al.*, 2001); review articles are uniformly positive
even though a recent meta-analysis by Curran *et al.* found a non-
significant odds ratio, i.e. a lack of association (Curran *et al.*, 2001).
   Studies of the Dopamine D4 (DRD4) receptor gene are widely
touted as positive, yet a study-by-study review reveals results that
are divergent, with both positive and negative studies (Faraone *et al.*,
2001; Grady *et al.*, 2003; Kustanovich *et al.*, 2003; Mill *et al.*, 2001).
Work by Faraone summarizing pooled odds ratios for eight candidate genes including dopamine receptors, dopamine transporter, and
dopamine beta-hydroxylase genes shows very small but significant
odds ratios ranging from 1.18 to 1.46 (Faraone *et al.*, 2005). He
concludes that 'the genetic architecture of ADHD is complex' and
states that 'these small and sometimes inconsistent effects' emphasize the need for future research to include larger sample sizes, and
'gene-environment interactions' (p. 1319). The laser-like focus on candidate genes related to ADHD drugs pervades the research on ADHD
'genetics'. However, probably the most significant problem with this
neuropsychiatric genetic approach has been summarized by Gottesman
and Gould, who state, as quoted by Pauls:

The reason there is so much difficulty is undoubtedly – in part – that psychiatry's classification systems describe heterogeneous disorders. In addition to the inherent complexity of psychiatric disorders...[it is clear that] the brain is the most complex of all organs...Furthermore, the brain is subject to complex interactions not just among genes, proteins, cells and circuits of cells but also between individuals and their changing experiences. (Gottesman and Gould, 2003 as cited in Pauls, 2005, p. 1310)

In other words, if a single diagnostic category, e.g. ADHD, describes a great variety of behaviours and individuals rather than a single condition, it is extremely unlikely that there is an identifiable genetic cause.

Apparent heritability may be due to genes or environmental influences. Faraone notes: 'More work from twin and molecular genetic studies is needed to determine if the increased familiality of persistent ADHD reflects the actions of genes or of familial environmental causes' (Faraone et al., 2004, p 303.) Factors associated with the diagnosis of ADHD include lower socioeconomic level, family conflict, parental affective disorders including maternal depression and anxiety, parental substance abuse, and parental disruptive and antisocial behaviours including delinquency (Biederman et al., 1995 and 1996; Chronis et al., 2003; Connor et al., 2003; Elgar et al., 2003; Faraone et al., 2004; Fisher, 1990; Johnston et al., 2001; Shaw et al., 2001). Certainly not all of these factors can be considered genetic. There has been increasing recognition of the importance and influence of the child's early environment on his or her chance of 'developing' ADHD. In a prospective study, the development of persistent hyperactivity in children observed from ages 2 to 7 was associated with maternal depression, 'hostile parenting practices' and maternal smoking during pregnancy (Romano et al., 2006). In a review of challenges for the next decade in ADHD research, Nigg notes that inadequate attention has been paid to 'the interplay of socialization and interpersonal process in early childhood along with the development of the self-regulatory abilities' (Nigg, 2005, p. 1433). He proposes that 'the neglect of this integration might in part be due to a misguided belief that because ADHD is highly heritable, socialization processes do not require intensive study. This belief is misguided because heritable effects are likely to be mediated at least in substantial part by socialization'. Without attention to the child's caregiving, family environment and parenting practices experienced, we are left with an inadequate and empty theoretical shell that does not account for observed symptomatology.

It is more plausible that environment, which includes psychosocial and socioeconomic factors, educational influences and home caregiving, interacts with the child's developing personality and intellectual and emotional makeup to 'produce' adaptive behaviours.

Neuropsychological research

Neuropsychological research into the etiology of ADHD is stepping back from the notion of a single definable cause for ADHD, with increasing use of all-embracing descriptors for ADHD, such as a 'multifactorial and clinically heterogeneous disorder', in which 'there isn't just one cause' (Biederman, 2005; AAP, 2005). Eric Taylor, head of the Department of Child and Adolescent Psychiatry at King's College, London, as quoted by Okie, states that there is not 'a single known physiological cause... there are many causes, each of small effect... and the model of a single disease is not well applied' (Okie, 2006, p. 2641). This more psychological line of inquiry suggests that even children with similar symptoms may have different underlying problems, and that a variety of behavioural difficulties do not have to result from a single unifying cause.

Initially ADHD was divided into a 'hyperactive' subtype and an 'inattentive' subtype, with some children said to show both features, but all phenotypes due to a single as yet unidentified neurocognitive defect. However, there is no pathognomonic profile on neurocognitive testing that is diagnostic of ADHD, and cognitive deficits found in subjects with ADHD are also observed in other neurologic and developmental disorders.

Pennington reviews evidence for the 'shortcomings of the single deficit model' (Pennington, 2005). At least four theoretical models of neuropsychological dysfunction are currently postulated, none of which alone appears to account for all cases of ADHD, but each of which is theorized as a new subtype and part of a possible new multiple deficit model. Originally it was hypothesized that deficits in executive function (EF), broadly defined as the ability to organize and supervise one's own thinking and behaviour, are responsible for ADHD. However, only about half of children diagnosed with ADHD have a deficit on the most sensitive measure of EF, about 20 per cent have no deficit on tests of EF, and about half of controls have at least a single deficit noted on EF testing (Nigg, 2005). So an 'EF subtype' of ADHD has been proposed to reconcile the data with the original hypothesis. Sonuga-Barke proposes a 'motivational dysfunction model' in which there is 'impaired signaling of delayed reward', and *ergo* suggests a 'motivational deficit subtype' (Sonuga-Barke and Edmund, 2005, p. 1235). Sergeant advances the 'cognitive-energetic model', which 'proposes that the underlying deficit in ADHD is an energetic dysfunction in the regulation of activation and effort needed to optimize ongoing information processing', and hence advance a 'cognitive-energetic subtype' of ADHD (Pennington, 2005, p. 1221; Sergeant, 2005). This last model is as yet untestable because direct measures of these 'energy pools' of arousal, activation and effort are not available. Finally, Kipp proposes a theory of 'cognitive inhibition' or 'the active suppression of cognitive contents' (Kipp, 2005; Pennington, 2005, p. 1223). Whether or not researchers will be able to patch these disparate academic theories into a unified and comprehensible 'multiple deficit model' of ADHD is not yet known.

There now appears to be recognition that ADHD is not a single disease or single condition. However, this veritable explosion of ADHD subtypes and theories has not brought clarity or transparency to the topic. The more researchers try to define and understand ADHD with novel neurocognitive models, the more complex and confusing the 'disease' appears. Also, as Pennington notes, 'research on ADHD has mostly lacked both a rich reciprocal relationship with basic developmental and cognitive science and the use of developmental designs' (Pennington, 2005, p. 1222). ADHD research has largely ignored emotional, developmental and personality factors, which have provided very fertile fields for the understanding of other childhood problems and pathologies. If a child manifests inattention, hyperactivity or impulsivity, or other behavioural symptoms, evaluation that considers environmental, emotional, and educational causes is compatible with the new 'multi-deficit model' thinking researchers are applying to ADHD.

Summary regarding causes of ADHD

Data regarding genetic loci, neuroanatomic lesions, and neurotransmitters are inconclusive. Unbiased review of the data reveals conflicting results. Neurocognitive and neuropsychological research has not produced a unifying theory. The symptoms of ADHD remain unexplained by single disease theories.

Diagnosis of ADHD

Almost a decade ago, the American Academy of Child and Adolescent Psychiatry (AACAP) formally recommended as an initial evaluation for ADHD: (1) an interview with the parents (to include the child's and the family's history); (2) use of standardized rating scales; (3) school information including results of academic testing; (4) a (psychiatric) child diagnostic interview; (5) a family diagnostic interview; (6) a complete physical examination; and (7) referral for additional testing as needed (Dulcan, 1997). In this approach, which uses structured interview and full testing as needed, many alternative diagnoses are considered, ranging from home and family stress and pathology to individual educational problems and psychiatric conditions. This method of evaluation is not recommended by the American Academy of Paediatrics (AAP, 2000, 2001). The current stated goal of rapid diagnosis is to provide prompt management with medication and/or behavioural therapy for treatment of targeted outcomes identified with 'input from parents, children, and teachers, as well as other school personnel' (ibid., p. 1037). A deeper understanding of the child's problems is not sought. The possibility of comorbid psychological or psychiatric conditions is raised very briefly, with a directive to 'evaluate for co-existing conditions... although the paediatrician may not always be in a position to make a precise diagnosis [of same]' (ibid., p. 1166). Since no diagnostic test is available for ADHD, clinicians are asked to use rating scales and behaviour checklists to make the diagnosis of ADHD. The AAP guidelines caution that these scales were tested under 'ideal' conditions, 'may function less well in primary care clinicians' offices', and '[the] questions on which these rating scales are based are subjective and subject to bias' (ibid., p. 1164).

In fact, there are significant problems with the available rating scales. The AAP Guidelines lists two 'ADHD-specific Checklists', the Conners parent and teacher rating scales for children aged 6–17 years, and an additional scale for females only (the SSQ-O-I Barkley's School Situations questionnaire). The original Conners Rating Scales suffered from high correlations (0.49–0.68) between items on the teachers' scale, and a high correlation on the parents' scale between conduct problems and hyperactivity (0.55) suggesting in both scales that the rated factors are not independent (Trites and Laprade, 1983; McGuiness, 1989). Major problems with the newer Conners Rating Scales-Revised are rarely discussed, but normative data are very limited and, even more troubling, the same population was used both to develop and validate the scale, which is a clear statistical 'no-no' (Gianarris *et al.*, 2001; Snyder *et al.*, 2004). Although a review by Collett *et al.* concluded that rating scales can 'reliably, validly and efficiently measure DSM-IV based ADHD symptoms in youth', Snyder *et al.* respond:

In the use of rating scales, the act of applying a cutoff and assigning qualitative (clinical) meaning to a score requires specific statistical tests to confirm the validity of the scale as used in common practice. Considering the insubstantial results of the two rating scales [Conners and ADHD-IV] that were tested for criterion validity and the lack of such testing of the other nine reviewed scales, Collett *et al.* lack sufficient evidence to conclude that rating scales can validly measure *DSM-IV*–based ADHD symptoms. (Collett *et al.*, 2003, p. 1015; Snyder *et al.*, 2004, p. 1189)

Validity is critical, since it asks, 'does the scale actually measure what we are trying to measure?' Certainly Snyder's position will be debated, but without other data available, it appears that the widely used Conners' Rating Scales-Revised have not yet been proven to measure ADHD symptoms.

The newer National Initiative for Childrens' Healthcare Quality (NICHQ) Vanderbilt Assessment Forms are available at the NICHQ website (<http://www.qualitytools.ahrq.gov/summary/summary.aspx? view_id=1&doc_id=6191&nbr=100552>, accessed 1 August 2006). These forms were developed jointly as guidelines by the AAP – Medical Specialty Society, the NICHQ, and the University of Chapel Hill for its Center for Children's Healthcare Improvement – Academic Institution. Sponsorship, i.e. funding, was provided by the Agency for Healthcare Research and Quality – Federal Government Agency [US] and McNeil Consumer and Specialty Pharmaceuticals, a Private For Profit Research Organization (Van Landeghem and Hess, 2005). McNeil manufactures Concerta™, an ADHD medication. The Vanderbilt assessment has separate teacher and parent forms, each with a 'symptom assessment' and an 'impairment in performance' checklist. The forms are also intended to screen for three prominent comorbidities, anxiety/depression, oppositional-defiant disorder and conduct disorder. During scale testing, suburban school teachers completed the Vanderbilt ADHD Diagnostic Teacher Rating Scale (VADTRS), with teacher report of a diagnosis of ADHD serving as the sole clinical validation, thus providing 'an approximation' of the diagnosis only, without an 'independent determination' (Wolraich *et al.*, 1996, pp. 149 and 150). The Vanderbilt ADHD Diagnostic Parent Rating Scale (VADPRS) validation was performed with a subset (241, 15.7 per cent) of parents who responded to an anonymous letter addressed to parents of students that had been *teacher-identified* as having ADHD without necessarily meeting DSM-IV criteria (Wolraich *et al.*, 2003).

Thus neither the teacher nor the parent Vanderbilt rating scales has direct clinical validation. Clinicians cannot be expected to research every form, checklist and scale that is recommended by a professional body; conversely they should expect that the process of examining reliability and validity has already been performed.

An additional problem with the use of rating scales is that information gathered is highly subjective. The purpose of obtaining information from two sources is to meet the formal DSM-IV criteria for ADHD of impairment in more than one setting. For most children, this means home and school, and the commonly used rating scales have separate parent and teacher versions. Pelham *et al.* (2005, p. 449) state that: 'The most efficient assessment method is obtaining information through parent and teacher rating scales; both...are needed for clinical purposes.' However, it is notable that parent and teacher ratings are frequently widely discrepant. Mitsis *et al.*, who describe evaluation of 74 referred children using the ADHD module of the Diagnostic Interview Schedule for Children, found parent – teacher concordance 'poor' with 'virtually no agreement for ADHD subtypes' (Mitsis *et al.*, 2000). Leslie *et al.* studied implementation of the AAP Guidelines and found that, of 159 consecutively evaluated children, 40 per cent had discrepant results on the parent and teacher versions of the Vanderbilt scales, 'with only the parent or teacher endorsing sufficient symptoms to meet the criteria of the Diagnostic and Statistical Manual of Mental Disorders, 4th ed.' (Leslie *et al.*, 2004, p. 129). Prior studies show similar results (Lahey *et al.*, 1987; Safer, 2000). Wolraich *et al.* (2004) screened 6171 elementary schoolchildren, of whom 1573 were identified as 'high risk' for ADHD, and evaluated 243 of these children, of whom 40 per cent had been diagnosed by 'health care professionals' as having ADHD. In this study concordance between parents and teachers was so low concerning ADHD symptoms and performance that 'when the two-setting requirement was strictly enforced, poor interrater agreement decreased diagnostic rates for all three types of ADHD'. Wolraich *et al.* concluded that using more 'lenient core symptom scores' could possibly decrease this effect. Another potential conclusion from these data would be that such high and persistent discordance indicates a need to reconsider the reliability and validity of the rating scales and/ or the diagnostic entity ADHD.

Another approach to the parent–teacher discrepancy issue has been articulated by Zhang *et al.* (2005) who advocate a clinician-based instrument to evaluate the severity of ADHD symptoms, the ADHD Rating Scale IV (ADHD RS), based on a trial with 'over 600' children and adolescents previously diagnosed with ADHD. The Zhang study comes from the Lilly Research Laboratories in Indiana; Eli Lilly manufactures the ADHD medication Strattera™. The repeatedly documented discordance between parent and teacher evaluation of ADHD symptoms should not become an inconvenience to be circumvented by increasing 'leniency' of criteria or changing the locus of progress evaluation to the health care provider. Rather, this is an opportunity to consider the real and significant impact of the environment, including structure and routine, and the attitudes and abilities of the adults interacting with the child, on the way a child behaves. It is also another opportunity to reconsider the possibility that ADHD is not a neurologic disease, like epilepsy, whose manifestations would be expected to be similar in all settings, but rather a group of behaviour symptoms manifested by a troubled child.

A significant obstacle to diagnosis of ADHD is the issue of comorbid conditions, which are highly prevalent and include childhood learning disabilities, conduct disorder and affective and mood disorders, as well as parental psychopathology including substance abuse and mood disorders. The rates of these conditions among children diagnosed with ADHD are estimated to range from 35 per cent to 60 per cent for oppositional or conduct disorder, from 12 per cent to 90 per cent for learning disabilities, from 18 per cent to 60 per cent for mood disorders including major depression, and from 25 per cent to 34 per cent for anxiety disorders (Brown, 2000; Butler *et al.*, 1995; Dankaerts and Taylor, 1995; Dilsaver *et al.*, 2003; Jensen *et al.*, 1993; MTA Cooperative Group, 1999; Pelham *et al.*, 1992; Pliszka, 2000 and 2003; Semrud-Clikeman *et al.*, 1992; Spencer *et al.*, 2003; Wilens *et al.*, 2002; Wolraich *et al.*, 1996). Hershorin states, 'In the presence of some comorbidities you can address the ADHD first. In the presence of certain comorbidities, we're obviously going to want to treat the ADHD second and go after the other symptoms first' (Hershorin, 2006, p. 39). The challenges to implementing this strategy are that: (1) 'ADHD symptoms' can look just like symptoms of each of the comorbidities; (2) treatment for these conditions is different from treatment for ADHD; (3) non-treatment can lead to poorer outcomes; and perhaps most importantly (4) paediatricians are not trained to recognize or treat childhood psychiatric disorders or learning disabilities (and express awareness of this issue themselves) (AAP, 2005; Connor *et al.*, 2003; Coyle, 2003; Pliszka, 2003; Waxmonsky, 2003).

Depression in childhood[1] can be difficult to recognize, and may present with different signs and symptoms than in adults (Coyle,

2003; Furman, 1992; Ryan, 2001). A recent consensus statement concluded that, 'more than 70% of children and adolescents with serious
mood disorders are either undiagnosed or inadequately treated', that
paediatricians have little to no training in diagnosis, and that age-
appropriate and validated diagnostic methods should be developed
(NIMH Blueprint Report, 2001). Stimulants may cause dysphoria and
dysregulation in major affective disorders, and treatment guidelines for
children with bipolar disorder specifically recommend 'to carefully use
the stimulants [in a child with 'coexisting ADHD'] if clinically indicated and *only after* [my italics] the child's bipolar symptomatology
has been controlled with a mood stabilizer.' (Kowatch *et al.*, 2005,
p. 227). Depression in childhood has a strong continuity with depression in adults, therefore recognition and treatment are important;
stimulants are contraindicated as initial treatment in most children
with mood disorders (Compton, 2004; Coyle, 2003; Delbello *et al.*,
2001; Lewinsohn *et al.*, 2002; NIMH, 2001).

There is a large overlap between conduct and oppositional defiant disorders, and ADHD. In fact, Pliska *et al.* state that 'Almost all
children younger than 12 years of age who meet criteria for ODD
[oppositional defiant disorder] or CD [conduct disorder] will almost
always meet criteria for ADHD' (Pliszka, 2000, p. 526) This degree of
symptom overlap suggests significant diagnostic confusion.

Anxiety is frequent in ADHD. In the widely quoted 'MTA Trial',
which compared medication and psychosocial or behavioural therapy,
34 per cent of children with ADHD met full diagnostic criteria for
an anxiety disorder, and this figure is in line with other work (MTA
Group, 1999, 2004; Wilens *et al.*, 2002). Based on current evidence,
the treatment of choice for anxiety in children is cognitive-behavioural
therapy, not stimulant medication (Compton, 2004). Most studies
show that significantly fewer children diagnosed with ADHD who
have anxiety, as compared to those without anxiety, respond to stimulants (30% as compared to 80% in a double-blinded study) (Pliszka,
1989) Diagnosis of anxiety may be difficult, possibly because the child
can experience emotional pain without having 'acting out' symptoms
that alert teachers and parents. Teachers are less likely to identify
children as anxious, and child and parent assessments are frequently
discrepant (Ford, 2003; Pliszka, 2000; Johnson, 2000). Identification is
important, however, because not only does the child suffer psychologically, but anxiety appears to predict future major affective disorders
including depression (Coyle, 2003; Pine, 1999 and 2001; Johnson
et al., 2000). Both diagnosis and treatment of anxiety will be easily

missed without careful and thorough assessment that goes beyond consideration of ADHD.

Learning disorders may be the most frequent 'comorbidity' in ADHD, probably because most children are referred by teachers who note behavioural and educational problems at school. In fact school referrals for ADHD are more frequent than parent referrals (Mulhern *et al.*, 1994; Shea *et al.*, 1996; Ullman *et al.*, 1994). Learning problems and low cognitive ability can lead to frustration and inattention, which may masquerade as ADHD. The strategy of stimulant treatment prior to educational assessment is supported by data showing that students with reading disability *and* ADHD who are treated with stimulants show improvement in reading scores, while those who have reading disability alone do not (McGee *et al.*, 1989; Richardson *et al.*, 1988). However, children with ADHD and learning disability respond significantly less well to stimulants than children with ADHD *without* learning disability (55% vs. 75% response rate) (Grizenko *et al.*, 2006). There is increasing evidence that early and intensive treatment of learning disorders improves later educational outcomes (Foorman *et al.*, 2003; O'Connor *et al.*, 2005). Thus, stimulant treatment without educational assessment for children with school failure or educational problems is an interference with timely and appropriate educational intervention.

There is good evidence that stimulant medications do not improve learning *per se*. Stimulants also do not distinguish children with 'ADHD' from normal children (Bernstein *et al.*, 1994; Rappaport *et al.*, 1978 and 1980). Motoric slowing and an improved attention span are proven responses to stimulant administration, and occur in children with and without the diagnosis of ADHD (ibid.). Older work showed that methylphenidate improves performance on tasks that require repetition and concentration, not on tasks involving learning new material (Barkley and Cunningham, 1978; Douglas *et al.*, 1986; Rie *et al.*, 1976). Volkow and colleagues recently studied the mechanism of methylphenidate's effect by comparing methylphenidate-induced dopamine release during performance on an 'academic' task (solving maths problems for a financial reward) with performance on a 'neutral task' (viewing nature cards with no financial reward) (Volkow *et al.*, 2004). Methylphenidate increased dopamine on the maths task but not the 'neutral task'. Subjects reported greater interest in the maths task when taking methylphenidate rather than placebo. In all cases increased interest in the task appeared to increase attention and performance. Volkow summarized, 'these results provide evidence that methylphenidate's effects on dopamine are sensitive to the conditions of its administration...methylphenidate enhanced the motivational saliency of the cognitive task, as evidence by the perception of the [remunerated] task as more interesting...methylphenidate's improvement of performance may be secondary to its motivational effects, which would explain why stimulants improve performance of a boring task in normal healthy individuals and why unmedicated ADHD children perform properly when the task is salient' (Volkow *et al.*, 2004, pp. 1178–9). Although the study has design weaknesses and a small sample size, it demonstrates that interest in task and contextual factors have as great an impact on attention and performance as stimulant treatment. Volkow *et al.* conclude that making schoolwork more interesting may be an effective 'non-pharmacologic' intervention for ADHD. This line of thinking can easily be extended: stimulant treatment should not replace or precede educational evaluation or intervention, and educational technique (how the teacher teaches) is a critical ingredient in childhood educational success.

Finally, other 'comorbid' problems such as occult mental retardation, hypervigilance due to fear or stress, and ongoing or past abuse, can also each manifest the same symptoms as ADHD (Furman, 2002; Levine, 1991; Murphy *et al.*, 1998). In these children, it appears that the conditions are not 'comorbid' but rather 'stand alone'. However, it is notable that symptom diagnosis alone would have produced an ADHD diagnosis without treatment for the underlying condition.

Treatment of ADHD

Although behavioural therapy is formally advocated in concert with medication treatment, many children receive medication only. The under-use of non-pharmacologic behavioural intervention has been documented (Concannon and Tang, 2005). Possible barriers include the belief that medication alone is effective, and difficulty accessing the mental health system. The MTA trial concluded that medication management was superior to behaviour modification therapy at 14 months but not at 36 months (Jensen *et al.*, 2007); however, it should be noted that behaviour modification therapy is only one of many types of psychotherapies, and that the therapeutic needs of all study participants were focused only on the ADHD diagnosis (MTA Group, 1999, 2004). The behaviour modification therapy as a 'one size fits all' therapy in the MTA trial may not be appropriate for children with symptoms diagnosed as ADHD but due to other etiologies.

Stimulant medications have come under increasing scrutiny for their safety and side-effect profiles. Certain ADHD medications, for instance pemoline (Cylert), have been entirely removed from the market, in this instance due to the unacceptably high risk of liver failure. Recently, amphetamines and methylphenidate came under FDA review because they are sympathomimetic amines, which reliably and significantly increase resting heart rate and blood pressure (Nissen, 2005, 2006; Wilens *et al.*, 2005). Related products including ephedra and phenylpropanolamine (PPA) have been associated with serious adverse effects and fatalities. Thirteen cases of sudden unexplained death due to amphetamines and eleven due to methylphenidate in children aged 1–18 years have been reported to the FDA's Adverse Event Reporting System (AERS) between January 1992 and February 2005 (McDonagh *et al.*, 2007). It is estimated that only about 1–10 per cent of certain types of adverse events are actually reported to AERS, and that reporting rates vary with time and event type (Hartnell and Wilson, 2004; Mosholder and Pamer, 2006; Nissen, 2006). Therefore it is possible either that these rates are the same as the 'baseline' rates for sudden death in children, or it is possible that reported events are a small percentage of actual events and the magnitude of risk is not yet known. It appears that children with cardiac disease are at highest risk and should not receive stimulants – children with *undiagnosed* cardiac disease are obviously also at risk. In addition, serious adverse neuropsychiatric events have occurred with use of stimulants, including psychosis, mania, hallucinations and unexpected aggression. The FDA's Drug Safety and Risk Management Advisory Committee voted 8 to 7 to include the strongest level of warning, a 'black box' warning, on the medications, while the Paediatric Advisory Committee rejected this conclusion and opted only for increased labelling.

An increase in blood pressure with acute or chronic stimulant treatment, known to be approximately 5 mmHg in adults receiving mixed amphetamine salts, would represent a significant population-wide increase in cardiovascular risk. This is in addition to the smaller risk of acute morbidity due to stroke or infarction or unexplained death with stimulant treatment. 'Long-term' studies in children have concluded that after two years of treatment with extended release mixed amphetamine salts (Adderall XR™) blood pressure elevations (systolic, 3.5 mmHg; diastolic, 2.6 mmHg) and pulse elevations (3.4 bpm) were 'clinically insignificant' (Findling *et al.*, 2005). Whether or not these increases accelerate or remain similar after five or ten years of treatment and their relevance to adult cardiovascular morbidity is actually not known. The other important long-term side-effect of stimulant medications is possible growth suppression. Data indicate this is due to appetite suppression. A recent study concluded that 'long-term' treatment (21 months) with long-acting stimulant medication (OROS methylphenidate or Concerta™) is safe and that its effects on growth were 'clinically insignificant' (Spencer et al., 2006). Actually, treated children were 0.23 cm shorter and on average 1.23 kg lighter than expected after 21 months of treatment; again, whether this effect would be the same, less or more after five or ten years of treatment is not known, and any differential medication effect during the child's pubertal growth spurt is also not known. The behavioural treatment effects of stimulant medications have not been shown to persist after medication is discontinued, and no subsequent improvement in psychological or personal health has been demonstrated after medication discontinuation, so studies about the consequences of stimulant therapy for much longer than two years are relevant and urgently needed (Jacobvitz et al., 1990; MTA Group, 1999, 2004; Steer, 2005).

Atomoxitine, a non-stimulant medication, has already received a 'black box' warning for an increased risk of suicidality. This medication has become increasingly popular since it is not a 'controlled substance' and can be prescribed without a DEA number with multiple refills on the same prescription. A recent study funded by Eli Lilly, the manufacturer of atomoxitine (Strattera™), and presented at Child and Adolescent Psychiatry meetings in Toronto, concluded it is as effective in a once-daily dose as twice-daily methylphenidate for reducing symptoms of ADHD (Wang, 2006). Side-effects were described as significantly more common in the atomoxitine group. What is most notable about the side-effects is their number and frequency (atomoxitine vs. methylphenidate): weight loss (1.2 kg vs. 0.4 kg), anorexia (37% vs. 25%), nausea (20% vs. 10%), somnolence (26% vs. 4%), dizziness (15% vs. 7%) and vomiting (12% vs. 6%).

A variety of side-effects are expected with ADHD medications. Those considered 'mild and tolerable' by the American Academy of Child and Adolescent Psychiatry were 'mild anxiety, mild depression, mild irritability, dull/tired/listless, mild picking at skin/nail biting, and fleeting tics' (Greenhill et al., 2002, p. 39S). One would normally expect these symptoms to be a reason for referral, not a result of treatment. A great degree of side-effect 'tolerance' appears to be expected of school-age children receiving stimulant medications that target their noxious behaviours. Although there are published adult testimonials of the pleasure and relief found in receiving the diagnosis of ADHD and beginning medication, there are no similar case reports or testimonials from children (Okie, 2006). There is no literature that studies children's feelings about their medication or diagnosis, nor is there a study that asks children receiving stimulants if the side-effects are worth the benefits. This is a concerning void. Non-compliance rates for school-age children treated with stimulant medication are reported to be 20–65 per cent (Swanson, 2003). Why are the voices of children not being heard? Adolescent non-compliance is a well-known phenomenon, and was the topic of a unique article that included commentaries on a case of a teen who chose to discontinue his ADHD medications. From the abstract: 'the commentaries highlight issues rarely discussed in the mainstream literature, including: the extent to which ADHD is erroneously portrayed and vigorously managed as a disease; the lack of validity of the ADHD construct in adolescence; the widespread use of stimulants as performance-enhancing drugs; the need to respect an adolescent's gut instinct and developing decisions; the importance of family dynamics in ADHD-like situations; the need to ease stimulant withdrawal effects; and the human rights of children prescribed psychotropic drugs' (Cohen et al., 2002, p. 189).

The choice of stimulant medication for any individual child is agreed to be a toss-up, with no evidence that amphetamines or methylphenidate are better for any predictable reason. Published research comparing outcomes may include cohorts whose medications were 'assigned by physician's choice'. A representative study, partially funded by Shire Pharmaceuticals (manufacturer of Adderall™), compared the efficacy of mixed amphetamine salts (Adderall™) and methylphenidate, and found that both drugs were efficacious for symptom improvement (Faraone et al., 2002). Possibly the most notable finding in this study was an 'important subgroup of placebo responders', which suggested a need for further study of the mechanism of the placebo effect in ADHD. Recent 'n-of-1 trials' conducted in paediatric practices in Australia shed further light on this phenomenon (Nikles et al., 2006). The intervention provided a 'within patient randomized double-blind crossover comparison' of stimulant vs. placebo and vs. alternate stimulants for patients on ADHD medication in whom treatment effectiveness was uncertain. Patients underwent six weeks of treatment periods, involving three sets of two-week comparisons between: original stimulant vs. placebo, original stimulant vs. new stimulant, and new stimulant vs. placebo. In 76 drug vs.

placebo comparisons, 29 subjects were 'responders' (defined as more favourable response to original stimulant in all three treatment sets), 12 were 'possible responders (defined as more favourable response to original stimulant in two of three treatment sets), and 28 were 'non-responders' (not specifically defined, but presumably original stimulant was no more effective in either of its head-to-head trials). Specific information on the number of patients responding to placebo is not provided. In 40 patients (63%), immediate post-trial management by doctor/family groups was consistent with trial results, while in 23 patients (37%) it was not. The study's purpose was to describe the use of the trials. Its inadvertent result was to highlight the importance of placebo effect, and possibly also the role played by personal belief, in ADHD 'treatment'.

Empiric trials of medications are often recommended. This approach frankly lacks scientific validity, and given recent information about serious medication side-effects and safety profiles, as well as the significant presence of placebo effect, may be unwise as well as uninfor-mative. Most concerning is the child who does not improve, improves only slightly, or experiences dysphoria, aggressive outbursts or mood dysregulation. Also concerning is the iatrogenic side-effect of stimulant 'rebound', a mimic of mood disorders, in which the child's symptoms worsen as the stimulant wears off (Sarampote et al., 2002). Clinicians and parents may conclude a child needs a higher dose of medication or a different medication(s), and it becomes increasingly difficult to dif-ferentiate under-treated symptoms, medication effects, and medication side-effects.

Pharmaceutical tentacles

In 1961 President Dwight Eisenhower warned about the 'conjunction of an immense military establishment and a large arms industry' in the United States, which he called the 'military industrial com-plex.' He urged Americans to 'guard against the acquisition of unwarranted influence, whether sought or unsought' by this complex (Eisenhower, 1961). In current times, Americans might be warned about a 'pharmaceutico-medical complex'. Pharmaceutical firms make millions of dollars selling medications that physicians prescribe. Whether ADHD is or is not a disease is absolutely critical to the pharmaceutical industry, and millions of dollars are spent advertising ADHD medications and supporting, via consultants' fees and research grants, both physicians and organizations that 'educate' the public about ADHD the disease. Financial support does not necessitate influence, but in the face of conflicting or inconclusive scientific evidence, bias may be unintentionally introduced. It is difficult to identify a review article about ADHD whose authors do not receive funding from a pharmaceutical company that manufactures ADHD medications (e.g. Spencer, 2005). Disclosure information for members of the AAP subcommittee on Attention-Deficit/Hyperactivity Disorder who co-authored the AAP Guidelines on ADHD was requested but not received. A representative responded that at the time the Guidelines were published this information was not required (Crane, 2006, personal communication). However, other information from the American Academy of Paediatrics on ADHD, including brochures, ADHD toolkit forms and other publications, is partially funded by McNeil Consumer and Specialty Pharmaceuticals, who manufacture Concerta™ with the McNeil Consumer and Specialty Pharmaceuticals logo and name stamped at the bottom of the ADHD toolkit forms and brochures (Van Landeghem and Hess, 2005; American Academy of Pediatrics, 2002, 2005).

Children and Adults with Attention Deficit Disorder (CHADD) is an organization that represents itself as educational and supportive. Use of medications for ADHD treatment is advocated by CHADD. In its annual budget of approximately $4.6 million (2004–5), 22 per cent of revenue comes from seven pharmaceutical companies that manufacture ADHD medications (CHADD, 2005). Finally, it was recently reported that 13 of the 21 individuals who set criteria for the DSM-IV diagnosis of ADHD have financial ties to pharmaceutical manufacturers of ADHD medications (Cosgrove *et al.*, 2006; Okie, 2006, p. 2641). There is reasonable evidence that ADHD is neither a disease nor a neurobehavioural disorder, which would make treatment with stimulant medications completely unnecessary, but whether the 'pharmaceutico-medical' complex will permit physicians, parents and educators to tumble to this conclusion is not yet clear.

Conclusions

Review of supporting literature for ADHD reveals no clear evidence for a discrete disease or condition. The 'core ADHD symptoms' of inattention, impulsivity and hyperactivity may result from numerous psychiatric, emotional and educational conditions that have been subsumed under the cloak of 'comorbidities.' There is no diagnostic test for ADHD, and widely used screening tools and criteria have not been validated. Stimulant medication trials do not diagnose ADHD, and the side-effect and safety profiles of these and other ADHD medications are concerning. A convergence of societal and financial pressures has created an ADHD industry which does not serve the interests of the individual child. These pressures include: (1) poor availability and accessibility of mental health resources; (2) decreased insurance coverage for mental health care; (3) stigmatization of emotional and social causes of mental health problems with emphasis on biological psychiatry; (4) increased economic pressures on families, leaving less time for any therapy that requires weekly or more frequent visits; (5) poor availability of educational testing in and out of the school system; (6) the inclusion in 1991 of ADHD as a reimbursable diagnosis for educational services under the Individuals with Disabilities Education Act Amendments of 1997 (increasing the financial incentive for school systems to diagnose this condition);and last, but not least, (7) well-funded and pervasive marketing of ADHD as a biological disease by pharmaceutical firms that manufacture ADHD medication.

Children deserve more than a checklist and a medication. Each child's symptoms deserve to be thoroughly and thoughtfully evaluated so he or she can receive the best and most appropriate intervention in a timely fashion. Full evaluation may include family assessment, educational and psychiatric or psychological testing, and may require multiple visits. Parents can be supported to advocate for their children's needs in the face of resource scarcity, and can be helped to understand that not all that ails a child either requires a pill or alternatively is the result of poor parenting. Children with difficulties can be encouraged to engage in treatment that supports personal mastery, which improves self-esteem, rather than receiving a lifetime label with daily medication.

Acknowledgements

Portions of this chapter were excerpted from L. Furman (2005) What is ADHD?, *Journal of Child Neurology* 20, 994–1003. Thanks are due to Dr Roger Brumback, Editor of *Journal of Child Neurology*, for permission to do so. Many of the ideas expressed here were the original work of Robert A. Furman, MD.

Note

1. It should be noted that many of the comorbid conditions (such as childhood depression and oppositional defiant disorder) are themselves the subject of debates with regard to their validity, cause and treatment.

References

American Academy of Paediatrics (2000) Clinical practice guideline: Diagnosis and evaluation of the child with attention-deficit/hyperactivity disorder. *Pediatrics* 105, 1158–70.

American Academy of Paediatrics (2001) Clinical practice guideline: treatment of the school-aged child with attention-deficit/hyperactivity disorder. *Pediatrics* 108, 1033–44.

American Academy of Pediatrics Arizona Chapter. ADHD Toolkit <http://www.azaap.org/for-health-care-providers/adhd.aspx> (accessed 1-26-08). Example of Toolkit form: D4 NICHQ Vanderbilt Assessment Scale – TEACHER Informant HE0351, copyright 2002 by American Academy of Paediatrics and National Initiative for Children's Healthcare Quality, 11-20/rev0303. <http://www.azaap.org/Common/Files/ADHDVanderbilt TeacherAssessment.pdf> (accessed 26 January 2008).

American Academy of Pediatrics (2005) What is ADHD anyway? Questions from teens (trifold brochure), HE50378.

American Psychiatric Association (1994) *Diagnostic and Statistical Manual of Mental Disorders, 4th edition (DSM-IV).* Washington, DC: American Psychiatric Association.

Barkley, R. A. and Cunningham, C. E. (1978) Do stimulant drugs improve the performance of hyperkinetic children? *Clinical Pediatrics* 17, 85–92.

Barr, C. L., Xu, C., Kroft, J., Feng, Y., Wigg, K. G., Zai, G., *et al.* (2001) Haplotype study of four polymorphisms at the dopamine transporter locus confirm linkage to attention deficit hyperactivity disorder, *Biological Psychiatry* 49, 333–9.

Bernstein, G. A., Carroll, M. E., Crosby, R. D., *et al.* (1994) Caffeine effects on learning, performance and anxiety in normal school-age children, *Journal of the American Academy of Child and Adolescent Psychiatry* 33, 407–15.

Biederman, J., Milberger, S., Faraone, S. V., Kiely, K., Guite, J., Mick, E., *et al.* (1995) Family-environment risk factors for attention deficit hyperactivity disorder: A test of Rutter's indicators of adversity, *Archives of General Psychiatry* 52, 464–70.

Biederman, J., Faraone, S., Milberger, S. *et al.* (1996) Predictors of persistence and remission of ADHD into adolescence: Results from a four-year prospective follow-up study, *Journal of the American Academy of Child and Adolescent Psychiatry* 35, 343–51.

Biederman, J. (2005) Attention-Deficit/Hyperactivity Disorder: A selective overview, *Biological Psychiatry* 49, 1215–20.

Bobb, A. J., Addington, A. M., Sidransky, E., Gornick, M. C., Lerch, J. P., Greenstein, D. K., Clasen, L.S., Sharp, W. S., Inoff-Germain, G., Wavrant-De Vrieze, F., Arcos-Burgos, M., Straub, R. E., Hardy, J. A., Castellanos, F. X. and Rapoport, J. L. (2005) Support for association between ADHD and two candidate genes: NET1 and DRD1, *American Journal of Medical Genetics, Series B (Neuropsychiatric Genetics)* 5, 67–72.

Brown, T. E. (ed.). (2000) *Attention-Deficit Disorders and Comorbidities in Children, Adolescents, and Adults.* Washington, DC: American Psychiatric Press.

Bush, G., Valera, E. M., and Seidman, L. J. (2005) Advancing the neuroscience of ADHD Functional Neuroimaging of Attention-Deficit/Hyperactivity Disorder: A review and suggested future directions, *Biological Psychiatry* 57, 1273–84.

Butler, S. F., Arredondo, D. E. and McCloskey, V. (1995) Affective comorbidity in children and adolescents with attention deficit hyperactivity disorder, *Annals of Clinical Psychiatry* 7, 51–5.

Carey, W. B. (2002) Is ADHD a valid disorder? in P. S. Jensen and J.R. Cooper, (eds), *Attention Deficit Hyperactivity Disorder: State of the Science. Best Practices.* Kingston, NJ: Civic Research Institute.

Castellanos, F. X., Giedd, J. N., Marsh, W. L., Hamburger, S. D., Vaituzis, A. C., Dickstein, D. P., *et al.* (1996) Quantitative brain magnetic resonance imaging in attention deficit hyperactivity disorder, *Archives of General Psychiatry* 53, 607–16.

Castellanos, F. X., Giedd, J. N., Berquin, P. C., Walter, J. M., Sharp, W., Tran, T., *et al.* (2001) Quantitative brain magnetic resonance imaging in girls with attention-deficit/hyperactivity disorder, *Archives of General Psychiatry* 58, 289–95.

Castellanos, F. X., Lee, P. P., Sharp, W., Jeffries, N. O., Greenstein, D. K., Clasen L. S., *et al.* (2002) Developmental trajectories of brain volume abnormalities in children and adolescents with attention-deficit/hyperactivity disorder, *Journal of the American Medical Association (JAMA)* 288 (2002), 1740–8.

Children and Adults with Attention Deficit Disorder (2005) Annual Budget Summary <http://www.chadd.org/AM/Template.cfm?Section=Reports1& Template=/CM/ContentDisplay.cfm&ContentID=1771>, accessed 19 July 2006.

Chen, C. K., Chen, S. L., Mill, J., Huang, Y. S., Lin, S. K., Curran, S., *et al.* (2003) The dopamine transporter gene is associated with attention deficit hyperactivity disorder in a Taiwanese sample, *Molecular Psychiatry* 8, 393–6.

Cheon, K., Young, H., Kim, Y., Namkoong, K., Kim, C. and Lee, J. (2003) Dopamine transporter density in the basal ganglia assessed with [123I]IPT SPET in children with attention deficit hyperactivity disorder, *European Journal of Nuclear Medicine and Molecular Imaging* 30, 306–11.

Chronis, A. M., Lahey, B. B., Pelham, W. E., Kipp, H. L., Baumann, B. L., Lee, S. S. (2003) Psychopathology and substance abuse in parents of young children with Attention-Deficit/Hyperactivity Disorder, *Journal of the American Academy of Child and Adolescent Psychiatry* 42, 1424–32.

Cohen, D. and Leo, J. (2004) An update on ADHD neuroimaging research, *The Journal of Mind and Behavior* 25, 161–6.

Cohen, D., Leo, J., Stanton, T., Smith, D., McCready, K., Laing, M. S., Stein, D. B., Oas, P., Kean, B., Parry, S. (2002) A boy who stops taking stimulants for 'ADHD': Commentaries on a Paediatrics case study, *Ethical Human Sciences and Services*. 4, 189–209.

Coles, G. (1987) *The Learning Mystique*. New York: Pantheon Books.

Collett, B. R., Ohan, J. L., and Myers, K. M. (2003) Ten-year review of rating scales. V: Scales assessing attention-deficit/hyperactivity disorder, *Journal of the American Academy of Child and Adolescent Psychiatry* 42, 1015–37.

Compton, S. N. (2004) Cognitive-behavioural psychotherapy for anxiety and depressive disorders in children and adolescents: an evidence-based medicine review, *Journal of the American Academy of Child and Adolescent Psychiatry* 43, 930–51.

Concannon, P. E. and Tang, Y. P. (2005) Management of attention deficit hyperactivity disorder: A parental perspective, *Journal of Paediatrics and Child Health* 41, 625–30.

Connor, D. F., Edwards, G., Fletcher, K. E., Baird, J., Barkley, R. A. and Steingard, R. J. (2003) Correlates of comorbid psychopathology in children with ADHD, *Journal of the American Academy of Child and Adolescent Psychiatry* 42, 193–200.

Cook, E. H., Stein, M. A., Krasowski, M. D., Cox, N. J., Olkon, D. M., Kieffer, J.E., *et al.* (1995) Association of attention deficit disorder and the dopamine transporter gene, *American Journal of Human Genetics* 56, 993–8.

Cosgrove L., Krimsky S., Vijayaraghavan M., Schneider L. (2006) Financial ties between DSM-IV panel members and the pharmaceutical industry. Psychotherapy and Psychosomatics, 75, 154–160.

Coyle, J. T. (2003) Depression and bipolar support alliance consensus statement on the unmet needs in diagnosis and treatment of mood disorders in children and adolescents, *Journal of the American Academy of Child and Adolescent Psychiatry* 42, 1494–503.

Curran, S., Mill, J., Tahir, E., Kent, L., Richards, S., Gould A., *et al.* (2001) Association study of a dopamine transporter polymorphism and attention deficit hyperactivity disorder in UK and Turkish samples, *Molecular Psychiatry* 6, 425–8.

Dankaerts, M. and Taylor, E. (1995) The epidemiology of childhood hyperactivity, in F. C. Verhulst and H. M. Koot (eds), *The Epidemiology of Child and Adolescent Psychopathology*. Oxford: Oxford University Press, pp. 178–209.

DelBello, M. P., Soutullo, C. A., Hendricks, W., Niemeier, R. T., McElroy, S. L. and Strakowski, S. M. (2001) Prior stimulant treatment in adolescents with bipolar disorder: Association with age at onset, *Bipolar Disorder* 3, 53–7.

Dilsaver, S. C., Henderson-Fuller, S. and Akiskal, H. S. (2003) Occult mood disorders in 104 consecutively presenting children referred for the treatment of attention-deficit/hyperactivity disorder in a community mental health clinic, *Journal of Clinical Psychiatry* 64, 1170–6.

Douglas, V. I., Barr, R. G., O'Neill, M. E. *et al.* (1986) Short term effects of methylphenidate on the cognitive, learning and academic performance of children with attention deficit disorder in the laboratory and the classroom, *Journal of Child Psychology and Psychiatry* 27, 191–211.

Dulcan, M. (1997) Practice parameter for the use of stimulant medication in the treatment of children, adolescents, and adults, *Journal of the American Academy of Child and Adolescent Psychiatry* 36 (10 Suppl.), 85S–121S.

Durston, S., Hulshoff Pol, H. E., Schnack, H. G., Buitelaar, J. K., Steenhuis, M. P., Minderaa, R. B., *et al.* (2004) Magnetic resonance imaging of boys with attention-deficit/hyperactivity disorder and their unaffected siblings, *Journal of the American Academy of Child and Adolescent Psychiatry* 43, 332–40.

Eisenhower, D. D. (1961) Military industrial complex speech. From *Public Papers of the Presidents' Dwight D. Eisenhower.* Available at http://coursesa.matrix.msu.edu/~hst306/documents/indust.html accessed 11–05–2008.

Elgar, F. J., Curtis, L. J., McGrath, P. J., Waschbusch, D. A., Stewart, S. H. (2003) Antecedent-consequence conditions in maternal mood and child adjustment: A four-year cross-lagged study, *Journal of Clinical Child and Adolescent Psychology* 32, 362–74.

El-Sayed, E. (1999) May a genetically determined slow maturational rate explain AD/HD and hyperkinetic disorders: A proposal of an alternate hypothesis and methodologic aspects. Licentiate Thesis. Stockholm: Karolinska Institutet.

El-Sayed, E., Larsson, J. O., Persson, H. E., Santosh, P. J. and Rydelius, P. A. (2003) 'Maturational lag' hypothesis of attention deficit hyperactivity disorder: An update, Acta paediatrica 92, 776–84.

Faraone, S. V., Short, E. J., Biederman, J., Findling, R. L., Roe, C. and Manos, M. J. (2002) Efficacy of Adderall and methylphenidate in attention deficit hyperactivity disorder: A drug-placebo and drug-drug response curve analysis of a naturalistic study,. *International Journal of Neuropsychopharmacology* 5, 121–9.

Faraone, S. V., Doyle, A. E., Mick, E. and Biederman, J. (2001) Meta-analysis of the association between the 7-repeat allele of the dopamine d(4) receptor gene and attention deficit hyperactivity disorder, *American Journal of Psychiatry* 158, 1052–7.

Faraone, S. V. (2004) Genetics of adult attention-deficit/hyperactivity disorder, *Psychiatric Clinics of North America* 27, 303–21.

Faraone, S. V., Perlis, R. H., Doyle, A. E., Smoller, J. W., Goralnick, J. J., Holmgren, M. A. and Sklar, P. (2005) Molecular genetics of Attention-Deficit/Hyperactivity Disorder, *Biological Psychiatry* 57, 1313–23.

Ford, T. (2003) The British child and adolescent mental health survey 1999: The prevalence of DSM-IV disorders, *Journal of the American Academy of Child and Adolescent Psychiatry* 42, 1203–11.

Findling, R. L., Biederman, J., Wilens, T. E., Spencer, T. J., McGough, J. J., Lopez, F. A. and Tulloch, S. J. SLI381.301 and .302 Study Groups (2005) Short- and long-term cardiovascular effects of mixed amphetamine salts extended release in children, *Journal of Pediatrics* 147, 348–54.

Fisher, M. (1990) Parenting stress and the child with attention-deficit/hyperactivity disorder, *Journal of Clinical Child Psychology* 19, 337–46.

Foorman, B. R., Breier, J. I. and Fletcher, J. M. (2003) Interventions aimed at improving reading success: An evidence-based approach, *Developmental Neuropsychology* 24, 613–39.

Furman, E. (1992) What is depression in childhood? *Child Analysis* 4, 101–23.

Furman, L. (2005) What is Attention-Deficit/Hyperactivity Disorder (ADHD)? *Journal of Child Neurology* 20, 994–1003.

Furman, R. A. (2002) Attention Deficit/Hyperactivity Disorder: An alternative viewpoint, *Journal of International Child and Adolescent Psychiatry* 2, 125–44.

Gianarris, W. J., Golden, C. J. and Greene, L. (2001) The Conners' Parent Rating Scales: A critical review of the literature, *Clinical Psychology Review* 21, 1061–93.

Gottesman, I. I. and Gould, T. D. (2003) The endophenotype concept in psychiatry: Etymology and strategic intentions, *American Journal of Psychiatry* 160, 636–45.

Grady, D. L., Chi, H. C., Ding, Y. C., Smith, M., Wang, E., Schuck, S., et al. (2003) High prevalence of rare dopamine receptor D4 alleles in children diagnosed with attention-deficit hyperactivity disorder, *Molecular Psychiatry* 8, 536–45.

Greenhill, L. L., Pliszka, S. R., Dulcan, M. K., Bernet, W., Arnold, V., Beitchman, J. et al. (2002) Practice parameter for the use of stimulant medication in the treatment of children, adolescents, and adults, *Journal of the American Academy of Child and Adolescent Psychiatry*, 41, 26S–49S.

Grizenko, N., Bhat, M., Schwartz, G., Ter-Stephanian, M. and Joober, R. (2006) Efficacy of methylphenidate in children with attention-deficit hyperactivity disorder and learning disabilities: A randomized crossover trial, *Journal of Psychiatry and Neuroscience* 31, 46–51.

Hartnell, N. R. and Wilson, J. P. (2004) Replication of the Weber effect using postmarketing adverse event reports voluntarily submitted to the United States Food and Drug Administration. Pharmacotherapy, 24, 743–9.

Hershorin, E. R. (2006) Co-morbidities in ADHD, presented at Masters in Paediatrics 2006 Leadership Conference, 25–30 January, Bal Harbour, Florida. Quoted in M. Rosenthal, Evaluate for coexisting morbidities when treating children with ADHD, *Infectious Diseases in Children* 2006; May, pp. 38–40 <http://www.idinchildren.com/200605/frameset.asp?article=children.asp>, accessed 9 February 2007.

Hill, D. E., Yeo, R. A., Campbell, R. A., Hart, B., Vigil, J. and Brooks, W. (2003) Magnetic resonance imaging correlates of attention-deficit/hyperactivity disorder in children, *Neuropsychology* 17, 496–506.

Horwitz, S. M., Kelleher, K. J., Stein, R. E. K., *et al.* (2005) Barriers to the identification and management of mental health issues in pediatric primary care. American Academy of Pediatrics, Division of Health Policy Research Periodic Survey #59: Executive Summary. Elk Grove Village, IL <http://www.aap.org/research/abstracts/05abstract1.htm>, accessed 26 January 2008.

Jacobvitz, D., Sroufe, L. A., Stewart, M. and Leffert, N. (1990) Treatment of attentional and hyperactivity problems in children with sympathomimetic drugs: a comprehensive review, *Journal of the American Academy of Child and Adolescent Psychiatry* 29, 677–88.

Jensen, P. S., Arnold, E., Swanson J. M. *et al.* (2007) 3-year follow-up of NIMH MTA study. *Journal of the American Academy of Child and Adolescent Psychiatry* 46, 988–1002.

Jensen, P. S., Shervette, R. E. III, Xenakis, S. N. and Richters, J. (1993) Anxiety and depressive disorders in attention deficit disorder with hyperactivity: New findings, *American Journal of Psychiatry* 150, 1203–09.

Johnson, J. G., Cohen, P. and Brook, J. S. (2000) Associations between bipolar disorder and other psychiatry disorders during adolescence and early adulthood: a community-based longitudinal investigation *American Journal of Psychiatry* 157, 1679–81.

Johnston, C. and Mash, E. J. (2001) Families of children with attention-deficit/hyperactivity disorder: Review and recommendations for future research, *Clinical Child and Family Psychology Review* 4, 183–207.

Kessler, R. C., Adler, L., Barkley, R., *et al.* (2006) The prevalence and correlates of adult ADHD in the United States: Results from the National Comorbidity Survey Replication, *American Journal of Psychiatry* 163, 716–23.

Kim, B. N., Lee, J. S., Cho, S. C. and Lee, D. S. (2001) Methylphenidate increased regional cerebral blood flow in subjects with attention deficit/hyperactivity disorder, *Yonsei Medical Journal* 42, 19–29.

Kim, B. N., Lee, J. S., Shin, M. S., Cho, S. C. and Lee, D. S. (2002) Regional cerebral perfusion abnormalities in attention deficit/hyperactivity disorder: Statistical parametric mapping analysis, *European Archives of Psychiatry and Clinical Neuroscience* 252, 219–25.

Kipp, K. (2005) A developmental perspective on the measurement of cognitive deficits in Attention-Deficit/Hyperactivity Disorder, *Biological Psychiatry* 49, 1256–60.

Kowatch, R. A., Fristad, M., Birmaher, B., Wagner, K. D., Findling, R. L. and Hellander, M., Child Psychiatric Workgroup on Bipolar Disorder (2005) Treatment guidelines for children and adolescents with bipolar disorder, *Journal of the American Academy of Child and Adolescent Psychiatry* 44, 213–35.

Kustanovich, V., Ishii, J., Crawford, L., Yang, M., McGough, J. J., McCracken, J. T., *et al.* (2003) Transmission disequilibrium testing of dopamine-related candidate gene polymorphisms in ADHD: Confirmation of association of ADHD with DRD4 and DRD5, *Molecular Psychiatry* 9, 711–17.

Lahey, B. B., McBurnett, K., Piacentini, J.C. (1987) Agreement of parent and teacher rating scales with comprehensive clinical assessment of attention deficit disorder with hyperactivity, *Journal of Psychopathological Behavaviour Assessment* 9, 429–39.

Leslie, L. K., Weckerly, J., Plemmons, D., Landsverk, J. and Eastman, S. (2004) Implementing the American Academy of Paediatrics attention-deficit/hyperactivity disorder diagnostic guidelines in primary care settings, *Pediatr* 114, 129–40.

Levine, K. (1991) Attention-Deficit/Hyperactivity Disorder – a non-organic point of view, presented at Psychiatry Grand Rounds, University Hospitals, Cleveland, OH.

Levine, M. (2006) All Kinds of Minds <http://www.allkindsofminds.org/index.aspx>, accessed 17 August 2006.

Lewinsohn, P. M., Rohde, P., Seeley, J. R., Klein, D. N. and Gotlib, I. H. (2002) Natural course of adolescent major depressive disorder in a community sample: Predictors of recurrence in young adults, *American Journal of Psychiatry* 157, 1584–91.

Llorente, A. M., Voigt, R. G., Jensen, C. L., Berretta, M. C., Kennard Fraley, J. and Heird, W. C. (2006) Performance on a visual sustained attention and discrimination task is associated with urinary excretion of norepineprhine metabolite in children with attention-deficit/hyperactivity disorder (AD/HD), *Clinical Neuropsychology* 20, 133–44.

Madras, B. K., Miller, G. M. and Fischman, A. J. (2005) The dopamine transporter and attention-deficit/hyperactivity disorder, *Biological Psychiatry* 57, 1397–1409.

Maher, B. S., Marazita, M. L., Ferrell, R. E. and Vanyukov, M. M. (2002) Dopamine system genes and attention deficit hyperactivity disorder: A meta-analysis, *Psychiatric Genetics* 12, 207–15.

Mattes, J. A. (1980) The role of frontal lobe dysfunction in childhood dyskinesis, *Compre Psychiatry* 21, 358–69.

McGee, R., Williams, S., Moffett, T., *et al.* (1989) A comparison of 13-year-old boys with attention deficit and/or reading disorder of neuropsychological measures, *Journal of Abnormal Child Psychology* 17, 37–53.

McGuiness, D. (1989) Attention deficit disorder: The emperor's clothes, animal 'pharm', and other fiction, in S. Fisher and R. P. Greenburg (eds), *The Limits of Biological Treatments for Psychological Distress*. Hillsdale, NJ: Lawrence Erbaum Associates, 151–87.

Mill, J., Curran, S., Kent, L., Richards, S., Gould, A., Virdee, V., *et al.* (2001) Attention deficit hyperactivity disorder (ADHD) and the dopamine D4 receptor gene: Evidence of association but no linkage in a UK sample, *Molecular Psychiatry* 6, 440–4.

Mitsis, E. M., McKay, K. E., Schulz, K. P., Newcorn, J. H. and Halperin, J. M. (2000) Parent-teacher concordance for *DSM-IV* attention-deficit/hyperactivity disorder in a clinic-referred sample, *Journal of the American Academy of Child and Adolescent Psychiatry* 39, 308–13.

Mosholder, A. D. and Pamer, C. A. (2006) Postmarketing surveillance of suicidal adverse event with pediatric use of antidepressants. *Journal of Child and Adolescent Psychopharmacology* 16, 33–36.

Muglia, P., Jain, U., Inkster, B. and Kennedy, J. L. (2002) A quantitative trait locus analysis of the dopamine transporter gene in adults with ADHD, *Neuropsychopharmacology* 27, 655–62.

Mulhern, S., Dworkin, P. H. and Bernstein, B. (1994) Do parental concerns predict a diagnosis of attention-deficit hyperactivity disorder? *Journal of Developmental and Behavioral Pediatrics* 15, 348–52.

Murphy, J. M., Wehler, C. A., Pagano, M. E., Little, M., Kleinman, R. E. and Jellinek, M. S. (1998) Relationship between hunger and psychosocial functioning in low-income American children, *Journal of the American Academy of Child and Adolescent Psychiatry* 37, 163–70.

MTA Cooperative Group (1999) A 14-month randomized clinical trial of treatment strategies for attention deficit/hyperactivity disorder, *Archives of General Psychiatry* 56, 1073–86.

MTA Cooperative Group (2004) National Institute of Mental Health Multimodal Treatment Study of ADHD follow-up: Changes in effectiveness and growth after the end of treatment, *Pediatrics* 113, 762–9.

MTA Cooperative Group (2004) National Institute of Mental Health Multimodal Treatment Study of ADHD follow-up: 24-month outcomes of treatment strategies for attention-deficit/hyperactivity disorder, *Pediatrics* 113, 754–61.

Nikles C. J., Mitchell G. K., Del Mar C. B., Clavarino A. and McNairn N. (2006) An n-of-1 trial service in clinical practice: testing the effectiveness of stimulants for attention-deficit/hyperactivity disorder, *Pediatrics*, 117, 2040–2046.

Nigg, J. T. (2005) Neuropsychologic theory and findings in attention-deficit/hyperactivity disorder: The state of the field and salient challenges for the coming decade, *Biological Psychiatry* 57, 1425–35.

Nigg, J. T., Willcutt, E. G., Doyle, A. E. and Sonuga-Barke, E. J. S. (2005) Causal heterogeneity in attention-deficit/hyperactivity disorder: Do we need neuropsychologically impaired subtypes? *Biological Psychiatry* 57, 1224–30.

NIMH Blueprint Report NIMH. National Advisory Mental Health Council Workgroup on Child and Adolescent Mental Health Intervention Development and Deployment (2001) *Blueprint for Change: Research on Child and Adolescent Mental Health.* Washington, DC: National Institute of Mental Health.

Nissen, S. E. (2005) Cardiovascular and renal drugs advisory committee. Report from the cardiovascular and renal drugs advisory committee: US Food and Drug Administration June 15–16, 2005, Gathersberg, MD. *Circulation* 112, 2043–6.

Nissen, S.E. (2006) ADHD drugs and cardiovascular risk, *New England Journal of Medicine (NEJM)* 354, 1445–8.

Oades, R. D., Sadile, A. G., Sagvolden, T., Viggiano, D., Zuddas, A., Devoto, P., Aase, H., Johansen, E. B., Ruocco, L. A. and Russell, V. A. (2005) The control of responsiveness in ADHD by catecholamines: Evidence for dopaminergic, noradrenergic and interactive roles, *Developmental Science* 8, 122–31.

O'Connor, R. E., Harty, K. R. and Fulmer, D. (2005) Tiers of intervention in kindergarten through third grade, *Journal of Learning Disabilities* 38, 532–8.

Okie, S. (2006) ADHD in adults, *New England Journal of Medicine*, 354, 2637–44.

Pauls, D. L. (2005) The genetics of attention-deficit/hyperactivity disorder, *Biological Psychiatry* 57, 1310–12.

Payton, A., Holmes, J., Barrett, J. H., Sham, P., Harrington, R., McGuffin, P., *et al.* (2001) Susceptibility genes for a trait measure of attention deficit hyperactivity disorder: A pilot study in a non-clinical sample of twins, *Psychiatry Research* 105, 273–8.

Pelham, W. E., Gnagy, E. M., Greenslade, K. E., and Milich, R. (1992) Teacher ratings of *DSM-III-R* symptoms for the disruptive behaviour disorders, *Journal of the American Academy of Child and Adolescent Psychiatry* 31, 210–18.

Pelham, W. E. Jr, Fabiano, G. A. and Massetti, G. M. (2005) Evidence-based assessment of attention deficit hyperactivity disorder in children and adolescents, *Journal of Clinical Child and Adolescent Psychology* 34, 449–76.

Pennington, B. (2005) Toward a new neuropsychological model of attention-deficit/hyperactivity disorder: subtypes and multiple deficits, *Biological Psychiatry* 57, 1221–3.

Pine, D. S., Cohen, E., Cohen, P. and Brook, J. (1999) Adolescent depressive symptoms as predictors of adult depression: Moodiness or mood disorder? *American Journal of Psychiatry* 156, 133–5.

Pine, D. S., Cohen, P. and Brook, J. (2001) Adolescent fears as predictors of depression, *Biological Psychiatry* 50, 721–4.

Pliszka, S. R. (1989) Effect of anxiety on cognition, behaviour, and stimulant response in ADHD, *Journal of the American Academy of Child and Adolescent Psychiatry* 28, 882–7.

Pliszka, S. R. (2000) Patterns of psychiatric comorbidity with attention deficit/hyperactivity disorder, *Child and Adolescent Psychiatric Clinics of North America* 9, 525–40.

Pliszka, S. R. (2003) Psychiatric comorbidities in children with attention deficit hyperactivity disorder: Implications for management, *Paediatric Drugs* 5, 741–50.

Pliszka, S. R. (2005) The neuropsychopharmacology of attention-deficit/hyperactivity disorder, *Biological Psychiatry* 57, 1385–90.

Rappaport, J. L., Buchsbaum, M. S. and Weingartner, H., *et al.* (1978) Dextroamphetamine: Cognitive and behavioural effects in normal prepubertal boys, *Science* 199, 560–3.

Rappaport, J. L., Buchsbaum, M. S. and Weingartner, H., *et al.* (1980) Dextroamphetamine: Its cognitive and behavioural effects in normal and hyperactive boys and men, *Archives of General Psychiatry* 37, 933–43.

Richardson, E., Kupietz, S. S., Winsberg, B. G., *et al.* (1988) Effects of methylphenidate dosage in hyperactive reading-disabled children: II. Reading achievement, *Journal of the American Academy of Child and Adolescent Psychiatry* 27, 78–87.

Rie, H. E., Rie, E. D., Stewart, S. and Ambuel, J. P. (1976) Effects of ritalin on underachieving children: a replication. *American Journal of Orthopsychiatry* 46, 313–22.

Romano, E., Tremblay, R. E., Farhat, A. and Côté, S. (2006) Development and prediction of hyperactive symptoms from 2 to 7 years in a population-based sample, *Pediatrics* 117, 2101–9.

Roth, R. M. and Saykin, A. J. (2004) Executive dysfunction in attention-deficit/hyperactivity disorder: Cognitive and neuroimaging findings, *Psychiatric Clinics of North America* 27, 83–96.

Ryan, N. D. (2001) Diagnosing paediatric depression, *Biological Psychiatry* 49, 1050–4.

Rydelius, P. A. (1994) Children of alcoholic parents: At risk to experience violence and to develop violent behaviour, in D. Chiland and J. G. Young (eds), *Children and Violence*. Northvale, NJ: Jason Aronson, pp. 72–90.

Safer, D. (2000) Commentary, *Journal of the American Academy of Child and Adolescent Psychiatry* 39, 989–92.

Sandberg, S. (1996) Hyperkinetic or attention deficit disorder, *British Journal of Psychiatry* 169,10–17.

Sarampote, C. S., Efron, L. A., Robb, A. S., Pearl, P. L. and Stein, M. A. (2002) Can stimulant rebound mimic paediatric bipolar disorder? *Journal of Child and Adolescent Psychopharmacology* 12, 63–7.

Semrud-Clikeman, M., Biederman, J., Sprich-Buckminster, S., *et al.* (1992) Comorbidity between ADDH and learning disability: A review and report in a clinically referred sample, *Journal of the American Academy of Child and Adolescent Psychiatry* 31, 439–48.

Sergeant, J. A. (2005) Modeling attention-deficit/hyperactivity disorder: A critical appraisal of the cognitive-energetic model, *Biological Psychiatry* 49, 1248–55.

Seidman, L. J., Valera, E. M. and Makris, N. (2005) Advancing the neuroscience of ADHD: Structural brain imaging of attention-deficit/hyperactivity disorder, *Biological Psychiatry* 57, 1263–72.

Shaw, D. S., Owens, E. B., Giovannelli, J. and Winslow, E. B. (2001) Infant and toddler pathways leading to early externalizing disorders, *Journal of the American Academy of Child and Adolescent Psychiatry* 40, 36–43.

Shea, K. M., Rahmani, C. H. and Morris, P. J. (1996) Diagnosing children with attention deficit disorders through a health department-public school partnership, *American Journal of Public Health* 86, 1168–9.

Smith, E. A., Russell, A., Lorch, E., Banerjee, S. P., Rose, M., Ivey, J., *et al.* (2003) Increased medial thalamic choline found in paediatric patients with obsessive-compulsive disorder versus major depression or healthy control subjects: A magnetic resonance spectroscopy study, *Biological Psychiatry* 54, 1399–1405.

Snyder, S. M., Drozd, J. F. and Xenakis, S. N. (2004) Validation of ADHD Rating Scales (letter to the Editor, discussion), *Journal of the American Academy of Child and Adolescent Psychiatry* 43, 1189–90.

Sonuga-Barke, E. J. S. and Edmund, J. S. (2005) Causal models of attention-deficit/hyperactivity disorder: From common simple deficits to multiple developmental pathways, *Biological Psychiatry* 57, 1231–8.

Spencer, T., Biederman, J. and Wilens, T. (2003) Attention-deficit/hyperactivity disorder and comorbidity, *Journal of the American Academy of Child and Adolescent Psychiatry* 46, 915–27.

Spencer, T. J., Biederman, J., Madras, B., Faraone, S. V., Dougherty, D. D., Bonab, A. A. and Fischman, A. J. (2005) In vivo neuroreceptor imaging in attention-deficit/hyperactivity disorder: A focus on the dopamine transporter, *Biological Psychiatry* 57, 1293–1300.

Spencer, T. J., Faraone, S. V., Biederman, J., Lerner, M., Cooper, K. M. and Zimmerman, B.; Concerta Study Group (2006) Does prolonged therapy with a long-acting stimulant suppress growth in children with ADHD? *Journal of the American Academy of Child and Adolescent Psychiatry* 45, 527–37.

Steer, C. R. (2005) Managing attention deficit/hyperactivity disorder: unmet needs and future directions, *Archives of Disease in Childhood* 90 Suppl, 19–25.

Swanson, J. (2003) Compliance with stimulants for attention-deficit/hyperactivity disorder: Issues and approaches for improvement, *CNS Drugs* 17, 117–31.

Taylor, E. (1995) Developmental psychopathology of hyperactivity, in J. Sargeant (ed.), *European Approaches to Hyperkinetic Disorder.* Zurich: Trumphimporteur, pp. 173–89.

Todd, R. D., Jong, Y. J., Lobos, E. A., Reich, W., Heath, A. C. and Neuman, R. J. (2001) No association of the dopamine transporter gene 3' VNTR polymorphism with ADHD subtypes in a population sample of twins, *American Journal of Medical Genetics*, 105, 745–8.

Trites, R. L. and Laprade, K. (1983) Evidence for an independent syndrome of hyperactivity, *Journal of Child Psychology and Psychiatry* 24, 573–86.

Ullmann, R. K., Sleator, E. K. and Sprague, R. L. (1984) ADD children: who is referred from the schools? *Psychopharmacological Bulletin* 20, 308–12.

Vaidya, C. J. , Austin, G., Kirkorian, G., Ridlehuber, H. W., Desmond, J. E., Gary, H., Glover, G. H., and Gabrieli, J. D. E. (1998) Selective effects of methylphenidate in attention deficit hyperactivity disorder: A functional magnetic resonance study, Proceedings of the National Academy of Sciences, 95, 14494–9.

Van Landeghem, K. and Hess, C. Children's Mental Health: An overview and key considerations for health system stakeholders. National Institute for Health Care Management *(NIHCM)* Foundation. *NICHM Issue Paper, February 2005, p. 20.* <http://www.nihcm.org/pdf/CMHReport-FINAL.pdf>, accessed 26 January 2008.

Viggiano, D., Ruocco, L. A., Arcieri, S. and Sadile, A. G. (2004) Involvement of norepinephrine in the control of activity and attentive processes in animal models of attention deficit hyperactivity disorder, *Neural Plasticity*, 11, 133–49.

Volkow, N. D., Wang, G. J., Fowler, J. S., Telang, F., Maynard, L., Logan, J., Gatley, S. J., Pappas, N., Wong, C., Vaska, P., Zhu, W. and Swanson, J. M. (2004) Evidence that methylphenidate enhances the saliency of a mathematical task by increasing dopamine in the human brain, *American Journal of Psychiatry* 161, 1173–80.

Volkow, N. D., Wang, G., Fowler, J. S. and Yu-Shin Ding, Y. (2005) Imaging the effects of methylphenidate on brain dopamine: New model on its therapeutic actions for attention-deficit/hyperactivity disorder, *Biological Psychiatry* 57, 1410–15.

Waldman, I. D., Rowe, D. C., Abramowitz, A., Kozel, S. T., Mohr, J. H., Sherman S. L., *et al.* (1998) Association and linkage of the dopamine transporter gene and attention-deficit hyperactivity disorder in children: Heterogeneity owing to diagnostic subtype and severity, *American Journal of Human Genetics* 63, 1767–76.

Wang, Y. (2006) Once-daily atomoxetine and twice-daily methylphenidate equally effective against ADHD. Poster presentation at joint annual meeting of the American Academy of Child and Adolescent Psychiatry and the Canadian Academy of Child and Adolescent Psychiatry, Toronto, Canada. Quoted by M. Sullivan in *Paediatric News* 40, 6.

Waxmonsky, J. (2003) Assessment and treatment of attention deficit hyperactivity disorder in children with comorbid psychiatric illness, *Current Opinion in Pediatrics* 15, 476–82.

Wilens, T. E., Biederman, J., Brown, S., Tanguay, S., Monteaux, M. C., Black, D. and Spencer, T. J. (2002) Psychiatric comorbidity and functioning in clinically referred preschool children and school-age youth with ADHD, *Journal of the American Academy of Child and Adolescent Psychiatry* 41, 262–8.

Wilens, T. E., Hammerman, P. G., Biederman, J. *et al.* (2005) Blood pressure changes associated with medication treatment of adults with attention-deficit hyperactivity disorder, *Journal of Clinical Psychiatry* 66, 253–9.

Wolraich, M. L., Hannah, J. N., Baumgaertel, A. and Brown, J. (1996) Comparison of diagnostic criteria for attention deficit/hyperactivity disorder in a county-wide sample, *Journal of the American Academy of Child and Adolescent Psychiatry* 35, 319–24.

Wolraich, M. L., Lambert, W., Doffing, M. A., Bickman, L., Simmons, T. and Worley, K. (2003) Psychometric properties of the Vanderbilt ADHD diagnostic parent rating scale in a referred population, *Journal of Pediatric Psychology* 28, 559–67.

Wolraich, M. L., Lambert, E. W., Bickman, L., Simmons, T., Doffing, M. A. and Worley, K. A. (2004) Assessing the impact of parent and teacher agreement on diagnosing attention-deficit hyperactivity disorder, *Journal of Developmental and Behavioral Pediatrics*, 25, 41–7.

Xu, X., Knight, J., Brookes, K., Mill, J., Sham, P., Craig, I., Taylor, E. and Asherson, P. (2005) DNA pooling analysis of 21 norepinephrine transporter gene SNPs with attention deficit hyperactivity disorder: No evidence for association, *American Journal of Medical Genetics, Series B (Neuropsychiatric Genetics)* 5, 115–18.

Zhang, S., Faries, D. E., Vowles, M. and Michelson, D. (2005) ADHD Rating Scale IV: Psychometric properties from a multinational study as a clinician-administered instrument, *International Journal of Methods in Psychiatric Research* 14, 186–201.

Chapter 2

ADHD and Genetics: A Consensus Reconsidered

Jay Joseph

Attention deficit hyperactivity disorder (ADHD) illustrates psychiatry's transformation of childhood misbehaviour into medical diagnosis, as seen in a 2002 'Consensus Statement on ADHD' by Russell Barkley and more than 80 other ADHD researchers (Barkley *et al.*, 2002. For a response to the Statement, see Timimi *et al.*, 2004). In their Statement, Barkley *et al.* claimed that there is 'no disagreement' among 'scientists who have devoted years, if not entire careers' to the study of ADHD, that it is a 'real medical condition'. Twin studies were said to have provided evidence that ADHD is 'primarily inherited', and that the importance of genetic factors influencing deficits in attention and inhibition are 'nearly approaching the genetic contribution to human height'. Barkley *et al.* went on to claim that one (unnamed) gene 'has recently been reliably demonstrated to be associated with this disorder', and that 'the search for more is underway by more than 12 different scientific teams worldwide at this time'.

By 2008, however, concerted worldwide efforts have failed to discover the genes presumed to cause ADHD and other major psychiatric disorders. It was expected that such genes would have been found in the current 'post-genomic era'. However, they have not been found. This has led to sobering assessments by psychiatric geneticists Kenneth Kendler and Peter Propping, who have based their careers on the argument that important genetic factors underlie psychiatric disorders. In 2005, Kendler concluded, 'The strong, clear, and direct causal relationship implied by the concept of "a gene for..." does not exist for psychiatric disorders. Although we may wish it to be true, we do not have and are not likely to ever discover "genes for" psychiatric illness'

(Kendler, 2005, p. 1250).[1] And in the same year, Propping wrote, 'Whereas genetically complex traits are being successfully pinned down to the molecular level in other fields of medicine, psychiatric genetics still awaits a major breakthrough' (Propping, 2005, p. 2). Thus, the field of psychiatric genetics may be approaching a period of crisis.

Barkley has written elsewhere that ADHD is a 'developmental failure in the brain circuitry that underlies inhibition and self-control' (Barkley, 1998, p. 67), which he linked to genetic factors. Comings et al. (2005, p. 13) also cited genetics in support of brain dysfunction theories of ADHD, writing, 'the finding that ADHD is a genetic disorder suggests the defective genes involved cause a dysfunction of the prefrontal lobes'. Thus, like other areas in psychiatry, questionable genetic theories and brain dysfunction theories of ADHD continue to cross-validate each other.

Reviewers of ADHD research often discuss the perceived importance of genetic factors, which they cite in support of a 'predisposition-stress' (diathesis-stress) model of causation. This model holds that ADHD is caused by an inherited predisposition combined with exposure to environmental triggers. However, Breggin and others have stressed the primacy of environmental factors and have questioned the validity of the ADHD diagnosis itself, seeing it as a label justifying the use of drugs to control children's behaviour (see Breggin, 1998, 2001a, 2001b; see also DeGrandpre, 1999; Leo, 2002).

In this chapter I will argue that genetic theories of ADHD, a diagnosis already of questionable validity, rest on very shaky foundations. In the process, I will show that the research cited in support of these theories is flawed on several critical dimensions rarely discussed in scientific papers, in the media, in textbooks, in scholarly reviews, or in popular works.

ADHD family studies

Research suggests that ADHD-type behaviours, like most human behaviours, tend to cluster in families (Biederman et al., 1986; Biederman et al., 1995; Biederman et al., 1990; Cantwell, 1972; Faraone et al., 1991; Morrison and Stewart, 1971; Nichols and Chen, 1981; Welner et al., 1977). However, although ADHD-type behaviour may be *familial* in the sense that it 'runs' or clusters in families, we cannot determine whether this clustering is caused by the greater *genetic* resemblance of family members, since families also experience similar environmental factors. As schizophrenia genetic researchers Gottesman and Shields (1982, p. 69) have written, 'that a disease is familial does not necessarily imply that it is genetic. Familial clustering can also be transmitted through culture, infectious sources, or learning.' And more recently, ADHD genetic researchers Faraone and colleagues (2005, p. 1313) observed that 'family studies cannot disentangle genetic from environmental sources of transmission'.[2] I agree with these assessments.

Twin research

Researchers' understanding that the familial clustering of ADHD can be explained on environmental grounds led them to seek other methods to determine whether genetic factors play a role. According to Faraone and colleagues (2005, p. 1313), 'adoption and twin studies [are needed] to determine whether genes account for the familial transmission of a disorder'.

All ADHD twin studies have used the 'classical twin method' (more commonly known as 'the twin method'). This research technique compares the resemblance of reared-together MZ twins (also known as monozygotic or identical twins; who share 100 per cent genetic similarity), versus the resemblance of reared-together same-sex DZ twins (also known as dizygotic or fraternal twins; who share an average 50 per cent genetic similarity). Based on the assumption that both types of twins experience the same kinds of environments, known as the 'equal environment assumption' or 'EEA', twin researchers argue that a statistically significant higher concordance rate (which means that both twins are affected) or correlation of MZ versus same-sex DZ twins is caused by the greater genetic resemblance of the former. There have been no studies of 'reared-apart' ADHD twins.

Although the twin method depends on additional assumptions,[3] the equal environment assumption has been the main area of contention between twin researchers and their critics. From the development of the twin method in the mid 1920s, until the early 1960s, twin researchers defined the EEA – without qualification – as the assumption that MZ and DZ twins share the same types of behaviour-influencing, physical, and treatment environments. I have called this the 'traditional EEA definition' (Joseph, 2004a). However, as most twin researchers now concede, the evidence clearly shows that MZ twins spend more time together, more often have the same friends, are treated more similarly by parents and others, and so forth (Kendler,

1983; Joseph, 2004a, 2006). Moreover, MZs share a closer emotional bond than DZs, and more often view themselves as being two halves of the same whole (that is, they experience what some psychologists call 'identity confusion'; see Ainslie, 1985; Jackson, 1960).

In the face of such evidence, twin researchers should have recognized that the twin method – just like a family study – is unable to disentangle the potential influences of genetic and environmental factors. Instead, while belatedly recognizing that MZ twins do indeed experience more similar environments than DZs, some twin researchers attempted to rescue the twin method by *redefining* the equal environment assumption. Behaviour geneticists and others have renamed the EEA as the 'equal trait-relevant environment assumption' (Carey and DiLalla, 1994), referred to here as the 'trait-relevant EEA'. According to Kendler and his colleagues, who define the EEA in the 'trait relevant' sense:

> The traditional twin method, as well as more recent biometrical models for twin analysis, are predicated on the equal-environment assumption (EEA) – that monozygotic (MZ) and dizygotic (DZ) twins are equally correlated for their exposure to environmental influences *that are of etiologic relevance to the trait under study* [emphasis added]. (Kendler *et al.*, 1993, p. 21)

By 'trait relevant', twin researchers mean aspects of the environment that have been shown to contribute to the psychiatric disorder in question. For example, exposure to trauma contributes to post-traumatic stress disorder. Table 2.1 outlines the two current definitions of the EEA.

Table 2.1 The two definitions of the equal environment assumption (EEA) used by contemporary twin researchers

The 'traditional' EEA definition
MZ twins and same-sex DZ twins experience equal environmental influences
The 'trait relevant' EEA definition
MZ twins and same-sex DZ twins experience equal environmental influences that are of etiologic relevance to the trait under study

Proponents of the trait-relevant EEA recognize that MZ twins experience more similar environments than DZs, but argue (e.g. Bouchard, 1993, 1997; Lyons *et al.*, 1991) or imply (e.g. Kendler, 1983) that *critics* of the twin method bear the burden of proof for demonstrating that MZ and DZ twins experience dissimilar trait-relevant environments. However, it has been observed that 'a basic tenet of science is that the burden of proof always falls squarely on the claimant, not the critic . . . Consequently, it is up to the proponents of these techniques to demonstrate that they work, not up to the critics of these techniques to demonstrate the converse' (Lilienfeld *et al.*, 2003, p. 3).

Thus, *twin researchers* bear the burden of proof for demonstrating that the greater environmental similarity of MZ versus same-sex DZ twins does not completely explain the common finding that MZs are more concordant for psychiatric disorders than are same-sex DZs. Several twin researchers (e.g. Hettema *et al.*, 1995; Kendler, 1983) have argued that the twin method is supported by a body of empirical 'EEA test' research. However, it has been shown elsewhere (Joseph, 2006; Pam *et al.*, 1996) that these studies do little to uphold the validity of the EEA and the twin method. Indeed, most twin researchers performing EEA test studies found that MZs experience much more similar environments than same-sex DZs (e.g. LaBuda *et al.*, 1997; Loehlin and Nichols, 1976; Morris-Yates *et al.*, 1990; Scarr and Carter-Saltzman, 1979).

It is noteworthy that Kendler and other twin researchers do not require critics to identify 'environmental influences that are of etiologic relevance to the trait under study' to invalidate genetic interpretations of *family studies*. In this case they recognize that, because family members share a common environment as well as common genes, family studies are unable to determine whether genetic factors are operating. Arbitrarily, contemporary twin researchers who define the EEA in the trait-relevant sense apply the trait-relevant requirement to the twin method, but *not* to family studies.

Therefore, despite previous attempts to redefine or test the EEA, the simple fact that MZ twins experience more similar environments and treatments than DZs invalidates genetic interpretations of MZ–DZ comparisons, for the same reason that genetic interpretations of family studies are invalid. There is no reason, therefore, to accept that the twin method measures anything other than the more similar environments of MZ versus DZ twins, and all conclusions in favour of genetic influences on psychiatric disorders (including ADHD) derived from the twin method must be disregarded (Joseph, 2004a, 2006).

ADHD twin studies

Nevertheless, twin studies constitute the most frequently cited evidence in support of a genetic basis for ADHD. According to Barkley (1998, p. 68), twin studies furnish 'the most conclusive evidence that genetics can contribute to ADHD'. Twin research has found consistently that MZ twins are more concordant for ADHD, or correlate higher for ADHD-type behaviours, than same-sex DZ twins. To date, more than 20 ADHD twin studies have been published (e.g. Cronk et al., 2002; Edelbrock et al., 1995; Gilger et al., 1992; Gillis et al., 1992; Heiser et al., 2006; Hudziak et al., 2003; Levy et al., 1997; Lopez, 1965; Saudino et al., 2005; Sherman et al., 1997; Thapar et al., 1995; Willcutt et al., 2000; Willerman, 1973).

Although most ADHD twin studies found greater MZ versus DZ resemblance for ADHD or ADHD-type behaviours, only Cronk et al. (2002) defined the EEA in the trait-relevant sense. Moreover, the majority of studies failed to mention the EEA, and no ADHD twin researchers other than Cronk et al. cited previous research or publications supporting the validity of the EEA. Thus, implicitly or explicitly, all but one group of ADHD twin researchers based their conclusions on the traditional assumption that the environments of MZ and DZ twins are equal, yet only Gillis and associates (1992) argued that these environments are actually equal.

An example of ADHD twin researchers who argue in support of the EEA are Thapar and colleagues, who defined the twin method in the traditional sense:

> The basic premise underlying twin research is that monozygotic (MZ) twins are genetically identical, whereas dizygotic (DZ) twins share on average 50% of their segregating genes. Thus, for a genetically influenced trait or disorder, MZ twins will be more similar than DZ twins, *assuming that MZ and DZ twins share environment to the same extent* [emphasis added]. In simple terms, we would expect the MZ correlation ... or concordance rate for a given trait or disorder to be greater than the DZ correlation. (Thapar et al., 1999, p. 106)

Thapar et al. ask us to conclude in favour of genetic influences on ADHD on the basis of the unsupported assumption that 'MZ and DZ twins share environment to the same extent', even as twin researchers in other areas of psychiatry have recognized that this is not true (e.g. Kendler *et al.*, 1993). Indeed, twin researchers Scarr and Carter-Saltzman (1979, p. 528) concluded more than 25 years ago that 'the evidence of greater environmental similarity for MZ than DZ twins is overwhelming'.[4]

ADHD genetic researchers Hay, McStephen and Levy (2001) have written that, although identical twins 'may well be treated more similarly than fraternal twins...this is far more a consequence of their genetic similarity in behaviour (and of ensuing responses by parents and others) than a cause of such similarity'. Like Kendler before them, who argued that 'MZ twins might *create* for themselves more similar environments' (Kendler, 1987, p. 706, emphasis in original), Hay and associates failed to understand that the *reason* MZ twins experience more similar environments than DZs is not relevant in assessing the validity of the twin method. For example, suppose that ADHD is caused solely by exposure to a toxic chemical. Because MZ twins spend much more time together than DZs, it is much more likely that both members of an MZ pair will be exposed to the chemical, and be subsequently diagnosed with ADHD, than it is that both members of a DZ pair will be exposed and diagnosed. However, even if MZs do indeed 'create' more similar environments than DZs because of their greater genetic similarity, it would be erroneous to conclude that higher MZ versus DZ concordance for ADHD is evidence that the condition has a genetic component. In this example – regardless of *why* MZs are together more often – higher MZ concordance is caused solely by MZs' propensity to be together more often than DZs, which leads them to be more similarly exposed to the toxic chemical that causes ADHD.

Thus, in order to invalidate genetic interpretations of ADHD twin data – in the same way that we can invalidate genetic interpretations of ADHD family data (Hay *et al.*, 2001, p. 12) – critics need only show *that* MZ and DZ environments are different.

Since the evidence overwhelmingly suggests that MZ twins are treated more alike, spend considerably more time together, and experience greater levels of identity confusion and closeness (Joseph, 2004a), we would expect MZ twins – on purely environmental grounds – to correlate higher than same-sex DZs on ADHD-related measures. Therefore, like ADHD family studies, ADHD twin studies are unable to disentangle the potential influences of genes and environment on ADHD-type behaviour.

As it turns out, MZ twins resemble each other more than same-sex DZs for most human behaviours, including many for which, intuitively, we would expect little if any genetic influence. For example, twin method results have been used to claim important genetic influences on loneliness (Boomsma *et al.*, 2005), the frequency of orgasm in women (Dawood *et al.*, 2005), the results of the United States 2004 presidential election (Alford *et al.*, 2005), perfectionism (Tozzi *et al.*, 2004), and breakfast eating patterns (Keski-Rahkonen *et al.*, 2004). Twin research in psychiatry, and in ADHD in particular, merely repeats the error of assuming that the greater resemblance of MZ versus same-sex DZ twins is the result of the former's greater genetic relationship, when a plausible alternative explanation holds that MZ's greater environmental similarity completely explains such results.

ADHD adoption research

Critics have argued for three generations that genetic theories in psychiatry are flawed because family *and* twin studies are confounded by environmental factors, and that we can draw no valid conclusions in support of genetics from the results of these studies. Psychiatric adoption studies were pioneered in the 1960s in order to eliminate these potential confounds. In theory, an adoption study is able to disentangle possible genetic and environmental influences on psychiatric disorders because adoptees receive their genes from one family, but are raised in the environment of another family.

Psychiatric geneticists Seymour Kety, David Rosenthal, Paul Wender, and their Danish associates published their first schizophrenia adoption studies in 1968 (Kety *et al.*, 1968; Rosenthal *et al.*, 1968). Their work was based on adoptions taking place in Denmark, and they had access to registers containing information on adoptions, and on people who had been admitted to a psychiatric facility. Kety and colleagues undertook this research on the basis of their astute observation that the evidence from schizophrenia family and twin studies was 'inconclusive', because 'it fails to remove the influence of certain environmental factors... In the case of monozygotic twins it has been pointed out that such individuals usually share a disproportionate segment of environmental and interpersonal factors in addition to their genetic identity' (Kety *et al.*, 1968, p. 345). Thus, adoption studies would not be necessary if, as proponents of the twin method claim, MZ–DZ comparisons provided unequivocal evidence in support of genetics.

While the logic of adoption studies might appear straightforward, the most important psychiatric adoption studies contained important methodological problems and were subject to several biases (Heston,

1966; Kety *et al.*, 1968, 1975, 1994; Rosenthal *et al.*, 1968, 1971; Tienari *et al.*, 1987, 2003, 2004; Wender *et al.*, 1974. For critical reviews of schizophrenia adoption research, see Boyle, 2002; Cassou *et al.*, 1980; Jackson, 2003; Joseph, 2004a, 2004b, 2006; Lewontin *et al.*, 1984; Lidz, 1976; Lidz and Blatt, 1983; Lidz *et al.*, 1981; Pam, 1995). Despite numerous flaws, however, schizophrenia adoption research possessed two qualities not found in ADHD adoption research: (1) the researchers made diagnoses blindly;[5] and (2) the researchers studied or had psychiatric records for adoptees' biological relatives.

The 'adoptive parents' method

As of this writing, ADHD adoption studies have been published by Alberts-Corush *et al.* (1986), Cantwell (1975), Morrison and Stewart (1973), Safer (1973), Sprich *et al.* (2000), and van den Oord *et al.* (1994). The results of these studies are frequently cited in textbooks, review articles, and scientific papers as supporting genetic theories of ADHD.

Because of the difficulty in obtaining the carefully guarded records of adoptees' biological families, which the Danish and American researchers were able to obtain through their access to national registers, the authors of the most frequently cited ADHD adoption studies had to rely on the 'Adoptive Parents' method, which Wender and colleagues (1968) developed in the 1960s. The Adoptive Parents method compares the psychiatric status of three (and sometimes four) types of families as follows:

(1) *BH (Biological Hyperactive)*. This group consists of non-adopted children diagnosed with ADHD who are reared in the homes of their biological parents.

(2) *AH (Adoptive Hyperactive)*. This group consists of adopted children diagnosed with ADHD who are reared by adoptive parents, with whom they share no genetic relationship.

(3) *BN (Biological Normal)*. This group typically consists of non-adopted normal (non-ADHD) children who are reared by their biological parents, and is designated as a control group.

(4) *AN (Adoptive Normal)*. The AN control group consists of adoptees having no record of ADHD or related diagnoses, who are reared by their adoptive parents. (Only Alberts-Corush and colleagues utilized this group.)

The authors of the four Adoptive Parents studies (Alberts-Corush et al., 1986; Cantwell, 1975; Morrison and Stewart, 1973; Sprich et al., 2000) assessed resemblance for ADHD among the relatives of groups 3 or 4 listed above. However, they had no information on their ADHD adoptees' biological relatives.

In fact, *no ADHD adoption study has investigated the biological relatives of adopted-away children,* meaning that their authors were unable to make direct comparisons between the biological and adoptive relatives of the same child. Kety and colleagues' schizophrenia adoption studies diagnosed the same adoptee's adoptive *and* biological relatives, whereas the ADHD Adoptive Parents studies compared diagnoses in a group consisting of *adopted-away ADHD children* and their adoptive families (AH), versus a group consisting of the families of *other* ADHD children living with their biological parents (BH).

Unfortunately, ADHD genetic researchers usually fail to discuss the severe limitations of the Adoptive Parents design unless compelled to do so by critics (for example see Faraone and Biederman, 2000, 2002). Too often, they fail to state clearly that researchers were unable to study adoptees' biological relatives, and sometimes write in potentially misleading ways about ADHD adoption research (Joseph, 2006). For example, Faraone and Biederman (2000, p. 57) wrote that a 'testable psychosocial theory' must be able to explain 'the elevated rates of ADHD and associated traits among the biological relatives of adopted away ADHD children', implying (incorrectly) that researchers obtained data on these biological relatives. And in a subsequent review article in which he discussed ADHD adoption research, Faraone (2004, pp. 305–6) wrote, 'By examining both the adoptive and biological relatives of ill probands, one can disentangle genetic and environmental sources of familial transmission.' This was the logic of Kety's schizophrenia adoption studies. However, no ADHD adoption study has examined the 'adoptive and biological relatives' of the same 'ill' adoptees. Authoritative ADHD experts such as Barkley (2003, p. 117) then write for a larger audience in technically accurate, yet potentially misleading ways: 'Cantwell... and Morrison and Stewart... both reported higher rates of hyperactivity in the biological parents of hyperactive children than in the adoptive parents of such children.'

Most reviewers and textbook authors have overlooked another important limitation of the Adoptive Parents model, which is that adoptive parents constitute a population screened for mental health as part of the adoption process. They are – by definition – a group in which we would expect to find fewer psychiatric disorders than in the general population. Thus, as behaviour geneticist Michael Rutter and his colleagues (Rutter *et al.*, 1990, p. 15) pointed out, low rates of psychological disturbance among adoptive parents in ADHD adoption studies 'could be no more than an artifactual consequence of the tendency to select mentally healthy individuals as suitable adopting parents'. Elsewhere, Rutter and colleagues (2001, p. 298) noted, 'Although claims are often made that adopting parents are typical of the general population... manifestly they are not', and that adoption studies in psychiatry 'are markedly constrained by the fact that adopting families are not representative of the general population and, in particular, involve a markedly restricted range of adverse rearing environments' (p. 301).

Therefore, the Adoptive Parents method's comparison of diagnoses among two groups of relatives – one in which parents are screened for psychopathology (AH), and another in which parents are not screened for psychopathology (BH) – provides no support for genetic theories of ADHD.

Yet another issue in ADHD adoption research is evidence that adoptees as a population are more likely than non-adoptees to receive an ADHD diagnosis (Deutsch, 1989; Deutsch *et al.*, 1982). If true, this casts further doubt on ADHD adoption researchers' already extremely shaky conclusions. If adoptees and non-adoptees constitute different populations with respect to ADHD, it would be difficult to generalize findings of an ADHD adoption study to the non-adoptee population. Although adoption researchers usually do not address this, many adopted children are psychologically scarred on the basis of having been abandoned by their primary caregivers. Thus, as Cassou and colleagues (1980) pointed out, a more evocative designation for adoption studies would be 'the study of abandoned children' (Les Études D'Enfants Abandonnés).

Having reviewed the individual ADHD adoption studies in detail elsewhere (Joseph, 2000a, 2002, 2006), I will merely list their main problems here. These include: (1) the researchers' failure to study adoptees' biological relatives; (2) researchers' use of non-blinded diagnoses, which they sometimes made on the basis of relatives' recollections; (3) inadequate definitions of ADHD; (4) researchers' inability to control for environmental confounds; (5) researchers' inability to control for the status of adoptive parents as a population screened for psychiatric disorders; (6) potential researcher bias; and (7) the use of late-separated adoptees.

Conclusions regarding ADHD adoption research

The Adoptive Parents method, used in four of the six ADHD adoption studies, provides no evidence in favour of genetics because, among other reasons, it does not assess the status of adoptees' biological relatives. In addition, the two studies using other designs (Safer, 1973; van den Oord et al., 1994) are flawed on other important dimensions (Joseph, 2000a, 2006). Behaviour geneticists Plomin and colleagues (2001, p. 228) recognized that ADHD 'adoption studies to date have been few and quite limited methodologically'. And Faraone and Biederman (2000, p. 570) acknowledged that ADHD adoption studies' 'relatively minor methodological problems...limit the strength of any inferences we can draw from these studies'. However, the methodological problems Faraone and Biederman dismissed as 'minor' are actually *massive*.

Heritability

The authors of textbooks and review articles frequently report that the heritability of ADHD is about 76 per cent, making it 'among the most heritable of psychiatric disorders' (Faraone et al., 2005, p. 1313). Twin researchers arrive at this figure by doubling the MZ–DZ correlation difference. For example, if MZs correlate at 0.90, and DZs correlate at 0.50, twin researchers would estimate heritability at 0.80 (80%). However, in addition to the fact that these estimates are based on the validity of the twin method's untenable equal environment assumption, heritability estimates in psychiatry and psychology are potentially misleading (Joseph, 2004a, ch. 5; Moore, 2001).

The heritability statistic was developed in agriculture to predict the results of a selective breeding programme (Joseph, 2004a; Lush, 1945, 1949). However, as Hirsch (1997, 2004) has argued, a numerical heritability estimate (coefficient) is not a 'nature–nurture ratio' of the relative contributions of genes and environment, and 'highly heritable' single-gene disorders such as phenylketonuria (PKU) can be prevented by a dietary intervention. Thus, even if genes play a role in ADHD, we cannot determine 'how much' of the 'ADHD phenotype' variation is attributable to genes because, like PKU, a timely (and possibly simple) environmental intervention could prevent a condition with a stated heritability as high as 1.0 (100%).

If we are to believe that ADHD is 'significantly heritable', we must also believe the same about loneliness (48% heritability; Boomsma *et al.*, 2005), the frequency of female orgasms when masturbating (51% heritability; Dawood *et al.*, 2005), breakfast eating patterns (approximately 60% heritability; Keski-Rahkonen *et al.*, 2004), perfectionism ('moderately heritable'; Tozzi *et al.*, 2004, p. 490), and political beliefs (32% heritability; Alford *et al.*, 2005). These examples again point to the faulty conclusions one can reach about genetics on the basis of twin research and accompanying heritability estimates.

The presumed genetic basis of ADHD rests on the results of family, twin, and adoption studies. However, although research seems to indicate that ADHD is familial, the fact that families share a common environment as well as common genes permits no valid conclusions in support of genetics. In addition, we have seen that twin and adoption studies also fail to provide scientifically acceptable evidence in support of a genetic basis for ADHD.

ADHD molecular genetic research

Genetic interpretations of the family, twin, and adoption studies I have just outlined have laid the basis for molecular genetic investigations in ADHD. In the early stages of this research, investigators such Thapar and colleagues justified the search for ADHD genes as follows:

> Overall, genetic factors have been shown to be important across a variety of studies. There is thus a compelling argument for now searching for susceptibility genes at a molecular level. (Thapar *et al.*, 1999, p. 108)

More recently, Faraone and colleagues (2005, p. 1313) argued that 'Family, twin, and adoption studies provide compelling evidence that genes play a strong role in mediating susceptibility to ADHD.' Thus, the ongoing search for 'ADHD genes' is based on the assumption that the condition's genetic basis has already been established. Interestingly, we will see that mathematical calculations used in some recent claims of gene findings are based on the very same questionable assumption.

As I have outlined previously (Joseph, 2006), the search for genes is based on mainstream psychiatry's assumptions and beliefs about ADHD. These include: (1) that ADHD is a valid diagnostic category that can be reliably diagnosed; (2) that ADHD is a familial disorder; (3) that ADHD involves a malfunction of the brain; (4) that the greater resemblance of MZ versus same-sex DZ twins on ADHD-related measures is the result of the former's greater genetic similarity; (5) that the results of ADHD adoption studies suggest the importance of genetic factors; (6) that researchers possess the technology to find genes; and (7) that gene discoveries would aid in the treatment or prevention of ADHD. However, there is little evidence supporting points 1, 3, 4, and 5, and point 7 is debatable.

Research methods

Molecular genetic researchers use linkage studies, genome scans, and association studies. In a *linkage* study, researchers search for genetic markers associated with a presumed disease gene among consanguineous family members. Findings are often represented as a logarithm of odds (LOD) score, which expresses the probability that the linkage occurred by chance. In general, an LOD score higher than 3 (1000:1 odds in favour of linkage) is necessary in order to claim statistically significant linkage. Linkage studies attempt to identify chromosomal regions where relevant genes might be located, but they are unable to identify actual genes. This is the task of follow-up studies. A *genome scan* analyses the complete genome of an individual against a set of markers whose positions on the chromosomes are known. A genome scan looks for common patterns of inheritance between these markers and the disease characteristics, and identifies linkage regions on the chromosomes. Unlike typical linkage analyses, which frequently are based on hypothesized 'candidate genes', genome scans make no assumptions about the possible location of genes. *Association studies* compare the frequency of genetic markers among unrelated affected individuals and a control group, and are performed with population-based case-control, or family-based samples. A genetic marker is a segment of DNA with an identifiable physical location on a chromosome, whose inheritance can be followed.

There are two main types of theorized genetic transmission for ADHD and other psychiatric disorders. The first is *Mendelian* inheritance, in which a trait or disorder is passed from parents to offspring by a single dominant, recessive, or sex-linked gene. However, most researchers now believe that it is very unlikely that ADHD is caused by a single gene (Comings *et al.*, 2005; Faraone *et al.*, 2005; Waldman and Gizer, 2006). The second is *polygenic* inheritance, meaning that many genes of varying effect sizes are believed to contribute to ADHD, in addition to unspecified environmental factors. Investigators then look for several genes, or individual genes thought to have a large-sized effect. According to one group of genetic researchers, 'The evidence suggests that ADHD is primarily a polygenic disorder involving at least 50 genes' (Comings et al., 2005, p. 3). As a critic pointed out, however, 'The argument that ADHD is "mediated by many genes acting in concert" is rather circular in that it is based primarily on the complete failure of molecular genetic studies to find such genes and replicate those findings' (Pittelli, 2002, p. 496).

Cause and effect

ADHD is frequently put forward as a 'multifactorial complex disorder', meaning that there is 'a complex interacting admixture of multiple genes and multiple environmental risk factors' (Rutter, 2001, p. 227). This is consistent with the previously discussed 'predisposition-stress' model of ADHD. However, the idea that ADHD is a complex disorder is merely a theory, not a fact. Psychiatric conditions such as ADHD remain 'complex disorders' even after initial gene-finding efforts come up empty, while subsequent gene-finding failures are explained on the basis of the 'complex' nature of the 'disorder'. Circular reasoning of this type is seen in a 2003 review of autism research, where the authors wrote that the 'current lack of success in finding genes for autism is similar to that of complex diseases' (Volkmar and Pauls, 2003, p. 1136). In fact, the 'lack of success' in finding genes is currently a *defining feature* of 'complex disorders' in psychiatry.

However, even if a gene is *associated* (correlated) with ADHD, it still doesn't mean that the gene contributes to its causation. For example, there is a strong correlation between having a Y chromosome and being the chief executive officer (CEO) of a Fortune 500 corporation. Yet, this does not mean that having a Y chromosome causes or predisposes someone to become a CEO. Most likely, the correlation is the result of social privileges granted to people with Y chromosomes (men) rather than the action of the chromosome itself. Furthermore, even if a gene is necessary for ADHD to appear, it still doesn't necessarily mean that the gene is a causative factor. As Ratner (2004, p. 30) pointed out, 'The fact that something is a necessary foundation for something does not mean that it causes it.'

Yet another problem is that, like twin and adoption studies, molecular genetic research depends on the acceptance of questionable assumptions. This is manifest not only in the investigators' decision to perform this research, but also because they factor assumptions about genetics into mathematical models of familial transmission. According to McGuffin (2004, p. 179), 'Unfortunately, conventional linkage requires several assumptions. These are that major gene effects (rather than just multiple small gene effects) exist, that there is some way of assuring genetic homogeneity, and that the mode of transmission of the disorder is known.' And Faraone and colleagues (1999, p. 131) have written, 'The main drawback of the LOD score method is that we must specify the mode of genetic transmission.' Thus, although ADHD molecular genetic researchers test multiple genetic models in computer analyses of their findings, all models assume that some type of genetic transmission is occurring. But what if *no* genetic transmission is occurring? The large number of false positive linkage findings in psychiatry in general, and ADHD in particular, may be another example of questionable assumptions leading researchers to the premature conclusion that genetic factors (or actual genes) exist. Their (subsequently non-replicated) results may be influenced by factoring false assumptions about genetic transmission into their LOD score calculations.

The fruitless search for ADHD genes

Like other areas of psychiatry, there have been a plethora of ADHD gene-finding claims in the past ten years. However, subsequent replication attempts have failed to confirm these claims. For example, in 1998 Plomin and Rutter (p. 1223) wrote optimistically that 'Genes associated with behavioural dimensions and disorders are beginning to be identified.' And in the fourth edition of their 2001 behavioural genetics textbook, Plomin, DeFries, McClearn, and McGuffin claimed that 'ADHD is one of the first behavioural areas in which specific genes have been identified' (Plomin *et al.*, 2001, p. 1). However, by 2005 Plomin recognized the ongoing failure of gene-finding efforts in psychiatry and psychology:

When are we going to be there [finding genes in child psychology and psychiatry]? Being an optimist, my response is 'soon'. But readers would be forgiven for being skeptical because they have heard this before...A small personal example of impatience and embarrassment about the slower-than-expected progress towards identifying QTLs [genes of varying effect sizes] is that my co-authors and I decided that we would not write the next edition of our [2001] behavioural genetics textbook...until we had some solid DNA results to present. The reason for this decision was that our 2001 edition had enthused about the field being on the cusp of a new post-genomic era in which DNA risk indicators would add great value to behavioural research. *We are still on that cusp* [emphasis added]. (Plomin, 2005, p. 1030)

This quotation shows, along with the statements by Kendler and Propping I quoted earlier, that at least three leading genetic researchers recognized in 2005 that no genes have been found that cause major psychiatric disorders such as ADHD.

Researchers currently focus on genes involved with the brain's dopamine receptors, which they view as candidate genes on the basis of an *a priori* hypothesis derived from neurochemical and neuropharmacological research (Asherson and Curran, 2001; Barr, 2001). The major areas of interest have been the DRD4 dopamine receptor gene, and the DAT1 dopamine transporter gene. In their 2000 response to my article on the genetics of ADHD (Joseph, 2000a), Faraone and Biederman (2000, p. 573) claimed that 'molecular genetic studies have implicated these two genes... in the etiology of ADHD'. However, although the original claims have found some support, several subsequent studies have failed to replicate an association between ADHD and the DRD4 or DAT1 genes (e.g. Bakker *et al.*, 2005; Langley *et al.*, 2005; Mill *et al.*, 2005; Ogdie *et al.*, 2003; van der Meulen *et al.*, 2005). In a detailed 2006 survey of the evidence in support of DRD4, DAT1, and other candidate genes, Waldman and Gizer (2006, p. 421) concluded, 'It should be clear... that for each [ADHD] candidate gene studied, there is a mixed picture of positive and negative findings'.

Several complete genome scans have also failed to find consistently replicated evidence in support of regions harbouring suspected ADHD genes (Arcos-Burgos *et al.*, 2004; Bakker *et al.*, 2003; Fisher *et al.*, 2002; Hebebrand *et al.*, 2006; Ogdie *et al.*, 2003). According to Faraone and colleagues, 'The handful of genome-wide scans that have been conducted thus far show divergent findings and are, therefore, not conclusive' (Faraone *et al.*, 2005, p. 1319). It is generous to state that these results are 'not conclusive'. It would be better to conclude that these genome scans found no replicated evidence that genes have anything to do with ADHD.

ADHD genetic researchers have resorted to citing meta-analyses (combining previous research) in support of associations between ADHD and chromosomal regions (e.g. Faraone *et al.*, 2001; Langley *et al.*, 2004; Li *et al.*, 2006). As Pittelli (2004, p. 1134) wrote, however, 'I find this trend of using meta-analysis to resurrect largely negative genetic linkage studies disturbing. It appears to be nothing more than a manipulation of data to obtain a desired result.' It does indeed appear to be such a manipulation, yet readers relatively unsophisticated in genetic research and terminology may well conclude that yet another 'ADHD gene' has been discovered. In fact, not one has been discovered.

We have seen prominent genetic researchers such as Robert Plomin argue that, although genes for ADHD and other disorders have not been found, we 'are on the cusp' of gene discoveries. What Plomin and other genetic researchers rarely consider in print, however, is the possibility that ADHD genes do not exist. Psychiatric geneticists and their supporters instead write optimistically about the great strides they have made, and how ADHD genes will soon be identified. They write as if they were searching for the cure of a deadly disease, or the virus causing an epidemic. But ADHD is simply a grouping of socially disapproved behaviours falsely passed off as a disease, and it is questionable whether finding genes would do anything to 'cure' these behaviours.

Generally speaking, these investigators substitute *language* for real gene findings. Thus, when they scan the genome and find no ADHD genes, they often write that genes are 'implicated', or that researchers are making 'enormous advances', or that genes are 'just beginning to be identified', or that studies 'suggest' the finding of genes, and so on. Plomin wrote in 2005 (p. 1030) that, although genes in psychiatry and psychology have not been discovered, this is 'an exciting time for child psychology and psychiatry. The field will be transformed as we move from finding genes to using them as genetic risk indicators in our research and eventually in our clinics.' And another researcher wrote in the same year, 'Uncovering the genomic underpinnings of ADHD is proving to be one of the most exciting stories in psychiatric genetics' (McGough, 2005, p. 1371). Ultimately, however, optimistic statements cannot eliminate the necessity of finding actual genes.

In other cases, it is mistakenly implied that several ADHD genes have already been identified (for example, see Asherson *et al.*, 2005; Barkley, 2003; Faraone, 2004, 2005; Goldstein and Schwebach, 2005; Kuntsi *et al.*, 2006; Pauls, 2005). The fields of behaviour genetics and psychiatric genetics have a long history of gene discovery claims which, although they certainly do produce headlines in the popular media, invariably fail to be replicated (Joseph, 2006).[6] As science writer John Horgan (2004) observed:

> Over the past 15 years or so, researchers have announced the discovery of 'genes for' attention-deficit disorder, obsessive-compulsive disorder, manic depression, schizophrenia, autism, dyslexia, alcoholism, heroin addiction, high IQ, male homosexuality, sadness, extroversion, introversion, novelty seeking, impulsivity, violent aggression, anxiety, anorexia, seasonal affective disorder, and pathological gambling. So far, not one of those claims has been confirmed.

We can add to this list a 2006 study in which the investigators claimed to have identified a chromosomal region harbouring genes for 'loneliness' (Boomsma *et al.*, 2006).

Biological markers (endophenotypes)

Biological markers in psychiatry (also known as 'endophenotypes'), have been defined as 'any neurobiological measure related to the underlying molecular genetics of the illness, including biochemical, endocrinological, neurophysiological, neuroanatomical, or neuropsychological markers' (Egan *et al.*, 2003, p. 277). For example, the results of a glucose tolerance test are a biological marker for diabetes. Gottesman and Shields introduced this concept into psychiatry in 1972, hoping that one day researchers would discover biological or behavioural markers for schizophrenia 'which would not only discriminate schizophrenics from other psychotics, but will also be found in all the identical co-twins of schizophrenics whether concordant or discordant' (Gottesman and Shields, 1972, p. 336). Three decades later, Gottesman wrote that because 'multiple genetic linkage and association studies using current classification systems [such as the DSM] . . . have all fallen short of success, the [endophenotype] term and its usefulness have reemerged . . . Endophenotypes are being seen as a viable and perhaps necessary mechanism for overcoming the barriers to progress' (Gotesman and Gould, 2003, p. 637).

Given the ongoing failure to find the genes presumed to underlie ADHD, researchers seek to identify biological markers in order to improve their ability to identify people who have the condition. A group of researchers investigating biological markers for ADHD believe that 'traditional nosological categories described in the DSM-IV . . . and ICD-10 . . . are suboptimal when it comes to describing who is affected and carrying susceptibility genes and who is not', and that to 'unravel the genetic constellation of ADHD, emphasis should be on the description of endophenotypes' (Slaats-Willemse *et al.*, 2003, pp. 1242–3). In other words, years of fruitless gene-finding attempts have led some researchers to conclude that they must find better ways than the DSM to define ADHD. Several traits have been proposed as possible markers to be studied (Doyle *et al.*, 2005; Waldman, 2005).

However, if the DSM definition of a disorder is inadequate for gene searches, it is also inadequate for biological marker searches (Joseph, 2006). In schizophrenia research, molecular geneticists M. F. Egan and colleagues (2003, p. 280) wrote, 'Most studies of intermediate phenotypes [endophenotypes] begin by looking for a difference between first-degree relatives and controls.' But these are the first-degree relatives of people diagnosed with DSM-defined schizophrenia, which is the same faulty diagnostic scheme that necessitated the search for biological markers in the first place. According to Merikangas and Risch (2003, pp. 627–8), 'Psychiatric disorder phenotypes, based solely on clinical manifestations without pathognomonic markers, still lack conclusive evidence for the validity of classification and the reliability of measurement.' But if ADHD and other psychiatric diagnoses are of questionable validity and reliability, this alone calls into question the results of previous family, twin, and adoption studies.

Breggin has observed that ADHD is 'simply a list of behaviours that require extra attention from teachers' (Breggin, 2001a, p. 203). In fact, most DSM diagnostic criteria, such as 'fidgeting', 'forgetting', and 'having difficulty awaiting turn' are found among most 'normal' children (APA, 2000, p. 92). The difference between 'normal' and 'ADHD' children, according to the DSM-IV-TR, is the *frequency* of these behaviours, denoted by the word 'often' (for example, 'is often forgetful in daily activities'). Given these criteria, what type of 'ADHD endophenotypes' could we expect to find? If both 'normal' and 'ADHD' children exhibit symptoms, albeit in differing degrees, how can a gene or biological marker know the difference between 'normal' and 'often' in a given culture?

Researchers will not be able to identify 'ADHD biological markers' because, unlike real diseases, there is little evidence that ADHD is caused by faulty biology. Even Plomin (2005, p. 1036) has written, 'I am not convinced that endophenotypes will prove to be useful for finding QTLs for what are quintessentially behavioural disorders such as autism, hyperactivity, and reading disability.' Thus, it is likely that

ADHD endophenotype research will soon arrive at the same *impasse* as ADHD molecular genetic research itself.

Is it necessary to find genes in order to study environmental factors?

Theoretically, the knowledge that children carry a genetic predisposition is useful to the extent that they can be helped to avoid environmental factors that might trigger ADHD. Thus, behaviour geneticists Hay and Levy (2001, p. 221) argued that if 'early behaviour genetic markers' or 'molecular markers' are discovered, 'they will only be of real use if acceptable interventions are available' while Cook (1999, p. 196) wrote that 'as the genetic risks are determined, it may become more feasible to determine specific environmental risk factors in the context of identified genetic risk'. However, 'early intervention' strategies are complicated by the potential impact of knowing that a child carries genes for ADHD. This knowledge could, in itself, be a life-altering event, affecting how parents, classmates, teachers, and others treat a child. And even in the unlikely event that presumed ADHD genes are found in the future, society might still decide to concentrate on eliminating environmental factors contributing to ADHD-type behaviour. These interventions would be aimed at all children in the same way that an anti-smoking campaign, which does not target its intended audience by genotype, can help reduce tobacco use.

The future of ADHD molecular genetic research

Propping (2005, p. 6) put forward some explanations for the embarrassing number of false positive results in psychiatric molecular genetic research. Among these he mentioned 'Premature publication because of competition pressure', 'Premature publication because of commercial interests', 'Selective publication of positive findings', and the 'Lower standard of investigators than in other fields'. Propping saw 'selective publication of positive findings to be the most threatening one for our field', and discussed the 'danger that journals preferentially publish positive findings, because a silent coalition exists between author and editor: both are interested in publishing positive findings'.

For Plomin (2005, pp. 1032–3), a major factor in failed gene-finding attempts has been that the genes he believes underlie conditions such as ADHD are of much smaller sized-effect than previously believed, and that the 'biggest effect' of any particular gene is 'not very big'. In his view, 'Underpowered studies are likely to be responsible for the widespread failure to replicate linkages and associations for common disorders, such as . . . hyperactivity and the DRD4 and DAT genes'. He called for the creation of 'more powerful vehicles with bigger engines: Huge samples of many thousands of individuals are needed to detect QTLs of very small effect size'. Regarding the predicted future discovery of genes, we have seen Plomin ask, 'When are we going to be there?' A major goal of this chapter has been to show that there is good reason to believe, as the saying goes, that 'there is no there, there'.

In 2000 I predicted that 'A gene (or genes) for ADHD will not be discovered, because it does not exist' (Joseph, 2000b, p. 587). Several years later, I see little reason to modify this prediction.

Conclusions

The presumed genetic basis of ADHD rests on the results of family, twin, and adoption studies. Although ADHD may be familial, the fact that families share a common environment as well as common genes permits no valid conclusions in support of genetics.

The twin method is no less confounded by environmental factors than are family studies because, as most people clearly understand, MZ twins experience more similar environments than DZs. Therefore, the greater resemblance of MZ versus same-sex DZ twins for ADHD, or ADHD-related tests, is completely explainable on non-genetic grounds.

ADHD adoption studies are greatly inferior to the flawed schizophrenia adoption studies that preceded them, and therefore offer no scientifically acceptable evidence in favour of genetic influences on ADHD. Finally, despite concerted worldwide efforts, researchers have been unable to find presumed ADHD genes. As I have argued here, it is unlikely that such genes exist. Similarly, investigators searching for the genes presumed to cause other major psychiatric disorders such as schizophrenia, bipolar disorder, and autism, have also come up empty-handed (Joseph, 2006). Clearly, future research should be directed towards environmental factors. Unfortunately, as Timimi *et al.* (2004, p. 60) point out, 'Research on possible environmental causes of ADHD type behaviours has largely been ignored, despite mounting evidence that psychosocial factors such as exposure to trauma and abuse can cause them.' A major reason that environmental factors have been overlooked is the widespread belief that faulty genes play a role in causing ADHD. In this chapter, I have attempted to show that there is little if any scientifically acceptable evidence supporting this belief.

Notes

1. However, in 2006 Kendler wrote, with more optimism, that 'we are beginning to identify and replicate susceptibility genes for psychiatric disorders' (Kendler, 2006, p. 1138).
2. Although most contemporary ADHD researchers understand that the results of family studies are explainable on environmental grounds, an author as influential as Russell Barkley (2003, p. 116) has written that 'ADHD clusters significantly among the biological relatives of children or adults with the disorder, strongly implying a hereditary basis to this condition.'
3. Additional assumptions of the twin method include: (1) that there are only two types of twins, MZ and DZ; (2) that investigators are able to reliably distinguish between MZ and DZ twins; (3) that the risk of receiving the diagnosis is the same among twins and non-twins (generalizability); and (4) that the risk of receiving the diagnosis is the same among individual MZ twins as a population, versus individual DZ twins as a population.
4. Another example of contemporary researchers defining the EEA in the traditional sense include Kuntsi and colleagues (2006, p. 14), who wrote, 'For shared environmental influences MZ and DZ twins are expected to correlate to the same extent.'
5. In ADHD adoption research, only Sprich et al. (2000) made blind diagnoses.
6. In their 1988 *Annual Review of Psychology* contribution, behaviour geneticists Loehlin, Willerman, and Horn (1988, p. 124) wrote, 'We are witnessing major breakthroughs in identifying genes coding for some mental disorders.' And 11 years before that, genetic investigators Julien Mendlewicz and John Rainer (1977, p. 327) claimed that 'A genetic vulnerability to manic-depressive disorder has been demonstrated by family, twin, and linkage studies.' Like ADHD, schizophrenia, and autism, however, manic-depression (bipolar disorder) genes remain undiscovered (Joseph, 2006).

References

Ainslie, R. C. (1985) *The Psychology of Twinship*. Lincoln: University of Nebraska Press.

Alberts-Corush, J., Firestone, P., and Goodman, J. T. (1986) Attention and impulsivity characteristics of the biological and adoptive parents of hyperactive and normal control children, *American Journal of Orthopsychiatry* 56, 413–23.

Alford, J. R., Funk, C. L., and Hibbing, J. R. (2005) Are political orientations genetically transmitted? *American Political Science Review* 99, 153–67.

American Psychiatric Association (2000) *Diagnostic and Statistical Manual of Mental Disorders, 4th edn, text revision.* Washington, DC: American Psychiatric Association.

Arcos-Burgos, M., Castellanos, F. X., Pineda, D., Lopera, F., Palacio, J. D., Palacio, J. D., Rapoport, J. L., Berg, K., Bailey-Wilson, J. E., and Muenke, M. (2004) Attention-deficit/hyperactivity disorder in a population isolate: Linkage to loci at 4q13.2, 5q33.3, 11q22, and 17p11, *American Journal of Human Genetics* 75, 998–1014.

Asherson, P. J., and Curran, S. (2001) Approaches to gene mapping in complex disorders and their application in child psychiatry and psychology, *British Journal of Psychiatry* 179, 122–8.

Asherson, P., Kuntsi, J., and Taylor, E. (2005) Unravelling the complexity of attention-deficit hyperactivity disorder: A behavioral genomic approach, *British Journal of Psychiatry* 187, 103–5.

Bakker, S. C., van der Meulen, E. M., Buitelaar, J. K., Sandkuijl, L. A., Pauls, D. L., Monsuur, A. J., van 't Slot, R., Minderaa, R. B., Gunning, W. B., Pearson, P. L., and Sinke, R. J. (2003) A whole-genome scan in 164 Dutch sib pairs with attention-deficit/hyperactivity disorder: Suggestive evidence for linkage on chromosomes 7p and 15q, *American Journal of Human Genetics* 72, 1251–60.

Bakker, S. C., van der Meulen, E. M., Oteman, N., Schelleman, H., Pearson, P. L., Buitelaar, J. K., and Sinke, R. J. (2005). DAT1, DRD4, and DRD5 polymorphisms are not associated with ADHD in Dutch families, *American Journal of Medical Genetics, Series B (Neuropsychiatric Genetics)* 132B, 50–2.

Barkley, R. A. (1998) Attention-deficit hyperactivity disorder, *Scientific American* (September), 66–71.

Barkley, R. A. (2003) Attention-deficit/hyperactivity disorder, in E. Mash and R. Barkley (eds), *Child Psychopathology, 2nd edn* (pp. 75–143). New York: The Guilford Press.

Barkley, R. A., Cook, E. H., Dulcan, M., *et al.* (2002) Consensus statement on ADHD, *European Child and Adolescent Psychiatry* 11, 96–8.

Barr, C. L. (2001) Genetics of childhood disorders: XXII. ADHD, Part 6: The dopamine D4 receptor gene, *Journal of the American Academy of Child and Adolescent Psychiatry* 40, 118–21.

Biederman, J., Faraone, S. V., Keenan, K., Knee, D., and Tsuang, M. T. (1990) Family-genetic and psychosocial risk factors in DSM-III attention deficit disorder, *Journal of the American Academy of Child and Adolescent Psychiatry* 29, 526–33.

Biederman, J., Faraone, S. V., Mick, E., Spencer, T., Wilens, T., Kiely, K., Guite, J., Ablon, J. S., Reed, E., and Warburton, R. (1995) High risk for attention deficit hyperactivity disorder among children of parents with childhood onset of the disorder: A pilot study, *American Journal of Psychiatry* 152, 431–5.

Biederman, J., Munir, K., Knee, D., Habelow, M., Autor, S., Hoge, S. K., and Waternaux, C. (1986) A family study of patients with attention deficit disorder and normal controls, *Journal of Psychiatric Research* 20, 263–74.

Boomsma, D. I., Cacioppo, J. T., Slagboom, P. E., and Posthuma, D. (2006) Genetic linkage and association analysis for loneliness in Dutch twin and sibling pairs points to a region on chromosome 12q23-24, *Behavior Genetics* 36, 137–46.

Boomsma, D. I., Willemsen, G., Dolan, C. V., Hawkley, L. C., & Cacioppo, J. T. (2005) Genetic and environmental contributions to loneliness in adults: The Netherlands Twin Register Study, *Behavior Genetics* 35, 745–52.

Bouchard, T. J., Jr (1993) Genetic and environmental influences on adult personality: Evaluating the evidence, in J. Hettema and I. Deary (eds), *Basic Issues in Personality* (pp. 15–44). Dordrecht, The Netherlands: Kluwer Academic Publishers.

Bouchard, T. J., Jr (1997) IQ similarity in twins reared apart: Findings and responses to critics, in R. Sternberg and E. Grigorenko (eds), *Intelligence, Heredity, and Environment* (pp. 126–60). New York: Cambridge University Press.

Boyle, M. (2002) *Schizophrenia: A Scientific Delusion? 2nd edn.* Hove, UK: Routledge.

Breggin, P. R. (1998) *Talking Back to Ritalin.* Monroe, ME: Common Courage Press.

Breggin, P. R. (2001a) Empowering social work in the era of biological psychiatry, *Ethical Human Sciences and Services* 3, 197–206.

Breggin, P. (2001b) What people need to know about the drug treatment of children, in C. Newnes, G. Holmes, and C. Dunn (eds), *This is Madness Too: Critical Perspectives on Mental Health Services* (pp. 47–58). PCCS Books: Ross-on-Wye, UK.

Cantwell, D. P. (1972) Psychiatric illness in the families of hyperactive children, *Archives of General Psychiatry* 27, 414–17.

Cantwell, D. P. (1975) Genetic studies of hyperactive children: Psychiatric illness in biologic and adopting parents, in R. Fieve, D. Rosenthal, and H. Brill (eds), *Genetic Research in Psychiatry* (pp. 273–80). Baltimore: The Johns Hopkins Press.

Carey, G., and DiLalla, D. L. (1994) Personality and psychopathology: Genetic perspectives, *Journal of Abnormal Psychology* 103, 32–43.

Cassou, B., Schiff, M., and Stewart, J. (1980) Génétique et schizophrénie: Réévaluation d'un consensus [Genetics and schizophrenia: Reevaluation of a consensus]. *Psychiatrie de l'Enfant* 23, 87–201.

Comings, D. E., Chen, T. J. H., Blum, K., Mengucci, J. F., Blum, S. H., and Meshkin, B. (2005) Neurogenetic interactions and aberrant behavioral co-morbidity of attention deficit hyperactivity disorder (ADHD): Dispelling myths, *Theoretical Biology and Medical Modelling* 2 (Published online 12/23/2005).

Cook, E. H., Jr (1999) Genetics of attention-deficit hyperactivity disorder, *Mental Retardation and Developmental Disabilities Research Reviews* 5, 191–8.

Cronk, N. J., Slutske, W. S., Madden, P. A. F., Bucholz, K. K., Reich, W., and Heath, A. C. (2002) Emotional and behavioral problems among female twins: An evaluation of the equal environment assumption, *Journal of the American Academy of Child and Adolescent Psychiatry* 41, 829–37.

Dawood, K., Kirk, K. M., Bailey, J. M., Andrews, P. W., and Martin, N. G. (2005) Genetic and environmental influences on the frequency of orgasm in women, *Twin Research and Human Genetics* 8, 27–33.

DeGrandpre, R. (1999) *Ritalin Nation*. New York: W. W. Norton.

Deutsch, C. K. (1989). Adoption and attention deficit disorder. In L. Bloomingdale and J. Swanson (eds), *Attention Deficit Disorder, Current Concepts and Emerging Trends in Attentional and Behavioral Disorders of Childhood, Vol. IV* (pp. 67–79). New York: Pergamon Press.

Deutsch, C. K., Swanson, J. M., Bruell, J. H., Cantwell, D. P., Weinberg, F., and Baren, M. (1982) Overrepresentation of adoptees in children with the attention deficit disorder, *Behavior Genetics* 12, 231–8.

Doyle, A. E., Willcutt, E. G., Seidman, L. J., Biederman, J., Chouinard, V. A., Silva, J., and Faraone, S. V. (2005) Attention-deficit/hyperactivity disorder endophenotypes, *Biological Psychiatry* 57, 1324–35.

Edelbrock, C., Rende, R., Plomin, R., and Thompson, L. (1995) A twin study of competence and problem behavior in childhood and early adolescence, *Journal of Child Psychology and Psychiatry* 36, 775–85.

Egan, M. F., Leboyer, M., and Weinberger, D. R. (2003) Intermediate phenotypes in genetic studies of schizophrenia, in S. Hirsch and D. Weinberger (eds), *Schizophrenia, 2nd edn* (pp. 277–97). Malden, MA: Blackwell.

Faraone, S. V. (2004) Genetics of adult attention-deficit/hyperactivity disorder, *Psychiatric Clinics of North America* 27, 303–21.

Faraone, S. V. (2005) The scientific foundation for understanding attention-deficit/hyperactivity disorder as a valid psychiatric disorder, *European Child and Adolescent Psychiatry* 14, 1–10.

Faraone, S. V., and Biederman, J. (2000) Nature, nurture, and attention deficit hyperactivity disorder, *Developmental Review* 20, 568–81.

Faraone, S. V., and Biederman, J. (2002) Drs Faraone and Biederman reply [Letter to the editor], *Journal of the American Academy of Child and Adolescent Psychiatry* 41, 1390–1.

Faraone, S. V., Biederman, J., Keenan, K., and Tsuang, M. T. (1991) A family-genetic study of girls with DSM-III attention deficit disorder, *American Journal of Psychiatry* 148, 112–7.

Faraone, S. V., Doyle, A. E., Mick, E., and Biederman, J. (2001) Meta-analysis of the association between the 7-repeat allele of the dopamine D4 receptor gene and attention deficit hyperactivity disorder, *American Journal of Psychiatry* 158, 1052–7.

Faraone, S. V., Perlis, R. H., Doyle, A. E., Smoller, J. W., Goralnick, J. J., Holmgren, M. A., and Sklar, P. (2005) Molecular genetics of attention-deficit/hyperactivity disorder, *Biological Psychiatry* 57, 1313–23.

Faraone, S. V., Tsuang, M. T., and Tsuang, D. W. (1999) *Genetics of Mental Disorders*. New York: The Guilford Press.

Fisher, S. E., Franks, C., McCracken, J. T., McGough, J. J., Marlow, A. J., MacPhie, I. L., Newbury, D. F., Crawford, L. R., Palmer, C. G. S., Woodward, J. A., Del'Homme, M., Cantwell, D. P., Nelson, S. F., Monaco, A. P., and Smalley, S. L. (2002) A genomewide scan for loci involved in Attention-deficit/hyperactivity disorder, *American Journal of Human Genetics* 70, 1183–96.

Gilger, J. W., Pennington, B. F., and DeFries, J. C. (1992). A twin study of the etiology of comorbidity: Attention-deficit hyperactivity disorder and dyslexia, *Journal of the American Academy of Child and Adolescent Psychiatry* 31, 343–8.

Gillis, J. J., Gilger, J. W., Pennington, B. F., and DeFries, J. C. (1992) Attention deficit disorder in reading-disabled twins: Evidence for a genetic etiology, *Journal of Abnormal Child Psychology* 20, 303–15.

Goldstein, S., and Schwebach, A. (2005) Attention-deficit/hyperactivity disorder, in S. Goldstein and C. Reynolds (eds), *Handbook of Neurodevelopmental and Genetic Disorders in Adults* (pp. 115–46). New York: The Guilford Press.

Gottesman, I. I., and Gould, T. D. (2003) The endophenotype concept in psychiatry: Etymology and strategic intentions, *American Journal of Psychiatry* 160, 636–5.

Gottesman, I. I., and Shields, J. (1972) *Schizophrenia and Genetics: A Twin Study Vantage Point*. New York: Academic Press.

Gottesman, I. I., and Shields, J. (1982). *Schizophrenia: The Epigenetic Puzzle*. New York: Cambridge University Press.

Hay, D. A., and Levy, F. (2001) Implications of genetic studies of attentional problems for education and intervention, in F. Levy and D. Hay (eds), *Attention, Genes, and ADHD* (pp. 214–24). East Sussex, UK: Brunner-Routledge.

Hay, D. A., McStephen, M. and Levy, F. (2001) Introduction to the genetic analysis of attentional disorders, in F. Levy and D. Hay (eds), *Attention, Genes, and ADHD* (pp. 7–34). East Sussex, UK: Brunner-Routledge.

Hebebrand, J., Dempfle, A., Sarr, K., Thiele, H., Herpertz-Dahlmann, B., Linder, M., Kiefl, H., Remschmidt, H., Hemminger, U., Warnke, A., Knölker, U., Friedel, S., Hinney, A., Schäfer, H., Nürnberg, P., and Konrad, K. (2006). A genome-wide scan for attention-deficit/hyperactivity disorder in 155 German sib-pairs, *Molecular Psychiatry* 11, 196–205.

Heiser, P., Heinzel-Gutenbrunner, M., Frey, J., Smidt, J., Grabarkiewicz, J., Friedel, S., Kuhnau, W., Schmidtke, J., Remschmidt, H., and Hebebrand, J.

(2006) Twin study on heritability of activity, attention, and impulsivity as assessed by objective measures, *Journal of Attention Disorders* 9, 575–81.

Heston, L. L. (1966). Psychiatric disorders in foster home reared children of schizophrenic mothers, *British Journal of Psychiatry* 112, 819–25.

Hettema, J. M., Neale, M. C., and Kendler, K. S. (1995) Physical similarity and the equal-environment assumption in twin studies of psychiatric disorders, *Behavior Genetics* 25, 327–35.

Hirsch, J. (1997) Some history of heredity-vs-environment, genetic inferiority at Harvard (?), and The (incredible) Bell Curve. *Genetica* 99, 207–24.

Hirsch, J. (2004) Uniqueness, diversity, similarity, repeatability, and heritability, in C. Coll, E. Bearer, and R. Lerner (eds), *Nature and Nurture: The Complex Interplay of Genetic and Environmental Influences on Human Behavior and Development* (pp. 127–38). Mahwah, NJ: Erlbaum.

Horgan, J. (2004) Do genes influence our behavior? *Chronicle of Higher Education* 26 November, retrieved online 1/2/2006, from <http://www.johnhorgan.org/work14.htm>.

Hudziak, J. J., Copeland, W., Rudiger, L. P., Achenbach, T. M., Heath, A. C., and Todd, R. D. (2003) Genetic influences on childhood competencies: A twin study, *Journal of the American Academy of Child and Adolescent Psychiatry* 42, 357–63.

Jackson, D. D. (1960) A critique of the literature on the genetics of schizophrenia, in D. Jackson (ed.), *The Etiology of Schizophrenia* (pp. 37–87). New York: Basic Books.

Jackson, G. E. (2003) Rethinking the Finnish adoption studies of schizophrenia: A challenge to genetic determinism, *Journal of Critical Psychology, Counselling and Psychotherapy* 3, 129–38.

Joseph, J. (2000a) Not in their genes: A critical view of the genetics of attention-deficit hyperactivity disorder, *Developmental Review* 20, 539–67.

Joseph, J. (2000b) Problems in psychiatric genetic research: A reply to Faraone and Biederman, *Developmental Review* 20, 582–93.

Joseph, J. (2002) Adoption study of ADHD [Letter to the editor], *Journal of the American Academy of Child and Adolescent Psychiatry* 41, 1389–91.

Joseph, J. (2004a) *The Gene Illusion: Genetic Research in Psychiatry and Psychology Under the Microscope*. New York: Algora. (2003 United Kingdom Edition by PCCS Books)

Joseph, J. (2004b) Schizophrenia and heredity: Why the emperor has no genes, in J. Read, L. Mosher, and R. Bentall (eds), *Models of Madness: Psychological, Social and Biological Approaches to Schizophrenia* (pp. 67–83). Andover, UK: Taylor & Francis.

Joseph, J. (2006) *The Missing Gene: Psychiatry, Heredity, and the Fruitless Search for Genes*. New York: Algora.

Kendler, K. S. (1983) Overview: A current perspective on twin studies of schizophrenia. *American Journal of Psychiatry* 140, 1413–1425.

Kendler, K. S. (1987). The genetics of schizophrenia: A current perspective, in H. Meltzer (ed.), *Psychopharmacology: The Third Generation of Progress* (pp. 705–13). New York: Raven Press.

Kendler, K. S. (2005) 'A gene for . . .': The nature of gene actions in psychiatric disorders, *American Journal of Psychiatry* 162, 1243–52.

Kendler, K. S. (2006) Reflections on the relationship between psychiatric genetics and psychiatric nosology, *American Journal of Psychiatry* 163, 1138–46.

Kendler, K. S., Neale, M. C., Kessler, R. C., Heath, A. C., and Eaves, L. J. (1993) A test of the equal-environment assumption in twin studies of psychiatric illness, *Behavior Genetics* 23, 21–7.

Keski-Rahkonen, A., Viken, R. J., Kaprio, J., Rissanen, A., and Rose, R. J. (2004) Genetic and environmental factors in breakfast eating patterns, *Behavior Genetics* 34, 503–14.

Kety, S. S., Rosenthal, D., Wender, P. H., and Schulsinger, F. (1968) The types and prevalence of mental illness in the biological and adoptive families of adopted schizophrenics, in D. Rosenthal and S. Kety (eds), *The Transmission of Schizophrenia* (pp. 345–62). New York: Pergamon Press.

Kety, S. S., Rosenthal, D., Wender, P. H., Schulsinger, F., and Jacobsen, B. (1975) Mental illness in the biological and adoptive families of adopted individuals who have become schizophrenic: A preliminary report based on psychiatric interviews, in R. Fieve, D. Rosenthal, and H. Brill (eds), *Genetic Research in Psychiatry* (pp. 147–65). Baltimore: The Johns Hopkins Press.

Kety, S. S., Wender, P. H., Jacobsen, B., Ingraham, L. J., Jansson, L., Faber, B., and Kinney, D. K. (1994) Mental illness in the biological and adoptive relatives of schizophrenic adoptees: Replication of the Copenhagen study to the rest of Denmark, *Archives of General Psychiatry* 51, 442–55.

Kuntsi, J., Neale, B. M., Chen, W., Faraone, S. V., and Asherson, P. (2006) The IMAGE project: Methodological issues for the molecular genetic analysis of ADHD, *Behavioral and Brain Functions* 2, 27, published on-line 8 March 2006, retrieved 8 November 2006.

LaBuda, M. C., Svikis, D. S., and Pickens, R. V. (1997) Twin closeness and co-twin risk for substance use disorders: Assessing the impact of the equal environment assumption, *Psychiatry Research* 70, 155–64.

Langley, K., Marshall, L., van den Bree, M., Thomas, H., Owen, M., O'Donovan, M., and Thapar, A. (2004) Association of the dopamine D4 receptor gene 7-repeat allele with neuropsychological test performance of children with ADHD, *American Journal of Psychiatry* 161, 133–8.

Langley, K., Turic, D., Peirce, T. R., Mills, S., van den Bree, M. B., Owen, M. J., O'Donovan, M. C., and Thapar, A. (2005) No support for association between the dopamine transporter (DAT1) gene and ADHD, *American Journal of Medical Genetics, Series B (Neuropsychiatric Genetics)* 139B, 7–10.

Leo, J. (2002). American preschoolers on Ritalin, *Society* 39, 2, January/February), 52–60.

Levy, F., Hay, D. A., McStephen, M., Wood, C., and Waldman, I. (1997) Attention-deficit hyperactivity disorder: A category or a continuum? Genetic analysis of a large-scale twin study, *Journal of the American Academy of Child and Adolescent Psychiatry* 36, 737–44.

Lewontin, R. C., Rose, S., and Kamin, L. J. (1984) *Not in Our Genes.* New York: Pantheon.

Li, D., Sham, P. S., Owen, M. J., and He, L. (2006) Meta-analysis shows significant association between dopamine system genes and attention deficit hyperactivity disorder (ADHD), *Human Molecular Genetics* 15, 2276–84.

Lidz, T. (1976) Commentary on a critical review of recent adoption, twin, and family studies of schizophrenia: Behavioral genetics perspectives, *Schizophrenia Bulletin* 2, 402–12.

Lidz, T., and Blatt, S. (1983) Critique of the Danish-American studies of the biological and adoptive relatives of adoptees who became schizophrenic, *American Journal of Psychiatry* 140, 426–35.

Lidz, T., Blatt, S., and Cook, B. (1981) Critique of the Danish-American studies of the adopted-away offspring of schizophrenic parents, *American Journal of Psychiatry* 138, 1063–8.

Lilienfeld, S. O., Lynn, S. J., and Lohr, J. M. (2003) Science and pseudoscience in clinical psychology: Initial thoughts, reflections, and considerations, In S. Lilienfeld, S. Lynn, and J. Lohr (eds), *Science and Pseudoscience in Clinical Psychology* (pp. 1–14). New York: The Guilford Press.

Loehlin, J. C., and Nichols, R. C. (1976) *Heredity, Environment, and Personality.* Austin: University of Texas Press.

Loehlin, J. C., Willerman, L., and Horn, J. M. (1988) Human behavior genetics, *Annual Review of Psychology* 39, 101–33.

Lopez, R. E. (1965) Hyperactivity in twins, *Canadian Psychiatric Association Journal* 10, 421–6.

Lush, J. L. (1945) *Animal Breeding Plans.* Ames, IA: Collegiate Press.

Lush, J. L. (1949) Heritability of quantitative characteristics in farm animals, *Hereditas (Suppl.).* G. Bonnier and R. Larsson (eds), 356–75.

Lyons, M. J., Kendler, K. S., Provet, A., and Tsuang, M. T. (1991) The genetics of schizophrenia, in M. Tsuang, K. Kendler, and M. Lyons (eds), *Genetic Issues in Psychosocial Epidemiology* (pp. 119–52). New Brunswick, NJ: Rutgers University Press.

McGough, J. J. (2005) Attention-deficit/hyperactivity disorder pharmacogenomics, *Biological Psychiatry* 57, 1367–73.

McGuffin, P. (2004). Behavioral genomics: Where molecular genetics is taking psychiatry and psychology. In L. DiLalla (Ed.), *Behavior Genetics Principles* (pp. 191–204). Washington, DC: American Psychological Association Press.

Mendlewicz, J., and Rainer, J. D. (1977). Adoption study supporting genetic transmission in manic-depressive illness. *Nature* 268, 327-329.

Merikangas, K. R., and Risch, N. (2003) Will the genomics revolution revolutionize psychiatry? *American Journal of Psychiatry* 160, 625–35.

Mill, J., Xiaohui, X., Ronald, A., Curran, S., Price, T., Knight, J., Sham, P., Plomin, R., and Asherson, P. (2005) Quantitative trait locus analysis of candidate gene alleles associated with attention deficit hyperactivity disorder (ADHD) in five genes: DRD4, DAT1, DRD5, SNAP-25, and 5HT1B, *American Journal of Medical Genetics (Series B, Neuropsychiatric Genetics)* 133B, 68–73.

Moore, D. S. (2001) *The Dependent Gene: The Fallacy of 'Nature vs. Nurture'.* New York: Times Books.

Morris-Yates, A., Andrews, G., Howie, P., and Henderson, S. (1990) Twins: A test of the equal environments assumption, *Acta Psychiatrica Scandinavica* 81, 322–6.

Morrison, J. R., and Stewart, M. A. (1971) A family study of the hyperactive child syndrome, *Biological Psychiatry* 3, 189–95.

Morrison, J. R., and Stewart, M. A. (1973) The psychiatric status of the legal families of adopted hyperactive children, *Archives of General Psychiatry* 28, 888–91.

Nichols, P. L., and Chen, T. C. (1981) *Minimal Brain Dysfunction.* Hillsdale, NJ: Lawrence Erlbaum Associates.

Ogdie, M. N., Macphie, I. L., Minassian, S. L., Yang, M., Fisher, S. E., Francks, C., Cantor, R. M., McCracken, J. T., McGough, J. J., Nelson, S. F., Monaco, A. P., and Smalley, S. L. (2003) A genomewide scan for attention-deficit/hyperactivity disorder in an extended sample: Suggestive linkage on 17p11, *American Journal of Human Genetics* 72, 1268–79.

Pam, A. (1995) Biological psychiatry: Science or pseudoscience? in C. Ross and A. Pam (eds), *Pseudoscience in Biological Psychiatry: Blaming the Body* (pp. 7–84). New York: John Wiley & Sons.

Pam, A., Kemker, S. S., Ross, C. A., and Golden, R. (1996) The 'equal environment assumption' in MZ-DZ comparisons: An untenable premise of psychiatric genetics? *Acta Geneticae Medicae et Gemellologiae* 45, 349–60.

Pauls, D. L. (2005) The genetics of attention-deficit/hyperactivity disorder, *Biological Psychiatry* 57, 1310–12.

Pittelli, S. J. (2002) Meta-analysis and psychiatric genetics [Letter to the editor], *American Journal of Psychiatry* 159, 496.

Pittelli, S. J. (2004) Genetic linkage for schizophrenia? [Letter to the editor], *American Journal of Psychiatry* 161, 1134.

Plomin, R. (2005) Finding genes in child psychology and psychiatry: When are we going to be there? *Journal of Child Psychology and Psychiatry* 46, 1030–8.

Plomin, R., DeFries, J. C., McClearn, G. E., and McGuffin, P. (2001) *Behavioral Genetics,* 4th edn. New York: Worth Publishers.

Plomin, R., and Rutter, M. (1998) Child development, molecular genetics, and what to do with genes once they are found, *Child Development* 69, 1223–42.

Propping, P. (2005) The biography of psychiatric genetics: From early achievements to historical burden, from an anxious society to critical geneticists, *American Journal of Medical Genetics, Series B (Neuropsychiatric Genetics)* 136B (1), 2–7.

Ratner, C. (2004) Genes and psychology in the news, *New Ideas in Psychology* 22, 29–47.

Rosenthal, D., Wender, P. H., Kety, S. S., Welner, J., and Schulsinger, F. (1971) The adopted-away offspring of schizophrenics, *American Journal of Psychiatry* 128, 307–11.

Rosenthal, D., Wender, P. H., Kety, S. S., Schulsinger, F., Welner, J., and Østergaard, L. (1968) Schizophrenics' offspring reared in adoptive homes, in D. Rosenthal and S. Kety (eds), *The Transmission of Schizophrenia* (pp. 377–91). New York: Pergamon Press.

Rutter, M. (2001) Child psychiatry in the era following sequencing the genome, in F. Levy and D. Hay (eds), *Attention, Genes, and ADHD* (pp. 225–48). East Sussex, UK: Brunner-Routledge.

Rutter, M., Bolton, P., Harrington, R., Le Couteur, A., Macdonald, H., and Simonoff, E. (1990) Genetic factors in child psychiatric disorders—I. A review of research strategies, *Journal of Child Psychology and Psychiatry* 31, 3–37.

Rutter, M., Pickles, A., Murray, R., and Eaves, L. (2001) Testing hypotheses on specific environmental causal effects on behavior, *Psychological Bulletin* 127, 291–24.

Safer, D. J. (1973) A familial factor in minimal brain dysfunction, *Behavior Genetics* 3, 175–86.

Saudino, K. J., Ronald, A., and Plomin, R. (2005) The etiology of behavior problems in 7-year-old twins: Substantial genetic influence and negligible shared environmental influence for parent ratings and ratings by same and different teachers, *Journal of Abnormal Child Psychology* 33, 113–30.

Scarr, S., and Carter-Saltzman, L. (1979) Twin method: Defense of a critical assumption, *Behavior Genetics* 9, 527–42.

Sherman, D. K., Iacono, W. G., and McGue, M. K. (1997) Attention-deficit hyperactivity disorder dimensions: A twin study of inattention and impulsivity-hyperactivity, *Journal of the American Academy of Child and Adolescent Psychiatry* 36, 745–53.

Slaats-Willemse, D., Swaab-Barneveld, H., de Sonneville, L., van der Meulen, E., and Buitelaar, J. (2003) Deficient response inhibition as a cognitive endophenotype of ADHD, *Journal of the American Academy of Child and Adolescent Psychiatry* 42, 1242–8.

Sprich, S., Biederman, J., Crawford, M. H., Mundy, E., and Faraone, S. V. (2000) Adoptive and biological families of children and adolescents with ADHD, *Journal of the American Academy of Child and Adolescent Psychiatry* 39, 1432–7.

Thapar, A., Hervas, A., and McGuffin, P. (1995) Childhood hyperactivity scores are highly heritable and show sibling competition effects: Twin study evidence, *Behavior Genetics* 25, 537–44.

Thapar, A., Holmes, J., Poulton, K., and Harrington, R. (1999) Genetic basis of attention-deficit and hyperactivity, *British Journal of Psychiatry* 174, 105–11.

Tienari, P., Sorri, A., Lahti, I., Naarala, M., Wahlberg, K., Moring, J., Pohjola, J., and Wynne, L. C. (1987) Genetic and psychosocial factors in schizophrenia: The Finnish adoptive family study, *Schizophrenia Bulletin* 13, 477–84.

Tienari, P., Wynne, L. C., Läksy, K., Moring, J., Nieminen, P., Sorri, A., Lahti, I., and Wahlberg, K. E. (2003) Genetic boundaries of the schizophrenia spectrum: Evidence from the Finnish Adoptive Family Study, *American Journal of Psychiatry* 160, 1587–94.

Tienari, P., Wynne, L. C., Sorri, A., Lahti, I., Läksy, K., Moring, J., Naarala, M., Nieminen, P., and Wahlberg, K. E. (2004) Genotype-environment interaction in schizophrenia-spectrum disorders, *British Journal of Psychiatry* 184, 216–22.

Timimi, S., and 33 co-endorsers (2004) A critique of the international consensus statement on ADHD, *Clinical Child and Family Psychology Review* 7, 59–63.

Tozzi, F., Aggen, S. H., Neale, B. N., Anderson, C. B., Mazzeo, S. E., Neale, M. C., and Bulik, C. M. (2004) The structure of perfectionism: A twin study, *Behavior Genetics* 34, 483–94.

Van den Oord, E. J. C. G., Boomsma, D. I., and Verhulst, F. C. (1994) A study of problem behaviors in 10- to 15-year-old biologically related and unrelated international adoptees, *Behavior Genetics* 24, 193–205.

Van der Meulen, E. M., Bakker, S. C., Pauls, D. L., Oteman, N., Kruitwagen, C. L. J. J., Pearson, P. L., Sinke, R. J., and Buitelaar, J. K. (2005) High sibling correlation on methylphenidate response but no association with DAT1-10R homozygosity in Dutch sibpairs with ADHD, *Journal of Child Psychology and Psychiatry* 46, 1074–80.

Volkmar, F. R., and Pauls, D. (2003) Autism, *Lancet* 362, 1133–41.

Waldman, I. D. (2005) Statistical approaches to complex phenotypes: Evaluating neuropsychological endophenotypes for attention-deficit/hyperactivity disorder, *Biological Psychiatry* 57, 1347–56.

Waldman, I. D., and Gizer, I. A. (2006) The genetics of attention deficit hyperactivity disorder, *Clinical Psychology Review* 26, 396–432.

Welner, Z., Welner, A., Stewart, M., Palkes, H., and Wish, E. (1977) A controlled study of siblings of hyperactive children, *Journal of Nervous and Mental Disease* 165, 110–17.

Wender, P. H., Rosenthal, D., and Kety, S. S. (1968) A psychiatric assessment of the adoptive parents of schizophrenics, in D. Rosenthal and S. Kety (eds), *The Transmission of Schizophrenia* (pp. 235–50). New York: Pergamon Press.

Wender, P. H., Rosenthal, D., Kety, S. S., Schulsinger, F., and Welner, J. (1974) Crossfostering: A research strategy for clarifying the role of genetic and experiential factors in the etiology of schizophrenia. *Archives of General Psychiatry* 30, 121-128.

Willcutt, E. G., Pennington, B. F., and DeFries, J. C. (2000) Etiology of inattention and hyperactivity/impulsivity in a community sample of twins with learning disabilities, *Journal of Abnormal Child Psychology* 28, 149–59.

Willerman, L. (1973) Activity level and hyperactivity in twins, *Child Development* 44, 288–93.

Chapter 3

A Critical Review of ADHD Neuroimaging Research[1]

Jonathan Leo and David Cohen

Some of the most often cited literature to support the idea that some children have abnormal brains that cause their 'Attention Deficit Hyperactivity Disorder' (ADHD) and to justify medicating children with stimulants such as amphetamine or methylphenidate comes from research utilizing modern neuroimaging techniques. Computerized tomography (CT) and magnetic resonance imaging (MRI) are used to produce pictures of various neuroanatomical structures. Images of glucose brain metabolism and cerebral blood flow are obtained using single photon emission computerized tomography (SPECT) and positron emission tomography (PET). Researchers in this field use these different imaging modalities to look for anatomical and physiological differences in the brains of children diagnosed with ADHD. Images published in scientific journals and in the media supposedly show abnormalities (or differences) in these children's brains. For clinicians, families, and the public who wonder whether or not the ADHD diagnosis points to an underlying disease, and whether its treatment requires drugs, the neuroimaging research and its accompanying images can be deciding factors.

Researchers have long tried to discover biological lesions in children diagnosed with ADHD. Principally using neuropsychological studies, pharmacological manipulations of brain chemistry, and attempts to find biochemical correlates of the ADHD behaviour cluster, investigators have produced 'a huge, diverse, and often conflcting literature', but 'no biological abnormality has ever been specifically and unambiguously linked to the disorder by conventional techniques' (Baumeister and Hawkins, 2001, pp. 3–4). However, in contrast to generally negative assessments of conventional research, assessments of the neuroimaging studies have been more positive. For example, a review by Faraone and Biederman concluded that 'taken together, the brain imaging studies fit well with the idea that dysfunction in the frontosubcortical pathways occurs in ADHD' (cited in Baumeister and Hawkins, p. 4).

Similarly, Giedd, Blumenthal, Molloy, and Castellanos (2001) summarized over 30 ADHD neuroimaging studies. Although Giedd *et al.* note that few findings have been replicated and most studies have inadequate statistical power, they conclude that, 'Taken together, the results of the imaging and neuropsychological studies suggest right frontal-striatal circuitry involvement in ADHD with a modulating influence from the cerebellum' (p. 44). Most of Giedd *et al.*'s review consists of six tables summarizing results from studies using different modalities (CT, MRI, SPECT, and PET) to compare the brains of 'ADHD' children to the brains of 'normal' children.[2] In each table, Giedd *et al.* identify the studies that have employed a particular technique, report on variables such as numbers of patients and controls, and summarize the key findings.

Although positive findings on neuroimaging studies of psychiatric disorders, including ADHD, are usually given wide coverage in scientific publications and the mass media, the fact remains that this body of research has not provided support for a specific 'biological basis' of ADHD. This is well noted by Baumeister and Hawkins (2001) who report, 'inconsistencies among studies raise questions about the reliability of the findings' (p. 2). These researchers noted that 'the complexity of many of these studies and [the] methodologic variation among them' make it 'difficult to discern whether these inconsistencies are apparent or real' (p. 4). Baumeister and Hawkins therefore isolated specific reported structural and functional abnormalities and examined the congruence among studies with respect to each. 'The principal conclusion is that the neuroimaging literature provides little support for a neurobiological etiology of ADHD' (p. 4). Writing, for instance, about the tendency for studies to find decreases in the size and activity of the frontal lobes, Baumeister and Hawkins summarize that:

> Even in this instance, however, the data are not compelling. The number of independent replications is small, and the validity of reported effects is compromised by a lack of statistical rigor. For example, several of the major functional imaging studies failed to employ standard statistical controls for multiple comparisons.

This means that many of the reported findings are almost certainly spurious. Moreover, considering the likely existence of bias
toward reporting and publishing positive results, the literature probably overestimates the occurrence of significant differences between
subjects with ADHD and control subjects. (p. 8, references omitted)

In addition, virtually all researchers in this field acknowledge that no
brain scan can currently detect anomalies in any given individual diagnosed with a primary mental disorder, nor can it help clinicians to
confirm such a diagnosis. For example, in his authoritative *Handbook
of Brain Imaging*, Bremmer (2005) states:

Unfortunately, we are not at a point where brain imaging can be
used routinely for the diagnosis of psychiatric conditions . . . We still
do not understand the patho-physiology or mechanisms of response
to treatment for most of these disorders. This lacunae is in contrast to our knowledge of neurological disorders, such as Parkinson's
disease, about which the pathophysiology was understood before
the advent of neuroimaging. In fact, we are only now using neuroimaging to attempt to understand the mechanisms underlying
neurological disorders . . . Most studies of psychiatric patients have
found that even when a particular finding characterized a patient
group, there remained as many as a third of patients who scored in
the range of the control subjects. Most investigators agree that these
patients should be not labeled as incorrectly diagnosed based on the
neuroimaging findings alone. (pp. 33–5)

Similarly, in the case of ADHD, Giedd *et al.* (2001) conclude unequiv-
ocally that:

MRI is not currently diagnostically useful in the routine assessment
or management of ADHD . . . The brain imaging studies . . . are not
currently specific enough to be used diagnostically . . . If a child has
no symptoms of ADHD but a brain scan consistent with what is
found in groups of ADHD, treatment for ADHD is not indicated.
Therefore, at the time of this writing, clinical history remains the
gold standard of ADHD diagnosis. (p. 45)

Given this crucial limitation of the neuroimaging data, what is its
utility in ADHD? Giedd *et al.* (2001) believe that it 'may help to
uncover the core neuropathology of the disease' (p. 45). However,

Giedd *et al.* do not provide in their tables information on a variable with undoubtedly weighty consequences on the interpretation of such research: *whether or not subjects diagnosed with ADD or ADHD had prior use of stimulant or other psychotropic medications.*

For investigators directly or not directly involved in neuroimaging research, information on the prior use of medication in the experimental subjects is simply too important to ignore. This is because an astronomical number of experimental and clinical studies on animals and humans find that almost every studied psychotropic drug consistently produces subtle or gross, transient or persistent effects on the functioning and structure of the central nervous system. The very definition of 'psychotropic' (acting on the central nervous system to produce changes in thinking, feeling, and behaving) presumes such effects. The effects vary depending on several factors, typically including dose and duration of use, as well as others such as the general state of the organism.

Sufficient evidence exists to view prior use of stimulants as a confounding factor in ADHD neuroimaging research. Research with rodents has documented that dopamine depletion is one of the intermediate and long-term effects of methylamphetamine and d-amphetamine treatment, but results about methylphenidate's effects have been mixed (Breggin, 1999; Wagner *et al.*, 1981; Wan, *et al.*, 2000; Yuan *et al.*, 1997). However, several studies have confirmed long-term pathology. In a study of young adult rats treated with methylphenidate twice daily for four days, there was evidence of 'attenuated presynaptic striatal dopamine function' 14 days after the end of treatment (Sproson *et al.*, 2001). In another experiment, methylphenidate was administered for two weeks to very young and older rats and the researchers found the density of dopamine transporters in the striatum (but not in the midbrain) to be 'significantly reduced after early methylphenidate administration (by 25% at day 45), and this decline reached almost 50% at adulthood (day 70), that is, long after termination of the treatment' (Moll *et al.*, 2001). Based on these findings Moll *et al.* (2001) concluded that 'long-lasting changes in the development of the central dopaminergic system [are] caused by the administration of methylphenidate during early juvenile life' (p. 15).

There have been several important studies on the effects of stimulants in humans. Volkow *et al.* (2001) utilized PET scans to look for functional changes following exposure to methylphenidate in healthy male subjects with no known psychiatric history and no past history of drug or alcohol abuse. Each subject underwent one scan 60 minutes after orally ingesting placebo and a second scan 60 minutes after orally ingesting 60 mg of methylphenidate. Methylphenidate induced large changes in the dopamine volume in the striatum (but not in the cerebellum). Volkow *et al.* (2001) conclude: 'These results provide direct evidence that oral methylphenidate significantly increases extracellular dopamine concentration in the human brain' (p. 3). If changes in the concentration of dopamine persist, however, they are likely to desensitize target areas to dopamine's effects, leading to a loss of dopamine receptors (downregulation). In this regard, in another study using SPECT to estimate striatal dopamine (D_2) receptor availability, non-drug treated children diagnosed with ADHD were scanned before and three months after methylphenidate treatment (Ilgin *et al.*, 2001). The investigators found 'D_2 availability reduced significantly as a function of methylphenidate therapy in patients with ADHD in all four regions of the striatum.' More to the point, the authors conclude: 'The effect of methylphenidate on D_2 receptor levels in patients with ADHD is similar to that observed in healthy adults: a downregulation phenomenon within 0 to 30%' (p. 755). Vles *et al.* (2003) similarly studied six boys diagnosed with ADHD: 'Three months after initiation of treatment with methylphenidate we found a down-regulation of the post-synaptic dopamine receptor with a maximum of 20% and a down-regulation of the dopamine transporter with a maximum of 74.7% in the striatal system' (p. 77). Given that no specific biological abnormality has been linked to ADHD, loss of neurotransmitter and receptors should be considered as drug-induced neuropathology. The word 'neuropathology' obviously has negative connotations and researchers commenting on stimulants' persistent effects generally prefer to use euphemisms, such as 'long-lasting neurochemical adaptations' or 'long-lasting neuro-adapations' (e.g., Fagundes *et al.*, 2006, p. 47; Martins *et al.*, 2006, p. 189).

The stimulant-specific findings briefly reviewed above illustrate the general point that, when striving to establish whether cerebral pathology or dysfunction is associated with a given psychiatric diagnosis, or to some symptoms or signs making up the criteria for a given diagnosis, it is critical to be able to rule out the probable impact on the brain of prior psychotropic drug use. This is especially the case in studies involving children, as significant changes occur in the number and patterning of brain cells well into adolescence (Vitiello, 1998). The clearest way to rule out such an impact is to select patients who have had no exposure to psychotropic medications, and to compare these patients to normal controls without the diagnosis.

In sum, we believe that a strong *prima facie* case exists, bolstered by much evidence, that the variable of prior medication exposure must be carefully considered in studies used to support the claim that cerebral pathology underlies the ADHD diagnosis in children. However, in the search for biological causes of behaviour disorders that characterizes psychiatric research – and perhaps to reassure themselves and others about the safety of widespread and long-term use of prescribed psychotropics – investigators have been prone to treat the variable of prior psychotropic drug use with less objectivity than its importance requires. They do so by 'mentioning' the variable but downplaying its impact, not discussing its impact, or by not mentioning the variable at all. These strategies or omissions are not used solely by authors who evaluate neuroimaging findings positively, as even Baumeister and Hawkins' (2001) highly critical review of 31 studies does not even raise the issue of medication status of ADHD subjects.

The question thus arises: how do researchers treat the confounding variable of prior drug exposure? To answer this question, we retrieved all the reports cited in Giedd *et al.*'s extensive review and extracted from each the relevant information. Below we present the same tables that Giedd *et al.* present, with additional columns indicating how many ADHD patients in each study were identified as having prior history of stimulant or other psychotropic drug use. Occasionally, we summarize or comment on some of the studies, highlighting what we judged to be noteworthy aspects or limitations not raised by Giedd *et al.* We then comment critically on several individual neuroimaging studies published since the Giedd *et al.* review, one of which made newspaper headlines to the effect that a biological basis of ADHD had been established. Finally, we conclude this chapter with a summary of our observations and a discussion of the possible meanings of this body of research and its future directions.

Findings

Computerized tomography

The six studies listed in Table 3.1 used computerized tomography (CT) to measure various regions of the cortex. Computerized tomography scanning was one of the first non-invasive brain imaging technologies developed, and the studies in Table 3.1 were all conducted before 1986. Only three studies included a control group. Four did not report

Table 3.1 Computerized tomography studies of attention deficit/ hyperactivity disorder, modified from Giedd *et al.* (2001)

Study	Patients	Controls	Findings	Medication history and status of patients
Bergstrom and Bille (1978)	46 (minimal brain dysfunction)	None	33% had 'abnormal' ventricles	Not reported
Thompson *et al.* (1980)	44 (minimal brain dysfunction)	None	4.5% abnormal	Not reported
Caparulo *et al.* (1981)	14 (DSM-III ADD)	None	28% abnormal	Not reported
Reiss *et al.* (1983)	7 (DSM-III ADD)	19 (neu-rological patients)	VBR larger	Unclear reporting
Shaywitz *et al.* (1983)	35 (DSM-III ADD)	27	None	Not reported
Nasrallah *et al.* (1986)	24 (hyperkinetic/ minimal brain dysfunction)	27	None	100% previously treated

Note: Tables 3.1–3.5 are from J. N. Geidd *et al.* (2001), Brain imaging of Attention Deficit/Hyperactivity Disorder, in J. Wassertein, L. E. Wolf and F. F. Lefever (eds), *Adult Attention Deficit Disorder: Brain Mechanisms and Life Outcomes* (vol. 931, pp. 33–49). New York: New York Academy of Sciences. Copyright © 2001 by New York Academy of Sciences, USA. Adapted with permission. To the original tables, we have added an additional column containing information on the medication history of the subjects.

the medication history of the patients, and in one study unclear reporting prevented making this determination.

Bergstrom and Bille (1978). The authors examined 50 children diagnosed with Minimal Brain Dysfunction (one of the immediate precursor terms of ADD/ADHD). Bergstrom and Bille reported various abnormalities in 15 cases, and provided detailed descriptions of three children, each manifesting 'hypotonia, traces of persisting neonatal reflexes, abnormal associated movements and motor and visuomotor incoordination after sensorimotor stress' (pp. 380–2). Case #1 was an 8-year-old boy who at birth weighed merely 1680 grams, had a one-minute APGAR score of 4, and suffered from perinatal asphyxia. On CT, he showed dilation of the left lateral ventricle and fissure of sylvius (p. 380). Case #2 was an 11-year-old boy whose CT showed dilation of the third ventricle. Case #3 was a 12-year-old boy who, at age seven, 'dribbled a lot' (p. 382). He also had 'a huge arachnoid cyst in the left temporal region' (p. 382). The children in this study have obvious neurological problems – some of which are suggestive of cerebral palsy, according to Shaywitz and colleagues (1983) – that go far beyond hyperactivity and inattention in typical classroom situations.

Shaywitz et al. (1983).   As Table 3.1 shows, under the column 'Findings' Giedd *et al.* (2001) reported 'None' for this study. This is somewhat misleading, as Shaywitz *et al.* (1983) actually did report finding *no difference* between the ADHD group versus controls. These authors stated unambiguously: 'Our findings suggest that when quantitative techniques, contrast populations, and blind analysis of CTs are employed, CTs of children with ADD are indistinguishable from contrasts. It further suggests that if anatomic abnormalities are present in ADD, they are not discernible using present-day CT technology' (p. 1502).

Thompson et al. (1980).   The brains of 44 children with minimal brain dysfunction and learning disabilities were scanned. Forty-two of these were normal and two (4.5%) exhibitied obvious organic pathology. Both these patients (4.5%) also had an obvious organic pathology. In the first, 'Delta CT examination of the brain revealed a focal area of decreased density deep in the right occipital region suggesting localized gliosis and atrophy that may have been ischemic or post-inflammatory in nature' (p. 49). In the second, agenesis of the corpus callosum was observed. Thompson *et al.* concluded: 'Most children evaluated with computed tomography can be expected to have normal scans. Little additional information will be provided from CAT scanning after neurologic and psychomotor testing' (p. 51).

Reiss et al. (1983).   This study compared 20 psychiatric patients, an unknown number of which had an ADD diagnosis, to controls. Thirteen of the patients had diagnoses ranging from borderline personality disorder to schizophrenia, including separation anxiety and Tourette's syndrome. Eleven patients had had one or more psychiatric hospitalizations and ten had been treated with psychoactive medications (including one with diphenylhydantoin for three months, and another with thioridazine for five years). The authors do not report how many patients were diagnosed with ADD, nor how many of these were treated with medication.

Nasrallah et al. (1986).　Again, under 'Findings', Giedd *et al.* (2001) report 'None' for this study, but this is incorrect. Nasrallah and colleagues measured four different physical characteristics: lateral ventricular size, third ventricle size, sulcal widening, and cerebellar atrophy. They found statistically significant differences for sulcal widening between patients and controls. In addition, they reported that 25 per cent of the patients had cerebellar atrophy, versus only 3.8 per cent of the controls. However, Nasrallah *et al.* do not interpret their results to support the hypothesis of ADHD-related neuropathology: 'since all of the hyperkinetic/minimal brain dysfunction patients had been treated with psychostimulants, cortical atrophy may be a long-term adverse effect of this treatment' (p. 245). Nasrallah *et al.* (1986) also took the bold step of suggesting that future studies should investigate whether stimulants result in structural brain changes. It is also important to mention that 7 of the 24 patients had a history of alcohol abuse.

Magnetic resonance imaging

The 14 studies listed in Table 3.2 all used magnetic resonance imaging (MRI). Two of the studies did not report on the issue of prior medication use by patients, and one did not report clearly. The 11 remaining studies involved a total of 259 patients and 271 controls, with 247 of the patients (95%) having had prior medication use. In only two studies did the authors actually discuss prior drug use (Castellanos *et al.*, 1994, 1996) but neither devoted more than two sentences to the topic.

It should be mentioned that four of the articles in Table 3.2 (Berquin *et al.*, 1998; Casey *et al.*, 1997; Castellanos *et al.*, 1994, 1996) used the same pool of experimental subjects (or a portion of). Furthermore, these subjects were originally part of yet another study, which compared methylphenidate to dextroamphetamine in children diagnosed with ADHD (Elia *et al.*, 1991). Such recycling of subjects from study to study strongly weakens the external validity of their findings.

Table 3.2 Magnetic resonance imaging studies of attention deficit/hyperactivity disorder, modified from Giedd et al. (2001)

Study	Patients/controls	Findings	Medication history and status of patients
Hynd et al. (1990)	10/10	Normal R>L anterior frontal width reversed in ADHD	100% previously treated
Hynd et al. (1991)	7/10	Anterior and posterior corpus callosum areas smaller in ADHD	100% previously treated
Hynd et al. (1993)	11/11	L caudate wider than R in normal subjects; reversed in ADHD	100% previously treated
Giedd et al. (1994)	18/18	Rostrum, rostral body of corpus callosum smaller in ADHD	Not reported, but patients recruited from day treatment programme at NIMH
Castellanos et al. (1994)	50/48	R caudate smaller and loss of normal R>L caudate asymmetry in ADHD	100% treated for 12 weeks prior to scans (78% longer treatment)
Semrud-Clikeman et al. (1994)	15/15	Splenium significantly smaller in ADHD group (posterior corpus callosum)	100% previously treated
Baumgardner et al. (1996)	13/27	Rostral body of corpus callosum smaller in ADHD	Not reported
Aylward et al. (1996)	10/11	Globus pallidus smaller in ADHD (significant on left)	100% previously treated, all on medication at time of scanning

Table 3.2 (Continued)

Study	Patients/controls	Findings	Medication history and status of patients
Castellanos et al. (1996)	57/55	Total cerebral volume, caudate, globus pallidus smaller in ADHD	93% previously treated
Filipek et al. (1997)	15/15	Caudates and R anterior superior white matter smaller in ADHD; posterior white matter volumes decreased only in stimulant non-responders	100% treated for at least six months prior to scans
Casey et al. (1997)	26/26	Performance on response inhibition tasks correlate with anatomical measures of frontostriatal circuitry, particularly on right	88.5% previously treated
Mataro et al. (1997)	11/19	Larger right caudate	None were receiving medication at time of experiment but unclear whether they had in the past.
Berquin et al. (1998)	46/47	Smaller posterior inferior cerebellar vermal volume	100% previously treated, 100% on medication during scanning
Mostofsky et al. (1998)	12/23	Smaller posterior inferior cerebellar vermal volume	58% previously treated with MPH, on medication at time of scanning

Mostofsky et al. (1998). In this study, 7 of the 12 boys diagnosed with ADHD had a prior history of psychotropic drug use. No discussion appears in this article about the potential problems with such use.

Castellanos et al. (1994). According to the authors, 'Fifty-three of [57 ADHD children] had been previously treated with psychostimulants, and 56 participated in a 12-week double-blind trial of methylphenidate, dextroamphetamine and placebo, as described elsewhere' (p. 608). In the discussion section of the paper the authors caution: 'Because almost all (93%) of the subjects with ADHD had been exposed to stimulants, we cannot be certain that our results are not drug related. A replication study with stimulant-naïve boys with ADHD is under way' (p. 614). This probably refers to the study by Castellanos *et al.* (2002) discussed below in detail.

Baumgardner et al. (1996). All of the ADHD children in this study were also diagnosed with Tourette's syndrome, making them atypical of the children being diagnosed with ADHD in North America. No medication history is reported.

Single photon emission tomography

The three studies cited in Table 3.3 (Lou *et al.*, 1984, 1990; Lou *et al.*, 1989), utilized single photon emission tomography (SPECT) scans. In the earliest study (Lou *et al.*, 1984), 6 of the 11 ADHD patients had a history of prior medication. In their follow-up, Lou *et al.* (1989) increased the patient sample and divided it into two groups. The first group of sixchildren was classified as 'ADHD' while the second group of 13 children was classified as 'ADHD Plus' because its children presented additional conditions. For instance, three of the children had IQs between 50 and 70, five had motor problems such as apraxia, and nine had various forms of dysphasia. Out of the 19 children in the two ADHD groups, 13 (68%) had a prior history of medication with methylphenidate.

These studies sought to answer two questions: (1) is there a difference in the brains of ADHD children compared to controls? (2) what is the effect of methylphenidate on the brains of ADHD children? The ADHD children in these studies who had been receiving methylphenidate discontinued their medication for one week prior to the study, an event that complicates answering both questions. Regarding the first question, any difference in the brains of the ADHD versus

Table 3.3 Single photon emission tomography studies using inhaled ^{133}Xenon, modified from Giedd *et al.* (2001)

Study	Patients	Control subjects	Findings	Medication history and status
Lou *et al.* (1984)	N = 13; 11 w/mixed ADD; 8 'dsyphasic'	N = 9, mostly siblings (3F)	Frontal hypoperfusion in all ADD; caudate hypoperfusion in 7/11 w/ADD; central perfusion increased in 6/6 after methylphenidate (MPH)	54% treated with 10 to 30 mg daily MPH, discontinued one week before scanning
Lou *et al.* (1989)	N = 6 'pure ADHD'; N = 13 ADHD plus other CNS dysfunction; 13 (includes 4 'pure ADHD') scanned pre- and post–MPH [total subjects: 19]	N = 9	'Pure ADHD': decreased R striatal perfusion, increased occipital and L sensorimotor and auditory regions; MPH significantly increased L striatal perfusion	68% treated in 'pure ADHD' group, 69% treated in other groups
Lou *et al.* (1990)	N = 9 'pure ADHD' (2F); N = 8 ADHD + dysphasia; (0 F)	15 contrast subjects (6 new, 7F)	Normalized striatal and posterior periventricular perfusion decreased in ADHD and ADHD+; occipital perfusion increased in 'pure ADHD'	Not reported

control subjects could be attributed to the medication. Regarding the second question, Lou *et al.* (1989) claimed they were examining the effect of methylphenidate on the brains of ADHD children. It would be more correct to say that the study examined the effect of methylphenidate on a group of children who had first been treated with methylphenidate (for an indeterminate time), then taken off the drug for a week of withdrawal, and then re-medicated. Thus, changes seen in the striatum of these patients could be attributed to long-term medication use, or withdrawal effects, or the effect of retreatment, or the entire sequence of treatment, withdrawal and re-treatment.

In the third, and most recent study, Lou *et al.* (1990) included 24 children but only ninewere placed in the 'pure' ADHD group. According to the authors: 'In retrospect, 11 of the children had a history of adverse, but mostly poorly described, antenatal and perinatal events such as vaginal haemorrahage, pre-clampsia, weak prenatal cardiac sounds, prolonged labor, and perinatal asphyxia. In 2 cases the probable cause of brain dysfunction was head trauma and measles encephalitis' (p. 8). Despite these obvious confounding factors, data from these 11 children's scans were not partitioned into a different group for more specific comparisons with controls or with the other ADHD subjects. Lou *et al.* do not mention prior medication use in the patients although it appears that some of them also participated in the previous studies (Lou *et al.*, 1984, 1989).

Positron emission tomography of glucose cerebral metabolism
The three articles in Table 3.4 were all published by Alan Zametkin's research group. The earliest study (Zametkin *et al.*, 1990) compared cerebral glucose metabolism between normal adults and adults with a history of hyperactivity in childhood. However, several authors (DeGrandpre, 1999; Reid *et al.*, 1994) have noted problems with this study. In particular, control females have a higher rate of cerebral glucose metabolism than control males, a finding that accounts entirely for the difference that Zametkin found between the ADHD patients and controls.

Zametkin *et al.* (1993) used ten adolescents diagnosed with ADHD, seven of whom had a history of prior medication use. Ernst *et al.* (1994) extended the 1993 study by adding ten more ADHD subjects, eight with a history of prior medication. The main finding of these studies was that in *adolescents* there was no difference in global brain metabolism between the ADHD patients and controls, unlike the findings in *adults* by Zametkin *et al.* (1990). Ernst *et al.* (1994) provide

Table 3.4 Positron emission tomography studies of glucose cerebral metabolism, modified from Giedd *et al.* (2001)

Study	Patients	Control subjects	Findings	Medication history and status of patients
Zametkin *et al.* (1990)	25 adults (7F)	50 adults (22F)	Global cerebral metabolism 8% lower in ADHD, with absolute significant decreases in 30 of 60 regions. Normalized differences all on left; superior posterior frontal, medial and anterior frontal and rolandic	None previously treated.
Zametkin *et al.* (1993)	10 adolescents (3F)	10 adolescents (3F; 7 were siblings of ADHD probands, only 2 in this study)	No differences in global metabolism. Normalized metabolism decreased significantly in 6 regions and increased in 1	70% previously treated 100% medication free for 3 weeks prior to scan
Ernst *et al.* (1994)	20 adolescents (6F); includes all subjects from study above	19 adolescents (5F)	No group differences in global metabolism; metabolism significantly lower in 6 ADHD females than controls of either sex or ADHD boys	80% previously treated 100% medication free for 2 weeks prior to scan

Note: One unpublished study omitted.

a list of reasons why a difference between the adolescent ADHD patients and controls might not have been detected; yet the authors never discuss the possibility that their results correctly show that there is *no difference between ADHD and control brains in adolescents.* Ernst *et al.* (1994) also looked at gender effect and did find a difference between the female ADHD patients and female controls, but not between male patients and male controls.

Functional imaging studies of cerebral blood flow in ADHD

With the exception of Amen and Paldi (1993), all articles in Table 3.5 were published after 1995, when it must have been clear to any researcher in the field that the issue of prior medication use was a variable that needed to be examined. Nonetheless, four of the seven articles do not mention whether the patients had prior medication use. *Amen and Paldi* (1993). Giedd *et al.* refer to a one-page abstract by Amen and Paldi (1993). This study was later expanded upon in a more detailed report (Amen and Carmichael, 1997), which is what we discuss here. The primary purpose of this study was to determine if there were similarities between reported PET and QEEG (quantified computerized EEG) findings in children diagnosed with ADHD. Because of dangers involved in exposing individuals to radioactive substances, the control subjects were patients from a psychiatric outpatient clinic who were diagnosed with a psychiatric condition but not with ADHD. Amen and Carmichael (1997) state that both ADHD and control patients were 'medication free', but no other details are provided.

Amen, who is prominent in the ADHD marketing enterprise, has received significant media attention based on his theory that there are six types of ADHD, each of which has distinctive behavioural symptoms with distinct neuroanatomical pathologies that can be visualized with SPECT scans (Amen, 2001). To our knowledge, Amen has not published a study showing that by using a brain scan he can tell the difference between the brain of an ADHD child and that of a normal child, or that he can use neuroimaging to diagnose any of his proposed six subdivisions of ADHD. Also problematic is that Amen uses SPECT scans as a regular tool to diagnose ADHD. Within psychiatry, neuroimaging is typically used for research, not diagnosis, because this technology involves low doses of radiation. Thus its use in children without life-threatening conditions is controversial, as Amen and Carmichael acknowledge (1997, p. 84). Amen is one of only a handful of practitioners who use neuroimaging as an aid in the diagnosis of ADHD.

Table 3.5 Functional imaging studies of cerebral blood flow in ADHD, modified from Giedd et al. (2001)

Study	Method	Patients	Controls	Findings	Medication history and status of patients
Amen and Paldi (1993)	[99m-TC] SPECT at rest & during maths stress test	54 (8F)	18 (8F)	Prefrontal deactivation significantly greater in ADHD (65% vs. 5%)	Unclear on prior history; medication-free during scan
Sieg et al. (1995)	[123-I] SPECT at rest	10 (3F)	6 (1F)	L (vs R) blood flow reduced in frontal and parietal regions in ADHD	Not reported
Teicher et al. (2000)	T2 relaxation times with MRI	11 children	6	Optimal dose methylphenidate significantly increased R caudate blood flow, decreased R frontal cortical flow	See Discussion and footnotes
Schweitzer et al. (2000)	[15O]water PET, neural activation related to working memory	6 male adults	6 male adults	Task-related changes in rCBF in men without ADHD were more prominent in the frontal and temporal regions, but rCBF changes in men with ADHD were more widespread and primarily located in the occipital regions	33% previously treated with MPH but had been medication-free for 2 and 10 yrs respectively

Table 3.5 (Continued)

Study	Method	Patients	Controls	Findings	Medication history and status of patients
Bush et al. (1999)	fMRI, Counting Stroop	8 adults	8 adults	ADHD subjects failed to activate the anterior cingulate cognitive division (ACcd) during the Counting Stroop. ACcd activity higher in control group. ADHD subject did activate a frontostriatal-insular network, indicating ACcd hypoactivity was not caused by globally poor neuronal responsiveness	100% previously treated with various ADHD medications. 48-hr washout prior to scans
Rubia et al. (1999)	MRI	7 males	9 males	ADHD adolescents showed lower power of response in the right medial prefrontal cortex during a stop task and a motor timing task, and in the R inferior pre-frontal cortex and L caudate during the stop task	Not reported
Vaidya et al. (1998)	fMRI, two go/no go tasks with and without drug	10 male children	6 male children	ADHD impaired inhibitory control on two tasks. Off-drug frontal-striatal activation during response inhibition differed between ADHD and healthy children	Patients had a 1 to 3 year history of medication

Teicher et al. (2000) [3].   This study used functional MRI relaxometry (fMRI) to assess blood volume in the striatum. It reportedly found differences in the putamen of 11 ADHD children compared to 6 healthy control children. Teicher *et al.* (2000) concluded: 'On average, T2-RT was 3.1% higher in ADHD children than control subjects in the left putamen...and 1.6% in the right putamen' (p. 471). However like many of the neuroimaging studies this conclusion is tempered by the issue of prior medication exposure. Some explanation of the experimental design of the Teicher *et al.* study is necessary.

The 11 children with ADHD were randomized to one of four groups: placebo, or methylphenidate at 0.5, 0.8, or 1.5 mg/kg in divided doses. The children received the appropriate dose for a week, after which they were tested for drug efficacy using objective measures of attention/activity and fMRI within 1–3 hours of their afternoon dose. The children then moved into the next group for a week, received the appropriate dose and were again scanned and tested. All children were cycled through all four groups but they started out in *different* groups. The researchers then compared the fMRI results of the unmedicated healthy control subjects and the ADHD subjects following their week of placebo treatment and it is this difference that is reported as significant. For instance, in a scatterplot (Teicher *et al.*, 2000, Figure 1, p. 472) the T2 relaxation times of the 11 ADHD children on placebo are compared to controls and Teicher *et al.* report that 'The increased T2 relaxation times in the ADHD sample indicate diminished regional blood volume' (p. 472). However, one problem with this scatterplot (and the experiment) is that the scans of the ADHD children performed during the week of the placebo treatment are not comparable. The *prescan* interval for each child might have been preceded by one, two, or three weeks of treatment with methylphenidate. A child randomized to placebo and then scanned is not comparable to a child administered three weeks of the drug followed by placebo and then scanned. Teicher and colleagues grouped children who *never* received drug treatment with children experiencing withdrawal from drug treatment. [4] Since exact treatment protocol is not supplied for each child, precise interpretation of the results is impossible.

Studies published since the Giedd et al. review
Two studies published since the Giedd *et al.* (2001) review are noteworthy for what they could have accomplished – but did not. Both

studies had the chance to compare non-medicated patients to appropriate controls yet merely addressed 'secondary' issues. Our analysis
of these studies focuses on sifting through the 'secondary' issues and
asking: what about the essential comparison between non-medicated
patients and controls? Again, we restate our incontrovertible point that
only such a comparison would provide unambiguous findings concerning any possible pre-existing brain anomaly in children diagnosed with
ADHD.

Kim et al. (2001).   These investigators used SPECT to examine rCBF
in 32 previously unmedicated ADHD children before and after eight
weeks of treatment with methylphenidate. Changes were detected in
the prefrontal cortex and the caudate nucleus. We have two concerns with this study. First, the drug-induced changes in the striatum
and frontal lobes are reported to occur in the same cerebral circuit
that Giedd *et al.* (2001) pointed to as the neuropathological locus
of ADHD. But whereas Giedd *et al.* attributed such findings to an
endogenous organic pathology, Kim *et al.* attributed their findings to
methylphenidate exposure. Second, the researchers did not include a
control group of 'normal' children to compare to the medication-free
ADHD children. Kim *et al.* appear to be one of the first research groups
to report on ADHD children not previously medicated, yet they have
not run the essential comparison between non-medicated children and
controls.

It would have been more fruitful to have divided the procedure into
two parts: the first part simply comparing the scans of ADHD children
to controls, and the second part examining the effect of medication
on the scans of ADHD children, as in the study by Lou *et al.* (1990).
Readers may be perplexed that the scans of the children diagnosed with
ADHD were not compared to controls. Kim *et al.* (2001) state that it
would have been unethical to examine the effect of methylphenidate
on a control group – and they are correct. However, their study would
have been more significant if, *prior to the drug administration*, they
had compared the scans of the ADHD children to a control group.

Castellanos et al. (2002).   This study, carried out between 1991 and
2001, reported that the brains of ADHD children are smaller compared to those of controls. The study is significant because of the
large size of the sample (291 participants) and because one third of
the patients never received medication. Three groups were constituted:
49 unmedicated patients, 103 medicated patients, and 139 controls.

Thus the authors had the opportunity to make numerous comparisons: unmedicated versus medicated, unmedicated versus controls, medicated versus controls, and ADHD versus controls. The most important – and we would say legitimate – comparison was between unmedicated patients and controls. However, compared to the controls, *the unmedicated patients were two years younger, shorter and lighter.*

Castellanos *et al.* state that height and weight did not correlate with brain size in their study.[5] Yet in that study these variables were significantly correlated with the diagnosis of ADHD. Thus, although finding three biological differences between the ADHD children and controls, the researchers focused on only brain size. Height and weight have never been shown to be part and parcel of ADHD, but the results from this study suggest otherwise. Conversely, if height and weight are only spuriously correlated with ADHD, then the appropriateness of the control group is called into question.

Consider the following data as shown in Figure 3.1: the entire ADHD patient group (medicated plus unmedicated) is significantly

	Entire patient group		Controls		
	Female N = 63	Male N = 89	Female N = 56	Male N = 83	P Value for patients vs. controls
Age, mean (SD) y,	9.4 (2.6)	10.5 (3.1)	10.0 (2.6)	10.9 (3.5)	0.13
Height, mean (SD), cm	134.9 (15.0)	141.7 (18.0)	140.2 (16.0)	147.3 (20.3)	0.01
Weight, mean (sd), kg	33.0 (12.2)	36.9 (14.4)	35.8 (12.5)	42.0 (16.5)	0.02

	Medicated patients	Non-medicated patients
Age*	10.9 (2.7)	8.3 (2.6)
Height	Not provided	Not provided
Weight	Not provided	Not provided

Figure 3.1 Participant's physical characteristics in the Castellanos *et al.* (2002) study.

Note: *P Value for medicated versus non-medicated 0.001.

shorter and lighter than the control group; for the most important comparison in the paper the subgroup of *unmedicated* patients is drawn from this already smaller and lighter group of patients; we are *not* told the height and weight of this subgroup of unmedicated patients but we are told that they are almost two years younger than the entire patient group; and for this reason the unmedicated patients are probably also significantly shorter and lighter than the control group. We say 'probably' because for this most important – in our view – comparison in the article the subjects' specific physical characteristics are not provided. The issue of height and weight is especially relevant here because most research on brain size has found it to be correlated with body weight. Gould has pointed out that in studies that have incorrectly associated brain size to other factors, the most common mistake has been in sample selection and that 'modern students of brain size have still not agreed on a proper measure to eliminate the powerful effect of body size' (1996, p. 138). We suggest that this effect was not eliminated in the Castellanos *et al.* (2002) study. Thus, besides a diagnosis of ADHD, the unmedicated children could have had smaller brains due to the fact that they were shorter, lighter, and younger. In fact, given all these other variables it would be noteworthy *if they did not have smaller brains.*[6]

To conduct a study to determine if there is something unique about the brains of ADHD children, one need not involve medicated children at all. The only apparent reason Castellanos *et al.* (2002) used medicated children was to answer questions about drug effects on the brain. To do so they compared unmedicated to medicated children: and they found no significant differences and concluded that the medications have no effect on brain size. However, this hardly seems the type of study to adequately address this issue, since the authors provided *no information* about medication use (such as doses, durations, or even types of drugs used) except this one sentence: 'At the time of the first scan, 103 patients (68%) were being treated with psychostimulants' (pp. 1742–3). We note also that, compared to medicated children, unmedicated children were not as severely affected by ADHD according to ratings by teachers and doctors.

In sum, what at first seems like a straightforward comparison of two groups of children reveals itself as a tangle of unnecessary complications, including secondary statistical analyses of subgroups, discussions about differences in amounts of white matter in 8-year-olds versus 10-year-olds, or concerns about height and weight as confounding variables. By itself, a simple comparison between unmedicated

ADHD children and controls would certainly have stood out as an important experiment. Peripheral questions could have been addressed as extensions of the primary question without complicating the experiment. But in this study peripheral questions did hopelessly confuse the essential comparison.

Our criticism of the experimental design of the Castellanos *et al.* (2002) study might seem excessive, but in light of the problems we have pointed out regarding selection of control groups, and considering that the study's patients and controls came from highly select populations, the concern seems justified. Yet, we would like to point out that the more straightforward comparison was – and still remains – well within the authors' grasp. The authors could still compare the scans of the non-medicated children to the scans of a control group matched for, among other things, height, weight, and age. This simpler comparison would be more direct and meaningful, and would not take 10 years to complete.

At the risk of belabouring the issue, we phrase it again, somewhat differently: in the past, researchers in this field had been unable to find unmedicated patients for their studies. Finally, here is one of the first research groups to overcome this obstacle, but immediately the question arises: why is the control group two years older, taller, and heavier than the group of unmedicated patients? It seems odd that, given 10 years and the resources of the National Institute of Mental Health (NIMH), these experienced researchers could not find a more appropriate control group. Ironically, previous studies were contaminated by a confounding medication factor; in this study the reverse is true: the control group is not comparable with the treatment group.

Nevertheless, the findings of Castellanos *et al.* (2002) will be more valuable if they are replicated with a more comparable set of controls – and will be of great interest to more than just ADHD researchers – for two reasons. If the findings are replicated they will be the first to correlate subtle differences in brain size with a behavioural trait, in this case activity level; and also the first to find that brain size is *not* correlated with height and weight.

Sowell et al. (2003).   This study, involving 27 ADHD and 46 normal control subjects, reported that ADHD children had smaller frontal lobes compared to the control subjects, but overall the ADHD subjects had more cortical grey matter (Sowell *et al.*, 2003). In our view, this study's significance derives not necessarily from this result, but – as with several previous ADHD neuroimaging studies – from important comparisons that researchers could have made, but *did not*.

As in the Castellanos *et al.* (2002) study, some of the ADHD subjects in the Sowell study were apparently medication-naïve. We say 'apparently' because specific descriptions were not provided: '15 of the 27 patients were taking stimulant medication at the time of imaging' (p. 1705). It is unclear how to categorize the remaining 12 patients. Did they have a history of medication use prior to the start of the study, and then stop taking their medication for 48 hours, or some other arbitrary time period before imaging? It surprises us that a study published in *The Lancet* could be so vague about one of the most important variables in the study. Conclusions based on a comparison of normal control subjects to medication-naïve ADHD subjects would be very different from conclusions based on a comparison of control subjects to ADHD subjects with varying durations of medication exposure or undergoing abrupt withdrawal.

The issue becomes considerably more muddled and confusing due to a brief concluding discussion by Sowell *et al.* (2003) of the potential role of stimulant medication on their findings. The authors first appropriately acknowledged that, since 55 per cent of their ADHD children were taking stimulants, 'the effects of stimulant drugs could have confounded our findings of abnormal brain morphology in children with [ADHD]' (p. 1705). The simplest way to evaluate this confounding effect properly would have been to compare the 15 medicated ADHD children with the 12 unmedicated ADHD children. However, Sowell *et al.* chose not to make that comparison: 'We did not directly compare brain morphology across groups of patients on and off drugs because the sample size was considerably compromised when taking lifetime history of stimulant drugs into account' (p. 1705). The authors further explained that this comparison, between unmedicated and medicated, is not needed because a prior study by Castellanos *et al.* (2002) suggested that medications do not affect brain size.

Sowell *et al.*'s methodological choice, and its justification, is both unconvincing and puzzling. First, although one can sympathize with their judgement that 'taking lifetime history of stimulant drugs into account' compromised their sample size, this judgement ignores the fact that for 30 years ADHD neuroimaging researchers have deemed it perfectly acceptable to compare ADHD subjects and normal controls *regardless of medication history*. Indeed, virtually all the studies that Sowell *et al.* cite to contextualize their own study and interpret their results exemplify this practice. Thus it is difficult to see why

Sowell *et al.* would feel that they should not compare medicated and unmedicated ADHD subjects. Clearly, just as they acknowledged limitations to their main study results, Sowell *et al.* could have reported the results of the more specific comparison with an acknowledgement of the appropriate limitations. Second, Sowell *et al.* cite Castellanos *et al.* to support the methodological choice of not comparing medicated and unmedicated ADHD subjects. But, third and most important, Sowell *et al.*'s data appear directly relevant to either support or refute the conclusions that Castellanos *et al* (2002) drew from their comparison. In fact, the results of the Castellanos *et al.*'s comparison of brain volumes of medicated and unmedicated ADHD children were deemed worthy of a major press release by the NIMH concerning stimulant drugs' effects on developing brains, yet the same comparison in the Sowell *et al.* study was considered insignificant and not even reportable.

The media paid significant attention to the Sowell *et al.* study. In one interview the study's last author stated: 'The next phase of the work will be to see whether the magnitude of the abnormalities in these individuals might influence the course of the condition, *their response to medication*, and which medications different children respond to' (cited in Edelson, 2003, italics added). We assume that this next phase of investigation will involve a comparison of medicated with unmedicated children – but how this will differ from their previous study, or from most of the neuroimaging studies, remains completely unclear.

The American Journal of Psychiatry (2006). In June 2006, the *American Journal of Psychiatry* published three articles (Pliszka *et al.*, 2006; Smith *et al.*, 2006; Tamm *et al.*, 2006) and an accompanying editorial about functional magnetic resonance imaging (Casey and Durston, 2006). The three studies conducted scans of children's brains during a specified task, and, importantly, all three studies had a group of medication-naïve ADHD children. However, when considered together, the three studies implicated an inordinate number of different brain regions, with little replication of the regions between studies. In brief, Smith *et al.* (2006) implicated the frontal, parietal, and temporal lobes, along with the striatum. Pliszka *et al.* (2006) implicated the anterior cingulate cortex and the left ventrolateral prefrontal cortex. Tamm *et al.* (2006) implicated the parietal lobes, the right precuneus, and the thalamus. One could almost ask: what area of the brain do they not implicate?

The accompanying editorial by Casey and Durston (2006) acknowledges these disparate findings. Rather than look at them as problematic for the ADHD neuroimaging field, however, Casey and Durston attempt to place the disparate findings within a theoretical construct largely based on the work of Barclay, who has suggested that cognitive deficits in ADHD are due to a deficit in inhibitory control. They state: 'Identification of core processes involved in a disorder can move a field from a disparate set of data-driven findings to a more theoretically coherent collection of studies' (p. 957). Does Casey and Durston's model provide a solid base for ADHD researchers to move forward, or is their explanation of these 'disparate' findings an attempt at salvaging a lack of reproducibility within the ADHD neuroimaging field? The model as proposed by Casey and Durston is that, 'basic learning systems are important in signalling top-down systems to adjust behaviour when predicted outcomes are violated'. This appears to be little more than a very general statement about learning. Although as a general statement it is hard to argue with it, it is so broad and all-encompassing that it makes room for almost every conceivable finding – and does little to explain how upwards of 10–15 per cent of the population has a disease. One test for whether a theory is too broad is to ask: what empirical findings would negate the theory? Casey and Durston have not proposed any findings (or types of findings) that would negate their theory, and, indeed, it is hard to imagine any that would negate it. For instance, in Figure 1 in their article, Casey and Durston hypothesize the involvement of the prefrontal cortex, the basal ganglia, the parietal cortex, and the cerebellum in ADHD. Yet none of the three accompanying studies even suggested that the cerebellum was involved. And, missing from Casey and Durston's schematic is the thalamus, which one study did implicate. Moreover, two of the studies were contradictory: Pliszka *et al.* found greater activity in ADHD subjects than controls in the inferior prefrontal cortex (p. 1059), while Smith *et al.* found less activity (underactiviation) in the mesial and front-parietal-temporal brain regions during the go/no go and switch tasks for the ADHD children. Yet, interestingly, while the imaging data for the ADHD children differed in these two studies, there was no difference in performance on the specified tasks between the ADHD children and controls. None of these issues are raised by Casey and Durston, and we are unsure how they could be fitted into the proposed model. Rather than a theory, what they have really proposed is a hypothesis.

Perhaps the most significant aspect of putting forth such a highly theoretical model of ADHD is that Casey and Durston are implicitly acknowledging that the more practical aspect of developing an imaging scan as a diagnostic tool is becoming more and more unlikely.

Volkow et al. (2007). This study utilized PET and compared dopamine transporter levels in 20 never-medicated adults to 25 controls. Dopamine transporter levels were lower in the left caudate and left nucleus accumbens in the ADHD subjects, but, most importantly, the dopamine transporter levels were not correlated with ADHD.

Discussion

We first undertook a reanalysis of the studies used in the review of ADHD neuroimaging studies by Giedd *et al.* (2001). Of the 33 relevant studies summarized in Tables 3.1 to 3.5, 29 included a control group of normal subjects, but only 19 reported on the ADHD patients' prior use of medication. These 19 studies involved a total of 356 patients and 365 controls, and all but one study found differences between ADHD and non-ADHD children. However, in each group of studies using an imaging modality, an average of 77 per cent of the ADHD children had prior exposure to medication. Prior exposure to medication serves as a distinctly confounding factor because it is widely recognized to cause at least 'long-lasting neurochemical adaptations' in the human and animal brain. Therefore, any suggestions about subtle structural or functional differences between the brains of 'ADHD' children and the brains of 'normal' children must await future, better conducted studies.

To their credit, several of the neuroimaging studies published since the Giedd *et al.* (2001) review used non-medicated children diagnosed with ADHD. Yet, inexplicably, most avoided a simple and straightforward comparison between these non-medicated children and appropriate controls. The Kim *et al.* (2001) study did not compare unmedicated children to controls; instead they started with unmedicated children, administered medications to them, and then performed scans. The most perplexing study was reported by Castellanos *et al.* (2002), who used unmedicated ADHD children who were younger, lighter, and shorter than the control group. Peripheral questions sidetracked each of these research groups from the more important comparison that, we maintain, would help to establish if any brain differences exist: that of unmedicated ADHD children to controls.

We are also concerned about how results are sometimes reported both in the Giedd *et al.* review and in the ADHD neuroimaging literature in general. For instance, in their review Giedd *et al.* (2001) categorize the findings of Shaywitz *et al.* (1983) as 'None' yet what Shaywitz *et al.* reported was that they found *no* significant differences between ADHD patients and controls. Readers of the Giedd *et al.* review who are trying to determine if neuroimaging researchers have found an anatomical basis for ADHD should be told if a study found no difference between ADHD patients and controls.[7] As another example, in adolescent males Ernst *et al.* (1994) found *no* difference in global cerebral glucose metabolism between ADHD and controls, but the researchers did find a difference in adolescent females. While the title of their paper – 'Reduced Brain Metabolism in Hyperactive Girls' – certainly conveys their findings, it would have been just as correct to have titled it 'Normal Brain Metabolism in Hyperactive Boys'. Apparently studies finding a difference between ADHD children and controls are more significant than negative studies, the former probably more likely to get published.

A simple way to illustrate the irrationality of dominant interpretations of neuroimaging research in ADHD is to compare it to interpretations of neuroimaging findings in the related field of research concerning the effects of illegal psychotropics. For example, in humans with persistent exposure to methylenedioxymethamphetamine (MDMA, commonly known as Ecstasy), brain imaging research is often cited as evidence that MDMA causes a deficit in serotonin-rich areas of the brain (Reneman *et al.*, 2001). In the case of MDMA, drug users are compared to controls and observed differences are attributed to *drug use*; but in the case of methylphenidate, drug users are compared to controls and differences are attributed to an *underlying organic pathology*.

Prior medication as a confounding variable
Slightly over half the papers in Giedd *et al.*'s (2001) review actually mention medication status of subjects; the rest do not inform readers about prior use. But most problematic is that not a single paper devotes more than a sentence (or two) to the topic. Prior medication use by ADHD subjects is virtually a 'non-issue'. Only one of the 33 studies even suggests that we actually study the effect of chronic stimulant treatment on the brain (Nasrallah *et al.*, 1986).

There is, of course, no such thing as a perfect experiment: if one looks long enough, flaws will be detected. Competing hypotheses can always be found. However, when investigating subtle neuroanatomical or metabolic changes in the brain, it is hard to imagine a more problematic variable than prior history of psychotropic drug use. In this light then, what are we to make of the fact that some researchers fail to even *mention* this variable?[8] Consider the variable of right- or left-handedness. In some studies researchers made a point of only using right-handed children (Rubia *et al.*, 1999) or of matching controls and patients for handedness (Geidd *et al.*, 1994). But the same researchers did not mention medication history. Researchers appear more concerned about handedness then they are about prior medication use.

At best, Giedd *et al.*'s (2001) concern with prior medication use is equivocal, illustrating how such concern is handled in the literature. On the one hand, in their 1994 study that purports to 'support theories of abnormal frontal lobe development and function in ADHD' (p. 655), Giedd *et al.* (1994) do not mention medication history of the patients even though this information must have been available because the patients were recruited from an NIMH programme. On the other hand, in their 2001 review Giedd *et al.* qualify Rubia *et al.*'s (1999) findings by stating, 'we must note that all the patients had been medicated with methylphenidate until 36 hours prior to their scans' and by noting that findings in control subjects scanned after an ingestion of MPH may 'reflect medication withdrawal effects' (p. 39). Also, in their final summary, Giedd *et al.* identify one limitation of this research as: 'none of the studies published to date has accounted for possible source of confounding such as prior medication exposure' (2001, p. 45). But clearly, if that is the case, the issue requires extensively more discussion and integration than four lines in a 13-page review article. Indeed, given the explicit warning from one of the earliest studies (Nasrallah *et al.*, 1986), why not remind readers of the confounding factor and immediately conduct studies without it? Perhaps the answer is found in Giedd *et al.*'s (2001) own explanation of the value of neuroimaging in ADHD: 'Imaging studies may help educate families and the public that ADHD is a biological entity' (p. 45).

For those researchers who feel that our concerns about prior psychotropic drug use are excessive it is important to remember how prior psychotropic use confounded the first experiments that tested the dopamine hypothesis of schizophrenia. Early reports that schizophrenic patients had more dopamine receptors than controls were eventually tempered by the realization that the patients in these studies had taken neuroleptics for years. Subsequent attempts to replicate the findings in medication-free patients have met with inconsistent results (Valenstein, 1998). And problematic for the field, the most straighforward study of all, a direct comparison between ADHD non-medicated and controls with no need for age-matching by Volkow *et al.* (2007), found that the dopamine transporter levels were not correlated with ADHD.

Conclusion

Imaging research is often used to justify the medication of children diagnosed with ADHD (Barkley *et al.*, 2002). For instance, Castellanos *et al.* (2002) state that based on their findings of smaller brain size in ADHD children, 'Future studies should focus on younger patients being enrolled into controlled treatment studies while in preschool' (p. 1747). However, we question the logic behind the idea that smaller brains justify drug treatment for younger children. If one follows this logic, what is one to make of the height and weight issues? Do height and weight differences also justify 'treating' preschoolers?

A comment in an earlier review of ADHD imaging research by two prominent researchers seems particularly instructive (Ernst and Zametkin, 1995). In addressing the fact that in the Nasrallah *et al.* (1986) study 7 of the 24 patients had a history of alcohol abuse, Ernst and Zametkin pointed out: 'Unfortunately, the inclusion of individuals with a history of alcohol abuse, representing 30% of the sample, confused the interpretation of the results, because the findings mirrored those reported in CT studies of alcoholic adults' (p. 1646). If interpreting results from a single study becomes confusing because 30 per cent of the sample had a prior history of alcohol abuse, then, undoubtedly, results from a field of research where over three-quarters of the patients were persistently exposed to a centrally active drug would be similarly compromised.

The necessary and definitive test to confirm the suggestion that ADHD children have a neuroanatomic pathology consists of using an appropriate brain scan to detect a difference between one 'typical' unmedicated ADHD child as found in the classroom, and a 'normal' child. As we pointed out at the beginning of this paper, there is virtual unanimity that this cannot be accomplished at present. Experiments with highly selective patient and control groups are, at best, only preliminary studies, and we have shown – in complement to the critical analysis by Baumeister and Hawkins (2001) – the findings of these studies must be called into question. In response to persistent pressure from earlier critics such as Baughman (1998) and Breggin (1991), it seems that neuroimaging researchers now acknowledge the importance of medication history.

Ruling out the effects of psychotropic medication is merely one of the tasks confronting researchers conducting neuroimaging research with ADHD patients. Even if the field accomplishes this task, however, several other important tasks remain. One of these will involve trying to make sense of findings of brain abnormalities or differences among some individuals diagnosed with ADHD. In October 2005, for example, the *New York Times* published an article by Benedict Carey entitled 'Can Brain Scans See Depression?' It contained interviews with prominent psychiatrists and child psychiatrists, many of whom have authored ADHD imaging papers. The *Times* article was notable for both its candour and frank assessment of the psychiatric neuroimaging field: 'Yet, for a variety of reasons, the hopes and claims for brain imaging in psychiatry have far outpaced the science, experts say.' And in the words of Paul Wolpe, a professor of psychiatry and sociology: 'The thing for people to understand is that right now the only thing imaging can tell you is whether you have a brain tumor.'

General theories about the neuroanatomical basis of learning are fascinating areas of research, and at some point scientists will likely clarify the neural circuits involved in learning. Just as with simple biological traits like height and weight, it may be possible that brain activation in a certain circuit can someday be measured, quantified, and plotted on a graph. And just as there is biological variation for simple traits, there will certainly be biological variation for activation of circuits. However, for the ADHD imaging researchers to achieve their goal (establishing the presence of idiopathic somatic pathology) they must go beyond plotting normal human biological variation and then labelling a portion of the population as 'diseased'. They must show a distinct difference between children diagnosed with ADHD and controls. As the ADHD imaging field moves from looking for anatomical landmarks to the development of highly theoretical models of ADHD, it has essentially acknowledged that the more practical matter of developing an imaging scan as a diagnostic tool is very unlikely. One could call it the ADHD neuroimaging paradox: as the brain imaging technology becomes more sophisticated, as more imaging studies are published and more regions of the brain added to an ever-expanding list of potential problem areas with little reproducibility between studies, and as theories of ADHD become more and more speculative, then the likelihood of using imaging as a practical diagnostic tool becomes smaller and smaller. While some would say that this is a sign that researchers are becoming more sophisticated, the other possibility is that they simply do not want to acknowledge the obvious.

Notes

1. Much of the material in this chapter was previously published in two papers in the *Journal of Mind and Behavior* (Leo and Cohen, 2003; Cohen and Leo, 2004). It has been updated for this chapter to include recent imaging studies.
2. Giedd *et al.* (2001) presented six tables. Since one of their tables summarized studies examining stimulant response we have not included it because we are primarily interested in studies investigating differences between ADHD and control subjects. Thus while the Giedd *et al.* review has six tables we only present five tables in our study.
3. Giedd *et al.* cite a 1996 paper by Teicher that is not concerned with brain imaging. We are not exactly sure which paper they meant to refer to but Teicher's most significant paper is the one that we discuss here.
4. It is difficult, if not impossible, to determine the exact design of this study – it is only by communicating directly with Teicher that we obtained information on the study design. He supplied only limited information so, while we have done our best to present his study fairly we are still unsure of the exact protocol. We also wonder how the reviewers of this paper were able to judge its merit given the limited explanation of the methodology.
5. Regarding the age discrepancy, the authors reported that they conducted a secondary analysis restricted to an age-matched subset of 24 unmedicated ADHD children and 54 controls and, 'All measures essentially remained unchanged' (p. 1745). However, given a more appropriate control group these types of secondary analyses would not have been required.
6. It would also be surprising if they did not have smaller skulls. If there is an association between skull size and ADHD then future studies could simply measure skull size.
7. Without entering into an elaborate discussion about the null hypothesis versus the research hypothesis (and the inability to prove the null hypothesis), suffice it to say that if you take two groups of people and compare a given trait and find no difference between the two groups it is quite possible that indeed there is no difference. Under 'findings' it would have been more accurate for Giedd *et al.* (2001) to say 'No Difference' rather then 'None' because this does relate to the research hypothesis of ADHD neuroimaging researchers.
8. For all studies with no information on medication history, we attempted to contact lead authors to obtain this information. Most did not respond.

One author replied: 'I am sorry, but I would have to go through all the files, and it is too time-consuming.' We do not know if this information was not reported because authors were unaware that prior drug use is a major confounding variable or, conversely, if authors were aware of it but realized that it lessened the validity of their findings to establish a biological basis for ADHD. Either possibility is a cause for serious concern.

References

Amen, D. G. (2001) Attention doctors, *Newsweek* (26 February), 137, 72–73.

Amen, D. G. and Paldi, J. H. (1993) Evaluating ADHD with brain SPECT imaging, *Biological Psychiatry*, 33, 44.

Amen, D. G. and Carmichael, B. D. (1997) High-resolution brain SPECT imaging in ADHD, *Annals of Clinical Psychiatry* 9, 81–6.

American Psychiatric Association (2000) *Diagnostic and Statistical Manual of Mental Disorders: Text revision (fourth edition)*. Washington, DC: American Psychiatric Association.

Aylward, E. H., Reiss, A. L., Reader, M. J., Singer, H. S., Brown, J. E., and Denckla, M. B. (1996) Basal ganglia volumes in children with attention-deficit hyperactivity disorder, *Journal of Child Neurology* 11, 112–15.

Barkley, R., Cook, E., Diamond, A., Zametkin, A., Tharpa, A., Teeter, A., *et al.* (2002) International consensus ctatement on ADHD, *Clinical Child and Family Psychology Review* 5, 89–111.

Baughman, F. (1998) Testimony at the NIH consensus conference on the treatment and diagnosis of ADHD. Washington, DC, 16–18 November.

Baumeister, A. A. and Hawkins, M. F. (2001) Incoherence of neuroimaging studies of attention deficit/hyperactivity disorder, *Clinical Neuropharmacology* 24, 2–10.

Baumgardner, T. L., Singer, H. S., Denckla, M. B., Rubin, M. A., Abrams, M. T., Colli, M. J., and Reiss, A. L. (1996) Corpus callosum morphology in children with Tourette syndrome and attention deficit hyperactivity disorder, *Neurology*, 47, 477–82.

Bergstrom, K. and Bille, B. (1978) Computed tomography of the brain in children with minimal brain damage: A preliminary study of 46 children, *Neuropaediatrie* 9, 378–84.

Berquin, P. C., Giedd, J. N., Jacobsen, L. K., Hamburger, S. D., Krain, A. L., Rapoport, J. L. and Castellanos, F. X. (1998) Cerebellum in attention-deficit hyperactivity disorder: A morphometric MRI study, *Neurology*, 50, 1087–93.

Breggin, P. (1991) *Toxic Psychiatry*. New York: St Martin's Press.

Breggin, P. (1999) Psychostimulants in the treatment of children diagnosed with ADHD: Part II – Adverse effects on brain and behavior, *Ethical Human Sciences and Services* 1, 213–41.

Bremmer, J. D. (2005) *Handbook of Brain Imaging*. New York and London: Norton.

Bush, G., Frazier, J., Rauch, S., Seidman, L., Whalen, P., Jenike, M., Rosen, B., and Biederman, J. (1999) Anterior cingulate cortex dysfunction in attention-deficit/hyperactivity disorder revealed by fMRI and the counting stroop, *Biological Psychiatry* 45, 1542–52.

Caparulo, B. K., Donald, M. S., Cohen, D. J., Rothman, S. L., Young, J. G., Katz, J. D., Shaywitz, S. E., and Shaywitz, B. A. (1981) Computed tomographic brain scanning in children with developmental neuropsychiatric disorders, *Journal of Abnormal Child Psychology* 20, 338–57.

Casey, B. J., Castellanos, F. X., Giedd, J. N., Marsh, W. L., Hamburger, S. D., Schubert, A. B., Vauss, Y. C., Vaituzis, A. C., Dickstein, D. P., Sarfatti, S. E., and Rapoport, J. L. (1997) Implication of right frontostriatal circuitry in response inhibition and attention-deficit/hyperactivity disorder, *Journal of American Academy of Child and Adolescent Psychiatry* 36, 374–82.

Casey, B. J., and Durston, S. (2006) From behavior to cognition to the brain and back: what have we learned from functional imaging studies of attention deficit hyperactivity disorder? *American Journal of Psychiatry* 163(6), 957–60.

Castellanos, F. X., Giedd, J. N., Eckburg, P., Marsh, W. L., Vaituzis, A. C., Kaysen, D., Hamburger, S. D., and Rapoport, J. L. (1994) Quantitative morphology of the caudate nucleus in attention deficit hyperactivity disorder. *American Journal of Psychiatry* 151, 1791–6.

Castellanos, F. X., Geidd, J. N., Marsh, W. L., Hamburger, S. D., Vaituzis, A. C., Dickstein, D. P., Sarfatti, S. E., Vauss, Y. C., Snell, J. W., Rajapakse, J. C., and Rapoport, J. L. (1996) Quantitative brain magnetic resonance imaging in attention-deficit hyperactivity disorder, *Archives of General Psychiatry* 53, 607–16.

Castellanos, F. X., Lee, P. P., Sharp, W., Jeffries, N. O., Greenstein, D. K., Clasen, L. S., *et al.* (2002) Developmental trajectories of brain volume abnormalities in children and adolescents with attention-deficit hyperactivity disorder, *Journal of the American Medical Association* 288, 1740–8.

Cohen, D. and Leo, J. (2004) An update on ADHD neuroimaging research, *The Journal of Mind and Behavior* 25, 161–6.

DeGrandpre, R. (1999) *Ritalin Nation*. New York: WW Norton and Company.

Edelson, E. (2003). Better brain images could lead to better ADHD treatment. Parent Center News Gutman, A. (2004). Introduction to new research: Navigating complex treatment options for ADHD (March 2004). Medscape from WebMD.

Elia, J., Borcherding, B. G., Rapoport, J. L., and Keysor, C. S. (1991) Methylphenidate and dextroamphetamine treatments of hyperactivity: Are there true nonresponders? *Psychiatry Research* 36, 141–55.

Ernst, M. and Zametkin, A. (1995) The interface of genetics, neuroimaging, and neurochemistry in attention-deficit hyperactivity disorder, in F. Bloom and D. Kupfer (eds), *Psychopharmacology* (pp. 1643–52). New York: Raven Press.

Ernst, M., Liebenauer, L., King, A., Fitzgerald, G., Cohen, R., and Zametkin, A. (1994) Reduced brain metabolism in hyperactive girls, *Journal of the American Academy of Child and Adolescent Psychiatry* 33, 858–68.

Fagundes, A. O., Rezin, G. T., Zanette, F., Grandi, E., Assis, L. C., Dal-Pizzol, F., Quevedo, J., and Streck, E. L. (2006) Chronic administration of methylphenidate activates mitochondrial respiratory chain in brain of young rats, *International Journal of Developmental Neuroscience* 25, 47–51.

Filipek, P. A., Semrud-Clikeman, M., Steingard, R. J., Renshaw, P. F., Kennedy, D. N., and Biederman, J. (1997) Volumetric MRI analysis comparing subjects having attention-deficit hyperactivity disorder with normal controls, *Neurology* 48, 589–601.

Geidd, J. N., Castellanos, F. X., Casey, B. J., Kozuch, P., King, A. C., Hamburger, S. D. and Rapoport, J. L. (1994) Quantitative morphology of the corpus callosum in attention deficit hyperactivity disorder. *American Journal of Psychiatry* 151, 665–9.

Giedd, J. N., Blumenthal, J., Molloy, E., and Castellanos, F. X. (2001) Brain imaging of attention deficit/hyperactivity disorder, in J. Wassertein, L. E. Wolf, and F. F. Lefever (eds), *Adult Attention Deficit Disorder: Brain Mechanisms and Life Outcomes* (vol. 931, pp. 33–49). New York: New York Academy of Sciences.

Gould, S. J. (1996) *The Mismeasure of Man* (revised and expanded edition). New York: W.W. Norton and Company.

Hynd, G. W., Semrud-Clikeman, M., Lorys, A. R., Novey, E. S., and Eliopulos, D. (1990) Brain morphology in developmental dyslexia and attention deficit disorder/hyperactivity, *Archives of Neurology* 47, 919–26.

Hynd, G. W., Semrud-Clikeman, M., Lorys, A. R., Novey, E. S., Eliopulos, D., and Lyytinen, H. (1991) Corpus callosum morphology in attention deficit-hyperactivity disorder: Morphometric analysis of MRI, *Journal of Learning Disabilities* 24, 141–6.

Hynd, G. W., Hern, K. L., Novey, E. S., Eliopulos, D., Marshall, R., Gonzalez, J. J., and Voeller, K. K. (1993) Attention deficit-hyperactivity disorder and asymmetry of the caudate nucleus, *Journal of Child Neurology* 8, 339–47.

Ilgin, N., Senol, S., Gucuyener, K., Gokcora, N., and Sener, S. (2001) Is increased D2 receptor availability associated with response to stimulant medication in ADHD? *Developmental Medicine and Child Neurology* 43, 755–60.

Kim, B., Lee, J., Cho, S., and Lee, D. (2001) Methylphenidate increased regional cerebral blood flow in subjects with attention deficit/hyperactivity disorder. *Yonsei Journal of Medicine*, 42, 19–29.

Leo, J. and Cohen, D. (2003) Broken brains or flawed studies? A critical review of ADHD neuroimaging research, *Journal of Mind and Behavior* 24, 29–56.

Lou, H. C., Henriksen, L., and Bruhn, P. (1984) Focal cerebral hypoperfusion in children with dysphasia and/or attention deficit disorder, *Archives of Neurology* 41, 825–9.

Lou, H. C., Henriksen, L., and Bruhn, P. (1990) Focal cerebral dysfunction in developmental learning disabilities, *The Lancet* 335, 8–11.

Lou, H. C., Henriksen, L., Bruhn, P., Borner, H., and Neilson, J. B. (1989) Striatal dysfunction in attention deficit and hyperkinetic disorder, *Archives of Neurology* 46, 48–52.

Martins, M. R., Reinke, A., Petronilho, F. C., Gomes, K. M., Dal-Pizzol, F., and Quevedo, J. (2006) Methylphenidate treatment induces oxidative stress in young rat brain, *Brain Research* 1078, 189–97.

Mataro, M., Garcia-Sanchez, C., Junque, C., Estevez-Gonzalez, A., and Pujol, J. (1997) Magnetic resonance imaging measurement of the caudate nucleus in adolescents with attention-deficit hyperactivity disorder and its relationship with neuropsychological and behavioral measures, *Archives of Neurology* 54, 963–8.

Moll, G., Hause, S., Ruther, E., Rothenberger, A., and Huether, G. (2001) Early methylphenidate administration to young rats causes a persistent reduction in the density of striatal dopamine transporters, *Journal of Child and Adolescent Psychopharmacology* 11, 15–24.

Mostofsky, S. H., Reiss, A. L., Lockhart, P., and Denckla, M. B. (1998) Evaluation of cerebellar size in attention-deficit hyperactivity disorder, *Journal of Child Neurology* 13, 434–9.

Nasrallah, H. A., Loney, J., Olson, S. C., McCalley-Whitters, M., Kramer, J., and Jacoby, C. G. (1986) Cortical atrophy in young adults with a history of hyperactivity in childhood, *Psychiatry Research* 17, 241–6.

Pliszka, S. R., Glahn, D. C., Semrud-Clikeman, M., Franklin, C., Perez, R., 3rd, Xiong, J., *et al.* (2006) Neuroimaging of inhibitory control areas in children with attention deficit hyperactivity disorder who were treatment naive or in long-term treatment, *American Journal of Psychiatry* 163(6), 1052–60.

Reid, R., Maag, J., and Vasa, S. (1994) Attention deficit hyperactivity disorder as a disability category: A critique, *Exceptional Children* 60, 198–214.

Reiss, D., Feinstein, C., Weinberger, D. R., King, R., Wyatt, R. J., and Brallier, D. (1983) Ventricular enlargement in child psychiatric patients: A controlled study with planimetric measurements, *American Journal of Psychiatry* 140, 453–6.

Reneman, L., Booij, J., de Bruin, K., Reitsma, J. B., de Wolff, F. A., Gunning, W. B., den Heeten, G. J., and van den Brink, W. (2001) Effects of dose, sex, and long-term abstention from use on toxic effects of MDMA (ecstasy) on brain serotonin neurons, *The Lancet* 358, 1864–9.

Rubia, K., Overmeyer, S., Taylor, E., Brammer, M., Williams, S. C. R., Simmons, A., and Bullmore, E. T. (1999) Hypofrontality in attention deficit hyperactivity disorder during higher-order motor control: A study with functional MRI, *American Journal of Psychiatry* 156, 891–6.

Schweitzer, J. B., Faber, T. L., Grafton, S. T., Tune, L. E., Hoffman, J. M., and Kilts, C. D. (2000) Alterations in the functional anatomy of working memory in adult attention deficit hyperactivity disorder, *American Journal of Psychiatry* 157, 278–80.

Semrud-Clikeman, M., Filipek, P. A., Biederman, J., Steingard, R., Kennedy, D., Renshaw, P., and Bekken, K. (1994) Attention-deficit hyperactivity disorder: Magnetic resonance imaging morphometric analysis of the corpus callosum, *Journal of the American Academy of Child and Adolescent Psychiatry* 33, 875–81.

Shaywitz, B. A., Shaywitz, S. E., Byrne, T., Cohen, D. J., and Rothman, S. L. (1983) Attention deficit disorder: Quantitative analysis of CT, *Neurology* 33, 1500–03.

Sieg, K. G., Gaffney, G. R., Preston, D. F., and Hellings, J. A. (1995) SPECT brain imaging abnormalities in attention deficit hyperactivity disorder, *Clinical Nuclear Medicine* 20, 55–60.

Smith, A. B., Taylor, E., Brammer, M., Toone, B., and Rubia, K. (2006) Task-specific hypoactivation in prefrontal and temporoparietal brain regions during motor inhibition and task switching in medication-naive children and adolescents with attention deficit hyperactivity disorder, *American Journal of Psychiatry* 163(6), 1044–51.

Sowell, E.R., Thompson, P.M., Welcome, S.E., Henkenius, A.L., Toga, A.W., and Peterson, B.S. (2003) Cortical abnormalities in children and adolescents with attention-deficit hyperactivity disorder, *The Lancet* 362, 1699–707.

Sproson, E. J., Chantrey, J., Hollis, C., Marsden, C. A., and Fonel, K. C. (2001) Effect of repeated methylphenidate administration on presynaptic dopamine and behaviour in young adult rats, *Journal of Psychopharmacology* (Oxford, England) 15, 67–75.

Tamm, L., Menon, V., & Reiss, A. L. (2006) Parietal attentional system aberrations during target detection in adolescents with attention deficit hyperactivity disorder: Event-related fMRI evidence, *American Journal of Psychiatry* 163(6), 1033–43.

Teicher, M. H., Anderson, C. M., Polcari, A., Glod, C. A., Maas, L. C., and Renshaw, P. F. (2000) Functional deficits in basal ganglia of children with attention-deficit/hyperactivity disorder shown with functional magnetic resonance imaging relaxometry, *Nature Medicine* 470–3.

Thompson, J. S., Ross, R. J., and Horwitz, S. J. (1980) The role of computed axial tomography in the study of the child with minimal brain dysfunction, *Journal of Learning Disabilities* 13, 334–7.

Vaidya, C. J., Austin, G., Kirkorian, G., Ridlehuber, H. W., Desmond, J. E., Glover, G. H., and Gabrieli, J. D. E. (1998) Selective effects of methylphenidate in attention deficit hyperactivity disorder: A functional magnetic resonance study, *Proceedings of the National Academy of Sciences* 14494–9.

Valenstein, E. (1998). *Blaming the Brain: The Truth about Drugs and Mental Health*. New York: The Free Press.

Vitiello, B. (1998) Pediatric psychopharmacology and interaction between drugs and the developing brain, *Canadian Journal of Psychiatry* 43, 582–4.

Vles, J. S., Feron, F. J., Hendricksen, J. G., Jolles, J., van Kroonenburgh, M. J., and Weber, W. E. (2003) Methylphenidate down-regulates the dopamine receptor and transporter system in children with attention deficit hyperkinetic disorder (ADHD), *Neuropediatrics* 4, 77–80.

Volkow, N. D., Wang, G. J., Fowler, J. S., Logan, J., Gerasimov, M., Maynard, L., Ding, Y. S., Gatley, S. J., Gifford, A., and Franceschi, D. (2001) Therapeutic doses of oral methylphenidate signigicantly increase extracellular dopamine in the human brain, *Journal of Neuroscience* 21(RC-121), 1–5.

Volkow, N.D., Wang, G.J., Newcorn, J., Fowler, J.S., Telang, F., Solanto, M.V., Logan, J., Wong, C., Ma, Y., Swanson, J.M., Schulz, K., and Pradhan, K. (2007) Brain dopamine transporter levels in treatment and drug-naïve adults with ADHD, *Neuroimage* 34, 1182–90.

Wagner, G. C., Schuster, C. R., and Seiden, L. S. (1981) Neurochemical consequences following administration of CNS stimulants to the neonatal rat, *Pharmacology, Biochemistry, and Behavior* 14, 117–19.

Wan, F. J., Lin, H. C., Huang, K. L., Tseng, C. J., and Wong, C. S. (2000) Systemic administration of d-amphetamine induces long-lasting oxidative stress in the rat striatum, *Life Sciences* 66, PL205–12.

Yuan, J., McCann, U., and Ricaurte, G. (1997) Methylphenidate and brain dopamine neurotoxicity, *Brain Research* 767, 172–5.

Zametkin, A. J., Nordahl, T. E., Gross, M., King, A. C., Semple, W. E., Rumsey, J., Hamburger, S. D., and Cohen, R. M. (1990) Cerebral glucose metabolism in adults with hyperactivity of childhood onset, *New England Journal of Medicine* 323, 1361–6.

Zametkin, A. J., Liebenauer, L. L., Fitzgerald, G. A., King, A. C., Minkunas, D. V., Herscovitch, P., Yamada, E. M., and Cohen, R. M. (1993) Brain metabolism in teenagers with attention-deficit hyperactivity disorder, *Archives of General Psychiatry* 333–40.

Part II
ADHD and Culture

Chapter 4

Why Diagnosis of ADHD has Increased so Rapidly in the West: A Cultural Perspective

Sami Timimi

ADHD remains so controversial there are very few areas in the literature that are uncontested. One fact that is agreed upon is that the diagnosis and prescription of stimulant medication for children receiving this diagnosis has gone through a very steep increase in the past few decades in most Western countries. Whilst this fact is not disputed the significance of this is interpreted differently by different theoretical stances. Those who believe ADHD to be a genetically inherited, neurodevelopmental disorder put the main reason as under-recognition of the disorder in the past (and, of course, in the majority of the non-Western world where ADHD remains a peripheral diagnosis). Thus, according to this depoliticized perspective there have always been children who are 'suffering' with this neurodevelopmental disorder, which causes hyperactivity, impulsivity, and poor concentration, but it is only as a result of recent scientific advances that we have discovered these to be symptoms of a medical condition that causes abnormal development and a chemical imbalance in the brain. In other words, ADHD has always existed but it is only recently that we have begun to realize this and so diagnose and treat it.

However, critics, such as myself, maintain that this reductionist stance is difficult to maintain in the absence of good evidence that supports the contention that ADHD is a physical condition resulting from abnormal development and a biochemical imbalance in the brain (for a summary of the critique of biological evidence see the various references in this book and some of my previous work such as Timimi, 2002, 2005, 2006). There are, of course, two other possibilities that could explain the dramatic increase in the diagnosis of ADHD in the West. The first is that there has been a real increase in ADHD-type behaviours in children leading to greater public scrutiny and concern about such behaviours, which, in turn, has resulted in a greater professional effort to understand and alleviate these behavioural problems. If there has been a real increase in these behaviours then understanding the causes of this would require us to turn our attention to changes in contextual factors within Western culture (where this epidemic of ADHD appears to be occurring) such as environment, society, economics and politics. Such an increase cannot be the result of genetics as, of course, genes do not change on such a large scale in only a couple of generations.

The second possibility is that there has not been a real increase in ADHD-type behaviours among young people but there has been a change in the way we think about, classify, and deal with children's behaviour – in other words our perception and the meaning we ascribe to children's behaviour. A move, from thinking about certain aspects of children's behaviour as boisterousness and therefore within the normal, expected realms for their behaviour, to thinking about these behaviours as symptoms of a medical disorder would be an example of a change in the way we think about certain behaviours. I have previously summarized how our view of childhood (and by implication our view of the role of parents, schools, welfare services, governments, and so on) has undergone some radical changes in the past few centuries in Western culture, as well as comparing the large differences between Western and many non-Western cultures' beliefs concerning childhood and child rearing (see Timimi, 2005). An examination of changes in the way we think about children and childhood also means an examination of contexts such as the social, cultural and political that shape our broad cultural discourses.

Both possible causes for the increase in diagnosis of ADHD (i.e. a real increase in these behaviours and a change in the meaning we ascribe to these behaviours) require an examination of contexts. Indeed the third, and in my opinion, most likely possibility that explains the increase in diagnosis, is an interaction between the above-mentioned two possibilities. In other words, it could be that changes in our cultural–environmental contexts are causing increases in ADHD-type behaviours and these, in turn, are changing our perception of childhood behaviour, and our perception of and the meaning we give to it is, in turn, changing the way we deal with it and our common cultural practices around children (such as child rearing and education), which in turn are further increasing these behaviours, and so on. There are potentially limitless variations of this interaction that may be operating at many different levels from the individual child right up to global organizations. In this chapter I want to revisit and further expand upon some of my previous analysis of the way contexts both change our perception and the meaning we ascribe to children's behaviour and effect their actual behaviour.

In parallel with the rapid increase in diagnosis of ADHD in Western culture there has been a paralleled growth in critical literature. This critical literature can be broadly divided into three areas. First, a critique of the evidence claiming that ADHD is a valid construct and that treatment with medication is both safe and effective. Secondly, literature that, in part, accepts the notion of ADHD but suggests more environmental causes for the condition (and therefore more environmental treatments). Thirdly, literature that views ADHD as having emerged from a change in the way we think about childhood and, thus, suggests reframing and re-conceptualizing the significance of behaviours we find in young people that we could label as ADHD. Of course, many of the authors involved write from across these three perspectives and, whilst there may be significant differences in their analysis of the evidence and conclusions they reach, as with the authors in this book they tend to be united by a deep concern about the scientific, clinical, ethical and public health implications of the continuing expansion in the number of children being diagnosed with ADHD and placed on powerful psychiatric medications for this.

Adverse environmental factors

In this section I wish to briefly summarize the critical literature that has arisen from the second of the above three areas – that is, critical perspectives on possible environmental bio-psycho-social causes of ADHD-type behaviours. In carrying out this summary I am mindful that, in order to maintain a logical, evidential link to the factual situation outlined at the beginning of the chapter (that there has been a rapid increase in the West in the numbers of children being diagnosed with ADHD in the past two decades), I will concentrate on factors thought to have undergone significant change in recent decades in the West.

Diet and nutrition

The content of children's diets in the West has undergone significant change, which, in turn, is related to changes in farming, food production, processing and marketing of products. Modern farming methods have moved farming towards more large-scale, intensive agriculture, involving a variety of technologies, from mechanisation to the use of fertilizers and pesticides, gene manipulation to artificially produced foods, and use of hormones and antibiotics in farm animals that are kept in progressively larger numbers in smaller places. This intensive farming produces greater yields and these are then subject to further processing and packaging for colour, taste and convenience. Finally, this is subjected to the dynamics of consumerism, which involves direct advertising to the young, and exploitation of our busy lifestyles including the resulting demand for convenient, fast foods.

The result has been a dramatic change in the nature of children's diets in just a few decades. Children's diets are now significantly higher in sugar, saturated fats, salt, and additives than even just a couple of decades ago. At the same time they are lower in fresh fruit and vegetables and essential fatty acids (such as from fish), all of which is contributing to an increase in a variety of physical (such as obesity), and possibly mental, health problems. Indeed an ecological study of national dietary patterns in relation to international variations in the outcome of some major mental health diagnosis, such as the outcome of schizophrenia and the prevalence of depression, showed an association between a higher national dietary intake of refined sugar and dairy products and a worse two-year outcome in schizophrenia at the same time as a high prevalence of depression being predicted by a low national dietary intake of fish and seafood (Peet, 2004). As summarized elsewhere in this book (see Chapter 12), there is a growing body of literature that is showing significant reductions in some ADHD-type symptoms, through various dietary interventions, including elimination of additives and the addition of supplements such as essential fatty acids and certain minerals and vitamins, can be achieved.

Family structure and lifestyle

Shifting economic structures have led to profound changes in the organization of family life. More mothers are employed outside the home, precipitating a renegotiation of power within the family. Suburbanization and the economic demands of successful market economies has resulted in greater mobility, less time for family life, and a reduction of contact and exchanges between members of the extended family.

Many families (particularly those headed by young women) are now isolated from traditional sources of child rearing information resulting in a greater 'ownership' by professionals of the knowledge base for the task of parenting (Zuckerman, 1975).

With increasing numbers of households in which there are two working parents or single parents following divorce, fathers and mothers are less available for their children through the day. Left increasingly to their own devices, children are more amenable to exploitation by the free market, which preys on their boredom and desire for stimulation (Kincheloe, 1998). In such an environment, a media that tells children that they are deficient without this or that accessory constantly confronts them. Western children respond to these influences by entering early, and without adult supervision, into the world of adult entertainments, becoming sexually knowledgeable and with earlier experience of drugs and alcohol (Aronowitz and Giroux, 1991).

One result of these changes in family structure is that families have become smaller, more emotionally intense units, as the number of relationships a growing child has to learn to negotiate are of a smaller number, making these relationships more intense and reducing the child's opportunity to discover the skills of negotiating multiple relationships more commonly found in extended family systems.

Breggin (1994, 1997) has put forward a strong case for the missing role of the absent father causing the ADHD-type behaviours seen in children with the diagnosis and has renamed the syndrome DADD (Dad's Attention Deficit Disorder). He believes that loving attention from their fathers is an effective curative factor for these children. In a similar vein, attachment theory suggests that the modern stressful social situation is having a dire and negative impact on the ability of parents to provide the sort of strong, secure and positive relationship children need with their parents. An accumulation of stresses on a family (such as lack of support, unresolved loss, poor relationship with father, insufficiently positive maternal model, pregnancy and birth complications, and difficult infant temperament), in some families, causes increasingly negative interactions to develop between a child and their parent(s), it is hypothesised, leading to exhaustion, frustration and irritability in the parent and challenging and hyperactive behaviour in the growing child, which in turn leads to a reinforcing demand–disatisfaction cycle (Stiefel, 1997).

Other 'brain development' researchers agree with this idea as more evidence is accumulating that shows that experience has physical/biological effects on the brain, which is now seen as an organ capable of undergoing reorganization in response to experiences, particularly in childhood but right up into adulthood (Greenough *et al.*, 1987; Valenstein, 1998; Bloom *et al.*, 2001). This model is not intended as a parent blame model nor does it seek to avoid the interpersonal realities of life, but it does point out that what is traumatic to an adult may not be traumatic to a child and vice versa (Offord, 1998).

Change in lifestyle of children
In addition to large changes in family structure in modern, Western society there have also been significant changes in children's lifestyles within these new family forms. A number of academics have turned their attention to some of these, including the increase in exposure to television, the impact of computers and computer games, the decrease in amounts of physical exercise, the decrease in amounts of unsupervised (free) play, all of which together is sometimes referred to as the 'domestication' of childhood.

The increasingly centre-stage role of electronic media that are fast paced, non-linguistic, and visually distracting, in front of which young children spend so many hours sitting, may literally have changed children's minds, making sustained attention to verbal input such as reading or listening far less appealing than faster-paced stimuli (Healy, 1998). Exposure to TV and computer games from a young age could then lead to a form of sensory addiction, leading to problems when children are asked to adapt to less stimulating environments such as school (De Grandpre, 1999). Interestingly, among the Amish, who are well known for their rejection of most modern indulgences such as computers and television, symptoms of ADHD appear to be uncommon (Papolos and Papolos, 1999). Recently, researchers at the University of Washington have discovered a strong association between the amount of early exposure to TV and subsequent attention span in early childhood, supporting previous research that showed an association between amount of TV watching and reduced reading ability and attention span (Christakis *et al.*, 2004).

Fears about children's safety, together with more 'in-house' entertainments such as computers and TV, has also led to many children growing up with a lack of fresh air and exercise, leaving those more active boys to behave like 'caged animals' (Panksepp, 1998a, b; Timimi, 2002). Indeed there is evidence from animal experiments to show that access to what the authors call 'rough-and-tumble' play promotes brain maturation and reduces levels of hyperactivity and impulsiveness in later life (Panksepp *et al.*, 2003; Gordon *et al.*, 2003).

The psychiatrist, Grace Jackson (2005), has concluded that, as a result, many of our children should be considered as suffering from 'dromospheric pollution' (where dromology is the study of speed). She believes that dromospheric pollution is creating children who are addicted to novel stimuli, multi-tasking, and speed as a result of early exposure to television, video games and the internet, causing changes not only psychologically but also possibly biologically too.

Changes in the education system

School is another big part of children's life where considerable changes have occurred that could promote ADHD-type behaviours. Modern teaching methods emphasize self-regulation and reject spoonfeeding (dependency), resulting in a difficult environment for children who have problems with organizing, ordering and learning and whose restlessness, in classroom environments that are highly stimulating, offer much choice and therefore (arguably) encourage distraction and poor concentration, is subsequently intensified (Timimi, 2002, 2005).

Emphasis has changed in schools in both North America and the United Kingdom. Schools are now expected to demonstrate better levels of academic achievement among their pupils and often have to compete with other schools in national performance league tables. As a result there are more standard tests and much of the curriculum is being pushed downward from older to younger children, with less time being set aside for more energetic and creative activities such as gym and music (Sax, 2000). Schools are anyway better set up for girls' development. Thus special-needs support is four times more likely to be given to boys, who lag behind girls in development of core school adaptive abilities such as reading and social skills. These latter two factors put together – more emphasis on academic achievement and differential rates of development – has put young-for-grade boys at a particular disadvantage, with as many as four-fifths of young-for-grade boys being prescribed stimulant medication in some areas of North America (LeFever et al., 1999; Ravenel, 2002).

Childhood abuse and trauma

Charles Whitfield (2006) points out that there is a large body of literature showing a link between childhood trauma or abuse and subsequent behaviour problems including ADHD-type behaviour. He believes that many who are erroneously diagnosed with ADHD/

ADD – and many who are accurately diagnosed with it – may have a history of abuse or trauma that has been overlooked. In his literature search he found 77 published reports of a significantly higher incidence of ADHD-type behaviours and ADHD among abused/traumatized children and found only one study that looked for it that reported a negative association between ADHD and trauma. Whitfield concludes that childhood trauma can lead to a multitude of health and social problems, including those that result from disrupted development of the brain and nervous system as a result of the physical effects of chronic stress on the developing brain.

Changes in the way we think about children's behaviour

The above list does not represent an exhaustive list of cultural changes in Western society that may be of relevance in causing ADHD-type behaviour in children, just as the list below is not an exhaustive list of changes in the way we conceptualize and give meaning to children's behaviour. Furthermore, these are not separate domains as changes in the meaning and significance we give to childhood behaviour interacts with actual changes in those environments. The separation I have made in this chapter is more for the sake of clarity and convenience in ordering my thinking about this topic than because these exist as natural, distinct and separate entities.

Our changing beliefs about parenting

I have summarized the enormous changes that have taken place in our view and understanding of the role of parents and the practice of child rearing that have taken place in Western culture over the centuries elsewhere (see Timimi, 2005). These have not been changes in mere details. For example, an unprecedented debate about childhood and child rearing emerged in late-seventeenth-century and early-eighteenth-century Europe, framed by the writings of John Locke and Jean Rousseau. Over the subsequent centuries several shifts in the position of mother and father have occurred and have accompanied shifts in the beliefs about the degree of interference, discipline and guidance that children need during their growing years. Thus, at various stages during the past few centuries the central figure in child rearing has shifted from mother to father and back again on several occasions. There have also been changes in ideas about the structure of the 'ideal' family and its relationship to both the State and the Church. Changes in our cultural beliefs about the role of the parents and the practice of child rearing in the past few decades in the West have been influenced by (and in turn influence) broader economic and political changes.

One feature that has changed dramatically over the past century of Western society is the amount of surveillance to which both parents and their children are subjected. The state has become more and more interventionist in family life, thus causing an increase in levels of anxiety among parents who may fear the consequences of their action to the point that any discernible influence on their part may likely be viewed as undue influence, making it more probable that those parents will leave essential socializing and guidance to the expertise of professionals (Maitra, 2006).

Life has become difficult for parents, who are caught in a double pressure when it comes to discipline. On the one hand there are increased expectations for children to show restraint and self-control from an early age. On the other hand there is considerable social fear in parents generated by a culture of children's rights that often pathologizes normal, well-intentioned parents' attempts to discipline their children. Parents are left fearing a visit from the SS (Social Services) and the whole area of discipline becomes loaded with anxiety. This argument holds equally true for schools. Parents often criticize schools for lack of discipline. Schools often criticize parents for lack of discipline. This double-bind has resulted in more power going to children. Parents are being given the message that their children are more like adults and should always be talked to, reasoned with, allowed to make choices, and so on.

There is also a lack of common ownership of rules and values with regard to the upbringing of children. Children may learn that only certain individuals have any right to make demands and have expectations regarding their behaviour. This relates to the way in which the task of parenting has come to be viewed in Western culture, as one that needs childcare expert's advice in order to get it right, with the involvement of others, be they extended family or the broader community, being viewed with increasing suspicion. A form of 'cognitive parenting' has arisen whereby parents are encouraged to give explanation and avoid conflicts (Diller, 2002). This hands-off, predominantly verbal model of parenting is both more taxing and less congruent with children's more action-based view of the world. In addition, some

parents may be motivated by discovering that ADHD is a new convenient way of getting a label from which you can get extra disability
benefits (Timimi, 2005; Breggin, 2002).

The normalizing perspective

Thom Hartmann is perhaps the best known author who espouses this
view. He points out that studies on children believed to have ADHD
are more interested in areas where these children perform poorly
compared to non-ADHD children and that they rarely look at those
areas of ability where 'ADHD' children may actually outperform non-
ADHD children, for example, in their ability to outscore their peers
in one of the new, high-stimulation video games or on a skateboard.
In other words the idea that ADHD is a medical disease shapes how
the research is then conducted in such a way that it is already primed
to discover that ADHD children are 'losers' (Hartmann, 2001). Whilst
viewing ADHD-type behaviours as being the product of a biological
difference, rather than viewing this difference as a sign of a 'disease',
he thus notes that this is sometimes advantageous to that individual.
Indeed, some authors have noted a striking similarity between descriptions of ADHD and descriptions of 'creative' children. For example
Professor Bonnie Cramond asks the question: 'There are so many similarities in the behavioural descriptions of creativity and ADHD that
one is left to wonder, could these be overlapping phenomena?' (quoted
in Hartmann 2001) After a thorough search of the literature in both
fields she concludes that the answer to that question is yes. Her idea
seems to be that both 'creative' and/or 'ADHD' children are individuals who have trouble with verbal learning but have a very imaginative,
visual manner of thinking. Whilst this can cause great problems in
the school environment, where verbal learning is highly valued but
visual/imaginative (as well as physical) learning isn't, it can prove to
be an advantage once the 'ADHD child' leaves school and embarks on
their career, in a way that pushes many of these 'ADHD sufferers' to
end up at the forefront of innovation in our society.

If we take our starting assumption that behaviours such as motor
activity, attention and impulsivity are normally distributed temperamental characteristics, then we can arrive at a different formulation
with regard to the relevance of biology. Viewing these behaviours as
temperamental characteristics as opposed to signs of a medical condition allows more attention to context. Research on children's temperament has shown that problems result from a mismatch between
the child's temperament and their environment (Thomas and Chess,

1977; Chess and Thomas, 1996). Even children who are highly diffi-cult temperamentally can become well adjusted behaviourally if their family and other social circumstances are supportive (Mazaide, 1989). Through this lens the behaviours we call ADHD are inherited in much the same way as other personality traits, whether these behaviours come to be perceived as a problem is mediated by psychosocial factors.

The normalizing perspective is essentially an attempt to place behaviour within its context. From this perspective any behaviour viewed in isolation, without considering the context in which it takes place, makes no sense and opens the door to all sorts of behaviours in isolation being viewed as abnormal. A boy (student A) pushing his classmate (student B) off his chair, if viewed as behaviour in isola-tion, may seem unintelligible, abnormal and perhaps a symptom of an illness that causes impulsivity within that individual. Knowledge of the context can quickly change the significance of this behaviour. Knowing that student B had written a derogatory remark on a piece of paper about student A, just seconds before student A had pushed him, changes the potential significance and meaning of the behaviour. Further knowing that student B is part of a group of friends who have been teasing student A over the past few months at an accelerating pace begins to shift the overall significance further. Perhaps at home student A's parents have been arguing, which A hears at night, mak-ing A feel unhappy and so on. The more contexts we know the more intelligible the behaviour becomes and the easier it is for us to relate to and understand this behaviour (in other words, the less mysteri-ous it becomes). This does not mean that the behaviour itself is not a problem and should not be dealt with in some way. However, it broadens our understanding of the nature of the problem, beyond that of a narrow focus on an unidentifiable, physical problem within stu-dent A. Narrow perspectives that have decided to divorce behaviour from its contexts causes a fundamental error in thinking that leads to a circular argument which goes something like this: this child is pre-senting with poor concentration, impulsivity, and hyperactivity. What is causing this? Answer: it is caused by ADHD. Question: how do you know it is ADHD? Answer: because he or she presents with poor concentration, impulsivity, and hyperactivity (Brown, 2005).

Why medicalization, why now?

I started this chapter by taking a fundamental fact in the ADHD con-troversy – that in Western culture rates of diagnosis and prescription of psychiatric medication for ADHD have increased dramatically in the past few decades. I proposed three possible reasons that can account for this: first, it is the result of increasing recognition of a previously unrecognized medical disorder; secondly, it is the result of increasing exposure to adverse, environmental circumstances; and thirdly, it is the result of a change in the way that we think about childhood and its problems (and, of course, a mixture of these three factors). I then reminded readers of the lack of evidence to support the first possible reason (of a previously unrecognized biomedical condition) and then discussed some of the evidence and literature that debates the second and third possible reasons. You will have realized that my interpretation of the evidence suggests to me that it is exploring the latter two reasons that are most likely to help us understand the reasons behind the current epidemic of ADHD in Western societies.

However, this leaves an important question to ponder; if, as I am suggesting, the current epidemic of ADHD has little to do with our becoming better at uncovering a previously unrecognized medical condition, why has the practice of diagnosing ADHD and prescribing psychiatric drugs to children for this become so popular, in other words, why this medicalization and why now? In attempting to answer this question it is helpful to refer to what the philosopher of science Thomas Kuhn (1970) calls 'paradigms' – that is whole systems of prejudice about what constitutes useful and respectable data, what form theories should take, what sort of language scientists should use, how they should go about their business, and so on. His view of the scientific paradigm (or interpretive framework, if you like) situates science itself within its social, cultural and political contexts. He suggests that underlying any scientific activity, theories and their application are often covert values and interests. Which paradigms then gain ascendancy within any context inevitably entails issues of power. These issues of values, interests and power in shaping which paradigms gain ascendancy are of particular relevance to psychiatry given the broad nature of the subject matter.

There are long-standing controversies about how best to understand human subjective life and its problems, and ongoing turf wars with regard to who has legitimate ownership over the territory that psychiatry claims. Furthermore, there is an interactive process going on between the paradigms used by those who hold positions of cultural power and the general cultural discourse. For example, ADHD is a concept that was first constructed by a culturally powerful discipline, namely medicine. Because of their high status, once doctors and medical scientists begin to use this construct, because it comes from a group with a strong and prominent voice in our culture, the idea of ADHD begins to seep into the everyday consciousness of the population by its popularization through various sources such as the media, visits to the doctor, setting up support groups, conversations between friends and relatives, and so on. As ADHD becomes part of daily discourse, so it gradually affects people's behaviour in a way that reinforces this concept by people's (such as parents, teachers, social workers, relatives, etc.) becoming concerned that a child may have this ADHD, thereby spurring on the demands for such a service which, in turn, expands the role of the doctor, and so on. In this sense, the relationship of power between certain high-status disciplines (in this case, medicine) and the general cultural discourse is an example of how a scientific paradigm (in this case, the idea that there is a brain disorder being called ADHD which causes certain behaviours in children) has the capacity to construct new realities and whole new ways of thinking. Below I expand on a number of factors that have contributed to acceleration of the process described above in recent decades in the West.

The role of the pharmaceutical industry

The drug industry has grown in profitability and influence in the past 20 years and is now second only to the arms industry in the US economy (Public Citizen, 2002). It controls much of the research agenda and employs sophisticated marketing strategies. Commercial rather than scientific concerns become the dominant driving force behind innovation. Within a system of capitalist global markets, drug companies have little choice but to do whatever works to increase the sales of their drugs, regardless of the impact on health care. Thus the hard sell is an inevitable consequence of the way that drug companies make money. Without strict regulation (and even with it) we should not be surprised to discover that some professionals notice that such a 'rich' industry provides many opportunities for greater personal wealth, which is reflected in the proliferation of links between individuals and the industry (Boyd and Bero, 2000).

Drug industry money is now everywhere, to the point where career advancement is clearly enhanced by a relationship with a drug company. Research confirms that marketing practices do influence prescribing habits (Wazana, 2000). Most doctors will claim that they are not influenced by drug industry promotion. However, those of us who feel immune from this may be especially vulnerable (Sagarin et al., 2002). Orlowski and Wateska (1992) studied hospital doctors who denied that going to all-expenses-paid seminars at popular vacation sites would influence them. However, these same doctors did significantly increase their prescribing of the promoted drugs starting from immediately after they received their invitations (Orlowski and Wateska, 1992).

Child psychiatry is especially vulnerable to the influence of the pharmaceutical industry for a number of reasons. There are no objective tests for external validation of disorders (like ADHD) that we purport to diagnose; therefore the boundaries of normality/disorder can be easily manipulated. In addition child and adolescent psychiatric diagnoses rely on reports of various adults in caring relationships with children, who understandably are looking for answers to the inevitable frustrations and fears that the complex task of child rearing produces. Simple one-word formulations (diagnoses) are therefore more attractive and easy to digest than complex multi-dimensional ones. Such a context within current fast-paced, time-stretched and stressful modern lifestyles can easily lead to complex personal, family and social problems being medicalized (Timimi, 2002, 2005). Finally, child psychiatric research is susceptible to the influence of vested interests, with design, conduct and reporting of research sponsored by industry almost inevitably being shaped to convey a favourable profile of the sponsor's drug (Safer, 2002; Melander *et al.*, 2003).

In the world of ADHD advocacy, Children and Adults with Attention Deficit Hyperactivity Disorder (CHADD), a large American-based 'parent support group', engages in lobbying and claims to provide science-based, evidence-based information about ADHD to parents and the public. Critics accuse CHADD of becoming a front for promoting stimulant medications manufactured by its corporate donors. Pharmaceutical companies donated a total of $674,000 in the fiscal year 2002–2003 (Hearn, 2004). In the UK the main parent support group ADDISS – Attention Deficit Disorder Information and Support Service – is also receiving significant funding from the pharmaceutical industry. For example, a recent educational campaign 'launched to support parents of children with ADHD' includes a glossy booklet on ADHD called *Family Stress Points*, which was produced using an educational grant from Ely Lilly (ADDISS, 2005).

The creation of new roles for doctors
It is also in the interests of certain groups of professionals to promote this discourse of medicalization. For example, the number of

consultant psychiatrists in the United Kingdom has more than doubled over the past 22 years with a parallel increase in the number of prescriptions being given; for example, anti-depressant prescriptions have more than doubled over the past decade (Double, 2002). This trend goes hand-in-glove with the pharmaceutical industry's marketing strategy where, for example, the anti-depressant Paroxetine™ is now licensed for the treatment of depression, generalized anxiety disorder, social anxiety disorder, panic disorder, obsessive compulsive disorder, and post-traumatic stress disorder. It is also worth mentioning that the numbers of disorders psychiatrists diagnose have continued to increase. The numbers of diagnostic categories have increased in the diagnostic and statistical manual of mental disorders (DSM) from 106 disorders in DSM-I in 1952 (American Psychiatric Association, 1952) to 357 in DSM-IV in 1994 (American Psychiatric Association, 1994).

The widespread establishment of right-wing monetarist policies in Western economies which promote ideals of growth, market expansion, and wealth creation, had a profound effect on the managed healthcare system in the USA. With the managed healthcare system being the bread and butter of the majority of psychiatrists and paediatrician's work, when the more labour-intensive psychotherapies lost favour with healthcare insurers, doctors soon realized they could make more money by going down the psychopharmacology route than the psychotherapy one. Managed health care has meant that an economic system has come to be built around DSM-IV diagnoses, with such diagnoses offering an easy way to organize the economic system of psychiatric health care. In order to obtain a legitimate ticket to a service, you need a DSM-IV diagnosis. Thus DSM-IV has become more than a mental health diagnostic manual; it is a legal, financial and ideological document, driving thinking about all sorts of emotions and behaviours, including those of our children, towards ever more medicalized notions.

The greater medicalization of American child and adolescent psychiatry together with its cultural power has resulted in child psychiatry in the UK also changing enormously in the last 10 years. Thus the UK's professional discourse has similarly become convinced that there are more personal and professional rewards to be gained by its adopting a more medicalized American-style approach (e.g. Goodman, 1997). This general trend towards believing that there are greater rewards both financially and in terms of professional esteem (constructs like ADHD allow the doctor to create a more 'traditional' doctor–patient script) has helped construct the field of 'neurodevelopmental' psychiatry which the public, trusting such high status opinions, has come to view as real.

The pervasive discourse of mother blame

Free market capitalism can be seen as the most complete and organized example of a political, social and economic system based on the values of masculinity that the world has ever seen. Its social and psychological values are based on aggressive competitiveness, putting the needs of the individual above those of social responsibility, an emphasis on control (rather than harmony), the use of rational (scientific) analysis, and the constant pushing of boundaries. Such a system produces gross inequalities (both within and between nations), has reduced the status and importance of nurture, and therefore the esteem attached to the role of mother. As a consequence more and more women are brought into the workplace – both to increase the workforce needed to service the market economies' demand for continuous growth, and to give women the self-esteem that was taken away from them as the role of motherhood lost its status. This movement out of the family sphere and into the public sphere has not been matched by a corresponding reverse movement of men out of the public sphere into more family and nurturing roles (quite the contrary in fact).

Thus, women have found themselves in a position where, unlike most non-Western cultures, the role of mother is no longer a source of social esteem, at the same time as continuing to bear most physical and emotional responsibilities for raising children. When put together with a long-standing focus in psychotherapy culture on the mother–child relationship, resulting in a, more often than not, mother-blaming focus, then we can see that when things go wrong with their children, mothers often end up perceiving themselves in a negative way.

The loss of esteem attached to the role of the mother, together with mother -blaming may be another important factor in the rise of the popularity of ADHD diagnoses. In this explanatory model, mothers who hear the negative judgements of school and other parents experience a sense of self-blame, failure, guilt and helplessness as well as anger and frustration with the child. When put in contact with the ADHD industry, such a mother may, at least temporarily, feel freed from the mother-blaming context that has been so oppressive. She is no longer a failed mother, but a mother battling against the odds with a disabled child. In this analysis, the primary problem is not seen as residing in the mother or the child (or the often absent father), but in the effects of the dominant discourses of psychology, psychiatry and patriarchy, which render parent and child as passive and separated from their abilities, competence and strengths (Law, 1997).

The moral panic about boys

Boys are underachieving in schools, more likely to be involved in violence, to be bullied or act as a bully, to be registered as having special needs, to be expelled from school, to abuse substances and to commit suicide (Rutter and Smith, 1995; Hey, *et al.*, 1998). The increase in these psychosocial problems, particularly among boys has been put down to a number of reasons, including lack of male role models for boys at school, a lack of clear goal setting and poor management at schools, economic changes effecting boys (especially working-class boys), a crisis of masculinity, incompatibility of the behaviour styles of boys with modern schooling, the impact of feminism, and a breakdown in family stability (Jackson, 1998; Pollack, 1998; Kryger, 1998; Hey *et al.*, 1998).

By the turn of the century a declining manufacturing sector has resulted in an increasing demand for an educated workforce and so schools are under greater pressure to increase the number of pupils gaining educational qualifications and moving on into higher education, and are subject to constant monitoring of their performance by governments. With fewer 'traditional' jobs available to boys at the end of their schooling, the link between self-esteem and academic achievement is greater than at any time in the past (Frosh *et al.*, 2002). Corporal punishment has been abolished in most Western countries (in UK state schools this happened in 1986) and there is a perception that modern schools are ruled by out-of-control boys in violent gangs. Rates of exclusion from mainstream schooling in the United Kingdom for boys has increased four-fold in the years since 1986 (Hey *et al.*, 1998). With the introduction of league tables to compare school performances and the poor levels of resource for schools resulting in large classes, together with a philosophy highly influenced by Western psychology of positive encouragement, independent learning and a high emphasis on verbal skills, boys' underachievement has become very visible. There has been a paralleled growth in special needs provision within the school and boys' have consistently dominated in this type of provision in the United Kingdom (Hey *et al.*, 1998; Cooper *et al.*, 1991).

At the same time as there has been a movement of adults out of the family; there has been a movement towards childcare becoming a professional (mainly female) activity. Thus, what appears to be happening in the psychological space of childhood is an increasing feminization in many aspects, particularly educational ones. There is now a large body of literature that attests to the fact that educational methods currently used in most Western schools (such as continuous assessment and socially orientated work sheets) are favoured more by girls than boys (Burman, 2005). This is then mirrored in national exam results where girls are now consistently achieving higher grades than boys even in some traditionally 'male' subjects like maths and science. With schools under market economy political pressure to compete in national league tables, and boys coming to represent a liability, it is hardly surprising that boys are seen as the 'failed' gender, provoking anxiety in their (primarily female) carers and teachers (Timimi, 2005).

The gender gap in the child population diagnosed with ADHD is matched by a significant and opposite differential among adults initiating the labelling process. While young males form the majority of those labelled with ADHD, it is overwhelmingly adult females, their mothers and teachers, who make the first determination that a child's behaviour falls outside the normal range of what little boys are expected to do. Though this differential reflects the adult females' more immediate involvement in the day-to-day care of children, mothers and fathers frequently disagree on the 'pathological' nature of their sons' behaviour. Surveys of stimulant use in the United States has shown that its use is highest in prosperous white communities where education is a high priority, where the educational achievement of both sexes is above the national average and, most importantly, where the gender gap in educational achievement favouring females is at its highest (Hart *et al.*, 2006). This ecological pattern is consistent with the view that ADHD can be seen as a barometer of social anxiety about boys' development, with stimulants being used as a (perceived) tool for educating boys'.

The search for quick fix solutions
One of the features of modern, economically developed, consumer societies is the continuous advance of technologies and our ever-greater reliance on them in modern life. When technologies are functioning properly, they operate in the background of our attention and their efficiency, function and use are thus taken for granted. The better the technology the less I have to think about it – it is there functioning just outside my awareness and making life easier for me. Thus, in our efforts to get from A to B we first had the bicycle, then the car which made the journey easier and more efficient. The car then evolved to

become faster, safer, smoother, and more comfortable and technology continues to evolve, so we get the automatic car, satellite navigation, lights that switch on and off automatically, a climate-controlled atmosphere, and so on. The attraction of technological advance has had a huge impact on our day-to-day life and, indeed, our consciousness. So attractive are the appeals of developing technologies which apparently make life easier, more efficient, and streamlined, that hardly a discipline can be found that has not turned to technology.

In this respect, medicine is a good example of a profession whose core value system has shifted from a primary focus on the care ethic towards a primary focus on a more technologically orientated ethic, which revolves around efficiency, accuracy, efficacy and economy (Sandler, 2005). Thus, the focus is on technical aspects rather than the human aspects of the job – as in the age-old cliché (which I remember to be true from my days as a medical student!) of the consultant on the ward round identifying patients through their ailment (this is a case of kidney stones, this is a case of heart failure, etc.), like objects rather than people.

This general technicalization of life has meant that we increasingly search for simple solutions where we rely on the technical expertise of various technicians in their trade. These 'experts' bring to bear their scientific, technical knowledge and devise a simple technical solution which requires minimum thought by the user and which, when applied, will fix the problem and render it to the background as all good technologies should. In this respect it is easy to see the appeal of the notion that the interpersonal problems which life inevitably brings can be reduced to a single, underlying disorder (such as ADHD) that can be fixed with a pill. It is also easy to see why, in such a cultural context, more time-consuming approaches such as psychotherapeutic ones that require thought, reflection, mental effort and great engagement with the subject matter have receded in their popularity.

Interestingly, the technicalization of modern culture has not been without its critics and, indeed, an ambivalent relationship with technology has been noted. Yes, we all want to own a car and drive one so that we can reach A from B efficiently, but we are also aware that this technology contributes to global warming so that this short-term gain may lead to long-term pain. Furthermore, the existence of mass means of transport, like the car, has had a profound effect on the mobility of people, which, in turn, has led to a weakening of social support structures as families and communities venture into all corners of the earth, often leaving behind them a sense of connection and belonging.

To bring it to a more personal level, it is great to have technology that allows me to wake up in the morning, lie in bed, and use the remote control to turn on the television in a house that is kept nice and warm with gas central heating which comes on automatically at certain times of the day. In fact it is so nice that I could stay there all morning, but my partner pulls me out of this technological comfort zone, persuading me to put on my coat and scarf and go out for a walk in the crisp, winter morning scenery. Not only is this invigorating but it forces me to re-engage with the simple human pleasures of being with, talking to and deepening a relationship with someone of far greater importance to my life than the central heating and television.

Simulated children and the fragmentation of childhood

The controversial philosopher, Jean Baudrillard (see Douglas, 1989) has suggested that modern culture is saturated with imagery through the media, advertising, television, and so on. The result of this, he argues, is that 'representation' has saturated reality to such an extent that experience is often taking place at a distance from reality. We thus experience the world through a kind of filter of preconceptions and expectations that have been fabricated in advance by a culture swamped with images. For example, how can you express your love for someone without that expression recalling in some way innumerable soap operas or Hollywood films in which our idea of love is constructed and played out daily. Baudrillard refers to this process as 'simulation'. Features of contemporary life as diverse as fashion, environmental design, opinion polls, emotions, lifestyles, and so on are all twisted and shaped by the saturation of imagery to such an extent that our relationship to everyday reality is fashioned as much by virtual reality as the physical one.

Simulation is not something that Baudrillard considers to be the opposite of truth; it is more that in Baudrillard's post-modern world there is no firm, pure reality left against which we can measure truth or falsity of any representations. For example, when we buy trainers, do we buy them for their practical function or because it possesses a brand image? Furthermore, how far has the function of these trainers become primarily the brand image rather than their function as a particular sort of footwear? Some of these themes are expanded upon by the American critic Fredrick Jameson (1991), who sees contemporary culture as constructing a reality that changes our focus from depth to the surface. He sees the commercialized space created by a consumer culture as causing a kind of detachment of the object from all meaningful connections (like the trainers in the example above, whose function has arguably become detached to a large extent from that of protective footwear) to the point where things are abstracted from their true origins and reused in meaningless and, often, trivial ways.

Such a consumerism creates a heightened awareness of appearance and style. The increasing invasion of images from media and advertising creates a dream world, a virtual reality to fantasize about, as commercials sell us images of ideal lifestyles that they attach to their products. Our culture has become so consumed by this perpetual imagery that we can now literally take off one identity and slip on another as we change our clothes, makeup, shoes, etc. We are seduced into becoming so concerned with our surface identity that we submit ourselves to long surgical procedures to change the shape and appearance of our bodies.

In the world of consumer capitalism everything becomes a potential object for exploitation and profit. Thus children become objects as advertising aimed specifically at children complements markets in toys, foods, educational equipment, fashion, sportswear, and so on. Indeed, I would argue that the dominance of the idea of mental 'health' (as opposed to say spiritual or social well-being) is a product, at least in part, of market economy consumer capitalism. Conceptualizing problems as 'health' individualizes suffering (thereby absolving and mystifying the role of social factors) and creates new markets (for example through the pharmaceutical industry). It is within the ideology that creates such fractured, superficial identities that we discover the same superficial labelling of identities on those decreed by modern institutions as 'mentally ill'.

Of course, none of these analyses is exhaustive and it would be a mistake to set them up as representing polarized opposites. Culture always exists in a fluid state and the cultural milieu is thus always subject to ongoing changes. Indeed, if anything, what the variety of current, analytical discourses on modern culture (as can be found, for example, in cultural studies) suggests is that if there is one thing on which there is general agreement, it is that the pace of cultural change has been accelerated, particularly with the advent of globalization over the past few decades. Therefore, the challenge, from a theoretical point of view is to keep theory on its toes so that it maintains flexibility that can adjust to changing circumstances and conditions that populations find themselves in, in order to remain relevant to informing practice.

Having mentioned this caveat, I am suggesting that one of the outcomes of current, cultural milieu is a move away from understanding based on depth and a connection with physical reality and everyday functionality, towards a culture where surface factors, such as image, appearance, the short-term and the immediate, has become more enduring and characteristic of current conditions. This impacts both on our view of children and their behaviour (which are thus more likely to be shaped by surface signs – such as ADHD, and a search for short-term, immediate solutions) as well as deeper effects on our consciousness (that includes, of course, children's consciousness).

Implications

What I have been undertaking in this chapter is an attempt at a different kind of diagnostic formulation. What I am referring to here is a more generic concept of diagnosis as being a word we use to 'characterize' our attempt to summarize our understanding of the broad question of 'what is going on here?'

I have set out in this chapter to explore the question; 'why has there been a dramatic increase in diagnosis of ADHD and prescription of stimulant medication for this in the past few decades in most Western countries?' In attempting to answer this question I proposed that three possible reasons needed further exploration: first that ADHD has always existed but it is only recently that we have begun to realize this and so diagnose and treat it; secondly that there has been a real increase in ADHD-type behaviours in children; and thirdly that there has not been a real increase in ADHD-type behaviours among young people but there has been a change in the way we think about, classify, and deal with children's behaviour (or of course a combination of all three). Having pointed out that there is little evidence to support the first possible reason (of a new discovery of a previously unrecognized medical disorder), I turned my attention to the other two possible reasons and presented some of the ideas and evidence from the critical literature that explores the latter two possibilities. Following this I discussed why these dynamics of medicalization are occurring in the way that they are, at this point in time. I have been careful throughout to avoid the mistake of going down the route of a simplistic 'grand narrative' that makes unsupportable claims about the 'truth' of the situation under study here. Thus, in answering the original question I have suggested a number of areas that may be useful to explore further as we try to put together a complex 'jigsaw puzzle' that answering this question is likely to require.

This has implications for both theory and practice. Research funds should be diverted from the (thus far) fruitless attempt at discovering the (possibly non-existent) biological underpinning of ADHD, and towards greater effort to further elucidate the relevance and role of contextual factors. This will require us to make greater efforts to develop more cross-disciplinary dialogue and collaboration. From the point of view of practice, moving theory out of a narrow reductionist neurodevelopment perspective will help move practice out of narrow assessments and excessive reliance on physical treatments (such as medication). As we develop more comprehensive contextualized accounts, so we open up the possibility for greater utilization of more diverse clinical approaches to the behaviour problems that children and their families present with that which we currently label as ADHD. From nutritional to lifestyle, from behavioural to cognitive, from family to systemic, dispensing with simplistic medicalized diagnoses in favour of more comprehensive and genuinely holistic diagnostic formulations allows us as practitioners to carry a bigger bag full of all sorts of instruments and tools (systems of knowledge) that we can use in a flexible manner depending on the unique circumstances of any particular child and their family.

References

ADDISS – Attention Deficit Disorder Information and Support Service (2005) available at <www.addiss.co.uk>, accessed 15 June 2005.
American Psychiatric Association (1952) *Diagnostic and Statistical Manual of Mental Disorders, First Edition (DSM-I)*. Washington, DC: APA.
American Psychiatric Association (1994) *Diagnostic and Statistical Manual of Mental Disorders, Fourth Edition (DSM-IV)*. Washington, DC: APA.
Aronowitz, S. and Giroux, H. (1991) *Post-modern Education: Politics, Culture and Social Criticism*. Minneapolis: University of Minnesota Press.
Bloom, F. E., Nelson, C. A. and Lazerson, A. (2001) *Brain, Mind and Behavior (Third Edition)*. New York: Worth Publications.
Boyd, E. A. and Bero, L. A. (2000) Assessing faculty financial relationships with industry, *Journal of the American Medical Association* 284, 2209–14.
Breggin, P.R. (1994) *The War against Children: How the Drugs Programmes and Theories of the Psychiatric Establishment are Threatening America's Children with a Medical 'Cure' for Violence*. New York: St Martin's Press.

Breggin, P. (1997) *The Heart of Being Helpful: Empathy and the Creation of a Healing Presence.* New York: Springer Publishing Company.

Breggin, P. (2002) *The Ritalin Fact Book.* Cambridge, MA: Perseus Publishing.

Brown, F. J. (2005) ADHD and the philosophy of science, in C. Newnes and N. Radcliffe (eds), *Making and Breaking Children's Lives.* Ross-on-Wye: PCCS Books.

Burman E. (2005) Childhood, neo-liberalism and the feminization of education, *Gender and Education* 17, 351–67.

Chess, S. and Thomas, A. (1996) *Temperament Theory and Practice.* New York: Brunner-Mazel.

Christakis, D., Zimmerman, F., DiGiuseppe, D. and McCarty, C. (2004) Early television exposure and subsequent attentional problems in children, *Pediatrics* 113, 708–13.

Cooper, P., Upton, G. and Smith, C. (1991) Ethnic minority and gender distribution among staff and pupils in facilities for pupils with emotional and behavioural difficulties in England and Wales, *British Journal of the Sociology of Education* 12, 77–94.

DeGrandpre, R. (1999) *Ritalin Nation.* New York: WW Norton.

Diller, L. H. (2002) ADHD: real or an American myth, presented at the 14th Annual Conference of the Associazone Cultural Pediatri. Rome: 10 October.

Double, D. (2002) The limits of psychiatry, *British Medical Journal* 324, 900–4.

Douglas, K. (1989) *Jean Baudrillard: From Marxism to Post-modernism and Beyond.* Cambridge: Polity Press.

Frosh, S., Phoenix, A. and Pattman, R. (2002) *Young Masculinities: Understanding Boys in Contemporary Society.* Basingstoke: Palgrave Macmillan.

Goodman, R. (1997) An over extended remit, *British Medical Journal* 314, 813–14.

Gordon, N., Burke, S., Akil, H., Watson, S. and Panksepp, J. (2003) Socially-induced brain 'fertilization': Play promotes brain derived neurotrophic factor transcription in the amygdale and dorsolateral frontal cortex in juvenile rats, *Neuroscience Letters* 341, 17–20.

Greenough, W. T., Black, J. E. and Wallace, C. S. (1987) Experience and brain development, *Child Development* 58, 539–59.

Hart, N., Grand, N. and Riley, K. (2006) Making the grade: The gender gap, ADHD, and the medicalization of boyhood, in D. Rosenfeld, and C. Faircloth (eds), *Medicalized Masculinities.* Philadelphia: Temple University Press.

Hartmann, T. (2001) Whose order is being disordered by ADHD? Available at <http://www.thomhartmann.com/whosorder.shtml>, accessed 13 July 2006.

Healy, J. M. (1998) *Failure to Connect.* New York: Simon and Schuster.

Hearn, K. (2004) Here kiddie, kiddie, available at <http://alternet.org/drugreporter/20594/>, accessed 15 June 2005.

Hey, V., Leonard, D., Daniels, H. and Smith, M. (1998) Boys' underachievement, special needs practices and questions of equity, in D. Epstein, J. Elwood, V. Hey and J. Maw (eds), *Failing Boys? Issues in Gender and Underachievement*. Buckingham: Open University Press.

Jackson, D. (1998) Breaking out of the binary trap: Boy's underachievement, schooling and gender relations, in D. Epstein, J. Elwood, V. Hey and J. Maw (eds), *Failing Boys? Issues of Gender and Underachievement*. Buckingham: Open University Press.

Jackson, G. (2005) Cybernetic children: How technologies change and constrain the developing mind, in C. Newnes and N. Radcliffe (eds), *Making and Breaking Children's Lives*. Ross-on-Wye: PCCS Books.

Jameson, F. (1991) *Postmodernism, or, the Cultural Logic of Late Capitalism*. Durham, NC: Duke University Press.

Kincheloe, J. (1998) The new childhood; Home alone as a way of life, in H. Jenkins (ed.), *Children's Culture Reader*. New York: New York University Press.

Kryger, N. (1998) Teachers understanding and emotions in relation to the creation of boys masculine identity, in Y. Katz and I. Menezes (eds), *Affective Education: A Comparative View*. London: Cassell.

Kuhn, T. S. (1970) *The Structure of Scientific Revolutions. Second Edition*. Chicago: The University of Chicago Press.

Law, I. (1997) Attention deficit disorder - therapy with a shoddily built construct, in C. Smith and D. Nyland (eds), *Narrative Therapies With Children and Adolescents*. New York: The Guilford Press.

LeFever, G. B., Dawson, K. V., and Morrow, A. D. (1999) The extent of drug therapy for attention deficit hyperactivity disorder among children in public schools, *American Journal of Public Health* 89, 1359–64.

Maitra, B. (2006) Culture and the mental health of children: The 'cutting edge' of expertise, in S. Timimi and B. Maitra (eds), *Contemporary Debates and New Directions in Child and Adolescent Mental Health*. London: Free Association Books.

Mazaide, M. (1989) Should adverse temperament matter to the clinician? An empirically based answer, in G. A. Khonstaum, V. E. Bates and M. K. Rothbart (eds), *Temperament in Childhood*. New York: Wiley.

Melander, H., Ahlqvist-Rastad, I., Meijer, G. and Beermann, B. (2003) Evidence b(i)ased medicine – selective reporting from studies sponsored by the pharmaceutical industry: Review of studies in new drug applications, *British Medical Journal* 326, 1171–3.

Offord, E. (1998) Wrestling with the whirlwind: An approach to the understanding of ADD/ADHD, *Journal of Child Psychotherapy* 24, 253–66.

Orlowski, J. P. and Wateska, L. (1992) The effects of pharmaceutical firm enticements on physician prescribing patterns: There's no such thing as a free lunch, *Chest* 102, 270–3.

Panksepp, J. (1998a) A critical analysis of ADHD, psychostimulants and intolerance of childhood playfulness: A tragedy in the making? *Current Directions in Psychological Sciences* 7, 91–7.

Panksepp, J (1998b) The quest for long term health and happiness: To play or not to play that is the question, *Psychological Inquiry* 9, 56–65.

Panksepp, J., Burgdorf, J., Turner, C. and Gordon, N. (2003) Modeling ADHD-type arousal with unilateral frontal cortex damage in rats and beneficial effects of play therapy, *Brain and Cognition* 52, 97–105.

Papolos, D. and Papolos, J. (1999) *The Bipolar Child.* New York: Broadway Books.

Peet, M. (2004) International variations in the outcome of schizophrenia and the prevalence of depression in relation to national dietary practices: an ecological analysis, *British Journal of Psychiatry* 184, 404–8.

Pollack, W. (1998) *Real Boys: Rescuing Our Sons from the Myths of Boyhood.* New York: Henry Holt.

Public Citizen (2002) *America's Other Drug Problem: A Briefing Book on the Prescription Drug Debate.* Available at <www.citzen.org/rxfacts>.

Ravenel, D. B. (2002) A new behavioral approach for ADD/ADHD and behavioral management without medication, *Ethical Human Sciences and Services* 4, 93–106.

Rutter, M. and Smith, D. (1995) *Psychosocial Disorders in the Young: Time Trends and their Causes.* Chichester: John Wiley and Sons.

Safer, D.J. (2002) Design and reporting modifications in industry sponsored comparative psychopharmacology trials, *Journal of Nervous and Mental Disease* 190, 583–92.

Sagarin, B. J., Cialdini, R. B., Rice, W. E. and Serna, S. B. (2002) Dispelling the illusion of invulnerability: The motivations and mechanisms of resistance to persuasion, *Journal of Personal and Social Psychology* 83, 526–41.

Sandler, J. (2005) *Values and Psychiatric Diagnosis.* New York: Oxford University Press.

Sax, S. (2000) Living through better chemistry? *The World and I* 15, 287–99.

Stiefel, I. (1997) Can disturbance in attachment contribute to attention deficit hyperactivity disorder? A case discussion, *Clinical Child Psychology and Psychiatry* 2, 45–64.

Thomas, A. and Chess, S. (1977) *Temperament and Development.* New York: Brunner-Mazel.

Timimi, S. (2002) *Pathological Child Psychiatry and the Medicalization of Childhood.* London: Routledge-Brunner.

Timimi, S. (2005) *Naughty Boys: Anti-Social Behaviour, ADHD and the Role of Culture.* Basingstoke: Palgrave Macmillan.

Timimi, S. (2006) The politics of attention deficit hyperactivity disorder, in S. Timimi and B. Maitra (eds), *Critical Voices in Child and Adolescent Mental.* London: Free Association Books.

Valenstein, E. S. (1998) *Blaming the Brain.* New York: The Free Press.

Wazana, A. (2000) Physicians and the pharmaceutical industry. Is a gift ever just a gift? *Journal of the American Medical Association* 283, 373–80.

Whitfield, C. (2006) Childhood trauma as a cause of ADHD, aggression, violence and ant-social behaviour, in S. Timimi and B. Maitra (eds), *Critical Voices in Child and Adolescent Mental*. London: Free Association Books.

Zuckerman, M. (1975) Dr. Spock: The Confidence Man, in C. Rosenberg (ed.), *The Family in History*. Philadelphia: University of Pennsylvania Press.

Chapter 5

Clinical Psychology and Attention Deficit Hyperactivity Disorder

Craig Newnes

Clinical psychology makes bold claims to be a scientist practitioner profession. It finds itself in the invidious position of also claiming expertise in human relationships whilst psychologists are not being noticeably better at human relationships than members of other professions. We are not alone in this paradox: builders and plumbers are notorious for rarely working on their own homes, general practitioners are not particularly healthy and many child experts have no children. The particular combination of wanting to appear as scientists and experts in people makes the profession vulnerable to criticism concerning both aspirations. British applied psychology's lead professional body, the Division of Clinical Psychology of the British Psychological Society, has embraced much of the rhetoric typical of professions (the need to 'protect the public', for 'accountability', etc.). In doing so, the Division has failed to examine scientifically whether this rhetoric translates into reality.

In the UK, the profession of clinical psychology has become adept at jumping on bandwagons. The profession assumes ownership of a variety of practices as they become fashionable and develop potential for paying our salaries. From psychometric assessment and psychotherapy to cognitive therapy and consultancy the profession has embraced different practices while claiming a scientific basis for its position of power. The enthusiasm with which the profession approaches powers under the new proposed Mental Health Act and a potential role in the Attention Deficit Hyperactivity Disorder (ADHD) explosion give cause for concern that, as a scientific discipline, clinical psychology has gone off the rails. As one more branch of the 'psy-complex' (Nicolas Rose's term for the group of professional vested interests in the psychology and psychiatry industries), however, its financial future is assured.

Before 1990 there were barely 5000 children in the UK diagnosed with ADHD. There are now over 200,000 (Wright, 2003). Ritalin™, a potentially brain-disabling drug, remains the commonest treatment. There are increasing claims that children who are difficult to manage have a neuro-developmental disorder. The phrase 'neuro-developmental disorder' is one aspect of a lexicon designed simultaneously to obscure meaning and give power to 'those that know' – in this case so-called child experts. In fact we have no idea how any given individual is meant to develop neurologically, nor can we know that a person is neurologically disordered from behavioural observation. Yet ADHD is solely diagnosed through such observation (of perfectly normal conduct – see, for example, Timimi and Radcliffe, 2005) and clinical psychologists then *infer* a neurological problem. This is perfectly in step with child psychiatrists who then prescribe drugs such as Ritalin™ in order to suppress the conduct. There are numerous examples of such practice amongst clinical psychologists.

Medicalizing conduct

Authoritative assertions abound from clinical psychologists. These are, of course, merely part of the rhetoric of professions which allows statements to appear true, when they can only ever be opinion. Murray, McKenzie, Brackenridge and Glen (2006), for example, state, 'There is broad support for the current medical definition of ADHD, and its sub-types among the general medical community.' They cite Goldman *et al.* (1998) and Taylor *et al.* (1996) in support of their statement. But what is meant by 'broad support'? Worse, in what sense is work cited from 1998 and 1996 current? Let us assume that some medical and related professions support a medical definition. It is tempting to conclude, 'They would, wouldn't they?' The authors continue, 'ADHD can be debilitating, impacting negatively on educational achievement, social behaviour, and family life.' There is no acknowledgement of the circularity of their position – we diagnose ADHD by observing behaviour and then claim that behaviour is *caused* by ADHD. This is an example of a category error common in mainstream psychiatry. A condition – depression, schizophrenia, Asperger's syndrome – is *inferred* from someone's conduct and then that same conduct is seen as arising from the inferred condition. It is like saying that chairs and tables (specific examples of a category) are furniture (the category) but also, somehow, *caused* by furniture. For categories such as ADHD, depression, and so on, any meaning of the observable conduct is obscured by a nonsensical confusion of category and cause. Such statements, by repetition, soon become the mainstay of professional writings and it can be difficult to enter the arena without participating in the rhetoric – an argument frequently used by authors to justify their use of diagnostic terminology. Such terminology can be promoted as a kind of 'short-hand', as if other professionals will immediately know what is meant. But if an expression is, by definition, meaningless, it will mean only what the reader thinks it does. Your 'depression' is not mine, one peron's understanding of 'ADHD' is rarely another's. If the reader or recipient of the diagnosis is unfamiliar with such terminology, then such medicalized statements boil down to: 'trust me, I'm a professional'.

Murray *et al.*'s paper is ostensibly about General Practitioners' knowledge of ADHD. The results of their survey of 40 GPs bear brief examination. Taking it as read that ADHD is a sensible way of labelling individuals, they asked GPs about diagnostic features, causes, effective treatment and the range of professionals to be involved. Only nine GPs were aware of all three diagnostic criteria (attention deficits, hyperactivity and impulsivity). Such knowledge tended to be voiced by more recently qualified practitioners. Murray and his colleagues reasonably suggest that such GPs have been more recently exposed to the growing literature on ADHD. Like any advertising campaign, such exposure is likely to lead to more so-called knowledge. Critically, the more the construct ADHD is used in medical literature, the more GPs are likely to accept it as an entity; the value of simple repetition has not been lost on those with a vested interest in promoting ADHD.

Unsurprisingly, 16 respondents identified genetic/biological origins of diagnosed conduct. Over half the GPs said they did not know the cause. Again, the proliferation of studies and journal articles on the theme of ADHD creates a context in which it is very difficult for GPs to question core constructs in their work – diagnosis being key. The older GPs are likely to have seen much of this before – in relation to so-called breakthroughs for a host of real (cancer, cystic fibrosis) and imagined (depression, schizophrenia) conditions. They may be used to the rhetoric and less swayed by the promotion of newer disorders, only to have their wisdom dismissed as a need for 'education'. Even the way the researchers frame the questions gives little room for manouevre on the part of their respondents. They ask about the cause of ADHD. They don't suggest that GPs might like to consider whether ADHD as a construct has validity.

Clinical Psychology Forum (CPF) is not typical of the literature scientist practitioners are exposed to. As a newsletter it publishes a high percentage of submissions. These are unconstrained by the conventions demanded of submissions to journals such as the *British Journal of Clinical Psychology*. As such, CPF can reveal a great deal more about the profession in the UK than other British journals. Authors can produce polemical, political and reflective pieces in addition to local studies. These can reflect the dominant discourse of scientism (where no statement can be made without recourse to a numbing range of studies) or can be reports of work that attempts to go against the mainstream. Such work tends to draw on theories and practice outside the dominant medical paradigm, notably social science, philosophy and political action. Papers of this type remain in the minority in *Clinical Psychology Forum*. Nonetheless, some examples are outlined below to show that there remain islands of practice in clinical psychology that continue to challenge the dominant discourse around ADHD.

Beyond the mainstream

The willingness to report work that goes beyond the parameters of accepted practice in the context of a medicalized National Health Service should not be undervalued. Clinical psychologists and other professionals find themselves ignored and insulted by colleagues on a regular basis for questioning virtually any practice (diagnosis, the use of medication and other physical interventions) that conforms to Foucault's conception of 'the Gaze'.

The clearest exposition of practice beyond mainstream psychological work with children is to be found in a special issue of *Clinical Psychology* edited by Nick Radcliffe, Scott Sinclair and myself (2004). This special issue morphed into the book *Making and Breaking Children's Lives* (Newnes and Racliffe, 2005). It includes papers examining ADHD as a construct (e.g. Brown, 2004; Spellman, 2004), different ideas about the kind of lives that might lead to children receiving the diagnosis (Vetere, 2004) and attempts to influence family life that do not frame conduct in diagnostic terms. Cobner *et al.* (2004) describes a clinical psychology service which deliberately maintains separation from the psychiatric arm of the Gwent Child and Adolescent Mental Health Service (CAMHS). Cobner and her colleagues offer telephone consultation to potential referrers which clarifies the service philosophy – 'the creation of alternative narratives'. Referrers preferring a diagnostic frame can be redirected to psychiatrists. Conversations with families then follow a three-stage model – in Cobner's terms 'deconstructing ADHD, exploring alternative narratives and thinking about the usefulness of diagnosis'. This last is considered from psychological (the usefulness of diagnosis in reducing uncertainty) and practical (the possibility that a diagnosis will lead to much-needed financial benefit via Disability Living Allowance) perspectives. Myatt, Rostill and Wheeldon (2004) use the concept of functionality (so-called problem behaviour maintains the status quo in any system) to re-direct parents' attention away from the conduct labelled as ADHD: 'If we were not talking about John's ADHD, what would we be talking about instead?' (p.36) Myatt and her colleagues remind us the 'For professionals, an ADHD description may render them powerless if they are non-prescribing' (p. 36). Their paper calls professionals to move beyond diagnosis and maintain a position of curiosity shared with the parents. In the same special issue, Woodhouse (2004) describes the work of the Cactus Clinic, founded by Steve Baldwin and committed to offering alternatives to medication for families with an ADHD diagnosis. In its assessment of a referred family the clinic considers a wide range of possibilities that might account for conduct deemed problematic. These include nutritional deficiency, metal intoxication, hormonal and metabolic disorders and genuine neurolgical conditions. Considerable information is offered concerning the adverse effects of drugs like Ritalin™ before children start on a drug withdrawal programme. This is followed by a caregivers' programme and a nutritional protocol. The clinic recognizes the modernist need for 'evidence' and researches and revises all its methods in a continuous programme. Outcomes are consistently excellent.

Southall (2006) begins her paper with: 'Children do not develop in a vacuum' (p. 33). Her critique of the diagnostic tendency focuses on ADHD and challenges clinical psychologists to rediscover environment and context as key to understanding any conduct. Ayling (2006) goes further and invokes the UN Convention on the Rights of the Child 1989 to protect the right of young people to independently access services when they feel unsafe in the family system in which they have become identified as 'the problem child'. It would be interesting to see the same Convention used to challenge the use of the ADHD diagnosis.

Analysing micro-neighbourhood referral patterns

Working in Birmingham, Carl Harris (2005) takes context, particularly physical context, very seriously indeed. Alongside specialist community development workers and a small group of residents, he has drawn up a new map of the locality. This map groups sections of local housing estates into 'micro-neighbourhoods'. Fifty-seven micro-neighbourhoods of varying shapes and sizes were constructed. Some are long and narrow, stretching along a road; others are compact, incorporating a number of defined 'closes' or 'groves'; others group together rows of high- and low-rise blocks of flats. On average there are around 200 people in each micro-neighbourhood.

Five (out of the 57) micro-neighbourhoods accounted for 29, or half, of referrals to a clinical psychologist. Two micro-neighbourhoods accounted for over a quarter of the referrals over an 18-month period.

These results fitted with information gathered from a health visitor who had been working in this area for 10 years. She was asked to put crosses on a map to indicate which parts of the patch she felt were most in need of support. She put five crosses on the map of the whole area, two of which were in the two already identified micro-neighbourhoods.

Bernardo Jiminez, Professor of Community Psychology from Mexico, visited the project and was shown the data. He was then taken on a drive around the estates and shown the houses in question. He provided a commentary on the houses in the context of their landscape and the houses' relationship to each other in their respective formations.

In the most modern estate, only separated from the area of high referral by a single-carriageway road, houses are grouped in horseshoe clusters frequently facing in towards a central (sometimes green) area. They appear to have a shared identity.

In the areas with the high referral rate the houses are arranged in a Radburn formation – in straight rows with the front doors of one row facing the back gardens of the next row or 'grove'. Inside, bedrooms, garages and front door are all at street level, while the living rooms and kitchen are on the first floor. Engels would have been unsurprised at this treatment of the working classes 150 years after his study of Manchester in post-industrial Britain.

The micro-neighbourhood analysis has an effect on the way we might understand the pattern of referrals to the community psychologist. The information was taken to a Neighbourhood Management meeting within the New Deal for Communities (NDC) organization. This team is a group of theme coordinators, each having a strategic responsibility for a different part of the programme – health, housing, education, employment, etc. At the meeting the data were presented and a discussion followed concerning:

- the hard to let nature of the housing,
- the consequent desperation of those who were likely to accept it,
- the difficult histories which some people may bring to the location,
- the reputation attached to the location,
- failure of services to deliver to those living there,
- the unorthodox, 'difficult' layout of the houses themselves,
- the environment surrounding the houses (which is an expanse of grass with no 'cues', e.g. paths or benches, as to how it should be used),
- the 'unsupervised' or 'un-overlooked' nature of a significant section of the rows of Radburn houses (which may then become a locus of behaviour that is difficult to manage),
- the absence of play facilities for young people,
- the 'barrack-like' nature of the housing layout which may not promote the development of a sense of community,
- the low levels of 'resources' of those living there, which will make it unlikely that they will be in a position to provide support to each other.

Implications for practice

Given the above, it must be asked whether clinical psychologists can side with children and families.

I have focused on Harris's work because it illustrates a position rarely taken by professional psychologists – that of a genuinely curious outsider who acknowledges that families and other local people, both professionals and neighbours, are likely to know what contributes to distress in their communities. The position places us, simultaneously, as part of 'the Gaze' and critical of it. As public employees such a position is likely to be both tenuous and short-lived. If psychologists can provide additional impetus for creating more healthful environments, then that is good enough. Harris, before qualifying as a clinical psychologist, studied the wider social sciences and philosophy. That background plus parenthood should, perhaps, be obligatory for those clinical psychologists who work in child services.

My analysis is likely to be seen as unbalanced. This is intentional. The dominant psychological and pseudo-medical discourse requires a balancing rather than balanced response. It would appear that many clinical psychologists, both in the Academy and clinical practice, tend towards a conservative maintenance of the status quo (crucially in the maintenance of their own status as experts) in relation to diagnosis of conduct they, like many psychiatrists, see as 'conditions' or 'syndromes'. Their vested interest as paid professionals makes it extremely difficult to challenge this dominant discourse relating to childhood (indeed, to living) seriously. There are, however, examples of practice which step beyond the confines of diagnosis and dustbin terms like 'disorder'. This practice draws on a rich history, both philosophical and sociological, which emphasizes the need for professional classes to take a humble and collaborative stance alongside that majority of citizens oppressed by a rich, frequently professional minority. Clinical psychologists can, and do, use their position of power and authority to draw attention to what millions already know – that society is organized to keep certain people in charge. Eschewing diagnosis and the possibility of 'treatment' for ordinary behaviour are but two small changes that clinical psychologists might make in their practice. They are likely to find allies in such an endeavour both within and beyond the usual confines of professional groups. It might be too much to ask that they have families of their own before they invade and observe the lives of others less privileged than themselves.

References

Ayling, R. (2006) Young people's independent access to child and adolescent mental health services, *Clinical Psychology Forum* 157, 8–11.

Brown, F. (2004) Scientific narratives and ADHD, *Clinical Psychology* 40, 17–20.

Cobner, R. (2004) Which road to understanding and change? *Clinical Psychology* 40, 30–3.

Goldman, L. S., Genel, M., Besman, R. J., and Slanetz, P. J. (1998) Diagnosis and treatment of attention deficit/hyperactivity disorder in children and adolescents, *Journal of American Medical Association* 279, 1100–7.

Harris, C. (2005) The Family Well-being Project: Providing psychology services for children and families in a community regeneration context, in C. Newnes and N. Radcliffe (eds), *Making and Breaking Children's Lives*. Ross on Wye: PCCS Books.

Murray, G. C., McKenzie, K., Brackenbridge, R., and Glen, S. (2006) General practitioner knowledge about psychological approaches to ADHD, *Clinical Psychology Forum* 158, 13–16.

Myatt, H., Rostill, H., and Wheeldon, S. (2004) Alternatives to Ritalin for looked after children: A culture shift, *Clinical Psychology* 40, 34–7.

Newnes, C., and Radcliffe, N. (eds), (2005) *Making and Breaking Children's Lives*. Ross on Wye: PCCS Books.

Radcliffe, N., Sinclair, S., and Newnes, C. (2004) *Clinical Psychology Forum* 40, Special issue: Children and ADHD: Sharing untold stories.

Southall, A. (2006) What have we learned from children? Or: Why we need a revolution in mental health, *Clinical Psychology Forum* 164, 33–6.

Spellman, D. (2004) Things to do in Denver when you're an ADHD 'denier', *Clinical Psychology* 40, 27–9.

Taylor, E., Chadwick, O., Hepinstall, E., and Danckaerts, M. (1996) Hyperactivity and conduct disorders as risk factors for adolescent development, *Journal of the American Academy of Academic Child and Adolescent Psychiatr*, 35, 1213–26.

Timimi, S., and Radcliffe, N. (2005) The rise and rise of ADHD, in C. Newnes and N. Radcliffe (eds), *Making and Breaking Children's Lives*. Ross on Wye: PCCS Books.

Vetere, A. (2004) (Why) Can't you sit still? The effects of domestic violence on children, *Clinical Psychology* 40, 14–16.

Woodhouse, D. (2004) The Cactus Clinic: An integrative approach to the treatment of ADHD, *Clinical Psychology* 40, 45–8.

Wright, O. (2003) Ritalin use and abuse fears, *The Times*, 28 July, p.3.

Chapter 6
ADHD in Australia: The Emergence of Globalization

Brian Kean

This chapter documents a brief history of the development of the ADHD diagnosis in the United States, the adoption of the ADHD diagnosis in Australia and the polarized views there over the condition, and reflects on the associated medical, social and educational discourses in the period. The emergence of use of the ADHD diagnosis in Australia illustrates broader forces structuring the globalization of the diagnosis. Critical issues for societies relating to its use, including children's rights and the risks associated with the rapid adoption of the use of drugs for the modification of child behaviour, are noted.

An abbreviated history of ADHD in the United States

Since the late 1960s in the United States millions of parents have been told that their children suffer from a condition known as Attention Deficit Hyperactivity Disorder (ADHD) or the antecedent labels for the condition, Attention Deficit Disorder (ADD) and the Hyperkinetic Reaction of Childhood. Parents are generally informed that ADHD is a proven neurological disorder (Green and Chee, 1994a, 1994b). The principal recommendation for treatment is management by pharmaceutical intervention (Barkley, 1990, 1998a; Diller, 1998, 2000; Edwards and Barkley, 1997; National Health and Medical Research Council [NH and MRC], 1997). The medical method of intervention for the condition was, and in general still is, the use of the amphetamine class of drugs. In the majority of cases, this involves using psychostimulant medications (amphetamine [dexamphetamine] or amphetamine-like drugs [methylphenidate hydrochloride]) for treatment (Barkley, 1990, 1998a; Diller, 1998; Edwards and Barkley, 1997; NH and MRC, 1997). Other types of psychiatric drugs are used as alternatives if the psychostimulant drugs prove ineffective in altering the child's behavioural responses (Breggin, 2001; Green and Chee, 1994a; NH and MRC, 1997).

In 1967 the use of drugs for behaviour modification was endorsed in an editorial in the *Journal of the American Medical Association* (1967) entitled 'Stimulant drugs and learning disorders in children' (see United States House of Representatives, 1970, 29 September). The behaviours identified as needing treatment were merged under the label of the hyperkinetic reaction of childhood. The hyperkinetic reaction of childhood category replaced the diagnosis of minimal brain dysfunction (MBD) that previously had been used to describe a broad range of behaviour and learning disorders (Barkley, 1990, 1998a; Schrag and Divoky, 1975). The distinction between the hyperkinetic reaction to childhood and the MBD category was the removal of the need to establish specific evidence of neurological damage. The requirement of evidence of neurological damage to the child was replaced by observations of the child's behaviour, generally reported to the medical practitioners by parents or teachers (Barkley, 1990, 1998a). The American Medical Association's definition of hyperactivity was linked with the claimed utility of amphetamine-type drugs to reduce the levels of motor activity and improve behaviour and classroom performance (United States House of Representatives, 1970, 29 September).

The re-conceptualization of the hyperkinetic reaction of childhood to ADD occurred with the release of the *Diagnostic and Statistical Manual of Mental Disorders* (DSM-III) in 1980, followed by renaming the condition ADHD in the DSM-IIIR in 1987, with further revision in the diagnostic criteria of the DSM-IV in 1994 and text revision by the American Psychiatric Association (APA) in the DSM-IV-TR in 2000 (APA, 1980, 1987, 1994, 2000). With each revision there has been an increase in prevalence level for the diagnosis (Goldman *et al.*, 1998). Reported prevalence levels vary between 1.7 per cent and 18.9 per cent of the child population depending on country, geographical location and the version of the DSM used (Goldman *et al.*, 1998).

During the 20-year period from 1970 to 1990, the number of children diagnosed with the condition in the United States doubled around every seven years (Divoky, 1989). Even though the use of amphetamine-type drugs had been accepted in the United States for over 20 years, the 1990s is characterized by significant increases in use of psychostimulant drugs for behaviour modification.

During the 1990s the United States continued as the main producer of methylphenidate consuming approximately 90 per cent of global consumption. Consumption increased by nearly 30 per cent in the first few years of 1990s followed by a plateau in growth of methylphenidate consumption in the middle of the decade. Towards the end of the 1990s consumption continued to climb with a 15 per cent increase from 1998 to 1999. Corresponding with the increase in consumption of methylphenidate was a rise in the use of amphetamine for the treatment of ADHD surging 100 per cent from 1997 to 1998, with a similar increase from 1998 to 1999. By 1998 amphetamine for the treatment of ADHD rose to one third of methylphenidate use in the United States. In 1999 amphetamine use exceeded the consumption of methylphenidate (International Narcotics Control Board [INCB], 2000).

For more than 30 years the diagnosis and treatment with amphetamine and other drugs of ADHD was a phenomenon almost unique to the United States and to a lesser degree, Canada (Diller, 1998). Before 1990, conflicting viewpoints in the medical profession resulted in dramatic differences between the level of use of drugs for treatment of ADHD in the United States and usage in the rest of the world (Barkley, 1990, 1998a). The redefinitions of the condition, as ADD (APA, 1980) and ADHD (APA, 1987), were not readily accepted by the international medical profession (Barkley, 1990, 1998a). In contrast to other scientific and medical advances, the recognition of the condition ADHD was only relatively recently adopted by any other countries. It was not until the last years of the 1980s that the international medical viewpoint on the condition changed and other countries began to use the APA's ADHD diagnosis (Barkley, 1990, 1998a; Rutter *et al.*, 1988).

Psychostimulant use in Australia

Australia was the first country to replicate the ADHD treatment model (INCB, 1995). During the 1990s there was a significant increase in the percentage of children who were diagnosed with the condition. Throughout the period the escalation in the use of the diagnosis in Australia led to several geographical areas reaching prevalence rates similar to the United States (Jacobs, 2002; Berbatis *et al.*, 2002).

Australia changed from almost nil use of psychostimulant drugs for the treatment of ADHD at the beginning of the 1990s to an overall treatment incidence of 1.8 per cent of 6–17 year olds by 1998

(Sawyer *et al.*, 2002). Prevalence data suggests that 7.5 per cent of Australian children aged 6–17 years have ADHD (Hutchins *et al.*, 2003). Because the treatment levels across Australia are significantly lower than treatment levels in the United States, arguments from prominent medical advocates of the ADHD diagnosis suggest that Australian children are not receiving adequate levels of drug treatment (Merson, 2002).

The variance between Australian states and across geographical areas within states is significant. Western Australia has the highest incidence of ADHD and drug treatment. The remaining states have similar levels to New South Wales, except for Victoria where incidence and drug treatments are approximately 20 per cent lower (Berbatis *et al.*, 2002).

Western Australia (WA) has the highest consumption of psychostimulants and in 2000 exceeded the United States in terms of the defined daily dose for statistical purposes (S-DDD) per 1000 inhabitants (Berbatis *et al.*, 2002). Berbatis and colleagues found that an estimated 18,000 or 4.2 per cent to 4.5 per cent of WA's population aged 4–17 years received psychostimulants for the treatment of ADHD in 2000. The rate of increase from 1984 to 2000 was 11 per cent per year.

In New South Wales (NSW) Berbatis and associates (2002) found a 1 per cent use in members of the population less than 18 years of age. However further analysis of the data used by Berbartis and associates suggested that the geographical area and age of the children created significant variance in the incidence of stimulant treatment. Salmelainen (2002) found that the rate of stimulant treatment for children between 7 and 11 years old in the NSW Hunter area in 2000 totalled over 30 per 1000 of children or 3 per cent of the population in that age group. With males in the 7–11 age range in the Hunter area the treatment rate was closer to 5 per cent of the cohort. In another six geographical areas of NSW the 7–11-year-old age treatment rate of males exceeded 3 per cent, and in another five geographical areas male treatment rates were approaching 3 per cent. There is wide variability in NSW for prescription levels based on geographical locations and age of the child (Salmelainen, 2002).

Data related to the use of other medications for treatment of ADHD that potentially include clonidine, antidepressants, neuroleptics and selective serotonin reuptake inhibiters (SSRIs) which can be prescribed by general practitioners in Australia as alternatives to psychostimulants are not included in estimates of overall medication intervention.

As noted in the study by Salmelainen (2002, p. 49) these medications 'are not formally monitored and are not restricted to specialist prescribing', and thus using psychostimulant data as a key indicator of the incidence of treatment of ADHD in children considerably underrates the actual number of children diagnosed with ADHD and treated with all classes of medication.

In congruence with patterns of prescribing in the United States, there is an increasing emphasis placed upon the use of the drugs in children under the age of 6 (Eccleston, 2006). The NSW data for 2000 indicated that for children under the age of 4, 0.2 children per 1000 population were already being treated. By 2004 the number had doubled with 0.4 children per 1000 population. In the 4-year-old age group the rate was 1.7 per 1000 population in NSW and 3.2 per 1000 population in WA. For the 5–6-year-old age group treatment rates were even higher, with 6.7 per 1000 population with a male/female ratio of 3.8:1 in NSW and 6.9 per 1000 population with a male/female ratio of 4.5:1 in WA. (Department of Health, 2005).

In the 1990s, dexamphetamine was the drug of choice for the treatment of ADHD in Australia due to its subsidy by the pharmaceutical benefits scheme (PBS). It was significantly cheaper than methylphenidate (National Health and Medical Research Council [NH and MRC], 1997). Since the inclusion of methylphenidate in the PBS, Australia's use of methylphenidate has almost equalled dexamphetamine (Commonwealth of Australia, 2006). In 2003, dexamphetamine was prescribed at 1.76 defined daily doses for statistical purposes (S-DDD) per 1000 inhabitants and methylphenidate at 1.34 S-DDD per 1000 inhabitants (INCB, 2004).

Over the past 16 years in Australia there has been an uptake of the ADHD diagnosis and significant increase in the use of psychostimulant drugs for treatment. There is significant variation between and within states in the level of use of dexamphetamine and methylphenidate. Reflecting trends in the United States there is a gender differential in the diagnosis with the male to female ratio being approximately 4:1. The actual treatment levels of ADHD with all drugs cannot be approximated as many other medications used in the treatment of ADHD are not officially documented. This would suggest that predicted incidence levels based upon using psychostimulant drugs as a guide underestimate the actual figures for the ADHD diagnosis and drug treatments. Analysis of the factors related to the uptake of the ADHD diagnosis in Australia will be reviewed after an overview of the global situation.

The globalization of ADHD

By the middle of the 1990s, other countries, including New Zealand, the United Kingdom and Germany, were adopting the ADHD diagnosis (INCB, 1996). In the 10-year period from 1990 to 2000, ADHD moved rapidly towards global acceptance. Berbatis, Sunderland and Bulsara (2002, p. 539) in analysing the licit, that is medically prescribed, consumption of psychostimulants in 10 countries in the period 1994 to 2000 found:

> For the 10 countries from 1994 to 2000, total psychostimulant consumption increased by an average of 12 per cent per year, with the highest increase from 1998 to 2000. Australia and New Zealand ranked third in total psychostimulant use after the United States and Canada. Australia consumed significantly more than the United Kingdom, Sweden, Spain, the Netherlands, France or Denmark.

As noted, in the 1990s, as they accept the United States' model of treatment other economically advanced countries have experienced similar trends to those in Australia. The increasing use of the ADHD diagnosis in other countries indicates that they will likely reach levels of amphetamine and amphetamine-like drug consumption comparable to those of the United States in the near future (INCB, 2000).

In the first few years of the twenty-first century the increased use of methylphenidate and amphetamine mainly for the treatment of ADHD continued and Australia's position as the third highest consumer of psychostimulant drugs changed to fifth as the United Kingdom and Iceland increased their use of methylphenidate (INCB, 2004). Table 6.1 details the combined use of amphetamine and methylphenidate mainly for the medical treatment of ADHD. Worldwide the trend is for increased use of both substances with dramatic variation between countries in the defined daily doses for statistical purposes per 1000 inhabitants per day.

In interpretation of the data the INCB (2004) noted that the amphetamines are mainly used for the treatment of ADHD and narcolepsy and the substantial increases can be attributed to the combined use of amphetamine and dexamphetamine in the United States for treatment of ADHD since 1988 (INCB, 2004). In the United States the change in the use of amphetamine and dexamphetamine is reflected in the INCB (2004) data indicating that in 1996 around 20 kg were needed for medical use; by 2003, 3.5 tonnes were manufactured for use mainly in the United States market.

Table 6.1 Consumption of psychostimulant drugs (amphetamine, dexamphetamine and methylphenidate) in defined daily doses for statistical purposes (S-DDD) for medical purposes per 1000 inhabitants per day

Country	1999	2001	2003
United States	9.25	9.37	11.44
Iceland	1.21	3.13	5.98
Canada	3.18	0.74	5.04
United Kingdom	0.75	1.15	3.97
Australia	2.28	2.43	3.1
Norway	0.45	0.85	2.26
Switzerland*	0.76	2.82	2.23
New Zealand	1.38	1.43	1.49
Netherlands*	0.91	1.11	1.36
Belgium	0.61	0.59	1.14
Germany*	0.27	0.67	0.99
Spain*	0.13	0.15	0.78
Sweden	0.2	0.36	0.57
Chile	0.5	0.52	0.53
Denmark*	0.14	0.22	0.4
Ireland*	0.26	0.06	0.36
Finland*	0.14	0.07	0.29
Japan*	0.14	0.19	0.29
Israel*	0.46	0.72	0.28
South Africa*	0.08	0.16	0.27
Total	23.3	27.14	43.47

Note: *Countries not listed by INCB (2004) as using amphetamine for medical use – data represents S-DDD for methylphenidate only.
Source: Data collated from INCB (2004), Comments on the Reported Statistics on Psychotropic Substances.

The worldwide use of methylphenidate over the past 15 years has also increased significantly. In 1990, 3 tonnes were produced rising to 8.5 tonnes in 1994 (INCB, 2005). The United States has also been the main producer of methylphenidate increasing production from 1.8 tonnes in 1990 to 21 tonnes in 2002, dropping moderately to 19 tonnes in 2003, mainly as a result of the increased use of amphetamine and dexamphetamine for the treatment of ADHD (INCB, 2004). The data clearly demonstrate significant increases in the use of psychostimulants for the treatment of ADHD and a trend towards globalization of the diagnosis.

Promotion of ADHD in the United States

Breggin (2001) defined the conglomerate effect of the interaction between drug companies, researchers, government agencies and medical organizations as the *psychopharmaceutical complex*. In this context, pharmaceutical company funding has organized a partnership with organized psychiatry where 'truth is the loser, along with the public and patients' (Breggin, 2001, p. 221). According to Breggin (2001) the six main elements of the *psychopharmaceutical complex* in the United States are:

- the pharmaceutical companies;
- the American Psychiatric Association (APA) and associated professional bodies;
- the Food and Drug Administration (FDA);
- the National Institute of Mental Health (NIMH);
- other government departments particularly the Department of Education; and
- community-based lobby groups given financial assistance from pharmaceutical grants for educational programmes.

Breggin (1993, 1997, 1998, 2001) and Breggin and Breggin (1994) have documented the role of community-based lobby groups and their links with pharmaceutical companies in various texts. In the United States, parental and community lobby groups were noted by Breggin to have various forms of financial links with pharmaceutical companies. In relation to ADHD, Breggin (1998, 2001) detailed the relationship between the United States Department of Education and Children and Adults with ADD (CHADD) that contributed to the distribution of information to schools, teachers and the wider community promoting a biopsychiatric view of child behaviour under the label of Attention Deficit Hyperactivity Disorder.

   Breggin (2001) suggested that associated with the increase use of the ADHD diagnosis there has been a form of conspiracy and collusion between the drug companies and the other elements of the *psychopharmaceutical complex* resulting in vastly increased pharmaceutical company profits. According to Breggin (2001) the *psychopharmaceutical complex* is fuelled by the power and money of the drug companies driving their own agenda – increasing demand and hence market share.

Through funding research, assisting ADHD parental lobby organizations, and also using their influence to create markets through the education system, the pharmaceutical companies have increased drug sales. Breggin's analysis has detailed the complexity of similar patterns of interactions between the FDA, NIMH, psychiatric experts and pharmaceutical companies in relation to a broad range of psychiatric drugs.

Breggin's analysis of the *psychopharmaceutical complex* is construed as a conspiracy theory by critics. Barkley (1998b), in a review entitled *ADHD, Ritalin, and Conspiracies: Talking Back to Peter Breggin*, refuted Breggin's analysis:

> Breggin claims that all are conspiring to 'drug' America's school children for the management of their ADHD, among other behavior problems. Left unaddressed by the author is precisely how such a complex conspiracy could ever be organised and kept secret, if it actually existed. No persuasive evidence of such a conspiracy is ever provided in the book, just the repeated assertion that an ADHD/Ritalin conspiracy exists. (p. 1)

However, Breggin's analysis has support illustrated by concerns raised by the United States Department of Justice, Drug Enforcement Administration (DEA). The DEA (1995) also questioned the appropriateness of the relationship between the pharmaceutical manufacturer of Ritalin™, Ciba-Geigy, and the parental support groups. The DEA reported that 'Ciba-Geigy (the manufacturer of Ritalin™) contributed $748,000 to CHADD from 1991 to 1994' (DEA, 1995, p. 3).

The circumstance of pharmaceutical company promotion under the guise of parental action support groups was detailed by the DEA (1995), which reported that:

> The DEA has concerns that the depth of the financial relationship with the manufacturer was not well-known by the public, including CHADD members that have relied upon CHADD for guidance as it pertains to the diagnosis and treatment of their children. (p. 4)

The relationship between the parent group and the pharmaceutical manufacturer was potentially breaching international law as indicated by the DEA:

> financial transfer from a pharmaceutical company with the purpose to promote sales of an internationally controlled substance would

be identified as hidden advertisement and in contradiction with the provisions of the 1971 Convention. (1995, p.4)

It is evident that there has been widespread promotion of the construct of a biological basis for ADHD and also direct promotion by medical experts in media, texts, and public meetings that has resulted in very significant increases in the use of the ADHD label and movement towards globalization in the use of the diagnosis that was idiosyncratic to the United States prior to 1990 (Kean, 2004). The interlinks between medical experts and parental lobby organizations whose promotional materials are claimed by critics as misleading raises questions concerning the scientific validity and reliability of the ADHD diagnosis and the role of the FDA, NIMH, pharmaceutical companies and researchers generally holding eminent positions in United States universities (Breggin, 2001; DEA, 1995; INCB, 1995; National Institutes of Health [NIH], 1998a; NIH, 1998b). The financial gains involved as a result of dramatic increases in treatment for ADHD also result in financial benefits to medical experts. This aspect does raise questions concerning the construction of knowledge, particularly in light of the claims promoting a proven biological/neurological basis for the disorder that has not been established in research (Baumeister and Hawkins, 2001; Breggin, 2001; Leo and Cohen, 2003; NIH, 1998a; NIH, 1998b).

Promotion of ADHD in Australia

As noted, Australia was the first country outside the United States and Canada to make significant use of the ADHD diagnosis and drug treatments for the behavioural control of children. Increases in the use of the diagnosis continued throughout the 1990s and was paralleled with numerous popular magazine articles, reports in the print and television media and the distribution of information concerning ADHD in the education system (Bailey and Rice, 1997). Were elements of the *psychopharmaceutical complex* evident in the period of introduction and increased use of the diagnosis? Breggin's (2001) construct can be generalized to the following components:

- The role of pharmaceutical companies and medical experts
- The role of government regulatory authorities
- The promotion by educational authorities
- The role of parental lobby groups.

The role of pharmaceutical companies and medical experts in Australia

In Australia in the early 1990s, the acceptance of the ADHD diagnosis began with a number of prominent paediatricians playing a major role in diagnosing large numbers of children with the condition and in the promotion of the diagnosis. Serfontein (1990, 1994), Green and Chee (1994a, 1994b), and Hutchins, Storm and Ngyuen (1995) all had significant roles in promoting the diagnosis of ADHD and made claims concerning the effectiveness of drug therapy for the treatment of the condition. Characteristic of their promotional stance were the statements by Green and Chee (1994a), who claimed:

Any professional who disputes the benefits of stimulant medication in ADD is very out of touch with the modern research literature. (p. 40)

Green and Chee (1994a) further emphasized in relation to psychostimulant drugs that:

This form of therapy is so well proven it is no longer worth our debating this point. Some people still believe the earth is flat, but that's not our problem. (p. 50)

The approach taken in the promotion of the ADHD diagnosis minimizes potential risks and provides medical reassurance that the drugs used to treat the condition are safe, regardless of the fact that long-term studies into the safety and efficacy of the treatment have not been established (Breggin, 2001; NIH, 1998b). Green and Chee (1994a, p. 40) claimed that 'stimulants are safe and parents are in charge of their continued prescription'. The claim that pyschostimulant drugs are safe contradicts the restrictions placed on distribution of the drugs that are listed in Schedule II substances in the United Nations Convention on Psychotropic Substances 1971 (United Nations, 1971). Even the manufacturer of Ritalin™ indicates 'Data on the safety and efficacy of long-term use of Ritalin™ are not complete' and notes that 'long-term therapy should be carefully monitored' (MediMedia, Australia, 2003, p. 365).

In combination with their written promotion of ADHD some of the paediatricians undertook media- and community-based activities to spread their viewpoint concerning the condition to the general public (Swanson, 1995). Dr Christopher Green held public meetings in Sydney, other capital cities and in country towns raising awareness of the general public to his particular viewpoints concerning ADHD. Another Australian paediatrician, Dr Paul Hutchins, also played a major role as a media commentator on the condition and regularly appeared on national television to respond to critics and promote the ADHD diagnosis (Swanson, 1995; Fanning, 2000). In promotion of the diagnosis of ADHD there is a downplaying of risks creating a perspective that the drug treatments are safe and effective, and that their use should not be questioned. In promotion of ADHD the paediatricians appear to make claims about safety that are not supported by the manufacturer's advice. They downplay risks and potential side-effects, and they support off-label use of methylphenidate in children under 6 years.

Green and Chee (1994a), in relation to children under the age of 6, suggested that 'The young child of three to six years metabolises the drug too quickly. Give four small doses each day, eg. at 8am, 11am, 1pm, 3.30pm'. Hutchins, Nunn and Hazell (2003, p. 168) also support the use of methylpenidate in children under 6 years, claiming that 'simulants are effective in preschool children, although evidence is limited to methylphenidate' for children under 4 years. In a similar fashion to Green and Chee (1994a), Hutchins and associates (2003, p. 168) suggest that with children under 6 the brain immaturity may make dosage regimes more complicated, requiring 'more frequent or higher doses'.

In relation to adverse drug reactions (ADRs) Green and Chee (1994a) downplay risks, suggesting that ADRs of suppression of appetite and wakefulness are easily reversible. They indicated that the only genuine concerns related to emotional lability, rebound behaviour and the possibility of tics and Tourette syndrome. They make the claim that these in fact may just be associated with ADD and may not be caused by medication. They note that 'along with the growing body of opinion, we believe the former to be true, but sometimes for medicolegal reasons, it is sometimes safer to disregard the truth' (Green and Chee, 1994a, p. 52). Hutchins and colleagues (2003, p. 166) noted appetite suppression and initial insomnia as ADRs and claim that 'they rarely persist to be too troublesome'. They also mention rebound and note that this can be overcome by using three doses a day or a long-acting medication. Hutchins and associates (2003, p. 116) also indicate that stimulants 'may precipitate or exacerbate tics, but the risk is overstated'. Depression is also mentioned; however, they claim that the role of stimulants as a cause is not proven and that it may be comorbid with the ADHD and just 'unmasked during stimulant treatment' (Hutchins *et al.*, 2003, p. 116).

In contrast to the brief specification of ADRs by Green and Chee (1994a) and Hutchins and associates (2003), the manufacturer of methylphenidate notes numerous potential ADRs related to the central and peripheral nervous system, gastrointestinal, cardiovascular, dermatological, haematological and list as other 'moderate reduction in weight gain and minor retardation of growth' (MediMedia, 2003, p. 366). In relation to the central and peripheral nervous system, the drug manufacturer detailed the following:

> Nervousness, insomnia and anorexia are the most common reactions occurring at the beginning of treatment and are usually controlled by reducing the dosage or omitting the drug in the afternoon or evening. Headache, drowsiness, dizziness, depressed mood, irritability, dyskinesia, difficulties in accommodation, and blurring of vision may also occur. Isolated cases of hyperactivity, convulsions, muscle cramps, choreoathetoid movements, tics, and Tourette syndrome have been reported. Isolated cases of toxic psychosis (some with visual and tactile hallucinations) have been reported, which subside when Ritalin™ is discontinued. (MediMedia, 2003, p. 366)

Support for the use of psychostimulant drugs for the treatment of ADHD is justified not only by its perceived effectiveness but also because of the paucity of access to alternative or supplementary interventions for treatment of the condition (Hutchins, 1997). This view was also supported by other paediatricians in the promotion of drug therapy, as indicated by Green and Chee (1994a), who reported:

> The official view is that all children with ADD must be treated in a multimodal way. This is a worthy sentiment, but with the 'rationalisation' of resources, many children will be lucky to get help in even one or two modes. (p. 42)

In Australia, contradicting the promotion of ADHD by advocate paediatricians, another group of paediatricians and psychiatrists have been critical of both the label and the associated use of medication for behavioural control. Critics indicated that other causes for the behaviours, other than having the condition of ADHD, are not given sufficient consideration in the approach taken in the DSM-IV

(Jureidini, 1996). Jureidini indicated that ADHD, as a collection of symptoms of overactivity, inattention and impulsivity does not withstand claims for descriptive trustworthiness and that 'description does not amount to explanation and reliability of identification does not entail validity of the disease' (1996, p. 201). The dominant medical belief that the demonstration of the symptoms indicates a pathological cause is challenged by Jureidini's (1996) analysis. He indicated that there are many reasons why a child may be overactive, impulsive or inattentive. Jureidini stated that:

> there is a wide range in activity of children, and in what is regarded as acceptable in a given family, social setting and culture. For any one child of given temperament, the current level of activity may vary, influenced by factors within the child, the family or the broader environment. (1996, p. 201)

The views expressed by Jureidini (1996) are reflected also in the comments by Oberklaid (1994 cited in Wallis, 1994, p. 33) who noted that the label and associated treatment led parents to believe their children's 'problems could be solved by a pill'. Oberklaid, a Professor at Melbourne's Royal Children's Hospital, claimed that 'You can have any symptom under the sun and you've got ADD, it's a way of avoiding responsibility' (cited in Wallis, 1994, p. 33).

With contradiction in medical opinion surrounding ADHD, a parent predisposed towards the diagnosis may be likely to seek an alternative medical practitioner to make the diagnosis if the first medical practitioner rejects the diagnosis. As a result, a parent significantly influenced by published material promoting the ADHD diagnosis may believe their child has ADHD and may pursue the diagnosis until they find a complying medical practitioner.

It should be of concern that a disorder that has the potential for misdiagnosis and overdiagnosis was promoted directly to the community. Are there hidden forces of power and money implicated in the motivation of a few paediatricians to educate the community about ADHD? One could speculate that perhaps the promotional activities announcing ADHD and promoting the use of medication were supported directly or possibly indirectly through research grants by pharmaceutical companies who stand to benefit financially through increased sales. Unfortunately, on their papers reviewed for this analysis the paediatricians do not declare one way or another any disclosures related to their publications.

In Australia there was also direct marketing of consumer information by the pharmaceutical companies that were supported by the NH and MRC (1997) who endorsed the publication by Ciba-Giegy of *Attention Deficit Hyperactivity Disorder and Learning Difficulties: Booklet for Parents*. Internet websites provide ongoing information for parents to access in relation to information concerning ADHD. The website <ADHDinfor.com> provides the pharmaceutical company with a website to distribute information about ADHD worldwide. Although there is a recommendation that the site is for US residents only, the information is accessible across the globe. On the site the pharmaceutical company provides information about ADHD, advice for parents, school personnel, ADHD resources and myths and facts concerning the condition (Novartis, 2006). In addition, it is noted that the information provided was approved by their advisory board composed of doctors, professionals, patients, and caregivers. This group of individuals was established and funded by the drug company as an educational service. On the website they inform teachers that 'Nine out of 10 children improve on a "stimulant drug", and to parents that 'ADHD is a physical disorder caused by differences in how the child's brain works' and that: 'stimulant medications are not addictive when used as directed. Studies have shown adequate treatment of ADHD may reduce the risk of substance abuse' (Novartis, 2006).

The role of Australian government regulatory authorities

In 1997 the Commonwealth of Australia published the findings by a panel of experts commissioned to review the diagnosis of ADHD, appropriate methods of management and the efficacy and long-term safety of stimulant drugs for treatment (NH and MRC, 1997). The terms of reference also included the formulation of advisory information for medical personnel, teachers, parents and consumer. This becomes a key document in Australia to support the increasing use of psychostimulants. The overall findings are best summarized in Recommendation 13 of the NH and MRC report:

> The use of stimulant medication should be considered as part of the management plan for most children with ADHD. The efficacy and safety of stimulant medication has been established for short-term use. (1997, p. 13)

Even though long-term safety and efficacy of psychostimulant treatment had not been established, the NH and MRC (1997) clearly support the drug treatments without any significant reservations.

The NH and MRC (1997) report on ADHD, providing national policy and guidelines for Australia, endorsed two key documents. The first, *Talk, Time, Teamwork: Positive and Practical Information for Schools: Collaborative Management of Students with ADHD*, was given strong endorsement and was recommended as a model for educational departments in Australia. It should be noted that Hutchins, the principal medical advisor involved in the development of *Talk, Time, Teamwork* , was also a member of the committee that produced the NH and MRC report (NH and MRC, 1997). The second document, endorsed by the NR and MRC (1997), was the publication of the Ciba-Geigy booklet, *ADHD – Attention Deficit Hyperactivity Disorder and Learning Difficulties: Booklet for Parents.*

The NH and MRC (1997) appear to take a non-critical viewpoint to any potential risks associated with children taking psychostimulants for the treatment of ADHD. For example, they noted that with the approval of the International Olympic Committee (IOC) Medical Commission, the Medical Advisory Panel (MAP) of the Australian Sports Commission advises that athletes with ADHD may continue their stimulant medication and compete in sports competitions until the age of 14 years and note that the MAP are seeking IOC approval for an increase of the age to 16 years. The NH and MRC (1997) only comment indicated that scientific research into the effects of stimulant medication on the performance of athletes with ADHD was strongly recommended.

The IOC Medical Commission and the World Anti-Doping Agency (WADA), *Drugs in Sport-IOC/WADA Guide*, clearly defines all amphetamines and methylphenidate as banned substances (MediMedia Australia, 2003, p. G-33). The banning of amphetamines in sport is a result of significant and serious risks associated with drug usage. The *IOC/WADA Guide* notes that stimulants are a category of drugs that increase alertness, reduce fatigue, and increase competitiveness and hostility. Their use has been associated with loss of judgement and has resulted in accidents in some sports. In a specific reference to amphetamines, the *IOC/WADA Guide* (2003) cited in MediMedia Australia (2003) notes that:

Amphetamine and related compounds have the most notorious reputation in producing problems in sport. Some deaths of athletes have occurred even when normal doses have been used under conditions of maximum physical activity (MediMedia Australia, 2003, p. G-33).

The NH and MRC (1997) report downplays the risks to children, from playing sport while affected by psychostimulant medications, instead of warning parents and sports personnel of the potential effects of the medication on heart rate, blood pressure and the potential for loss of judgement increasing risks of accidents.

Following the NH and MRC (1997) report, there have been many government inquiries and reports in various states concerning ADHD. Increasingly there has been a more critical view of the ADHD label. In the state with the highest use of psychostimulants the report of the WA Parliament, Education and Health Standing Committee (2004) *Attention Deficit Disorder in Western Australia* in findings noted that:

> During their training, paediatricians have not been adequately informed about the extent of alternative diagnoses and treatment methods, and are therefore more likely to use drug therapy in the first instance in the management of ADHD. (p. xxi)

> The behavioural symptoms underlying the diagnosis of ADHD are a key factor in the controversy surrounding the condition as many are within the range of 'normal' childhood behaviour. (p. xxii)

> The clinical diagnosis of ADHD is most often based on reported behavioural observations made by parents and/or teachers. There are no tests that identify the existence of ADHD in a biological sense. This is one of the reasons for the divergent views on the existence of ADHD as a clinical entity. (p. xxiii)

> There is a paucity of evidence on the long-term effects of psychostimulant medication on children. (p. xxiii)

A more critical view of ADHD particularly related to overdiagnosis of the condition reflected in the WA inquiry may be one factor that has led to a moderation in the increases in the use of psychostimulants since 2001 in Australia. Although it is still increasing, the rate of increase of psychostimulant drug use has slowed considerably in the period 2001 to 2004.

The promotion by Australian educational authorities

In Australia, the recognition and acceptance of ADHD as a valid area of special education had received considerable resistance and even initially evoked sceptical responses. Condon (1995) in a review of the literature on ADHD found that not only did problems exist in the interpretation of the criteria for diagnosis, and in the credibility of the use of teacher and parent rating scales, but also in the utility of the diagnosis for educational interventions. Condon (1995) claimed that the diagnosis often overlooked primary educational issues that will not be resolved by labelling the child as ADHD.

A review of Australian texts in Special Education from the early 1990s reveals a non-acceptance or total avoidance of ADHD as a category of special education intervention. Cole and Chan (1990), in their text *Methods and Strategies for Special Education*, provided a fleeting reference to ADHD as a subcategory of the now virtually unrecognized category of minimal brain dysfunction syndrome (MBD). They dismissed the label indicating that it has 'few implications for treatment' (p. 233). They indicated, that 'much more needs to be known about the child before a program of treatment can be organised' (p. 233).

Ashman and Elkins (1994), in the text *Educating Children with Special Needs*, again included only a brief reference to ADHD in the section of the text dealing with students with behavioural and emotional disorders. In dealing with the incidence of behavioural disturbance they made a specific reference to the controversy surrounding use of the ADHD label, claiming that 'political or interest group pressure can inflate prevalence figures by arguing for the inclusion of students with specific labels such as Attention Deficit Hyperactivity Disorder (ADHD)' (p. 301). Ashman and Elkins (1994) further criticized the utility of the classification and the usefulness for educational intervention:

> Prime amongst these is the debate on Attention Deficit Disorder (ADD) which has been linked or not linked with hyperactivity. From an educational perspective, the diagnostic label provides little (if any) value to the classroom teacher or specialist teacher in terms of educational remediation. (p. 303)

In Australia, in general, academics working in the area of Special Education have been reluctant to accept the hegemonic medical model of ADHD. For 20 years Australian education has been moving towards inclusive educational practice and acceptance of diversity in the classroom without the need for labelling of the individual with special educational needs (Foreman, 2001). However in the mid 1990s there comes a significant change influenced by medical practitioners, who appear to have acted as promotional agents for the ADHD diagnosis. They have had significant impact in influencing educational policy and in distributing informational material to teachers, schools and the wider community. Hutchins (1997), an Australian paediatrician, provided insight into the influence he has extended over the education system in NSW to promote ADHD and the associated treatment with medication.

In 1995 the New South Wales (NSW) Department of School Education (DOSE) distributed free to all schools a promotional text entitled *Talk, Time, Teamwork: Positive and Practical Information for Schools: Collaborative Management of Students with ADHD* (NSW DOSE, 1995). The text contains a range of proformas and decision-making procedures with a focus on screening children for referral to medical practitioners for ADHD diagnosis.

The authors of the document were indicated in the text by the statement that 'The Department of School Education has developed Talk, Time, Teamwork: Collaborative Management of Students with ADHD in conjunction with specialist medical practitioners' (NSW DOSE, 1995). The actual authors were not listed. However, one author who is self-acknowledged as Hutchins (1997), revealed:

As discussed in the document 'Talk Time and Teamwork', prepared by this author with the NSW Department of School Education (1995) medication use is not essential in AD/HD and is relative to other approaches for diagnosis and management. These may be unavailable, have long waiting lists, or be less effective. This inevitably emphasises the place of medication and the significance of a therapeutic trial with potential rapid benefits. (p. 65)

In the 'NSW DOSE Charts' section of the publication a two-page chart detailed the benefits of medication for:

behaviour, emotions, school performance, some learning tasks, improved peer and family relationships, enhanced multimodal behavioural and remedial intervention, aggression and delinquency, work output, socialisation, family function, enhance effectiveness of support teaching, cognitive behaviour therapy and counselling, learning and subtle language functions (NSW DOSE, 1995).

The claims in the document are overstated, since the only benefit demonstrated through treatment with methylphenidate or dexamphetamine are short-term changes in behaviour for some students only. The broad claims made in the statement indicate that ADHD medication is a cure-all for all types of behavioural problems, social and educational issues and effectively enhances other interventions ranging from support teaching, to remedial intervention, cognitive behaviour therapies and even to subtle language functions.

Distribution of material of this nature that details claims that are not substantiated in research to date in order to influence teacher beliefs, needs to be questioned. Furthermore, the financial links and interests that have resulted in these outcomes need public exposure and debate in order to establish the credibility and trustworthiness of the role of educational departments in Australia paralleling similar approaches in the United States (Breggin, 2001). Given the known potential for overdiagnosis and misdiagnosis of the disorder, systematic promotion aimed at screening children for the condition appears to have been premature in the context of controversy in the scientific and medical community over the nature of the disorder and effectiveness of the hegemonic medical interventions for treatment (NIH, 1998a, 1998b).

Associated with the acceptance of the ADHD diagnosis and claimed benefits of psychostimulant medications was the development of Children's Hospital Educational Research Institute (CHERI) (CHERI, 2006). Dr Paul Hutchins, Head, Child Development Unit, the Children's Hospital at Westmead played a significant role in its development. The key purpose of the organization was to assist children with 'significant medical, developmental and psychological conditions achieve their full potential through a partnership between health and education' (CHERI, 2006). The collaborative approach of linking the fields of medicine and education reflects the construct of the psychopharmaceutical complex linking organizations resulting in increasing pharmaceutical sales.

The role of parental lobby groups in Australia

In Australia, during the period of expansion of the ADHD diagnosis, the activities of parental support groups also became evident. Wallis (1994) described this development in Australia stating that:

Support groups-where parents meet for advice and sympathy – are popping up in country towns and suburban centers, and although there is no formal network, this week a newly formed committee will publish the first edition of what they hope will become a national newsletter called *Order in the House*. They have collected almost 200 addresses of local groups across Australia. (p. 32)

In many instances, these new groups amalgamated with existing parental support groups for children who have learning disabilities. These parental support/lobby groups obtained most of their information concerning ADHD from the United States (Swanson, 1995). The information presented by the support groups to parents included CHADD information sheets, publications, reports, reviews and texts by United States ADHD researchers. An increasing number of publications by Australian medical practitioners, promoting the hegemonic medical model of ADHD, supplement the United States ADHD information (Green and Chee, 1994a, 1994b; Serfontein, 1990, 1994). The Australian publications directly replicated the hegemonic United States medical model and information concerning ADHD.

As in the United States, medical advocates for ADHD in Australia were also supporting the role of the parental organizations. Paediatricians Green and Chee (1994a) indicated the importance of the role that parental support groups played in the process of gaining acceptance of and for the promotion of the ADHD diagnosis. Green and Chee (1994a) highlighted the forces behind the increases in diagnosis rates and the spread of the acceptance of ADHD treatment. They reported that:

The current interest in attention deficit disorder and the recognition of the importance of stimulant medication did not come from the teaching of our academic institutions or from professional colleges. The enlightenment came about as a result of the energy of parent support groups who demanded that the professions provide up-to-date treatment for their children (p. 38).

Green and Chee (1994a) confirmed the role that parental support groups have played in promotion of the diagnosis in Australia. However, such strong support, indicating the changes to be an enlightenment based upon parental demand and pressure through specific lobby groups, could not be described as a scientific approach to a serious

medical issue. In negating the role of academic institutions, professional colleges and thus scientific studies, one questions the validity of
the support given to the parental lobby groups by the paeditricians.

By 1997 there was an overall national peak organization ADHD
Network of Australia (ADDnet) and various state and regional organizations through Australia. The development and spread of parental
lobby organizations for ADHD in Australia again illustrates another
element of Breggin's psychopharmaceutical complex operating during the period of rapid uptake and ongoing increased use of the
ADHD diagnosis. This societal development was predicted by Barkley,
the world's most well-known advocate of the ADHD diagnosis, who
predicted (1990) that:

> Fortunately, the explosive growth of parent support/political action
> associations for ADHD arose almost simultaneously with this public
> controversy over Ritalin™; at this writing, they promise to make the
> education of ADHD children a national priority at the start of this
> last decade of the 20th century. These associations also offer the best
> hope that the general public can be provided with a more accurate
> depiction of ADHD and its treatment. (p. 37)

Emerging globalization

DeGrandpre (2000) proposed an explanation for the international differences based on different cultural perspectives. DeGrandpre (2000)
suggested that the differences between countries in the use of drug therapy for ADHD were a result of differences in social cohesion and that
'it is essentially unheard-of in France, where family structure is intact'
(p. 14). DeGrandpre (2000) also noted that in France behavioural
problems were more likely to be assessed as a child development or
psychosocial issue and not medical disorder or disease.

DeGrandpre (2000, p. 15) stated that the United States was experiencing an 'epidemic of behavioural and emotional problems with
children'. He proposed that instead of dealing with the psychosocial
factors contributing to the epidemic that there had been a total reliance
on drug therapy as the solution. As a result, DeGrandpre believed that
the United States society had taken the pathway of medicating children, under the guise of the ADHD label, with Ritalin™ and other
drugs to make them compliant rather than addressing the more challenging educational, family and societal factors he suggested were the
cause of the behavioural problems.

In the United Kingdom, Baldwin (2000) identified four main factors responsible for the increase in the use of the ADHD diagnosis and associated pharmaceutical intervention. Baldwin (2000) claimed that the increases were due to:

- pharmaceutical company promotion;
- ill-conceived medical treatments for attention problems that do not account for developmental stages and needs of children;
- the creation of a climate within the educational system that promoted the diagnosis and treatment by drug therapy;
- and lack of alternative treatment programmes, particularly those with a behavioural of psychosocial basis.

Baldwin (2000) linked marketing and promotional strategies of pharmaceutical companies combined with a lack of alternative treatments as key factors for the recent increased use of the diagnosis in the United Kingdom. As with Australia, elements of the psychopharmaceutical complex are apparent. In Iceland, which has recently become the second-highest consumer of psychostimulants behind the United States, the presence of parental lobby groups is also evident with the Parent Association for MBD recently changing their name to the Icelandic ADHD Association (Icelandic ADHD Association, 2006).

This issue of parental lobby associations becoming a key factor in globalization was first raised by the INCB (1996), where review of the changes in psychostimulant medication worldwide triggered criticism of the misdiagnosis and overdiagnosis of the condition of ADHD in the United States and a warning to other countries to avoid replicating the situation that had occurred in the United States. In particular the INCB (1996) noted a specific threat coming from parental organizations based in the United States taking their promotional activities into the international arena.

Conclusions

ADHD has become the most intensively studied and researched area of child development (Barkley, 1998a). The number of articles published on hyperactivity in scientific literature grew from 31 in the last three years of the 1950s to 7000 in the last three years of the 1970s (Divoky, 1989). Since the late 1970s there has been an even greater publication rate in the area, with the major emphasis being on studies demonstrating the efficacy of medication as opposed to other forms of treatment

(Divoky, 1989) and there have been even further increases in research output in the 1990s (Barkley, 1998a). The focus of the research has been on the supposed benefits to children and not on ensuring the safety and efficacy of the treatment in the long term. Emphasis has been placed strongly on utility of medication in treatment with the use of simple behavioural interventions as an adjunct. Although the efficacy of methylphenidate and dexamphetamine for reducing the core symptoms of hyperactivity, impulsiveness and inattention in the short term has substantial research in support, the effectiveness of long-term treatment and the overall benefit in terms of prognosis from diagnosis and pharmaceutical intervention are far from being resolved (Vitiello, 2001).

The use of the diagnosis of ADHD and treatment of children with drugs for behavioural control has increased dramatically in the last decade. The practice has also spread from being unique to North America to include Australia and an increasing number of developed societies. Medical practitioners who are very much in favour of the treatment may be prescribing to a large number of children based upon very short assessments and as a result overdiagnosing and misdiagnosing the condition. Elements of the psychopharmaceutical complex appear associated with the increased use of psychostimulant drugs. In particular advocate paediatricians, direct and indirect pharmaceutical company marketing, government endorsement, community-based lobby groups and promotion of ADHD in the educational system are elements contributing to the escalation in use and globalization of the diagnosis. Review of the elements contributing to the increased use of the ADHD diagnosis in Australia suggests that medical specialists, educational systems and parental lobby group actions paralleled elements of the psychopharmaceutical complex documented by Breggin (2001) in the United States.

The diversity of opinion within the medical community indicates that the very diagnosis itself is not definitive or perhaps even credible. Other medical, developmental, social and educational problems may be being masked and therefore not treated by using drugs to suppress symptoms. The expediency of suppression of behaviours through the use of drugs may also be leading to practitioners not adequately investigating the cause of the child's problems and consequently failing to develop interventions to address behavioural and learning problems in the long term. Marketing practices involving complex interactions between parental lobby groups, medical specialists promoting the benefits of the medications, education departments and pharmaceutical companies suggest a selective transmission of knowledge resulting in a belief that the drugs provide a long-term solution for a complex range of behaviour and learning problems in the diverse group of children labelled as ADHD.

References

American Psychiatric Association (APA) (1980) *Diagnostic and Statistical Manual of Mental Disorders, Third Edition.* Washington, DC: (APA).

American Psychiatric Association (APA) (1987) *Diagnostic and Statistical Manual of Mental Disorders, Third Edition, Revised.* Washington, DC: (APA).

American Psychiatric Association (APA) (1994) *Diagnostic and Statistical Manual of Mental Disorders, Fourth Edition.* Washington, DC: (APA).

American Psychiatric Association (APA) (2000) *Diagnostic and Statistical Manual of Mental Disorders, Fourth Edition, Text Revision.* Washington, DC: (APA).

Ashman, A. and Elkins, J. (eds) (1994) *Educating Children with Special Needs.* Sydney: Prentice-Hall.

Bailey, J. and Rice, D. (eds) (1997) *Attention Deficit/Hyperactivity Disorder: Medical, Psychological and Educational Perspectives.* Sydney: The Australian Association of Special Education Inc.

Baldwin, S. (2000) Impact evaluation of mass media public education campaign on clinic service provision for minors diagnosed with ADHD/ADD: Audit survey of 1000 index families, *International Journal of Risk & Safety in Medicine* 13, 203–219.

Barkley, R. A. (1990) *Hyperactive Children: A Handbook for Diagnosis and Treatment.* New York: The Guilford Press.

Barkley, R. A. (1998a) *Attention-Deficit Hyperactivity Disorder: A Handbook for Diagnosis and Treatment.* New York: The Guilford Press.

Barkley, R. A. (1998b) *ADHD, Ritalin, and Conspiracies: Talking Back To Peter Breggin.* CHADD website, retrieved 11 December 2001, from <http://www.chadd.org/news/Russ-review.htm> [Document no longer accessible].

Baumeister, A. A., and Hawkins, M. F. (2001) Incoherence of neuroimaging studies of attention deficit/hyperactivity disorder, *Clinical Neuropharmacology* 24, 2–10.

Berbatis, C. G., Sunderland, V. B. and Bulsara, M. (2002) Licit psychostimulants in Australia 1984 to 2000: International and jurisdictional comparison, *Medical Journal of Australia* 177, 539–43.

Breggin, P. R. (1993) *Toxic Psychiatry: Why Therapy, Empathy and Love Must Replace the Drugs, Electroshock and Biochemical Theories of the 'New Psychiatry'.* HarperCollins: London.

Breggin, P. R. and Breggin, G. R. (1994) *Talking Back to Prozac: What Doctors Aren't Telling You about Today's Most Controversial Drug*. New York: St Martin's Press.

Breggin, P. R. (1997) *Brain Disabling Treatments in Psychiatry: Drugs, Electroschock and the Role of the FDA*. New York: Springer.

Breggin, P. R. (1998) *Talking Back to Ritalin: What Doctors Aren't Telling You about Stimulants and ADHD*. Monroe (ME): Common Courage Press.

Breggin, P. R. (2001) *Talking Back to Ritalin: What Doctors Aren't Telling You about Stimulants and ADHD, Revised Edition*. Cambridge: Perseus Publishing.

Children's Hospital Educational Research Institute (CHERI) (2006) *Our History*. Retrieved 8 August 2006, from <http://www.cheri.com.au/history.html>.

Cole, P. G., and Chan, L. K. S. (1990) *Methods and Strategies for Special Education*. Sydney: Prentice-Hall.

Commonwealth of Australia (2006) *Schedule of Pharmaceutical Benefits for Approved Pharmacists and Medical Practitioners*. Canberra: Author. Retrieved 8 August 2006, from <http://www.health.gov.au/internet/wcms/ publishing.nsf/ Content/ 906DE64065A8A57CCA256F180047F029/ $File/schedule_aug06.pdf>.

Condon, D. (1995) ADHD: Maybe not the precision that is often implied, *Special Education Perspectives* 4, 3–10.

DeGrandpre, R. J., (2000) *Ritalin Nation: Rapid-Fire Culture & the Transformation of Human Consciousness*. New York: Norton, W.W. & Co. Inc.

Department of Health (2005) *Stimulant Prescribing and Usage Patterns for the Treatment of ADHD in Western Australia (1 August 2003–31 December 2004)*. Pharmaceutical Services Branch, Department of Health, Western Australia.

Diller, L. H. (1998) *Running on Ritalin: A Physician Reflects on Children, Society and Performance in a Pill*. New York: Bantam Books.

Diller, L. H. (2000) United States House of Representatives, Subcommittee on Early Childhood, Youth and Families. Hearing: 16 May 2000. *Ritalin Use among Youth: Examining the Issues and Concerns*. Chairman Congressman Castle. Retrieved 27 August 2001, from <http://edworkforce.house.gov/ hearings/106th/ecyf/ritalin51600/diller.htm>.

Divoky, D. (1989) Ritalin: Education's fix-it Drug? *Phi Delta Kappa International* 70, 599–605.

Drug Enforcement Administration (DEA) (1995) *Methylphenidate: A Background Paper*. Washington, DC: Drug and Chemical Evaluation Section, Office of Diversion Control, DEA, US Department of Justice.

Eccleston, R. (2006) Preschoolers' Ritalin set for approval, *The Australian – Health*. Retrieved 8 August 2006, from <http://www.theaustralian.news.com.au/story/ 0,20867,19750113-23289,00.html>.

Edwards, G. H. and Barkley, R. A., (1997) Attention Deficit-Hyperactivity Disorder: history, diagnosis, and current concepts, in J. Bailey and D. Rice (eds), *Attention Deficit/Hyperactivity Disorder: Medical, Psychological and Educational Perspectives*, pp. 1–18. Sydney: The Australian Association of Special Education, Inc.

Fanning, E. (2000) The magic pills: How good are they? *60 Minutes*, 9 October, Ninemsn. Retrieved 31 October 2000, from <http://community. ninemsn.com.au/chat/60minutesD.asp> [No longer accessible].

Foreman, P. (ed.) (2001) *Integration and Inclusion in Action (2nd Edition)*. Sydney: Harcourt Australia.

Goldman, L. S., Genel, M., Bezman, R. J. and Slanetz, P. J. (1998) Diagnosis and treatment of attention-deficit/hyperactivity disorder in children and adolescents, *Journal of the American Medical Association* 279 (14), 1100–7.

Green, C. and Chee, K. (1994a) Management of attention deficit disorder: A personal perspective, *Modern Medicine of Australia* (Feburary), 38–53.

Green, C. and Chee, K. (1994b) *Understanding ADD*. Sydney: Doubleday.

Hutchins, P. (1997) Attention deficit-hyperactivity disorder: Collaboration between teacher and doctor – tuning teaching, management and medication, in J. Bailey and D. Rice (eds), *Attention Deficit/Hyperactivity Disorder: Medical, Psychological and Educational Perspectives*, ch. 3, pp. 49–87. Sydney: Australian Association of Special Education Inc.

Hutchins, P., Nunn, K., and Hazell, P. (2003) Attention Deficit Hyperactivity Disorder: Child & Adolescent Mental Health Statewide Network (2003), *Psychotropic Prescribing in Children and Adolescents*, pp. 162–71. Sefton, Sydney: Child & Adolescent Mental Health Statewide Network.

Hutchins, P., Storm, V., and Ngyuen, R. (1995) Realities of stimulant treatment of attention deficit hyperactivity disorder in NSW – the hype stops here! *Journal of Paediatrics and Child Health* 31, A9.

Icelandic ADHD Association. (2006) *The Icelandic ADHD Association*. Retrieved 20 August 2006, from <http://www.adhd.is/default.asp?sid_id= 11431&tre_rod=015%7C&tId=1>.

International Narcotics Control Board (INCB) (1995) *Annual Report 1995*. United Nations Publications: No E.96.XI.1. Retrieved 7 August 2006, from <http://www.incb.org/incb/en/annual_report_1995_chapter2.html#IIB4>.

International Narcotics Control Board (INCB) (1996) Control of Use of Methylphenidate in the Treatment of ADD: Expert Meeting on Amphetamine-Type Stimulants, Shanghai, 25–29 November. Vienna: INCB.

International Narcotics Control Board (INCB) (1997) *INCB Sees Continuing Risk in Stimulant Medication Prescribed for Children*. INCB Annual report background note no. 4. Vienna, Austria: INCB .

International Narcotics Control Board (INCB) (2000) *Report of the International Narcotics Control Board for 2000*. Retrieved 1 August 2006, from <http://www.incb.org/incb/en/annual_report_2000.html>.

International Narcotics Control Board (INB) (2004) *Comments on the Reported Statistics on Psychotropic Substances*. Retrieved 1 August 2006, from <http://www.incb.org/pdf/e/tr/psy/2004/psychotropics_comments.pdf>.

International Narcotics Control Board (INCB) (2005) Report of the International Narcotics Control Board for 2005. Retrieved 1 August 2006, from <http://www.incb.org/incb/en/annual_report_2005.html>.

Jacobs, B. (2002) *Queensland Children at Risk: The Overdiagnosis of 'ADHD' and the Overuse of Stimulant Medication*. Brisbane: Youth Affairs Network of Queensland.

Jureidini, J. (1996) Annotation: Some reasons for concern about attention deficit hyperactivity disorder, *Journal of Paediatric Child Health* 32, 201–3.

Kean, B. (2004) The Risk Society and Attention Deficit Hyperactivity Disorder (ADHD): A Critical Social Research Analysis Concerning the Development and Social Impact of the ADHD Diagnosis. Unpublished doctoral thesis. Lismore: Southern Cross University.

Leo, J. and Cohen, D. (2003) Broken brains or flawed studies? A critical review of ADHD neuroimaging research, *The Journal of Mind and Behavior* 24, 1, 29–55.

MediMedia Australia (2003) *MIMS Annual: Australia*. pp. 365–6. St Leonards: MediMedia Australia.

Merson, J. (2002) The wild ones, *The Sun Herald: Good Weekend Magazine* (Sunday, 11 May), pp. 20–6.

National Health and Medical Research Council (NH and MRC) (1997) *Attention Deficit Hyperactivity Disorder*. Canberra: Australian Government Publishing Service.

National Institutes of Health (NIH) (1998a) Diagnosis and treatment of Attention Deficit Hyperactivity Disorder, *NIH Consensus Statement 1998* (draft). Rockville, MD:. Retrieved 21 November 1998, from <http://www.odp.od.nih.gov/consensus/cons/110/110_statement> [Document no longer accessible].

National Institutes of Health (NIH) (1998b) Diagnosis and treatment of Attention Deficit Hyperactivity Disorder (ADHD), NIH Consensus Statement 16(2))(16–18 November). William H. Natcher Conference Center: National Institutes of Health. Bethesda, MD.

New South Wales Department of School Education (DOSE) (1995) *Talk, Time, Teamwork: Collaborative Management of Students with ADHD*. Sydney: NSW Department of School Education.

Novartis (2006) *ADHD info.com: School Personnel*. Retrieved 20 August 2006, from <http://www.adhdinfo.com:80/info/school/about/sch.jsp>.

Rutter, M., Tuma, A. H., and Lann, I. S. (eds) (1988) *Assessment and Diagnosis in Child Psychopathology*. New York: The Guilford Press.

Salmelainen, P. (2002) *Trends in the Prescribing of Stimulant Medication for the Treatment of Attention Deficit Hyperactivity Disorder in Children and Adolescents in NSW*. Sydney: NSW Department of Health.

Sawyer, M. G., Rey, J. M., Graetz, B. W., Clark, J. and Baghurst, P. A., (2002) Use of medication by young people with attention deficit/hyperactivity disorder, *Medical Journal of Australia* 177, 21–5.

Schrag, P. and Divoky, D. (1975) *The Myth of the Hyperactive Child.* New York: Pantheon.

Serfontein, G. (1990) *The Hidden Handicap: Dyslexia and Hyperactivity in Children.* Sydney: Simon and Schuster.

Serfontein, G. (1994) *ADD in Adults.* Sydney: Simon and Schuster.

Swanson, N. (1995) Speed for breakfast, *Four Corners.* Sydney: ABC Broadcasting, 12 February.

United Nations (1971). *Convention on Controlled Substances, 1971.* Retrieved 8 August 2006, from <http://www.incb.org/pdf/e/conv/convention_1971_en.pdf>.

United States House of Representatives (1970) *Federal Involvement in the Use of Behavior Modification Drugs on Grammar School Children of the Right to Privacy Inquiry: Hearing before a Subcommittee of the Committee on Government Operations,* 29 September Washington, DC: US House of Representatives.

Vitiello, B. (2001) Methylphenidate in the treatment of children with attention-deficit hyperactivity disorder, *Canadian Medical Association Journal* 27, 165 (11). Retrieved 20 November 2002, from <http://www.cmaj.ca/cgi/content/full/165/ 11/1505>.

WA Parliament, Education and Health Standing Committee (2004) *Attention Deficit Disorder in Western Australia.* Perth: State Law Publisher.

Wallis, C. (1994) Life in overdrive: Doctors say huge numbers of kids and adults have attention deficit disorder: Is it for real? *Time,* 5 September, pp. 31–42.

Chapter 7

ADHD and Globalization

Sami Timimi and Begum Maitra

Introduction

In a London clinic

A 7-year-old mixed-'race'[1] British boy was referred to a London Child and Adolescent Mental Health Service (CAMHS) by his GP at the request of his mother. She believed his 'demanding' behaviour, and refusal to settle at school, to be attributable to 'ADHD'. Resentful of the school's repeated calls to take him home for 'disrupting' the class, and of her perception that she was being blamed for poor parenting, she had been struck by conversations with a friend whose child was receiving medication for ADHD. She had looked up the condition on the internet, and anxiously hoped that medication would solve both their problems.

Assessment revealed a long history of extreme domestic violence between the parents resulting eventually in a successful criminal prosecution and the father's imprisonment. The child, born soon after, was inextricably linked in the mother's mind with these painful memories. Further complicating this was a complex conflict-laden history of multi-generational inter-racial (white British-African) relationships in the mother's family that had left the mother (herself of mixed race) with a number of unresolved, conflicting and largely unconscious negative stereotypes and expectations connected with 'race'. The most striking finding was that of the mother's rejection of her son, and her belief that his behaviours were proof of his 'genetic' links with his violent father.

In urban India

On visits to India one of the authors (BM) found that she was increasingly being consulted by parents anxious that their children might be suffering from a particular set of conditions – specifically, ADHD, autism or Asperger's syndrome. A 3-year-old girl was brought for an opinion. The apple[2] of her parents' eye and uncontested ruler of the extended household, she was the only child in an upwardly mobile family. Like innumerable other urban families, the parents had chosen[3] to have only one child in the belief that they would be unable to provide for the extensive material needs (for the best foods, health care and education) of more than one child. The mother eyed the little girl worriedly as she scampered about the room, overturning articles and scrawling on the walls confident that the new adult observing her would be no less indulgent over such obvious liberties. She (the mother) asked whether BM thought the child too thin or, perhaps, suffering from vitamin/dietary deficiencies, or some other more mysterious lack. Despite the absence of any evidence to support these notions the complex rules of social exchange required BM to make a sufficiently convincing enquiry into the child's diet and daily routines. As the questions limped into silence the mother hesitantly produced a prescription. The paediatrician[4] she had consulted previously had recommended a number of multivitamin preparations, dietary supplements and a small dose of methylphenidate. Asked what she had understood of the rationale for the last drug, the mother reported that the doctor had wondered whether her child might suffer from 'ADHD'.

Community research subjects in inner-city London

Presented with vignettes of a number of common clinical presentations to child mental health services, Bangladeshi and white British mothers in a council estate in West London in the latter part of the 1980s showed interesting similarities and differences in their explanatory models (Maitra, 1995). White British mothers thought restlessness in young children who were also unresponsive to parental rules and discipline was likely to be due to intrinsic factors within the child, resulting in 'ADHD/Hyperactivity', or due to extrinsic agents, such as 'E' factors in foods. Bangladeshi mothers were more inclined to cite physical illness first, followed closely by 'social' factors such as poor parental 'teaching' (*shiksha*, also implying 'discipline'), and, somewhat more hesitantly (since the researcher was a medical professional), malign influences arising from others in the social environment, or from the spirit world. When considered together with responses to other vignettes (of 'emotional disorder' and 'conduct disorder') the major difference lay in the absence of a purely 'psychological' model among the Bangladeshi mothers. While both groups saw the emotional states of children as reactive to their social environments, Bangladeshi mothers seemed genuinely puzzled by the idea that any separation needed to be made between a young child's emotional state and some underlying state or process. Thus, when asked why a 6–7-year-old might be withdrawn and tearful, white British mothers frequently spoke of 'depression' but Bangladeshi mothers seemed puzzled. After running through the possibility of the child's being unwell (and excluding hunger as a cause in affluent Britain, their adoptive country), they would ask whether the child had no parents. The implication seemed to be that the presence of parents (and the improved material resources in this country) was sufficient to ensure that a child's needs would be met.

These vignettes demonstrate the to and fro movement of ideas about childhood behaviours, whether or not these are considered problematic, by whom, how responsibility is attributed, and the relationships between public and professional systems of attribution. This chapter suggests that 'culture' is central to these systems of exchange. In this discussion culture is not limited to futile attempts to pin down 'ethnic identities', a position that has regrettably settled into British health policy and provision, but includes considerations of dominant ideologies, local and distant, and on how these travel globally exerting their influence in often unexpected ways and places, such as the impact of consumerist culture on health practice, or the impact of cultural beliefs about selfhood on parental and professional attitudes towards child care. We hope to show how the global movements of people and ideas offer an opportunity to reconsider the basic premises of our professional beliefs about children and the construct of ADHD.

Globalization

The ever-increasing abundance of global connections and our understanding of them constitute globalization[5]. This 'compression of the world' has led to an intensification of consciousness of the world and a shortening of distance and time across the globe. Many forces have been at play to bring about the globalization we are so familiar with today, including the extension of world capitalist economy, industrialization, increasing surveillance (most notable through global information systems) and the world military order (Giddens, 1990, 1991). Global recession hastened a renewed globalization of world economic activity involving the speed up of production and consumption turnover. Over the last 35 years the volume of global migration has doubled. Hardly a society is left that can call itself 'monocultural'. In Western Europe, for example, 8–10 per cent of the population is of non-European origin, most arriving in recent decades. Providing adequate services for populations who may have different spiritual and cosmological as well as lifestyle beliefs and practices to that of the host culture is thus something that no society can afford to ignore.

Globalization from above

One important recent aspect of globalization is the neo-colonial character of the way the world economy has become organized (often referred to as neo-liberalism). This economic system has resulted in glaring inequalities between the 'developed' and 'developing' worlds and, from a human rights perspective, it can be argued that the global economic system is guilty of human rights violations and bears a large responsibility for man-made problems, such as poverty, starvation, lack of health care, militarization and regional conflicts.

Edward Said (1978, 1981) illuminates the 'structural' and societal character of racism in his description of 'Orientalism' as a set of Western discourses of power that constructed an Orient in ways which reproduced the positional superiority and hegemony of the West – a general group of ideas impregnated with European superiority, racism and imperialism to be found in a variety of Western texts, media and practices. Said (1981), for example, argued that the Western media represents Islamic people as irrational fanatics led by messianic and authoritarian leaders, at the same time as Islamic women are portrayed as oppressed, not allowed to speak for themselves and of lacking a sense of personal agency.

United States and other Western countries' controlled corporations dominate global communications industries. Some argue that as a result, mass media fit into the world capitalist system by providing the necessary ideological support for the imposition of the values it requires for continuous capitalist expansion on a global scale (Schiller, 1969). Thus, the commodity culture necessary for continuing market expansion penetrates all spheres of life with the creation of niche markets and the advertising of idealized and fantasy lifestyles on which to attach products. The consequence is that the choice between values and lifestyle then becomes a matter of taste and style. This causes a heightening of a focus on individuality and self-concern, at the expense of social values and identities (Crook *et al.*, 1992; Featherstone, 1991). The eventual aim of such a market system is to g*et all* cultures to submit to its logic and, by implication, to the values required for promoting continued consumption globally. Thus, McDonald's, Coca Cola, Nike, and so forth become global brands, representing more than just the product they are selling.

In the post '9/11' world, the topics of assimilation, integration and multiculturalism have re-emerged with gusto, as concerns have grown about the danger to our society that some ethnic minority groups (particularly Muslims) pose. Undercurrents of anxiety and hostility interweave as old colonial arguments emerge in a new form, persuading us that we have shown too much tolerance to migrants and should make greater efforts to force migrants to assimilate into Western value systems.

In the last two to three decades of the twentieth century, policies of assimilation gradually gave way to those of 'multiculturalism', as it became apparent that many communities had not 'assimilated' as had been hoped, but instead had learned to defend and discover value in their own cultural legacy. Increasing racial tension, coupled with the visible social and economic deprivation of many minority communities contributed to a growing appreciation of how racism had kept many non-whites out of positions of power and influence. Eventually this led to the gradual abandonment of monoculturalism, with new policies aimed at integration rather than assimilation, in which it was more accepted that minority groups would keep their cultural identities. It is of course apparent that the move towards integration and multiculturalism has not resolved many of the issues surrounding how we adapt to the era of globalization and the multicultural character of modern societies. Ballard (2007) points out that 'fair-weather multi-culturalists' may well cite the recent spate of terrorist acts in Britain as a reason to return to dreams of community cohesion, and presents a passionate argument for plurality.

A more subtle impact of the neo-liberal character of globalization is the export of Western value systems to countries with value systems born from different traditions. This can result in undermining the stability of traditional beliefs and practices in many communities that have served their children well, at the same time producing points of conflict, antagonism and contradictions as the merits of different value systems clash (Ang, 1996). All too often these conflicts are resolved in favour of the more powerful and influential culture (i.e. that of the industrialized West).

Globalization from below

However, the politics of neo-liberal globalization paradoxically also offers certain opportunities. As Appadurai (1993) writes, the centre–periphery model of globalization cannot account for these other complex, overlapping and disjunctive variations which result in differing regional concerns together with new forms of cultural hybridism and multiplicity. Thus, neither the economic or cultural flow has been all one way. Globalization has arguably brought many aspects of non-Western cultures, from cuisine to medicinal, and from spiritual to aesthetic into the mainstream. The emergence of powerful new economies in other regions, such as the so-called 'tiger' economies of the Far East, demonstrates the successful translation of local tradition and social values into the workplace (such as corporate loyalty to and protection for workers in return for their conformity and hard work for the company) and enhanced the competitiveness of these economies (Ellington, 2004).

This multidirectional cultural flow makes possible an unexpected series of new and hybrid forms – of identities, beliefs and practices, and can reinvigorate 'traditions', albeit changing meanings and the relationships between component parts of the belief systems. Fernea (1995) describes how, despite prolonged attempts at influencing public opinion in the Arab Middle East and North Africa, attitudes have moved towards the reaffirmation of a regional, Muslim identity, and a hardening against Western value systems. Children in multicultural communities, both indigenous and minority ethnic, are exposed to such an array of cultural influences that they appear to adopt a 'pick-and-mix' attitude towards traditions, and develop multiple, hybrid 'identities' that perform an instrumental function within the immediate contexts where these children operate (Maitra, 2006). The rapid increase in exposure to global influences may create conflict between contradictory values systems. While this may give rise to parental difficulties and the possibility of emotional or behavioural problems in children, it can also lead to innovative solutions (Banhatti *et al.*, 2006).

Global exchange and the mental health disciplines

A comparative perspective of medical systems in diverse cultures highlights two key premises embedded in Western biomedicine, and therefore in Western psychiatric theory and practice – disease 'essentialism' and disease 'universalism' (Fabrega, 1996; Kleinman, 1996). Thus hypertension may vary in incidence and even clinical presentation from locale to locale and ethnicity to ethnicity, but, at least in principle, hypertension should occur anywhere (universalism), and retain its core characteristics such as pathophysiological patterns, course and outcome (essentialism). These underlying assumptions that operate in current psychiatric classifications raise not only practical issues concerning the usefulness of current nosology in clinical work, research and training, but also a deeply moral one. This ethical question concerns the appropriateness of using Western 'ethno-psychiatry' in settings where it may make little sense and potentially undermines more useful local nosologies and practice.

In critiquing the assumption of universalism it can be noted some conditions may descriptively resemble current psychiatric categories but may not be disorders at all in some cultures. Thus a person with 'schizotypal personality disorder' or even frank schizophrenia as categorized in Western ethno-psychiatry, can be a seer, prophet, artist, shaman, or even a healer in another culture (Littlewood, 1996; Okasha, 2000). In such a setting, what the West calls 'psychosis' may be interpreted (for example in some Islamic cultures) as a spiritual response to religious stagnation, where aspects of the psychosis are believed to confer positive mystic insights (Okasha, 2000).

We can see similar problems with the idea of disease essentialism. For example, Kleinman (1988) poses the question of how cultural overlap and cultural variation affects our understanding of the underlying processes. Kleinman compares the concept of neurasthenia, commonly used in regions of China, and the concept of major depression, commonly used in the West. He notes that the treatment approaches for these apparently overlapping (some would say corresponding) conditions differs significantly. Further, if we are to accept the essentialist underpinning of these diagnoses, then this must cast some doubt on the relevance of one or other diagnosis.

'Ethno-psychiatry' and anthropologically informed transcultural psychiatry

The chequered history of multiculturalism and its relationship with transcultural psychiatry has been summarized elsewhere (Kirmayer and Minas, 2000). It was during the latter half of the era of multiculturalism that the now well-recognized sub-specialty of transcultural psychiatry (or cultural psychiatry) began to take indigenous beliefs and practices, with regard to behavioural disturbance and mental distress, seriously. Moreover, in doing so, not only were the new transcultural psychiatrists trying to increase understanding of mental health nosologies and practices in other parts of the world, but, just as importantly, the new paradigms asked serious questions about the allegedly universal applicability of Western biomedical psychiatric theory and practice, and thus the very founding assumptions on which Western psychiatry is based. From this perspective Western psychiatry could now be viewed as a product of a particular society's history, philosophy, and ideology and thus a form of 'ethno-psychiatry'.

Another problem, as pointed out by Jadhav (2004), is that while this new anthropologically informed trancultural psychiatry, with its attendant critique of modern mainstream psychiatric practice, has taken hold in significant sections of Western psychiatric research, training and practice, in the non-Western world, from which much of this new insight is essentially derived, psychiatric practice remains rooted in the exported colonial model (i.e. of Western ethno-psychiatry). He gives the example of India, a nation of over a billion people, which has produced Booker Prize winners, but not yet a single textbook of psychiatry that is genuinely predicated on local psychological and social insights and realities. As a result, he points out, phenomenologies of rich bodily experiences are pushed into the black box of 'somatization', with the somatic experiences of patients being recorded in English by local mental health professionals on mental state examination forms derived from Maudsley (a famous psychiatric institute in London). This exclusion of culture systematically abolishes the ability to consider the role of major social and cultural variables that may well provide a phenomenological template to shape more appropriate local nosologies of distress (Kirmayer and Young, 1998).

The more context-rich paradigm of the 'new transcultural psychiatry' (Littlewood, 1990) illuminates many of the operating assumptions of Western traditional psychiatry and problematizes them. For example, reflecting Western cultural value systems, Western psychiatry views the self as being governed by internal desires, thoughts and feelings that are essentially autonomous. Conversely, in many non-Western cultures the individual is viewed (and is more likely to perceive themselves) as governed by social relationships, duties, responsibilities, and the behaviour and feelings of others. Coker (2003) illustrates some of the contradictions that can occur when the individualistic view of the self is juxtaposed with the social one. In her study of psychiatric patients in Egypt, she found that, whereas many Egyptian patients and their families viewed the presenting problems as residing within the fragmentation of interpersonal relationships and social structure, the doctor had to convert these into disembodied symptoms belonging to the individual, in order to be able to categorize the problems according to the Western psychiatric classification system that was being used. In his book *Mining Civilizational Knowledge,* Goonatilake (1998) points out that there is a wealth of knowledge held in non-Western cultures that has been almost completely overlooked and bypassed as the assumption of the inherent superiority of Western culture has been embedded in Western thought for many centuries now. For example, there are many different ways of conceptualizing the 'unconscious'. South Asian philosophies have for centuries had a wide-ranging and vibrant set of ideas on the nature of the unconscious, in contrast to Western culture that has grasped at trying to understand this only really in the last century or so. A wide variety of South Asian theories of mind, such as those arising from Buddhist and Upanishadic philosophies, have long been familiar with the relative nature of 'reality', and the distorting properties of 'perception'. The recognition of these limitations of the mind has long been required as the first step towards a 'true' knowledge of the nature of reality (Goonatilake, 1998).

With regard to our visions of childhood, those dreamt up by Western professionals and governments are not only imposed upon Western citizens, but also on populations worldwide who are viewed as in need of civilization and development (according to Western ideals). The export of Western notions of childhood, socialization and education is inextricably connected to the export of modern Western constructions of gender, individuality, and family amongst other things (Stephens, 1995, Comaroff and Comaroff, 1991). As particular conceptions of 'normal' childhood are exported, so are particular conceptions of 'deviant' childhoods. Western perceptions of the different lives that children lead in the developing world are dominated by stigmatizing notions, such as poverty (or 'need', as it is more politely described) materially and psychologically, with local peculiarities often seen as 'abusive' because these allegedly deprive children of what the West constructs as their 'birthright' or indeed their 'childhood'. Not surprisingly, these views justify continued efforts to export Western visions of childhood around the world (Stephens, 1995).

Just as narrow notions of child development, and the kind of rearing that best facilitates it, are being imposed on countries of the South, so also are highly problematic notions of mental disorders in children. The need of market economies continually to expand markets has allowed drug companies to exploit new, vague and broadly defined childhood psychiatric diagnoses, resulting in a rapid increase in the amount of psychotropic medication being prescribed to children and adolescents in the West (Timimi, 2002, 2005). Evidence is emerging that this trend is spreading to countries of the poorer South where growth in the prescribing of psychotropic medications to children is occurring (Wong *et al.*, 2004). Little research has been done on the safety and efficacy of psychotropic drugs in such children, with prescribing patterns in children often being based on information drawn from research in adults (Wong *et al.*, 2004). This suggests that the Western individualized biological/genetic conception of childhood mental health problems is spreading to the countries of the South and may be undermining more helpful indigenous belief systems (Timimi, 2005).

What is most obviously missing from the debates that are found in much contemporary academic literature on children's mental health is the non-Western perspective. Many non-Western cultures have long established theories and practices that consider child development, the contributions of parents, wider society and a number of factors that, framed in the language of Western culture, lie outside the social-psychological realm and more within the moral-ethical realm. When labelled 'spiritual', as these matters often are, they are quickly dismissed by the self-conscious professional Western view as marginal, if not bordering on the suspect. Labelled 'religious', these considerations are either viewed in reductionist categoric terms (as Islamic, Hindu, Catholic), or as problematically introducing the political-fundamentalist perspective into the favoured picture of health professions (where the fantasy is that our theories and practices are essentially apolitical).

It would be useful to enquire into what these systems of thought, at first glance unfamiliar and even alarmingly prescriptive, provide for the developing child. In the Indian tradition the human life cycle is conceptualized as unfolding in a series of stages each having unique tasks, with *samskaras* – expressive and symbolic performances – that mark the child's transition from one stage to another (Kakar, 1994; Banhatti *et al.*, 2006). Middle Eastern ideas on child development, heavily influenced by Islamic thought, have been formed, and debated by Islamic scholars, for many centuries (Gil'adi, 1992). Various stages of cognitive development are identified, which revolve around sophisticated concepts such as *tamyiz* (facility for discernment), *addab* (respect/ public manners) and *aql* (mindfulness or social intelligence) the development of which in a child is seen as evidence of readiness to progress to the next developmental phase (Timimi, 2005; Davis and

Davis, 1989; Fernea, 1995). Both these cultural systems emphasize religious duties and social values such as cooperation, truthfulness, helping the elderly, obeying parents, and the importance of the body in ensuring spiritual and psychological health.

Our lack of engagement with these cross-cultural perspectives represents a rather hidden form of institutionalized racism (or more accurately, institutionalized cultural hegemony) that has infected Western academic and political endeavours for too long. Not only does this present real dangers to the traditions and knowledge bases in existence in the non-Western world but it means that, in addition, the populations in the Western world are being denied the opportunity to benefit from the positive effects that embracing non-Western knowledge, values and practices may bring.

ADHD and globalization

The problem with current psychiatric classification system is more than just the misapplication of Western ethno-psychiatric categories in non-Western settings. Foregrounding the importance of cultural context has implications for practice in Western countries too. For example, although the social symbolic character of 'anorexia nervosa' is recognized, as well as its scarcity in countries where starvation is common and body weights labelled 'obese' by current Western criteria are valued as a sign of prosperity, this understanding seems to do little in deterring, undermining, or rethinking the category away from viewing it as a natural medical disorder (with biological underpinning). Using a culture-rich paradigm means wondering about the wisdom of so much effort being directed towards finding the neuro-biological substrate for anorexia rather than campaigning and consciousness-raising in the cultural discourse that over-idealizes the slimness of women.

Transcultural psychiatry and ADHD

Despite the continued failure to incorporate the insights of transcultural psychiatry into much of mainstream psychiatry, it has become impossible to discount this growing sub-specialty. There are now many prominent, senior and influential psychiatrists who are associated with this new anthropologically informed transcultural psychiatry 'movement', and its influence is thus visible in many training schemes and service provisions (in the West). Within the field of child and adolescent psychiatry, however, there is little to suggest that mainstream research, training, theory and practice is paying anything more than superficial lip service to the cultural dimension. Given that the young of any society are reliant on various care-providing adults to make decisions on their behalf, and thus ineluctably embedded in the broader context of social relationships, this is particularly disappointing as one might have expected that this specialty would take the lead in developing more context-rich paradigms.

A large body of sociological and anthropological literature already exists that explores the differing beliefs and practices which exist and change over time and across cultural groups with regard to the nature of childhood and child rearing. That such literature has been almost completely overlooked is more a testament to existing power hierarchies and vested interests than its lack of relevance to child and adolescent mental health (see Timimi, 2005 for further discussion). Instead the reverse has happened and the narrow deterministic biomedical template developed by adult psychiatry has been imported into child and adolescent psychiatry, leading to recent epidemics in conditions such as ADHD.

This drive to 'discover' biomedical templates within which to place various children's behaviours that are considered socially difficult, has resulted in the exclusion of cultural meaning and local significance of these behaviours and the adoption of 'universalizing' and 'essentializing' approaches. What currently passes for mainstream ADHD is completely embedded in such thinking, seemingly without being able to reflect critically on the implications such an approach has when working in the multicultural settings that we all now practise in. An example of this can be found in a recently produced document, written by a group of 15 prominent researchers and clinicians and entitled 'Global consensus on ADHD/HKD' (Global Working Group, 2004). It takes a universalizing approach, stating ADHD to be a valid neuro-developmental disorder that is found in all cultures, and an essentializing perspective, stating ADHD to be a genetic condition, with core aetiological and pathophysiological features, which is thus amenable to developing a uniform treatment approach (mainly medication) that can be applied across the world. Nowhere is there any evidence that the authors have taken seriously, or even acknowledged, that there are differing beliefs, attitudes and practices with regard to our understanding and approach to behavioural problems in the young. Indeed, despite presenting a detailed template on how to make a diagnosis of ADHD and how to plan treatment (using a flow chart), which the authors state can be used across the globe, the only treatment study referred to in the document is the now largely discredited

MTA group 14-month trial (MTA Co-operative Group, 1999) which took place in the USA (see Timimi, 2006, for a discussion of the critiques of this study). It is of great concern that documents such as the above, claiming that ADHD is under-diagnosed and under-treated across the world and basing their recommendations for intervention on one flawed study that took place in a Western country, can be published unchallenged in a peer-reviewed international journal. In our opinion, such a document could be deemed institutionally racist as a result.

The dangers of this uniform 'one-size-fits–all' approach to theory and practice is illustrated in David Walker's (2006) study of the practice of labelling native American Indian children from Yakama Nation tribes reservations with ADHD. Walker describes the long history of oppression to which the Yakama tribes have been subjected, apparently based on notions of the flawed 'genetic make-up' of American Indian 'races' that warranted the institution of eugenic measures. In the first half of the last century it prompted the forced admission of Yakama parents into mental institutions (and frequently the sterilization of mothers) and children to institutions where many were labelled as 'feebleminded', often subjected to physical and sexual abuse, and forced to do long hours of manual labour. Walker also documents the Yakama Nation's resilience in the face of this unremitting onslaught on their way of life and cultural ideals and the efforts by many community elders to keep traditional language, beliefs and practices alive. This complex colonial history has left a legacy of ambivalence in the community's relationship to mainstream institutions in the US including its schools, but also an invidious impact on the community's response to its own members, and their successes within the mainstream idiom. Walker tells of a young man who scored 99 per cent marks in an exam, and of an uncle who retorts, 'Huh, I'll bet you think you're better than us now'. Walker discusses the development of an 'oppositional identity' (Walker, 2006, p. 72) engendered by these ambiguities. Success at learning the language and behaviour codes of the White public school systems may be seen as a threat to minority cultural identity, and lead to a risk of being charged with being an 'apple' – 'red' ('Indian') on the outside and 'white' on the inside. Since the advent and increasing popularity of the ADHD label in the reservation health centres, schools have had an easy 'get out' clause when faced with the disrupting effects of these dynamics. Children may now be referred for evaluation for ADHD. In Walker's opinion the ADHD label has come to signify the new 'feebleminded'. The

bio-deterministic model of ADHD simply has no chance of notic-
ing these dynamics, let alone trying to address them. Indeed, its very
function would seem to be that of masking these problematic socio-
cultural factors, effectively serving the function of maintaining the
status quo.

An approach that is properly informed and inclusive of cultural variety (of the normal and of what is considered problematic) would need
to challenge this universalism and essentialism. This means including
cross-disciplinary and cross-cultural perspectives in research in order
to lay the foundations for a more thorough overhaul of the diagnostic
category, and the project to extend its use globally. This will require
an extensive questioning of the cultural assumptions underlying the
construct itself. How do we instil alertness to cultural contexts into
notions of deficit? Is it even possible to develop universal agreement on
what is sufficient attention (and what is not) or sufficient stillness (and
what is too much activity) without admitting that these judgements
are essentially context-dependent, varying with the daily activities and
expectations of children?

Despite attempts at standardizing criteria and assessment tools
in cross-cultural ADHD studies, major and significant differences
between raters from different countries are apparent (Mann *et al.*,
1992). There are also significant differences between raters when raters
rate children from different ethnic minority backgrounds (Sonuga-
Barke *et al.*, 1993). One replicated finding is an apparently high rate
of hyperactivity in China and Hong Kong (Shen *et al.*, 1985; Luk
and Leung, 1989). In these studies nearly three times as many Chinese as English children were rated as hyperactive. A more detailed
assessment of these results suggested that most of the 'hyperactive'
Chinese children would not have been rated as hyperactive by most
English raters and were a good deal less hyperactive than English children rated as 'hyperactive' (Taylor, 1994). One suggestion for such a
consistently large disparity in hyperactivity ratings between Chinese
and English children is that it may be due to the great importance of
school success in Chinese culture leading to an intolerance of much
lesser degrees of disruptive behaviour (Taylor, 1994). Whatever the
reason(s), it demonstrates that hyperactivity and disruptiveness is a
highly culturally constructed entity.

Thus, whatever part of conditions such as ADHD is biological,
how we construct meaning out of this is a cultural process. Brewis
and Schmidt (2003) studied a middle-class Mexican school with over
200 pupils. Using standard diagnostic criteria, they found that about

8 per cent of the children could be diagnosed as having ADHD, yet there was only one child in that school who had been given the diagnosis. Through interviews with parents and teachers they discovered that these carers regarded ADHD-type behaviours as within the boundaries of behaviours viewed as normal and expected for these children's ages.

This raises the question of the alleged suffering that children with ADHD experience, and that diagnosis and treatment would release them from. In other words, it charges those who fail to diagnose and treat it with failing in their professional responsibilities towards children. The issues raised are complex, and raise questions about the value and significance to be given to children's suffering, and how it is to be weighted by contextual considerations. For example, if we examine the category of 'deliberate self-harm', we find it contains a mixed bag of cases – of children who are hoping to draw attention to problems that are difficult to speak of more directly, and some whose intentions appear to be less the solution of dilemmas than the desire to use moral pressure to coerce others around them into acceding to their wishes. What proportion of the children who appeared markedly overactive and inattentive are unduly imprisoned by the extremely narrow range of behaviours acceptable within urban Western environments? That some of these children, 'hyperactive' in early life when they are less able to verbalize their frustration, grow into older children with 'conduct disorders' (or fall into the much-cited complexities of the 'dual-diagnosis' category) can scarcely be remarkable. A proportion of children will indeed be soothed by the knowledge that their fears have eventually been proven to be true and that the problem lies in them (and not their adverse parenting or social contexts). Whether or not medication makes a significant difference to their 'condition' or how they feel about their lives, it leads to conversations between their carers and professional systems, and activities that absorb them – investigations, dose monitoring, checklists and such – that takes some of the 'heat' off them.

A small group of children may well genuinely benefit from the medication. The question is whether the current pressures on mental health clinicians – to fill their 'quotas' for diagnosing ADHD led by prevalence statistics based on questionable criteria, and the anxieties about conformity within their disciplines – is the most useful climate in which to consider whether it is ethical to use medication because we do not feel able to alter the lopsidedly stringent expectations we impose on children. In another cultural framework it may be seen as more important to ensure, in non-negotiable terms, that children do not engage in sexual activity (because of risks to health and collective moral values, and to prevent pregnancies among those who lack the individual ability or collective support necessary to rear children of their own) than to ensure that children spend a fixed number of hours in school whether they wish to or not. In other words differing cultural contexts produce differing sets of expectations with regard to childhood and child rearing, which produce differing areas of concern, focus, attention, and practice. Whilst attention levels in a school setting may become the focus for a great deal of angst which produces particular social and professional systems of practice (such as ADHD clinics and stimulant prescription), for other cultural contexts attention levels in a school may have a much lower priority (and therefore much lower evidence of social and professional practices that focus on it). Who has the authority to decide which of these areas of focus produces practices that are 'better' for children than others?

Implications

This chapter suggests that understanding 'culture' is central to the task of understanding how systems of meaning and practice become constructed around certain childhood behaviours (in this case those that construct ADHD), particularly within the rapidly changing face of our socio-cultural contexts since the acceleration of globalization in the last few decades. Ideologies, local and distant, travel globally, exerting their influence in often unexpected ways and places, such as the impact of consumerist culture on health practice, or the impact of cultural beliefs about selfhood on parental and professional attitudes towards child care. These global movements of people and ideas offer an opportunity to reconsider the basic premises of our professional beliefs about children and the construct of ADHD. To do this we examined some of the macro-dynamics of globalization, its relevance to psychiatry more generally, and then ADHD specifically.

A more appropriate and ethical approach to understanding and dealing with 'poor' attention and 'hyper' activity in children (and for that matter adults) requires us to step back from the assumptions that shape current theory and practice, in order to ask more searching questions that could help us develop a better understanding of more regional beliefs and practices around these phenomena, which in turn is likely to undermine fatally the construct itself as it reveals the more relative (as opposed to universal and essential) nature of ADHD-type behaviours.

We need to ask questions like: what are the various important behavioural norms and ideals found in differing settings and across different historical periods, in particular with regard to categories such as age and gender? What developmental models exist and how do these vary in and between different cultural groups? How do different cultural groups (and children themselves) view the use of medicine for behavioural problems? What relation, if any, exists between moral 'good's and 'bad's (for example, is there a dualism such as between the mad and the bad, as exists in Western culture)? How is the self conceptualized and what are the goals this self is perceived to be developing towards? And so on. Such an approach to the problematic concept of ADHD can help produce a greater diversity in our understanding and hopefully result in a more sophisticated approach to the way we deal with what is essentially a loose collection of qualitatively normal behaviours found in most children at some time in their lives.

Notes

1. This older term is used (unrepentantly) in preference to the current use of 'mixed-heritage' which, as a recent refinement to the terminology, hopes to eliminate the problematics of skin colour and race by referring to other inheritances. It is our view that it merely moves the battle lines into increasingly vague, and self-referential, territory.
2. In the idiom of their language the parents spoke of her, with embarrassed pride, as the *moni/* 'jewel' of their eyes.
3. The moral authority of this position did not arise within the family, or from the beliefs of elders, nor indeed from within their own emotional convictions. This conviction grew out of contemporary public opinions in urban India shaped by overwhelming media images of what Western societies believed children were entitled to.
4. Health service provision in India covers a wide array of medical/healing systems, including Western medicine. The last may be delivered through private clinics (with the fees covering a wide range), or government hospitals/ clinics, where treatment is free or hugely subsidized. Other systems of medicine, including homoeopathic, Ayurvedic and Unani, may variably combine elements of Western biomedical care. At the other pole are systems that closely integrate physical and spiritual health in techniques that may loosely be termed 'religious' healing.
5. Globalization was defined by sociologist Roland Robertson (1992) as 'The compression of the world and the intensification of the consciousness of the world as a whole.'

References

Ang, I. (1996) *Living Room Wars*. London: Routledge.

Appadurai, A. (1993) Disjuncture and difference in the global cultural economy, in P. Williams and L. Chrisman (eds), *Colonial Discourse and Post-Colonial Theory*. Hemel Hempstead: Harvester Wheatsheaf.

Ballard, R. (2007) Living with difference: A forgotten art in urgent need of revival? In J. R. Hinnells (ed.), *Religious Reconstruction in the South Asian Diasporas: From One Generation to Another*. London: Palgrave Macmillan.

Banhatti, R., Dwivedi, K. and Maitra, B. (2006) Childhood: An Indian perspective in S. Timimi and B. Maitra (eds), *Critical Voices in Child and Adolescent Mental Health*. London: Free Association Books.

Brewis, A. and Schmidt, K. (2003) Gender variation in the identification of Mexican children's psychiatric symptoms, *Medical Anthropology Quarterly* 17, 376–93.

Coker, E. (2003) Narrative strategies in medical discourse: Constructing the psychiatric 'case' in a non-western setting, *Social Science and Medicine* 57, 905–916.

Comaroff, J. and Comaroff, J. (1991) Africa observed: Discourses of the imperial imagination, in J. Comaroff and J. Comaroff (eds), *Of Revelation and Revolution: Christianity, Colonialism and Consciousness in South Africa, Vol. 1*. Chicago: University of Chicago Press.

Crook, S., Pakulski, J. and Waters, M. (1992) *Postmodernization*. London: Sage.

Davis, S. S. and Davis, D. A. (1989) *Adolescence in a Moroccan Town*. New Brunswick, NJ: Rutgers University Press.

Ellington, L. (2004) *Learning from Japan*. Available at <http://www.indiana.edu/~japan/digest15.html>, accessed 27 September 2005.

Fabrega, H. (1996) Culture and historical foundations of psychiatric diagnosis, in J. E. Mezzich, A. Kleinman, H. Fabrega and D. L. Parron (eds), *Culture and Psychiatric Diagnosis: A DSM-IV Perspective*. Washington, DC: American Psychiatric Press.

Featherstone, M. (1991) *Consumer Culture and Postmodernism*. London: Sage.

Fernea, E. W. (ed.) (1995) *Children in the Muslim Middle East*. Austin: University of Texas Press.

Finkelhor, D. and Korbin, J. (1988) Child abuse as an international issue, *Child Abuse and Neglect* 12, 3–23.

Giddens, A. (1990) *The Consequences of Modernity*. Cambridge: Polity Press.

Giddens, A. (1991) *Modernity and Self-Identity*. Cambridge: Polity Press.

Gil'adi, A. (1992) *Children of Islam: Concepts of Childhood in Medieval Muslim Society*. Oxford: Macmillan.

Global Working Group (2005) Global consensus on ADHD/HKD, *European Journal of Child and Adolescent Psychiatry* 14, 127–37.

Goonatilake, S. (1998) *Mining Civilizational Knowledge*. Bloomington: Indiana University Press.

Jadhav, S. (2004) How 'culture bound' is 'cultural psychiatry'? *International Psychiatry: Bulletin of the Board of International Affairs of the Royal College of Psychiatrists* 4 (April), 6–7.

Kakar, S. (1994) *The Inner World of the Indian Child*. New Delhi: Oxford University Press.

Kirmayer, L. and Young, A. (1998) Culture and somatization: Clinical, epidemiological and ethnographic perspectives, *Psychosomatic Medicine* 60, 420–30.

Kirmayer, L. J. and Minas, H. (2000) The future of cultural psychiatry: An international perspective, *Canadian Journal of Psychiatry* 45, 438–46.

Kleinman, A. (1988) *Rethinking Psychiatry: From Cultural Category to Personal Experience*. New York: The Free Press.

Kleinman, A. (1996) How is culture important for DSM-IV? In J. E. Mezzich, A. Kleinman, H. Fabrega and D. L. Parron (eds), *Culture and Psychiatric Diagnosis: A DSM-IV Perspective*. Washington, DC: American Psychiatric Press.

Littlewood, R. (1990) Review article: From categories to contexts: A decade of the 'new cross-cultural psychiatry', *British Journal of Psychiatry* 156, 308–27.

Littlewood, R. (1996) Psychiatry's culture, *International Journal of Social Psychiatry* 42, 245–68.

Luk, S. L. and Leung, P. W. L. (1989) Conners teachers rating scale – a validity study in Hong Kong, *Journal of Child Psychology and Psychiatry* 30, 785–94.

Maitra, B. (1995) Lay schemas for health and illness – Bangladeshi and English mothers. Conference Proceedings, Working with Families in a Multi-Ethnic Society: Confronting Racism and Taking Acount of Culture, June, Institute of Family Therapy, London.

Maitra, B. (2006) Culture and the mental health of children: The 'cutting edge' of expertise, in S. Timimi and B. Maitra (eds), *Critical Voices in Child and Adolescent Mental Health*. London: Free Association Books.

Mann, E. M., Ikeda, Y., Mueller, C. W., Takahashi, A., Tao, K.T., Humris, E., Li, B. L. and Chin, D. (1992) Cross-cultural differences in rating hyperactive-disruptive behaviours in children, *American Journal of Psychiatry* 149, 1539–42.

MTA Co-operative Group (1999) A 14-month randomized clinical trial of treatment strategies for attention deficit/hyperactivity disorder, *Archives of General Psychiatry* 56, 1073–86.

Okasha, A. (2000) The impact of Arab culture on psychiatric ethics, in A. Okasha, J. Arboleda-Florez and N. Sartorius (eds), *Ethics, Culture, and Psychiatry: International Perspectives*. Washington, DC: American Psychiatric Press.

Robertson, R.(1992) *Globalization: Social Theory and Global Culture*. London: Sage Publications.

Said, E. (1978) *Orientalism*. London: Routledge.

Said, E. (1981) *Covering Islam*. London: Routledge.

Schiller, H. (1969) *Mass Communications and the American Empire*. New York: Augustus.

Shen, Y. C., Wong, Y. F. and Yang, X. L. (1985) An epidemiological investigation of minimal brain dysfunction in six elementary schools in Beijing, *Journal of Child Psychology and Psychiatry* 26, 777–88.

Sonuga-Barke, E. J. S., Minocha, K., Taylor, E. A. and Sandberg, S. (1993) Inter-ethnic bias in teacher's ratings of childhood hyperactivity, *British Journal of Developmental Psychology* 11, 187–200.

Stephens, S. (1995) Children and the politics of culture in 'Late Capitalism', in S. Stephens (ed.), *Children and the Politics of Culture*. Princeton: Princeton University Press.

Taylor, E. (1994) Syndromes of attention deficit and over-activity, in M. Rutter, E. Taylor and L. Hersov (eds), *Child and Adolescent Psychiatry, Modern Approaches: Third Edition*. Oxford: Blackwell Scientific Publications.

Timimi, S. (2002) *Pathological Child Psychiatry and the Medicalization of Childhood*. London: Brunner-Routledge.

Timimi, S. (2005) *Naughty Boys: Anti-Social Behaviour, ADHD, and the Role of Culture*. Basingstoke: Palgrave Macmillan.

Timimi, S. (2006) The politics of ADHD, in S. Timimi and B. Maitra (eds), *Critical Voices in Child and Adolescent Mental Health*. London: Free Association Books.

Walker, D. (2006) ADHD as the new 'feeblemindedness' of American Indian children, in G. Lloyd, J. Stead and D. Cohen (eds), *Critical New Perspectives on ADHD*. Abingdon: Routledge.

Wong, I. C., Murray, M. L., Camilleri-Novak, D. and Stephens, P. (2004) Increased prescribing trends of paediatric psychotropic medications, *Archives of Disease in Childhood* 89, 1131–2.

Chapter 8

Social Deprivation or Brain Dysfunction? Data and the Discourse of ADHD in Britain and North America

Nicky Hart and Louba Benassaya

Contrasting images of ADHD in Britain and North America

Popular knowledge and public concern about the state of children's mental health takes different forms in developed societies depending on political culture, medical ideology, and the institutional framework of health care. In North America, the rising incidence of Attention Deficit and Hyperactivity Disorder (ADHD) features prominently in debates about the psychological well-being of children in contemporary society. It is the mental disorder singled out by the Centers for Disease Control and Prevention (CDC) Mortality and Morbidity Weekly Report (MMWR). Data from the 2003 National Survey of Children's Health (NSCH)[1] reported as many as 10 per cent of US boys and almost 5 per cent of girls affected by this disability making it the most prevalent and publicized mental disorder of childhood.[2] These are estimates. The *true* incidence of ADHD in the US is not known with certainty because it is not a reportable condition and the NSCH statistics come from superficial self-reported survey data (see below pp. 235). The number of prescriptions for Ritalin™ and other ADHD drugs is the most certain indicator of rising trends. During the 1990s the production of Ritalin™ and related drugs rose by as much as 900 per cent to supply an afflicted population which is now so numerous that schools and even summer camps

218

have had to make special provision to dispense children's *meds* to ensure that the vast supply in circulation is not diverted to illicit recreational use.[3]

The signs of an ADHD epidemic out of control have occasioned some anxious speculation including concern that the promotional efforts of pharmaceutical corporations might be inflating demand for childhood medications.[4] Politicians periodically voice concern and White House conferences have been called to help lawmakers figure out what is going on. These occasions inevitably provide a convenient platform for the nation's leading paediatricians to reiterate their surprisingly upbeat view of the epidemic. The fact that a growing proportion of children now depend on continuous medication to help them cope both at home and in an increasingly competitive classroom environment is not *officially* viewed as an indicator of worsening relations between parents and children, overcrowded classrooms or of a child-unfriendly post-modern culture. Instead the impression emerging from professional literature is that paediatricians are becoming more effective at identifying children with congenital problems that need treatment. And the treatment of choice is chemotherapy, specifically psycho-stimulant drugs which are claimed to compensate efficiently for the deficiencies of mother nature. Collective professional confidence in chemotherapy is evidenced in the repeated observation that only a fraction of children who could benefit from these wonder drugs are currently under treatment.

Publicity about the tribulations of modern childhood takes a different form across the Atlantic. In Britain, deteriorating trends in youth delinquency, anti-social behaviour and self-harm generate a high level of public concern as well as legislation aimed at outlawing breaches of unacceptable behaviour. Though these are prime political and social issues, they are also part of the national discourse of health as is evidenced in a recent British Medical Association (BMA) report which highlighted their relationship to worsening trends in children's mental health (BMA, 2006). This report estimates a doubling since 1975 of the incidence of depression, eating, sleeping, learning and conduct disorders to highlight the shortage of medical services for dealing with them. The symptoms of ADHD or Hyperkinetic Disorder (HD), as it is known in the UK, are submerged within this list. They are notable because HD is the only mental disorder likely to be treated with prescription medicine in the UK (see p. 226 below). Though the British media frequently carries reports of rapidly increasing rates of medication, the best estimates of prevalence (see p. 222 below) indicate that it is still only a fraction of the US rate (1.5% overall, 2.6% in boys and 0.4% in girls) and the disorder does not occupy anything like the same cultural space in the debate about childhood and its discontents in modern times as it does in the USA.

In Britain, the issue of social inequality has played a major role shaping the political and professional discourse of health since New Labour became the party of government. This may account for the greater availability of systematic and comprehensive evidence of the *social distribution* of all the mental disorders of childhood in the government's own statistical output. Though many paediatric psychiatrists in the United Kingdom probably share an inclination to construct the symptoms of ADHD as a congenital phenomenon, the picture that emerges from national data draws attention to the fact that social deprivation is a primary factor of childhood health and illness, both physical and mental. The children most at risk live in poverty and social disadvantage and awareness of this fact brings a potential ethical issue to the debate about the safety of administering powerful psycho-active drugs to children. Recent high-profile reports of suicide attempts among medicated children have made doctors more cautious about the short, let alone long-term, safety of drugs which claim to manage emotional insecurity and, though it is often argued that Ritalin™ has a proven safety record based on more than three decades of use, this reputation is not founded upon a prospective longitudinal study of the kind which finally revealed, once and for all, the lethal nature of cigarettes. Safety issues aside, the evidence that mental disorder in childhood is socially stratified raises the question of whether doctors should be dispensing drugs to manage the fallout of social inequality. Though at the current rate of medication in the UK, this thought is probably not a significant deterrent, it would undoubtedly loom larger if the ADHD epidemic crosses the Atlantic.

The important point here is that the institutional framework of health policy in Britain backed by appropriate epidemiological evidence leaves more space for an environmental explanation. This leads to an interesting paradox. Even though British paediatric psychiatry employs the more stringent World Health Organization (WHO) diagnostic criteria which identify only the more severe symptoms of disorder, the resulting medical discourse is still more likely to recognize a causal role for social deprivation. In the US, psychiatrists employ their own diagnostic checklist to diagnose ADHD and this has been repeatedly modified in recent decades to permit a larger percentage of children to be qualified as learning disabled (see p. 223). Though this has undoubtedly fuelled an increase in the numbers of children identified and treated, it has not shifted the orthodox medical view that the disorder is basically an intrinsic disability of congenital origins.

So we get two different accounts of the meaning and manifestation of ADHD on each side of the Atlantic Ocean. These accounts are variously informed by social science data. In this chapter, we attempt to paint an accurate picture of the incidence and distribution of the symptoms of ADHD in the two nations. We are aware that the evidence available to us from the United Kingdom is based on a carefully conducted government-sponsored face-to-face study. The evidence for the United States is also drawn from a government survey, which, though conducted by telephone, covered more than 100,000 households in 50 states. Ours is a secondary analysis of these data that are in the public record and are therefore potentially part of the contemporary discourse in the two nations. The prevailing view of the problems of childhood in contemporary society is constructed from many different sources, some more reliable than others. In this chapter we have restricted ourselves to the best available empirical evidence in an attempt to construct an accurate comparison of how far the disorder has developed in each population. As sociologists, we believe in an empirical reality, accessible by systematic data. We emphasize here that our aim is to go beyond popular discourse, or even adjudicate it. High-quality survey data are an essential ingredient of this effort.

In the USA, research on ADHD is largely confined by a bio-medical and clinical perspective. Studies conducted within this paradigm are frequently funded by pharmaceutical companies and they rely on case control methods to investigate either the somatic peculiarities of afflicted children or the effectiveness and efficiency of drug therapy. In the UK, the availability of a much richer body of evidence gathered within the framework of social epidemiology produces an alternative environmental account which has a better chance of competing with biological or genetic reductionism. These different research orientations generate the 'scientific substance' for revealing the truth about ADHD. They in turn produce different kinds of discourses of the meaning of the disorder pointing to different strategies for policy makers and practitioners in each setting. This chapter explores these different discourses of ADHD in the two nations, along with the data and the political processes by which they are generated. Let us start with data.

ADHD prevalence in Britain and North America

In 2004, the estimated incidence of ADHD in the US was 7 per cent with 2.5 boys afflicted for every one girl. In Britain the term hyperkinetic disorder (HD) is employed for children who exhibit the symptoms of ADHD and in the same year, i.e. 2004, only 1.6 per cent of British children met the criteria for a positive diagnosis in a respective gender ratio of 6 to 1. These estimates are taken from government-sponsored surveys in each country. Figure 8.1 summarizes the international difference indicating also the proportion of children in each nation treated with powerful psycho-active medicines to control their symptoms of disorderly and distracted behaviour.

The percentage of afflicted children given psycho-stimulant medicine to control their behaviour is 55 per cent in the US compared to 43 per cent in Britain. In real terms, the much higher incidence of ADHD in North America means that many more children routinely live 'under the influence' of amphetamine-type medications to calm them down at home and help them cooperate, if not compete diligently in the classroom. This is brought out in Figure 8.1, which shows clearly by just how much the percentage of medicated children in the US dwarfs the British incidence.

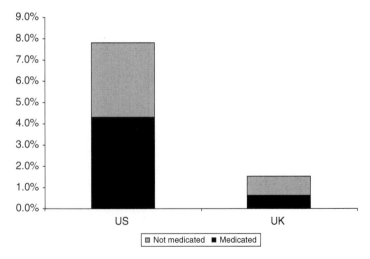

Figure 8.1 Total incidence of ADHD/hyperkinetic disorder according to whether child is medicated

Sources: Green *et al.* (2005; adapted from table 7.10) and Visser and Lesesne (2005).

Between 1997 and 2003/2004, the incidence of ADHD in the US National Child Health Survey rose from 5.5 to 7.2. The rate climbed 25 per cent among boys and 54 per cent among girls, a difference which helped close the gender gap in what has been traditionally thought of as a male affliction. The increasing incidence of ADHD among girls in the US made an important contribution to the rising trend, shifting the nation even further away from the European norm. In Britain, less than half of one per cent of girls get labelled ADHD and there was no discernible increase in prevalence between 1999 and 2004. Figure 8.2 summarizes gender differences in ADHD/HD within each national population. It shows the narrowing gap in the US in contrast to the widening gap in the UK. It also includes the gender gap in emotional disorders for the UK as a reference point to indicate that the wider gender gap in childhood only applies to the symptoms of ADHD.[5] Each column measures the ratio of male to female prevalence, which does not reveal the actual incidence in either society.

Between 1999 and 2003, as the rate rose overall, the gender gap in the US narrowed from 3.1 to 1 to 2.5 to 1. In a similar period (1999–2004), the overall rate was pretty static in the UK, but the gender gap went in the opposite direction, widening slightly from

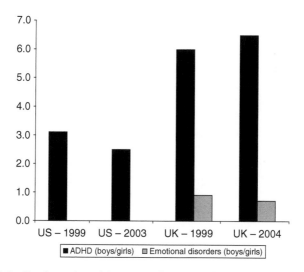

Figure 8.2   Gender ratios of ADHD and emotional disorders
Sources: Green *et al.* (2005; adapted from tables 4.1 and 4.2) and Visser and Lesesne (2005).

6:1 to 6.5:1. A large excess of the disorder among boys is in line with the gender distribution manifested in the US in 1960/70 when the doctors began to break the taboo on administering drugs like Ritalin™ to children. At that time very few girls received a prescription; the gender gap was more than 10 boys to every girl (Conrad, 1976). In this early period, hyperactivity was the diagnosis, and boys were much more likely to be a target of medication. The narrowing of the sex difference since then is a response to a greater willingness among paediatricians to give small children medicines which act on the central nervous system, a disposition which developed in concert with a broadening of the range of *disabling* traits included in the diagnostic checklist.[6] The most important development here was the inclusion of *distractability* or attention deficit among the signs of troubling child behaviour. Bringing this into the picture allowed day-dreaming girls to be declared learning disabled. This is the key factor diminishing the gender gap in the US; it also plays a major part in explaining why the numbers afflicted and the rate of medication are so much higher.

The terminology 'ADHD' is a product of American medical culture. It is a hybrid diagnosis which assembles all of the 'symptoms' on which drugs like Ritalin™ claim to exert a beneficial effect. In the United States, doctors currently depend on the Diagnostic and Statistical Manual IV (DSM-IV) which is more flexible and inclusive than the ICD (International Classification of Disease) which Britain and the rest of Europe employ to classify mentally disordered children. Compared to the ICD, the DSM makes it much easier to become ADHD. Whereas eligible children in the US must *either* exhibit signs of hyperactivity-impulsivity *or* inattention, in the UK, they have to meet *both* criteria to get labelled hyperkinetic (Green *et al.*, 2005). Though the term ADHD is gaining currency in Europe including Britain,[7] the term hyperkinetic disorder (HD) has continued to be employed to identify developmentally deviant children. The increased willingness to label children as learning-disabled and eligible for drug therapy in the US is therefore influenced by milder diagnostic criteria which turn out to be much more inclusive from a gender perspective. Figure 8.1 does not disaggregate medication rates by gender; however, there is no statistically significant difference between medication rates of males and females in the US (Visser and Lesesne, 2005), which indicates the greater willingness of American doctors to medicate children, irrespective of gender.

Though the national difference in Figures 8.1 and 8.2 appears striking by any standard, its epidemiological significance is ambiguous.

Nobody knows for sure whether the current incidence of 10 per cent of boys with ADHD represents an increase over rates prevailing before 1997. The strong probability that it does is increased by the fact that the use of the psycho-stimulant drugs to suppress the symptoms multiplied by a factor of 8 or 9 during the 1990s.[8] This is spectacular evidence of an underlying epidemic and it has sparked political and public concern that the numbers of children being prescribed psycho-stimulant medicine are excessively high and deeply troubling. This view is expressed by a disparate group of writers, cultural critics, politicians, *dissident* practising paediatricians and medical and social science academic/researchers and physicians concerned about or intrigued by the recent epidemic scale of the ADHD trend. The character of the reaction may be gauged from the words of cardiac specialist Steven Nissen MD, a member of the Drug Safety and Risk Management Advisory Committee (9 February 2006) assembled to review 24 cases of sudden cardiac deaths reported among young patients taking ADHD drugs. As he put it: 'I want the physicians' hands to tremble a bit when they write a prescription for these drugs' (FDA, 2006).[9] Nissen, in company with other expert members, was alarmed by evidence presented to the meeting of a spectacular increase in the number of prescriptions written for ADHD medicines between 1999 and 2003. It was the rising rate of medication, rather than the evidence of adverse effects which triggered an unanticipated proposal to put a bold warning on the medications to alert family practitioners to the fact that psycho-stimulant medicine acts directly on the circulatory system, raising blood pressure and heart rate in ways that could have long-term deleterious effects.[10]

As noted, the number of prescriptions per head of population for ADHD in the US is up to 7 or 8 times the European rate. This means that many more US children are given medicine to control their behaviour, and the exposed population is more socially diverse (i.e. it is evenly spread throughout the social hierarchy). The narrowing gender gap in ADHD is one dimension of this and, as we have seen, it has been facilitated by broadening the diagnostic checklist to admit many more children to the population of 'learning-disabled' youngsters. Among those convinced that the trend is a social phenomenon, we find two distinctive versions of environmentalism. The first is that the epidemic is a product of rampant pharmaceutical capitalism, the second, possibly connected, that it signifies a sea change in the experience of growing up in a fast-changing society in which there is less and less time for family life and fewer resources for labour-intensive parenting, including the provision of nutritious home-cooked meals eaten around the family dinner table. Putting these impressions together sees the rising toll of kids with ADHD as the product of too much junk food, too much TV, not enough quality time with parents, too much sedentary indoor leisure and too much reliance on prescription drugs to solve all the problems of troubling social relationships in contemporary society.[11]

The symptoms of ADHD in Britain go under the heading hyperkinetic *disorder* and the empirical evidence for interpreting trends are more developed. We can gauge the changing prevalence of all kinds of mental disorders from a series of national cohort studies established to monitor changes in child welfare in 1946, 1958, 1970 and 1999. These longitudinal surveys report a sustained deterioration in children's mental health during the last quarter of the twentieth century, a period which witnessed fundamental change in family life and parent–child relations.[12] The clearest signs of deterioration involve depressive illness, self-harm and behaviours which go under the heading '*conduct disorders*'. Conduct disorders including delinquent and anti-social behaviour both alone and in groups rose from 6.8 per cent to 14.9 per cent between 1975 and 2000, the parallel rise for emotional problems was from 10.2 per cent to 16.9 per cent.[13] The evidence for ADHD is more equivocal in these longitudinal studies though the number of prescriptions issued for its treatment are known to have risen sharply in the last five years.

In Britain, hyperkinetic disorder is the only mental disorder of childhood which is likely to be treated with prescription medicines. As Figure 8.1 reveals, 43 per cent of those identified with HD were receiving medication in 2004. This is compared with a 13 per cent medication rate for autism, 9 per cent for conduct disorders (mostly for co-morbid hyperkinetic disorder) and 7 per cent for emotional disorder (approximately half of it co-morbid hyperkinetic disorder). Comparable figures for the US are not published in this issue of the MMWR, though reports suggest that US paediatricians feel less constrained about supplying the whole repertoire of psychotropic drugs, including anti-depressants, to school and even pre-school age children.[14]

Congenital anomaly in the medical discourse of ADHD

The medical discourse of ADHD in the USA sends strong signals that the symptoms are the product of a *congenital* anomaly.[15] The word congenital is employed cautiously to mean literally a condition that is present at birth (con = with, genital = birth). It could be the product of genetic inheritance, physiological idiosyncrasy or the result of birth injury. The signals pointing to fundamental organic causes are emitted by a research literature which is: (a) oriented to uncovering differences in the size, structure and functioning of the brains of afflicted children; (b) focused on evaluating the efficacy of medication versus other therapies; and (c) in the routine use of the term *ADHD children* which conveys the impression that we are dealing with a specific category or sub-type of human being. This impression is strengthened by the absence of any *serious* countervailing epidemiological account of the social distribution of the disorder. If the paediatric profession was concerned that ADHD had external causes, it would surely have pressurized the government to establish a more sophisticated apparatus for measuring the incidence and social contours of the disorder. The absence of even an accurate count of the number of children under treatment is the most telling sign that ADHD is viewed as an intrinsic disability. One consequence is the lack of a population denominator for gauging the safety of ADHD drugs (see p. 225). Though the percentage of the child population identified with ADHD has been estimated at between 3 per cent and 7 per cent for more than three decades, only recently has there been an organized national effort to count the incidence, monitor trends and use national data to explore the social context in which the disorder arises. In 1997, the Centers for Disease Control and Prevention (CDC) set in place a survey instrument for estimating the size of the afflicted population and highlighting its salient social characteristics. These data are examined below and compared with the available British evidence.

Speculation about the determining role of genes in socially stratified health outcomes is a touchy business (though becoming less so) and many medical researchers understandably shy away from the explanations which might be construed as simply *eugenic. Gene environment* interaction is the respectable contemporary framework for discussing and researching genetic inheritance as one among many factors of disease or disorder but this idealized approach is belied by a terminology which continues to rely on a label designating clinical characteristics in the afflicted population as the means of capturing the essence of ADHD and by the lack of research on the influence of the social environment. The same impression is conveyed by the absence of any *significant* concern in the professional/research literature on the scale of medication or the ethics of using prescription medicines to compensate for problems arising in the social environment.[16] The lack of this concern testifies to the belief that the phenomenon is not environmental.

The theory that ADHD is the product of brain peculiarities has been around in one form or another for decades. The acronym MBD has served as a flexible shorthand for changing ideas on this theme. It can be translated as *minimal brain damage*, *minimal brain dysfunction*, or *minimal brain disorder*. In each case, the physiological source is *too minimum* to be detected. Despite its longevity, the theory of MBD has proved consistently resistant to empirical proof.[17] In 1998, the National Institutes of Health Consensus Conference on ADHD concluded that there was '*no independent, valid test for ADHD*' nor '*any data to indicate that ADHD is due to a brain malfunction*' (National Institutes of Health Consensus Development Conference Statement, 2000). When untreated, there is still no evidence of the disorder leaving an unambiguous bio-chemical 'footprint' in a child's body. Considerable research effort over three decades has been dedicated to the quest to uncover a physiological basis for ADHD, but there is still no objective test of abnormality (Leo and Cohen, 2003).

Researchers have tried to prove that children displaying the symptoms of ADHD are constitutionally different, e.g. they have smaller or less developed brains. Since the practice of medication got under way in the 1960s, the technology for investigating brain function has gotten more sophisticated with the emergence of MRI. But still adequate proof of congenital disability remains as elusive as it does for autism, whose origins in a somatic neuro-pathology have also yet to be demonstrated. Some studies claim to have uncovered signs of a statistically significant somatic abnormality but then it turns out that the affected children *may* have been on powerful drugs which act on the central nervous system including the brain for months or even years. Prior medication is a significant confounding factor yet many papers reporting statistical associations fail even to mention whether the research design controlled for this variable. This makes it impossible to separate *congenital* characteristics from the effects of bio-chemical therapy on the young developing brain. If the goal is to demonstrate a 'natural' difference between groups of children, the necessity to recruit both research and control samples who have not yet been exposed to bio-chemically based therapy would seem obvious and yet a large volume of resources has been expended on investigations where the researchers not only failed to obtain samples of untreated children but perhaps even failed to recognize the necessity of doing so. Paradoxically, this applies to a majority of publications (Leo and Cohen, 2003).

Despite the lack of sound evidence, the impression that ADHD is a congenital abnormality has strengthened in recent years in the context of the emerging belief that it is an inherited trait which runs in families and is therefore a permanent disability requiring treatment throughout life. This is obviously good news for the pharmacy business and many sufferers and their parents also find comfort in an account which eradicates the thought that the disorder is someone's fault. In keeping with a congenital interpretation, the rapid rise of the disorder is constructed as a story of scientific progress in which paediatricians become increasingly skilled at uncovering hidden disability that can be easily remedied. This is facilitated by the normalization of disability, a cultural development fuelled by legislation against discrimination in all its forms which also helps explain medical complacency in the face of an epidemic of learning disability. Orthodox medical opinion dismisses a link between rising prescriptions and trends of diminishing mental well-being in the child population. The evidence of large geographical variation in ADHD across the 50 states is more likely to be seen as the product of regional or class disparity in access to paediatric care than as a sign that the disorder is the product of variations in the social environment in different places (LeFever *et al.*, 2003).

MBD theory is tenacious because it serves as a justification for the treatment of children with amphetamine drugs, a practice which originally met strong professional resistance.[18] The practice of administering powerful psychoactive drugs to children whose brain is still developing is more easily rationalized if the central nervous system of the patient is believed to be fundamentally defective. The treatment was cautiously pioneered in the US in the 1960s and once the cultural barriers were down, the willingness to medicate accelerated. During the 1990s, the number of US children given drugs to manage the central nervous system more than tripled and even spread to pre-schoolers aged 3–4 despite the fact that there is no FDA mandate for this use and product labels specifically warn against it. It is hard to imagine that any responsible doctor would advocate giving amphetamines to a 3- or 4-year-old *except* in the context of an irremediable congenital anomaly.

ADHD and health inequality

The statistical evidence generated by the British government as part of its policy making function runs against the impression that ADHD is best thought of as a bio-medical phenomenon. The social distribution of the disorder follows the contours of a class mortality gradient. In other words, it fits the classic profile of health inequality: low prevalence at the top, and high prevalence at the bottom of the social hierarchy. Children exhibiting the symptoms of emotional and conduct disorders, and those afflicted with the troubling symptoms of attention deficit and hyperactivity disorder are much more likely to be poor, to be raised by single and/or unemployed parents, to grow up in neighbourhoods scarred by the signs of underprivilege and to be exposed to stressful life events and social relationships in their early lives.

Figure 8.3 displays the class gradient of *psychiatric morbidity* as a whole in British children. The rate is around 4 per cent among children in families where the main breadwinners are employed in higher professional occupations (e.g. lawyers, doctors, professors). It is four times higher (16 per cent) in families where parents are either chronically unemployed or have never worked at all.

This group includes single-parent families headed by young women with no labour market experience prior to becoming mothers. The rate of ADHD British style (hyperkinetic disorder) follows the same course. It increases from 0.5 per cent in professional families to 2.6 per cent in households with no attachment to the labour market, a five-fold increase. In between these two poles of social privilege and underprivilege, the risk of mental disorder is around 6 per cent in

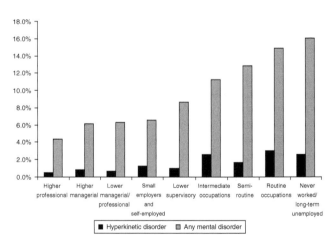

Figure 8.3   Social class and mental health in childhood, England and Wales 2004
Sources: Green *et al.* (2005; adapted from table 4.14).

other middle-class strata before 'jumping' to more than 8 per cent in the lower supervisory/technical occupations; from this point onwards, it rises steadily on each successive downward rung of the social hierarchy. If we take the lower supervisory occupational category in Figure 8.3, as the division between the middle- (white collar) and working-class (blue collar) strata of British society (containing respectively 56 per cent and 44 per cent of the population), we can conclude that social class is strongly associated with children's mental well-being. Working-class kids face a much higher probability of experiencing the symptoms of mental disorder in all its forms than their peers in middle-class homes; hyperkinetic disorder is no exception.

The occupational class gradient of ADHD can be translated to another variable representing the social and economic geography of health inequality. This variable is based on the ACORN classification which uses the census characteristics of the area where a child lives (the postal code) to summarize its salient social characteristics. Figure 8.4 classifies the same sample of children by the quality of their living environment. In a literal sense this variable represents the social and economic environment of daily life and therefore the differential opportunities for physical and intellectual development in childhood.

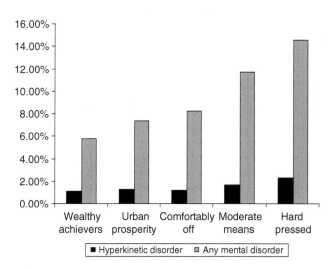

Figure 8.4 Health inequality in childhood and the social geography of disadvantage
Sources: Green *et al.* (2005; adapted from table 4.19).

Once again, we find the social gradient so typical in the health inequality research literature. The symptoms of childhood psychiatric morbidity in areas populated by wealthy families are only half the rate of areas where families with moderate means make their homes. The gap is even wider between the most advantaged and the least disadvantaged neighbourhoods and it applies to all mental, as well as hyperkinetic, disorders. These findings recur irrespective of the social indicator used to stratify the population as following Figure 8.5 shows.

Whether it is education, income or occupational class, the result is virtually the same. The simple measures of social stratification in Figure 8.5 divide the national population into two segments of approximately 60 per cent and 40 per cent growing up respectively in more propitious and less propitious circumstances. In each case, children who grow up in good socio-economic circumstances are much less likely to exhibit symptoms of all kinds of mental disorder including ADHD British style. From these data, we get an unmistakable impression that the gap in mental health, including ADHD, between the two segments of British society is strongly related to life chances as these are shaped by the structures of social inequality.

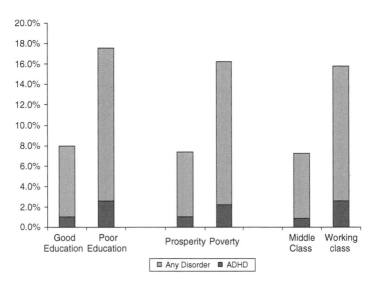

Figure 8.5   Social inequalities in childhood mental health summary indicators
Sources: Green *et al*. (2005; adapted from tables 4.10, 4.12, and 4.14). Population divisions: 44 per cent working class, 39 per cent poverty, and 32 per cent poor education.

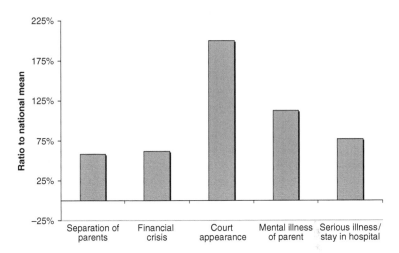

Figure 8.6   Prevalence of hyperkinetic disorder by stressful life events, UK 2004
Sources: Green *et al.* (2005; adapted from table 7.20).

The British survey evidence also gives us a close-up view of how structured social inequality translates into negative experiences in early life. Figure 8.6 displays the ratio of stressful life events in childhood in children identified with HD compared with the national mean. It reveals that the risk of developing the symptoms of HD is more than 50 per cent higher where a child is exposed to the separation of parents or to a financial crisis in the family. The ratio rises to 75 per cent excess in cases of serious illness requiring hospitalization and to 100 per cent where a parent reports their own mental illness. The highest excess of all is where a parent is in trouble with the law – reports of a court appearance by a parent raises the risk by almost 200 per cent.

British children who display symptoms of hyperkinetic disorder are more likely to be exposed to troubling events in early life. This comes out clearly in Figure 8.6. These data are suggestive, not conclusive. Even in a sample of 10,000 families (see below), the incidence of HD is too small to achieve statistical significance except using simplified variables of the kind displayed in Figures 8.3–8.5. Nor do the reported associations with specific life events allow us to separate cause and effect with any certainty; this could only be achieved in a prospective study based on a large sample of children. But the pattern in Figure 8.6 reinforces the importance of investigating the causal connections between symptoms of mental illness/disability in children and their daily living environment and, given the rising incidence of ADHD in the US, it highlights the importance of asking the same questions there. How far is the pattern observed in Britain also true of the USA?

Disparity versus inequality in childhood mental health: contrast and correspondence in the UK and the US

The social distribution of psychiatric morbidity replicated in Figures 8.3–8.6, is based on a large purpose-designed survey conducted under the auspices of the British Department of Health in 2004.[19] It was a repeat of an earlier survey conducted in 1999. The researchers drew on a sample of more than 10,000 families drawn from the records of the child benefit system. Child benefit is a non-means tested income transfer distributed to every household with children. Since it is not tied to household income, but is rather an economic citizenship entitlement, there is a high uptake which means the sampling frame would have included virtually all households with children. At 76 per cent, the response rate was comparatively high and, especially so, in view of the time it took to gather the evidence. The face-to-face interviews lasted between 90 and 120 minutes, even longer where children were old enough to be recruited as additional informants. The survey design involved identifying the symptoms of mental disorder both from questions and prompts, and, where appropriate, from direct observation. In addition a questionnaire was mailed to the teacher of every child in the survey. This generated a variety of reports and observations of possible morbidity whose relevance was determined by a team of clinical coders. The two surveys conducted five years apart revealed little change in the incidence of psychiatric morbidity between 1999 and 2004. The prevalence of ADHD British style, 1.5 per cent and 1.6 per cent among children 5–16 years old, was virtually the same on both dates.[20] These observations instil some confidence that the survey data used to construct Figures 8.2–8.6 drew on evidence collected with considerable care and attention.

Government statistics designed to monitor trends in childhood disorders are also available in the US from a survey covering more than 100,000 households from all 50 states and the District of Columbia. The National Survey of Children's Health (NSCH) was conducted between January 2003 and July 2004 by the Centers for Diseases Control and Prevention's National Center of Health Statistics, which used the State and Local Area Integrated Survey (SLAITS) programme to gather data on all aspects of child health including learning disabilities and mental disorders. SLAITS surveys use the sampling frame of the National Immunization Survey (NIS) to randomly sample households with children under 18 years old (US Department of Health and Human Services HRSA, Maternal and Child Health Bureau, 2005). For the NSCH, interviews were conducted over the *telephone* and were designed to take an average of *25 minutes* to complete.[21] In households with more than one child under 18 years old, one child was randomly selected as the focus of the interview. The respondent was identified as the adult knowing the most about the child's health and health care and 5.9 per cent of the interviews (6,035) were conducted in Spanish; all of the remaining interviews were conducted in English. The response rate was 68.8 per cent, resulting in 102,353 completed interviews.

These two national surveys evidently use quite different methods to arrive at the respective national estimates of the numbers of children who are learning disabled. Despite this, they at least provide a preliminary opportunity to compare the incidence and social distribution of ADHD. The first question of interest is whether an equivalent social gradient in the distribution of HD is also found for ADHD in the US. To answer this question, we draw upon three indicators of social hierarchy: race, income, and parental education, which are recorded in both surveys.[22]

Figure 8.7 compares the race distribution of ADHD in the US and the UK.[23] The comparison is confined to children classified as either black or white in the two nations i.e. it excludes other race/ethnic categories. The data are displayed as ratios to the national mean in each case. Using ratios disguises the different incidence in the two nations but it brings out clearly the extent of race disparity. In the UK, we can see that ADHD is overwhelmingly a white male disorder. White British boys have the highest ratio to the national average (2.9:1.6) whereas white British girls exhibit the lowest (0.4:1.6). The equivalent ratios among British black boys and girls reinforce the impression that HD is a highly gendered and racialized disorder in the UK. Children of both sexes in the black population record below average rates of hyperactivity disorder (0.6 per cent and 0.7 per cent), their profile is close to that of British white girls. It is white boys who are 'out on a limb' as far as the troubling symptoms of ADHD are concerned.

The picture in the US is quite different. There we see an equivalent gender differential in both the black and the white population. Irrespective of race, approximately 12 per cent of boys were reported as suffering from ADHD in 2004, compared with 5 per cent of white

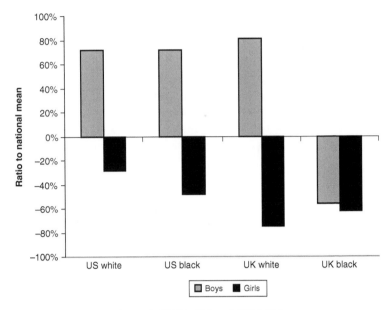

Figure 8.7   Race, gender and ADHD, US and UK 2004
Sources: Green *et al.* (2005; adapted from table 4.6) and Visser and Lesesne (2005).

girls and 3.6 per cent of black girls. ADHD is not distinctively white in the US and compared with the UK, it is fast becoming less distinctively male. It is worth noting that despite the singularity of white male children in the UK, their rate of HD (2.9 per cent) is still below even the female incidence of ADHD in the US.

These data indicate that race inequality does not yet appear to be an important *axis of economic stratification* in the symptoms of ADHD in either the UK or the US. This stands in contrast with what we have observed already of the distribution of the disorder by all the orthodox indices of structured social class in the UK child population. What about the US? How far is ADHD class stratified there? Figure 8.7 tries to answer this question by comparing the distribution of the disorder in each nation in relation to the poverty line.

We have already seen the distinctive socio-economic pattern of hyperkinetic disorder in the UK. How does the US compare? Figure 8.8 uses ratios to the poverty line defined as 60 per cent of the national average wage to divide the population into three income brackets.[24] It gives a strong impression that income has a greater effect on ADHD rates in the UK than in the US. While both nations exhibit

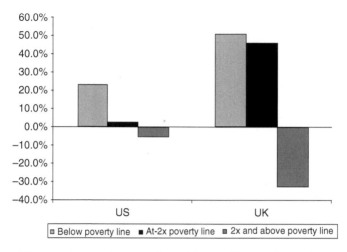

Figure 8.8 Prevalence of ADHD/hyperkinetic disorder by socioeconomic status, compared to the national average
Sources: Green *et al.* (2005; adapted from table 4.12) and Visser and Lesesne (2005).

a class gradient in the same direction with the risk of learning disability inversely proportional to income, the relationship with income in Britain is magnified. For example, American children below the poverty line record a rate of ADHD 23.1 per cent above average; in the comparable British category, the risk is 50 per cent higher. The reverse is also true – the most economically advantaged children in the UK are much more protected against an HD diagnosis than their American counterparts (−32.7 per cent versus −5.1 per cent, respectively).

Figure 8.8 indicates that income is a less important source of disparity in learning disability, or at least in detected learning disability, in the US. Compared with the UK, the ADHD income gap is relatively narrow and the difference stands out particularly in the intermediate group (up to twice the poverty level). In the UK this group exhibits an excess of 46 per cent while in the US it is only 2.6 per cent, not far off the rate recorded by the rest of the population in more prosperous material circumstances. A sharp difference is also apparent among children in the most economically secure category. In Britain, these children are far less likely to display the symptoms which lead to a diagnosis of hyperactivity. Their rate is more than 30 per cent below average, compared with a deficit of only 5 per cent in the equivalent US section of the population. Although these data are not disaggregated by gender, we can note here another interesting pattern in the US, with girls below the poverty line exhibiting slightly lower rates of ADHD (4.2 per cent) than both girls at the poverty level (4.7 per cent) and at two times above the poverty level (4.5 per cent); in contrast, British females display the same class gradient as males. These data further support the impression that social class matters greatly in the UK but has a more muted and mixed impact in the US.

Parental education is our third indicator of social stratification and once again, in Figure 8.9, we see a more consistent class-related pattern in the UK. British children of less educated parents are much more susceptible to being diagnosed hyperkinetic. Once again, we emphasize that our international comparison refers to relative not absolute risk.

Three simple categories of educational achievement are used to divide the child population into social classes based on education: less than high school, high school and more than high school.[25] The impression of a wider class gradient in Britain is once again the striking feature of Figure 8.9. Compared with the national average, children whose parents fail to complete the basic national educational course have a 73.3 per cent higher chance of being identified hyperactive; their counterparts in the US actually record the lowest rate.[26] The intermediate group in the UK – children whose parents have a high

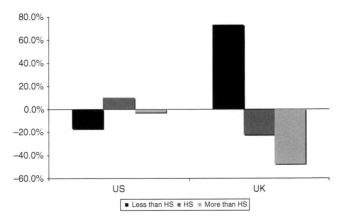

Figure 8.9 Prevalence of ADHD/hyperkinetic disorder by parents' education compared to national average

Sources: Green *et al.* (2005; adapted from table 4.10) and Visser and Lesesne (2005).

school diploma or the equivalent – exhibit a deficiency of HD (−22.0 per cent), while their American counterparts are the only group to have an excess of ADHD (10.3 per cent). Again, the US data are mixed and difficult to interpret. Several questions are raised that cannot be answered with these data – how is it that children whose parents have not completed high school (−16.7 per cent), and are therefore assumed to be concentrated in the lower SES strata, are the most protected whereas those below the poverty line (Figure 8.6) are most at risk? One possible reason is that the poverty population contains a disproportionate number of migrants who are culturally resistant to the idea that children need medication to control their emotions and who, by lacking health insurance, are cut off from the mechanisms which smooth entry to the ADHD identity. The children of first-generation migrants are known to record lower rates of ADHD but more research is needed to determine the relationship between the various indices of social inequality in the United States and their intersection with the process of labelling children as learning disabled.

The UK dataset is much more in-depth, relying on parent and child in-person interviews, teacher questionnaires, as well as clinical coders. It obviously provides a richer, deeper view of the social distribution of HD. Although the US data are drawn from a much larger sample, they are more superficial, relying on parents' self-reports during a relatively short phone interview. This constrains the type of analysis we can perform as well as the confidence to be placed in reported experience and it leaves us with many unanswered questions such as those posed above. There is some evidence suggesting that ADHD is a product of the social environment in the US but it is not good enough to allow us to get close to understanding the distribution of the disorder in the social hierarchy.

These observations illustrate the important role that high-quality data can play in constructing the meaning of health and well-being. The environmental perspective sponsored by the British culture of social policy/social medicine is validated by a richer body of data which demonstrate the connections between social deprivation, psychiatric morbidity and child development. In the presence of these data, it is much more difficult to resort to a knee-jerk congenital model of the disorder. It is easier to do this in the US in the absence of sound socio-demographic evidence and in the presence of a large body of evidence assembled within a framework of clinical investigation and treatment.

ADHD, social policy and the disability environment in Britain and the US

By examining the different discourses on ADHD in the US and UK, we can begin to understand how two nations at the same level of social and economic development produce different impressions of the character and causes of variations in child mental health. The evidence in Figures 8.7–8.9 lead us to a third issue: what incentives, if any, are associated with being labelled an 'ADHD child in each society?' Does the disability environment as shaped by political culture and social policy also play any part in structuring the social distribution of ADHD?

In Esping-Anderson's (1990) classification of welfare state systems, Britain and the United States are classified together as examples of the Liberal Welfare State Regime. This type of regime operates a minimum safety net programme of benefits designed primarily to maintain the work ethic rather than equalize life chances in the manner associated with the social democratic regimes of Scandinavia. The joint classification of Britain and the US as examples of the Liberal Welfare Regime is the legacy of a shared heritage of liberal political economy which emphasizes personal initiative and self-sufficiency. This features in the incentives given off by what we term the *disability environment* in each nation. At the same time there are important differences in welfare state institutions between the UK and the US which come out strongly in the context of the state's responsibility for doing something about child mental health.

One big contrast has already been highlighted: the fact that Britain has a comprehensive national health system while the US, alone among advanced nations, still permits the market to play a substantial role in distributing health care to its youngest citizens.[27] Beyond this are other differences. State guarantees of economic citizenship to children are much more developed in the UK. One prime example is the child benefit allowance which is paid for *every child* in Britain from birth to maturity and designed as a public contribution to the costs of bringing up children. The British child benefit payment must not be confused with the American TANF (Temporary Assistance for Needy Families).[28] Child benefit is not means tested; it is cash income, paid as of right for every child in the population and in addition to any other monetary 'means tested' benefits distributed to unsupported families. The allocation system provided a convenient sampling frame for the British data used in this chapter.

These observations express a major difference of political economic culture between Britain and the United States. The institutions
of the welfare state are more highly developed and have more cultural legitimacy in the UK. This difference gains expression in the
benefit incentives which structure the experience of children with disabilities. In the US, state intervention to compensate individuals for
proven disabilities are primarily implemented through education and
the workplace. Disability benefits for children with ADHD are primarily in the form of educational accommodations and there are few direct
financial incentives.[29]

The Education for all Handicapped Children Act passed in 1976
established the Individualized Education Program (IEP), guarantee-
ing children with disabilities the right to an educational programme
tailored to their needs. This translates into any of the following,
depending on their needs: extended time on class assignments and
tests, access to a resource centre, a tutor, and a counsellor. This Act
was extended in 1986 to include an early childhood component and
its name was changed in 1990 to the Individuals with Disabilities
Education Act (IDEA) (N. Halfon, personal communication, 2007).

While the benefit environment in the US is geared towards ensuring parity in schools, colleges and universities for disabled students,
the British welfare state directly compensates households for the financial burden of more labour-intensive parenting of children with mental
health disorders. The numbers of children with ADHD whose parents receive these cash benefits are difficult to calculate but, in the
2004 survey used here, 27 per cent of children recorded with HD
children lived in a household receiving at least one disability benefit.
This compared with 8 per cent of households in the population as a
whole. Figure 8.10 shows how far families with a child identified as
exhibiting the symptoms of HD benefited from the various types of
welfare benefits distributed to individuals and families with disabilities
in Britain.

As Figure 8.10 reveals, in the survey used in this chapter, households
with a child identified as fitting the symptoms of HD had a 300 per cent
greater chance of living in a household receiving one or other of these
two benefits. Eligibility for the carer's allowance is restricted to people
who actually perform the work themselves and is therefore unlikely
to be claimed by a parent in gainful employment. Indeed the idea of
this allowance in the context of caring for a disabled child is that the
duty of care prevents the parent from being employed. The disability
living allowance is intended as a compensation for the excess costs of

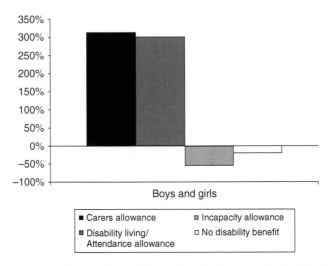

Figure 8.10 Prevalence of hyperkinetic disorder by type of disability benefit compared to national average, UK 2004
Sources: Green *et al.* (2005; adapted from table 4.13).

child raising in a context where a child has a certified disability. From Figure 8.10 it is clear that both types of benefits are distributed to families containing a child with a diagnosis of HD, though the principles governing the allocation of either allowance are impossible to determine with these data. The financial value of the benefits is very modest and at a level that the incentive for seeking a diagnosis to secure eligibility would decrease in due proportion to the alternative income-generating opportunities of the parent or family.

Variation in the disability environment probably plays a part in shaping the contrasting social demography of ADHD and HD in the US and the UK. The living standards of low-income parents in Britain, especially mothers with no market income, are undoubtedly raised if they are in receipt of a carer's allowance or if their child is certified eligible for a disability living allowance. The incentive to seek either of these benefits is evidently less for more prosperous families in Britain and this may contribute to the observed class gradient. The opposite rationale applies in the US. There, the emphasis on educational accommodation and the right to additional resources including an individualized programme of instruction is much more likely to attract parents anxious that their child do well at school or at least does not fall behind their peers. Higher-income parents who are more knowledgeable about manipulating the educational system to maximize their children's chances may look upon ADHD as a useful tool for negotiating additional resources for their children in the class and exam room. This may contribute to the extension of the diagnosis to include milder symptoms of disability and to the ambiguous, if not outright absence of a relationship with the various indices of social inequality.

The available published evidence for the US does not allow us to explore variations in the social and economic settings in which children get labelled ADHD. However, we may hypothesize that different principles may be operating in different socio-economic settings. The incentive to seek an ADHD label for a troublesome child in a context of relative social deprivation may come from a hard-pressed teacher who knows that the removal of the child to a special classroom, or failing that, medication will reduce her problems of discipline in the classroom. In more privileged contexts, the parent is the more likely agent actively seeking to obtain a positive diagnosis so that their child may receive the educational benefits that they are legally granted under IDEA and Section 504 of the Rehabilitation Act. There is some Geographical Information Systems (GIS)-type evidence for the US (Bokhari *et al.*, 2005) suggesting that prescriptions for ADHD are higher in census areas where more affluent, white families with health insurance reside.

Different modes of managing the disability may thus arise from different incentive contexts, though this is an under-researched area. It also conceivable that school administrators with fixed budgets will resist labelling students as disabled because, once they are defined as having special needs, they will have to find additional resources to conform with IDEA. Their interests may be at odds with individual teachers coping with discipline problems in an overcrowded classroom. At the aggregate level it is known that special-needs spending in US schools puts a major strain on school budgets. For example, New York records one of the highest per pupils expenditures on education but much of it is consumed by the substantial minority who claim additional resources on grounds of disability (Hart *et al.*, 2004). Under these circumstances it is easy to appreciate why rates of medication have risen so sharply since the revisions to IDEA in 1990, for psychostimulant treatment is the quickest and cheapest means of maintaining order and discipline in overcrowded classrooms, while creating the appearance if not the reality that the disability is under control. If the medicine really works, then it neutralizes the claims of students seeking special accommodations.

There is less pressure emanating from schools in the UK because children who are disruptive can simply be excluded for up to 45 days a year or even permanently (Malacrida, 2004). Malacrida (2004, p. 71) calls this British policy of exclusion 'non-medical social control'. A British school can also resort to exclusion if it is unable to provide the special-needs instruction that a child with any kind of disability including HD might need. As a result, there is less incentive for screening and medicating children. Indeed British teachers have a reputation for resisting attempts by parents seeking an ADHD diagnosis for their child (ibid.). Several British parents interviewed by Malacrida in her 2000 comparison of ADHD in Britain and Canada claimed that UK educators were extremely reluctant to cooperate with the diagnosis of children with ADHD, telling parents that 'ADHD is just another American fad that's come over here' and 'The ADHD label should *never* be applied to a child' (ibid.). These observations suggest a fundamental divide between the average British teacher and his or her American counterpart who has been identified as the single most likely person to initiate the process of labeling a child with ADHD.

The option to exclude children in British schools is popularly associated with disruptive, undisciplined behaviour than with medical disorders or disability. When a school excludes a child, it is up to the local political administration to provide a substitute as soon as possible. However, excluded children may find themselves off the roster for a considerable time and the number of children temporarily or permanently excluded on grounds of unacceptable behaviour or needs has become a novel social barometer for monitoring the state of the family, the indiscipline of youth or the competence of government. This is one means whereby the issue of children, their behaviour and their well-being stays at the head of the political agenda. It is an important stimulus for the kind of research which we have used in this chapter.

Concluding remarks: the data and discourse of ADHD

This chapter has reviewed the social distribution of the symptoms of Attention Deficit Hyperactive Disorder in two nations. As we have emphasized, our analysis is based on the best available empirical evidence. The incidence of the disorder and rate of medication in the United Kingdom is taken from a carefully designed government survey conducted in 1999 and replicated in 2004. The term ADHD is not used in this survey. At each date, hyperkinetic disorder (HD) is employed for the symptoms classified as ADHD in the DSM-IV.

Drug-dispensing statistics assembled by the Department of Health in the UK suggest that a substantial increase in the prescription of ADHD medications has taken place over the half decade possibly alongside an increased willingness to embrace the US diagnostic terminology (DSM-IV), which includes milder symptoms of the disorder (S. Timimi, personal communication, 2007). The evidence in this chapter cannot be used to throw light on this possible trend because it is not drawn from the medical care delivery system. Our measure of incidence was derived directly from the decisions of clinical coders on the basis of informant reports gathered in face-to-face interviews with parents, including observations of the child in the home setting. These are the type and quality of sociological data which give us confidence that the incidence of the disorder in the UK did not change in the first quinquennium of the twenty-first century.

The rate of prescription for methylphenidate medication was recorded only in the 2004 replication survey. This is the estimate which appears in Figure 8.1. We cannot rule out that the possibility that the rate of medication increased alongside a stable incidence of symptoms between 1999 and 2004. Starting from a low base, it is conceivable that a large percentage increase in the use of drugs to treat children took place in the years leading up to 2004. However, on the basis of replicated survey evidence of an unusually high quality, we have no warrant for inferring that a substantial increase in the symptoms was evident between 1999 and 2004 in the UK. In future replications, it would be important to monitor any change in the rate of medication and perhaps incorporate a mechanism for flagging sample members' use of prescribed medicines in the NHS central record-keeping system.

On the basis of the evidence we have assembled, we are confident that the disorder known as ADHD is far more prevalent in the United States than in the UK. Indeed, the US is probably home to more children suffering from this disorder than the rest of the world altogether. In light of the argument developed in this chapter, this sentence should perhaps be rephrased as 'the US is home to more children *who are aware* that they are ADHD'. In this vein of thought we might add that there is currently something of a roller coaster effect in the US. Not only is the number of school children (ages 5–17) exhibiting symptoms five times higher than the European average, but also in recent years the proportion of the afflicted population has swollen as the diagnosis has been extended to people outside the school age band. *Adult ADHD* is currently depicted as the most profitable market for new ADHD drugs in the US but as a 'no go' in Europe by the leading investors' website (<www.datamonitor.com>).

Why are so many more people being labelled learning disabled in one place compared with another? This chapter offers a relatively simple answer to this question. The social profile of the ADHD population is more diverse in the USA because the process of classifying the disorder is more flexible and inclusive. This generates a larger pool of patients displaying the symptoms necessary for a positive diagnosis. In the UK, a smaller proportion of the population are diagnosed, they are more likely to be male and they are more heavily concentrated in socially disadvantaged circumstances. The scarcity of ADHD in Britain occurs because more stringent rules are employed to identify people in need of treatment. This international contrast is therefore a product of different medical discourses backed up by different approaches to research and different kinds of bodies of scientific data.

Contrary to expectations, the singling out of people displaying the most extreme symptoms does not restrict the discourse to a congenital representation of the disorder. The contrasting images of ADHD on each side of the Atlantic therefore run counter to what would be predicted from the diagnostic script. In the US, the willingness to treat 'milder' symptoms is *not* associated with an environmental view of disability, while in Britain, a more stringent diagnostic regime is no more likely to produce a congenital account; indeed, quite the opposite, the available evidence continues to suggest that the symptoms of ADHD, like many other diseases and disabilities, are the product of health inequality arising from social disadvantage in early life.

These contrasting impressions are the product of different approaches to research and treatment in different medical cultures. In the UK, recognition that disparities in mental well-being are socially distributed is more readily accepted, perhaps even expected, by the medical profession as evidenced in the recent BMA report (see p. 219). If this report may be taken as the '*conscience collective*' of the nation's physicians, we may deduce that the problem is viewed as the product of the social environment. The high and increasing incidence of mental ill health and its concentration among socially disadvantaged children is the highlight of this chapter.

The existence of the National Health Service is an additional important reason why an environmental perspective gets more of a hearing in Britain. Cost-effective and politically accountable health policy can be determined only in the light of valid statistical evidence which increases the pressure to monitor trends in population health status. One effect is the stream of official statistics generated by the health care system itself and charting the increase in depression and conduct disorder which fuels public concern that the incidence of unhappy, unruly, undisciplined and delinquent behaviour is an increasing and worrying trend. Though the prevalence of ADHD is much lower in the UK, there is still public anxiety that it represents a deterioration in child well-being, particularly among those growing up in disadvantaged social circumstances. The view of ADHD as the product of the social environment is more in keeping with the political and medical culture and history of the United Kingdom.

The absence of a comprehensive health care service for children sponsored and funded by the state reduces the pressure on government to monitor trends with the same degree of precision and leaves more space for the medical profession itself to create and maintain the reality of disorders like ADHD. Though this might be applauded on the grounds that politics should be kept out of medical research, it would be naïve to claim that the research findings coming out in the USA generate more scientifically neutral knowledge. The impression that ADHD is a congenital phenomenon is fortified by research funded by pharmaceutical corporations who have direct financial interest in sustaining an orthodox clinical view of the disorder. This view sits more easily with individual drug-based therapy and must be a powerful factor in sanctioning the high rates of medication currently reported.

Notes

1. The NSCH is sponsored by the CDC Centers for Disease Control.
2. The NSCH recorded between 1 per cent and 2 per cent of pre-school children with the disorder in 2004. Beyond the opposite end of the expected age range, an increasing number of adults are self-diagnosing ADHD and finding physicians willing to legitimate their eligibility for psychostimulant medicine, which has also added to the population of people relying on prescription medicine to cope with the social relations of daily life.
3. ADHD drugs are among the top 10 stolen substances in the US and have become a problem of abuse.
4. It should also be noted that there is some scepticism, if not outright cynicism, about the epidemic spread of ADHD, including criticism of the part played by pharmaceutical capitalism fuelling demand for treatment by sponsoring academic research and self-help movements among the parents of disabled children.

5. Up to the age of 13, there is gender parity in the incidence of *mental/ emotional* disorder. Thereafter, females record higher rates.
6. See Healy (1997) for observation on the declining professional resistance to psychiatric chemotherapy.
7. As Timimi (2002: 88) points out, the UK is increasingly using the term ADHD in lieu of hyperkinetic disorder.
8. Part of the increase is explained by a new trend of diagnosing and treating ADHD as a disorder of adulthood, not merely among grown-up ADHD kids but also among adults who discover their disability only when they enter university or the job market. See Conrad and Potter (2000).
9. See FDA, 2006 and also Nissen, 2006.
10. Adverse events such as heart attacks appearing to be associated with medicines are reported to the FDA on a voluntary basis. It is estimated that only 10 per cent of such outcomes are notified. The FDA panel was presented with a brief detail of reported deaths but the information was difficult to interpret – because of its incompleteness. Dr Nissen's caution arose from a sense that the reported mortality might be the tip of an iceberg. The so-called 'black box' warning was not implemented because of pressure from the American Psychiatric Association, which argued that a warning would have an adverse effect on access to vital treatment for children with severe learning disabilities.
11. Greg Critser's (2005) book *Generation RX* charts the increasing dependence of the US population on bio-chemical methods of coping with life's stresses.
12. See Collinshaw *et al.*, 2004.
13. In 1999, as many as 20 per cent of adolescent girls in Britain were reported as experiencing emotional problems in 1999. Ibid., p.1352.
14. According to a report in the *Los Angeles Times*, Saturday, 1 May 1999, between 1994 and 1997, the number of child prescriptions for Prozac and related drugs rose 114 per cent in the US from 343,000 to 735,000 per annum.
15. It is our impression that proportionately there has been less research effort to prove the congenital origins of ADHD in Britain. From preliminary searches we believe that the majority of the research coloured by this emphasis has been performed in the US rather than Europe but this is a comparative question that needs more systematic research.
16. It is not just the lack of research with an environmental focus, but even outright hostility to such research. One noted researcher Gretchen LeFever had difficulty publishing findings of a study reporting rates of medication as high as 20 per cent among boys in a Virginia school district and she later experienced a temporary suspension from her university post following an accusation of unethical research practice by an anonymous telephone caller (Lenzer, 2005A; Lenzer, 2005B).
17. See Leo and Cohen (2003).

18. Healy (1997) observes that the resistance was not confined to children. The idea of using chemicals to manipulate the mind was controversial for patients of all ages.

19. The findings of this survey were widely drawn on by the BMA in its recent report.

20. For 1999, the survey was administered to children 5–15 years old.

21. The mean interview length was 23:25 minutes and 28:53 minutes for NIS-eligible and NIS-ineligible households, respectively.

22. In the NSCH, ADHD-related questions were put to respondents whose child was at least 24 months. Data were then weighted to estimate rates for children between 4 and 17 years old.

23. Multiracial children were included in the 'Black' category in the UK data.

24. In 2003, the Federal Poverty Level (FPL) in the US was $18,400 for a family of four. In the UK, we defined £199 per week and lower as 'below the poverty level', £200–399 'at 2 x the poverty level', and £400 and above as '2 x and above the poverty level'. To determine the excess or deficiency compared with the national average, we divided the prevalence rate per income bracket by the overall ADHD/HD rate for that country, and then subtracted 100 per cent.

25. For the UK, we constructed the following categories: (1) 'less than high school' – GCSE grades D-F (or equivalent) and those with no qualifications; (2) 'high school' – A-Level (or equivalent) and GSCE grades A–C (or equivalent); and (3) 'more than high school' – degree level and teaching/ HND/nursing level. Similar to the income analysis above, we divided the prevalence rate per education bracket by the overall ADHD/HD rate for that country, and then subtracted 100 per cent to obtain the excess or deficiency per educational level.

26. It is much more difficult to make international comparisons based on education than on income.

27. Interestingly, one of the strongest census indicators of ADHD in the US is access to health insurance.

28. On 1 July 1997, TANF replaced AFDC (Aid for Families with Dependent Children), which was available only for the children of single-parent families in poverty and paid partly as food stamps. TANF requires parents receiving welfare assistance to work a certain amount of hours per week. Families now receive food stamps through the Food Stamp Program.

29. The 1990 *Sullivan* v. *Zebley* Supreme Court decision also coincided with the new IDEA law. Prior to the *Zebley* decision, Social Security Income (SSI) benefits were administered to only elderly, blind, and disabled individuals; however, *Zebley* established new criteria that gave cash or Medicaid benefits to children with disabilities who were not functioning or behaving at an appropriate age-level (Garrett and Glied, 1997, pp. 1, 5). Since the list of disabilities was expanded to include more mental disorders, children with ADHD became eligible for these cash benefits

(ibid., p. 5). For the first time, there were financial benefits for children being diagnosed with ADHD. Between 1989 and 1992, the number of children who received SSI increased from approximately 300,000 to 750,000, and was mostly due to the enrolment of children diagnosed with ADHD and mental retardation (Bass and Mosley, 2001, p. 3). However, these benefits only lasted a few years. In 1996, the Clinton administration passed the Personal Responsibility and Work Opportunity Act (PRWOA), which altered the criteria for SSI eligibility and effectively prevented most children with ADHD from receiving cash benefits (ibid., p. 4). As a result, parents of children with ADHD have educational benefits through the Individuals with Disabilities Education Act (IDEA) and Section 504 of the Rehabilitation Act of 1973, which prevents discrimination against disabled students and allows special accommodations for children with special needs.

References

Bass, L. and Mosley, J. (2001) Assessing the implications of welfare reform for children's SSI receipt', paper presented at the Joint Center for Poverty Research/HHS Grant Conferences, 6–7 September, Washington, DC, 2 December 2001.

Bokhari, F., Mayes, R. and Scheffler, R. (2005) An analysis of the significant variation in psychostimulant use across the U.S, *Pharmacoepidemiology and Drug Safety* 14, 4, 267–75.

British Medical Association (BMA) (2006) *Child and Adolescent Mental Health: A Guide for Healthcare Professionals*. London: BMA.

Collinshaw, S., Maugha B., Goodman, R. and Pickles, A. (2004) Time trends in adolescent mental health, *Journal of Child Psychology and Psychiatry* 45, 8, 1350–62.

Conrad, P. (1976) *Identifying Hyperactive Children: The Medicalization of Deviant Behavior*. Lexington: Lexington Books.

Conrad, P. and Potter, D. (2000) From hyperactive children to ADHD adults: Observations on the expansion of medical categories, *Social Problems* 47, 4, 559–82.

Critser, G. (2005) *Generation Rx: How Prescription Drugs are Altering American Lives, Minds, and Bodies*. Boston: Houghton Mifflin Company.

Esping-Anderson, G. (1990) *The Three Worlds of Welfare Capitalism*. New Jersey: Princeton University Press.

Food and Drug Administration (2006) *Minutes of the Meeting Held February 6th 2006*, <www.fda.gov/ohrms/dockets/ac/06/transcripts/2006-4202t1.pdf>.

Garrett, A. B. and Glied, S. (1997) The effect of US Supreme Court ruling: *Sullivan v. Zebley* on child SSI and AFDC enrollment, NBER Working Paper Series (Working Paper 6125). Cambridge, MA: National Bureau of Economic Research, August.

Green, H., McGinnity, Á., Meltzer, H., Ford, T. and Goodman, R. (2005) *Mental Health of Children and Young People in Great Britain, 2004*. Office for National Statistics, Department of Health and the Scottish Executive. Basingstoke: Palgrave Macmillan.

Hart, N., Grand, N. and Riley, K. (2004) Making the grade: The gender gap, ADHD, and themedicalization of boyhood, in Dana Rosenfeld and Christopher A. Faircloth (eds), *Medicalized Masculinities*. Philadelphia: Temple University Press, 132–64.

Healy, D. (1997) *The Anti-Depressive Era*. Cambridge, MA: Harvard University Press.

Lefever, G. B., Arcona, A. P and Antonuccio, D. O. (2003) ADHD among American schoolchildren: Evidence of overdiagnosis and overuse of medication, *The Scientific Review of Mental Health Practice* 2, 1, available on-line: <www.srmhp.org/0201/adhd.html>.

Lenzer, J. (2005) Researcher to be sacked after reporting high rates of ADHD, *British Medical Journal* 330, 691 (26 March).

Lenzer, J. (2005) Researcher cleared of misconduct charges, *British Medical Journal* 330, 865 (15 October).

Leo, J. and Cohen, D. (2003) Broken brains or flawed studies? A critical review of ADHD neuroimaging research, *The Journal of Mind and Behavior* 24, 1, 29–56.

Malacrida, C. (2004) Medicalization, ambivalence and social control: Mothers' descriptions of educators and ADD/ADHD, *Health: An Interdisciplinary Journal for the Social Study of Health, Illness, and Medicine* 8, 1, 61–80.

National Institutes of Health Consensus Development Conference Statement (2000) Diagnosis and treatment of attention-deficit/hyperactivity disorder (ADHD), *Journal of the American Academy of Child and Adolescent Psychiatry* 39, 2, 182–93.

Nissen, S. (2006) ADHD drugs and cardiovascular risk, *New England Journal of Medicine* 354, 14, 1445–8.

Timimi, S. (2002) *Pathological Child Psychiatry and the Medicalization of Childhood*. New York: Brunner Routledge.

US Department of Health and Human Services HRSA, Maternal and Child Health Bureau (2005) *The National Survey of Children's Health (2003)*. National Center for Health Statistics. *Vital Health Statistics* 1, 43.

Visser, S. N. and Lesesne, C. A. (2005) Mental health in the United States: Prevalence of diagnosis and medication treatment for Attention-Deficit/Hyperactivity Disorder in United States, 2003, *Centers for Disease Control, MMWR Weekly* (2 September, 2005), 54, 34, 842–7.

Part III
ADHD Drug Therapies

Chapter 9

The Case against Stimulants

Grace E. Jackson

The development of the human brain is one of the great miracles in the universe.

Beginning in the first weeks of life in a developing embryo, the organ of consciousness unfolds through six stages of development (Rice and Barone, 2000):

- proliferation (the embryo gives rise to new cells called neuroblasts or stem cells)
- differentiation (the stem cells assume special roles as neurons and glia)
- migration (the neurons travel to new locations in their expanding surroundings)
- synaptogenesis (the neurons reach out to make connections with their neighbours)
- myelination (neuronal extensions receive a special fatty coat called myelin, which accelerates the speed of brain signalling)
- pruning (the brain trims away unnecessary cells and synapses).

Each of these stages is unique in its timing and vulnerability to disruption.

Although it was once believed that so-called 'critical periods' of neurodevelopment were limited to gestation and infancy, it is now known that many growth processes remain vital across the lifespan. Armed with this knowledge, scientists have come to appreciate the fact that early and even limited exposures to environmental toxicants (such as pharmaceuticals) can result in delayed or prolonged declines in cognitive or behavioural functions.

Most significantly, research in the fields of neuroscience and developmental psychology has revealed the importance of protecting the normal development of youth and teens. Normal growth rates are essential for at least three reasons. First, the maximization of brain size during childhood is associated with greater intellectual capacity at all ages, and may present a defence against dementia in old age (Gale *et al.*, 2004; Mori *et al.*, 1997; Rushton and Ankney, 1996). Second, the emergence of intellectual and emotional maturity depends critically upon the formation of white matter (myelin) in the brain regions which may underlie the capacity for self-control and abstract thought (Fields, 2005; Fuster, 2002; Nagy *et al.*, 2004; Travis, 1998). Third, the maintenance of normal development prevents the necessity of postponed or 'catch-up' growth – a phenomenon that has been linked by some investigators to long-term deficits in adult cognition (Fisher *et al.*, 2006).

A tragic history

For more than 40 years, research involving the study of humans, animals, and cell samples has demonstrated the disruptive effects of stimulants upon development and growth. Tragically, the *reality* and *implications* of this toxicity have been ignored.

Due to the privileged and redundant publication of studies with egregious methodologies and assertions, opinion leaders in psychiatry and paediatrics have stated that prescription stimulants are *not* a cause of growth delay. For example, in 1996 and 2003, clinicians affiliated with Massachusetts General Hospital (Biederman *et al.*, 2003; Spencer *et al.*, 1996) claimed that the deficits observed in their young patients were the manifestations of an underlying phenotype, rather than the byproduct of chemical therapy. Even then, as the following discussion shows, the evidence for such a claim was weak.

The suppression of growth

As early as 1969, Uehling reported the effects of oral d-amphetamine (Dexedrine) administered to juvenile rats at the relatively low dose of 2 mg/kg per day (Uehling, 1969). Weight measurements of these animals were obtained at five-day intervals over a course of treatment, which spanned seven months (>250 days). Findings were remarkable for significant weight loss in the medicated animals, with weight reduction worsening over time.

In 1980, Greeley and Kizer documented the effects of a three-week course of methylphenidate (Ritalin™) upon the growth and endocrine functions of neonatal and juvenile rats (Greeley and Kizer, 1980). Varying doses of the stimulant (1, 3, 10, 35, 100 mg/kg) were administered to males and females via subcutaneous injections given twice a day. Statistically significant reductions were found in weight *and* length (35 and 100 mg/kg), along with a variety of endocrine abnormalities across the entire range of doses. For the female rats specifically, exposure to methylphenidate in both age groups was associated with a delay in the onset of puberty and a decline in the frequency of oestrous cycling. Following the termination of drug treatment, these abnormalities resolved.

By 1986 and 1987, Pizzi and colleagues had described similar results for neonatal (male and female) and peri-adolescent (male) rats exposed to a 20-day course of methylphenidate (Pizzi *et al.*, 1986; Pizzi *et al.*, 1987). Subcutaneous injections (35 mg/kg) were administered on a daily or twice-a-day schedule. Significant and dose-related reductions in skeletal length and body weight were observed. These changes reversed following a 30-day period of drug cessation.

In 2003, graduate students at George Mason University reported the results of their unique research protocol (Wheeler *et al.*, 2003) in which juvenile male rats were administered a daily oral dose (1 mg/kg) of methylphenidate for a period of 40 days. Based upon a finding of slower weight gain among the medicated animals versus drug-free controls, the investigators concluded that a *commonly used dose of stimulant* had induced growth delay, since none of the rats in their experiment had been bred to display the symptoms of ADHD.

While the human implications of these and other animals studies must always be interpreted with caution – due to the anatomic, genetic, and metabolic differences which exist between species – the medical community's consistent failure to appreciate this body of research has contributed to a long period of journalistic obfuscation. Two extensive reviews on this subject (Poulton, 2005, 2006) provide formidable analyses of the methodological flaws which have characterized the dominant papers in the medical literature, undermining advances in the integrity of clinical care and the pace of scientific investigations of this subject.

Methodological flaws in the stimulant growth suppression literature

- Cross-sectional rather than longitudinal study design (i.e., omission of intra-individual variations over time)
- Enrolment of previously medicated subjects
- Outcome analysis using static height or weight, rather than changes in *growth rates*
- Outcome analysis using percentiles, rather than z-scores or paired measurements
- Inappropriate normative standards (out-of-date growth charts)
- Inappropriate controls (e.g. previously medicated or younger comparison groups)
- Inappropriate drug dose (use of lower than standard dose)
- Non-continuous drug therapy (limited or interrupted duration of therapy)
- Inadequate power (unable to detect statistically significant differences in growth patterns due to small sample size relative to the duration of study).

When higher-quality studies have appeared, their findings have confirmed the developmental aberrations observed in non-humans. The largest American investigation to date, known as the MTA (Multimodal Treatment of ADHD) study, examined the effects of four different treatment protocols in 579 children between the ages of 7 and 10 (MTA Cooperative Group, 1999). Although the study enrolled its first subjects in 1991, a *naturalistic analysis* of growth effects (based upon actual medication use, rather than assigned treatment) was not forthcoming until 2004 (MTA Cooperative Group, 2004). Only at that time did investigators announce data from both 14- and 24-month assessment points, including the finding that *stimulant use in childhood was associated with a persistent reduction in growth rate* (see Table 9.1).

Several findings in the MTA study invalidated the hypothesis that growth deficits were a component of ADHD. At baseline, the ADHD subjects exceeded the population norms for height and weight. Average z-scores[1] *increased* over time for the children who remained drug-free. In contrast, average z-scores for height and weight *decreased* over time in the chronically medicated subgroup, suggesting that these growth deficits were indeed a product of the chemical intervention.

Table 9.1 Growth reduction on stimulants, MTA study

Months 1–14	Months 14–24	Estimated ht suppression with continuous drug therapy
−0.90 cm per year	−1.04 cm per year	~1 cm per year (~½ inch)
−2.55 kg per year	−1.22 kg per year	~1.25 kg per year (~3 lb)

Source: MTA Cooperative Group (2004).

The more recent Preschool ADHD Treatment Study (aka, PATS) examined the effects of methylphenidate in 140 previously unmedicated children under the age of 5 (Swanson *et al.*, 2006). Measurements at baseline revealed an experimental cohort which exceeded the population norms (86th percentile, based upon z-scores for height and weight). Following a four-week placebo controlled treatment phase, stimulant recipients were maintained on drug therapy for an additional 10 months. Annual *growth rates* were smaller than expected after the initiation of stimulant therapy, based upon a variety of outcome measures.

Preschoolers remaining on stimulants experienced a 20 per cent lower than expected gain in height (based upon an expected gain of 6.79 cm/yr) and a 55 per cent lower than expected gain in weight (based upon an expected gain of 2.39 kg/yr) when compared to the reference population. Due to the pre-treatment body size of the sample, the research team rejected the notion that these growth deficits were a product of a pre-existing maturational delay.

Table 9.2 Growth reduction on stimulants, PATS

Growth rate deficit units	Change in percentile points	Change in z-units
−1.38 cm/yr (height)	−7.53 points per year (height)	−0.26 per year (height)
−1.32 kg/yr (weight)	−13.18 points per year (weight)	−0.49 per year (weight)

Source: Swanson *et al.* (2006).

The implications of these and other studies (Charach *et al.*, 2006; Dickinson *et al.*, 1979; Lisska *et al.*, 2003; Poulton and Cowell, 2003) are three-fold. First, the findings leave little doubt about the fact that it is stimulant medication, rather than ADHD, which produces a persistent reduction in skeletal development when drugs are initiated before puberty. Second, it should concern the medical profession substantively that the mechanisms responsible for this growth phenomenon remain unknown. Third, the studies underscore the ambiguous nature of the medical community's guidelines, as clinicians are encouraged to monitor children more closely, while they are concurrently dissuaded from withdrawing drug treatment. Meanwhile, the 'elephant in the room' which most healers perpetually ignore remains the unproven assumption that it is possible pharmaceutically to restrict the growth of a child's skeleton, without simultaneously impairing the growth of that child's brain.

The impairment of neurodevelopment

Normal development: a primer

Before examining the evidence that stimulants suppress the growth of the human brain, it is necessary to appreciate the stages and appearance of normal development. Research in this area has been aided not only by the traditional techniques of microscopy and tissue exam (neuropathology), but increasingly, by the evolution of sophisticated neuroimaging technologies (e.g. MRI, PET, SPECT). Only recently have the latter methods been used by investigators to catalogue the sequence of changes associated with healthy ageing. Key findings from this body of research (Courchesne *et al.*, 2000; Giedd *et al.*, 1999; Sowell *et al.*, 2003; Toga *et al.*, 2006) suggest that brain volume expands through adolescence. *Grey matter* (so-named for the appearance of neuronal cell bodies, dendrites, and glia) proliferates rapidly in infancy and early childhood, assumes a more gradual rate of development through adolescence (peaking at different times in different regions), and then plateaus until the seventh decade of life. *White matter* (so-named for the appearance of myelin, the fatty layer of insulation which speeds transmission along the axons of the brain) increases from birth until well into middle age. The complex period of adolescence is marked by extensive remodelling involving two processes: pruning, whereby surplus cells and pathways are excised; and plasticity, whereby new connections and myelination progress. During this time, the ratio of grey to white matter declines. Similar events occur during adulthood and senescence, as a gradual process of degeneration (tissue loss in both grey and white matter) may be opposed or delayed by regional changes, which include cellular proliferation (neurogenesis) and synaptogenesis (new cell–cell connections).

Street drugs shrink the brain

All animals are created equal, but some are more equal than others. (George Orwell, *Animal Farm*)

All stimulants are created equal, but some are more equal than others. (Grace E. Jackson, MD)

Historically, the medical profession has expressed concern about street drugs in terms of their degenerative effects upon the intact brain. However, with the discovery in the 1990s that neural development continues throughout the lifespan, along with the realization that early chemical exposures may cause delayed but important brain changes, the field of addiction medicine – in contrast to paediatrics and psychiatry – has openly acknowledged the potential toxicity of stimulants upon the growth of the brain.

Cocaine and amphetamine
Two studies led by scientists at UCLA have examined the brain effects of commonly abused stimulants. In 2000, Bartzokis *et al.* published the results of their investigation of stimulant effects upon the brain structure of young adults (ages 23–35). In this limited analysis involving a sampling of the frontal and temporal lobes, ten subjects dependent upon cocaine (mean duration of addiction: 7.9 years) and nine subjects dependent upon amphetamine (mean duration of addiction: 6.7 years) were compared to age-matched, non-addicted volunteers. After controlling for variations in education, ethnicity, and head size (intracranial volume), the researchers observed an association between dependence upon both stimulants and significantly reduced volume and grey matter density in the temporal lobe.

In a follow-up study (Bartzokis *et al.*, 2002), the researchers again employed magnetic resonance imaging (MRI) to compare the anatomy of 37 cocaine-dependent subjects (average duration of addiction: 8.8 years) and 52 non-addicted controls. Although the project was limited by the fact that each subject was scanned at one point in time, the investigators used their data to compare the brain morphology of the cocaine users (age range: 25–47) against age-matched, healthy controls (age range: 19–44). Several findings were remarkable. First, the cocaine-dependent subjects failed to demonstrate the expected age-related increase in white matter. In fact, a statistical trend was noted in the opposite direction: the white matter of cocaine users declined prematurely in the frontal and temporal lobes. Second, the rate of grey matter loss (again, an expected component of normal ageing) was accelerated for the users of cocaine. While the research team conceded their inability to prove causality in a cross-sectional study design, they expressed concern about the potential for cocaine to suppress maturation in the frontal and temporal lobes. In particular, they noted the compatibility of their findings with other research (Clarke *et al.*, 1996; Gollub *et al.*, 1998; Kaufman *et al.*, 1998; Strickland *et al.*, 1993), and they discussed possible mechanisms responsible for this effect (such as the impairment of astroglial development and the reduction of cerebral blood flow).

Prescription stimulants shrink the brain

> A foolish *in*consistency is the hobgoblin of little minds. (Ralph Waldo Emerson) (My addition in italics)

While it is not difficult to locate studies in which neuroscientists contemplate the toxicity of street drugs, such as those which have been mentioned above, it is almost impossible to locate studies in which medical professionals concede that prescription stimulants inflict the same kinds of chemical harm. An excellent example of this phenomenon is the notable absence of any citation within the National Library of Medicine's major database (PubMed), in which any researcher has ever reported the postmortem brain findings from a human autopsy following chronic treatment with a psychostimulant.

As this chapter is written, many medical researchers have performed *cross-sectional* neuroimaging analyses on the brains of children diagnosed with ADHD. Yet some of these authors have not divulged the *raw data* from the scans of children who were chronically medicated, versus those who remained drug free. Whether intentional or otherwise, this limits the capacity of the critical reader to assess the developmental toxicity of psychostimulants. Nevertheless, the results which have been published provide consistent evidence that prescription stimulants do nothing to 'normalize' the size (or functioning) of the maturing brain.

For example, Mostofsky and colleagues used a semi-automated MRI approach to examine the volumes of functionally significant brain regions in 12 males with ADHD (ages 8–14) versus 12 age- and gender-matched controls (Mostofsky *et al.*, 2002). Ten of the twelve patients (83 per cent) had received previous treatment with psychostimulants. Findings were remarkable for statistically significant reductions in total brain size, total white matter, total grey matter, and frontal lobe volume in the ADHD subjects. Although two of these children had never received stimulant drug therapy, the research team did not divulge the raw data for that subgroup.

Sowell and colleagues examined regional brain size differences of 27 ADHD patients and 46 non-ADHD controls, ranging in age from 8 to 18 (Sowell *et al.*, 2003b). High resolution MRI demonstrated reduced white matter volume in the ADHD subjects, along with age-inappropriate cortical reductions (grey matter) in the frontal and temporal lobes. Although the investigators conceded (p. 1705) that 'the effects of stimulant drugs could have confounded the findings of abnormal morphology' (56 per cent of the ADHD children were taking stimulants at the time of their scans), they did not compare brain scan results for ADHD subjects according to medication status ('on' or 'off' drug) due to the fact that the lifetime history of stimulant exposure had been so high.

Ashtari and colleagues performed a magnetic resonance analysis of ADHD children using diffusion tensor imaging (DTI) to quantify white matter (Ashtari *et al.*, 2005). In this investigation, 18 ADHD subjects (mean age: 8.94) were compared with 15 controls (mean age: 9.13). Thirteen of the patients (72 per cent) had received prior treatment with psychostimulants for an average duration of therapy lasting 1.5 years. As a group, the ADHD children displayed significant reductions in the white matter development of many regions of the brain (frontal motor cortex, basal ganglia, pons, parieto-occipital cortex, and cerebellum). The investigators did not divulge raw data for the white matter changes observed in the five children who were stimulant naïve (never medicated).

Carmona and colleagues applied an automated MRI technique (Carmona *et al.*, 2005) to compare regional and global brain differences in 25 ADHD subjects (ages 6–16) and 25 controls (21 males, 4 females in each group). ADHD patients demonstrated significantly smaller total brain volumes (5.4 per cent) and decreased grey matter by volume (5.2 per cent). Reductions were also noted in total white matter and cerebrospinal fluid, although these differences just missed the cut-off for statistical significance due to the power of the study (small sample size). Details about medication history were limited to methylphenidate, but the authors conveyed the impression that all 25 children received medication in this study. The authors' conclusion was striking:

> It is improbable that our findings could be attributed to the psychostimulant treatment. In other studies, ADHD [grey matter] abnormalities did not differ significantly between medicated and unmedicated patients. (Carmona *et al.*, 2005, p. 92)

To support the contention that stimulants do not impair the developing brain, the authors cited just *one* other study (Castellanos *et al.*, 2002), but they seemed oblivious to its flaws and erroneous conclusions.

The Castellanos study

To date, the only longitudinal brain scan study of ADHD children to appear in the medical literature is the Castellanos study. Now the linchpin of the American 'ADHD industry', this is the crucial study, which declared, 'There is no evidence that stimulants cause abnormal brain development' (Castellanos *et al.*, 2002, p. 1747).

Widely hailed by its creators as the first neuroimaging study to include a substantial number of unmedicated children, the project enrolled 152 patients (49 never medicated, 103 with present or past exposure to stimulants) and 139 controls. The goal of the study was the collection of serial brain scans at two-year intervals across a period of ten years (1991–2001). In reality, only 60 per cent of the participants returned for more than one head scan, necessitating the integration of cross-sectional and longitudinal data (see Table 9.3).

The data were further limited by another notable exclusion. Due to motion artefact, 11 per cent of the head scans obtained from ADHD

Table 9.3 Castellanos longitudinal brain scan study

Headscans	1	2	3	4
ADHD subjects (n = 152)	40%	40%	13%	7%
Normal controls (n = 139)	37%	40%	21%	2%

Source: Castellanos *et al.* (2002).

subjects were rejected (vs. 6 per cent of the head scans obtained from controls). Even the research team acknowledged the fact that this omission quite likely removed data from the more symptomatic ADHD patients. Such data would have added clinically (and perhaps statistically) important variance to the developmental trajectories when graphs were later constructed to compare brain changes over time.

Another confounding factor involved age matching, which had to be estimated due to unequal numbers of ADHD subjects (152) and healthy controls (139). The control group was approximately one year older than the ADHD subgroup as a whole, and older by about three years than the 49 patients who had never received stimulant drug therapy. These age disparities introduced the most significant confounding factor into the study, because they led to repeated comparisons between older and younger participants, rather than between 'diseased' vs. 'non-diseased' or 'drugged' vs. 'drug-free' children.

The age disparity was crucial to the summary claim that stimulants are not a cause of brain reduction, as older medicated children were compared repeatedly to drug-free subjects who were two years younger than themselves, and who therefore displayed age-appropriate lags in brain size and myelination. In an attempt to compensate for this confounding variable, the research team performed a separate but unpublished age-matched analysis comparing growth rates according to age *and* medication status. Unfortunately, the age-matched analysis included brain scan results from only 24 of the 49 (49 per cent) drug-free subjects. In their published paper, the investigators did not divulge the raw data from this portion of the study.

The most celebrated feature of the Castellanos study is the pictorial depiction of growth trajectories showing changes in brain volumes for children and teens (age range: 5–16 for females, 5–19 for males). After alleging at the start of the paper that ADHD was the cause of smaller brain size at baseline (based upon the research team's failure to compare *all* of the unmedicated subjects with *all* of their age-matched and medicated peers), the investigators constructed predicted growth curves using a 'fitted polynomial' technique. First, longitudinal and cross-sectional data were combined using sophisticated statistical procedures (the 544 images which were used to make the curves included the subjects who provided one head scan). Second, data were omitted from all but the central 90 per cent of each sample's age range. In other words, 10 per cent of the dataset was excluded, based upon the investigators' concern (Castellanos *et al.*, 2002, p. 1746) that the resulting curves would otherwise have been 'too heavily influenced by extreme findings'.

Aided by these manipulations, the investigators produced growth curves which showed consistently larger brain volumes in the control group versus children with ADHD. However, based upon the overall shapes of the growth curves in the two groups of participants (a mildly sloping, inverted U), the research team made an extraordinary conclusion:

> longitudinal growth curves are roughly parallel, suggesting that the fundamental developmental processes active during late childhood and adolescence are essentially healthy in ADHD. (Castellanos *et al.*, 2002, p. 1747)

Parallel curves do not always mean healthy growth

Although the researchers claimed that the parallel curves were proof of 'essentially healthy' growth processes, since it implied that the ADHD and non-ADHD children were progressing at *steady rates* of development, this interpretation was invalid for many reasons. First, there was insufficient evidence to accept the premise that the ADHD growth curves were anything but normal until the start of stimulant drug therapy.

Second, there was no reason to celebrate the fact that the growth curves of medicated children were persistently suppressed. A parallel growth curve does not necessarily invalidate the existence of underlying growth pathology. The research team overlooked the fact that many of the ADHD children had probably entered the study during a period of canalization. In the endocrine literature, canalization refers to the tendency of the human body to maintain a narrow and predictable track of growth (Boersma and Wit, 1997). This can occur even while the organism is growing in a restricted fashion, in the context of illness, malnutrition, or endocrine defects.

Third, the investigators had presumably missed the window of the earliest and most abrupt reductions in growth velocity, since medication effects upon skeletal development are most apparent in the first three years of drug treatment.

Fourth, the mixing of data from pre-pubertal, pubertal, and post-pubertal children doubtlessly compromised the ability of the investigators to detect growth rate divergence, since the pubertal growth spurt in ADHD patients and controls, combined with the 'catch-up' growth spurt in children who stopped taking their stimulants, must have over-whelmed the data from younger subjects who were still medicated, and still exposed to drug-related endocrine dysregulation.

Fifth, the researchers did not display neurodevelopmental trajectories in terms of one particularly meaningful parameter. For example, the outcomes might have looked far different if the researchers had constructed growth curves in terms of a changing *ratio* of grey matter to white matter density. Such an analysis might have been more reflective of age-related maturation (the decline in grey matter being strongly outpaced in puberty by the expansion of myelination), leading to highly divergent rather than parallel growth curves.

Stimulant-related growth suppression

Mechanisms

Even if physicians deny the possibility that stimulants are a *cause* of growth suppression, it should be clear from the previous studies that the drugs fail to normalise the development of ADHD children. The catastrophic failure of the current Zeitgeist is the notion that the growth impairment which occurs during stimulant therapy is simply a 'minor' or 'transient' annoyance. This belief speaks to an epidemic of professional misinformation, in which the behaviours of healers deny the seriousness and implications of the mechanisms which are responsible for growth dysfunction.

Disruption of cartilage formation

As early as 1979, paediatricians at the University of Arkansas were alarmed by the discovery that a stimulant called pemoline (Cylert) was causing growth delays in their ADHD patients (Dickinson *et al.*, 1979). In response to this clinical observation, the professionals were motivated to examine the effects of pemoline upon the development of the immature skeleton (Kilgore *et al.*, 1979). The research protocol involved the incubation of varying concentrations of stimulants (pemoline, methylphenidate, and methamphetamine) with cartilage obtained from the long bones and pelvic rudiments of chicken embryos. Following a sixteen-hour period of drug exposure, the cartilage fragments were analyzed for changes in chemical processes. The researchers found that all of the stimulants exerted significant, inhibitory effects upon the enzyme processes that play an essential role in the formation of cartilage – the essential precursor of skeletal bones. While the Arkansas findings demonstrate a plausible mechanism of stimulant-related bone delay, they do not resolve the question of stimulant-related brain delay. Potential explanations for this phenomenon, however, are found in other equally under-appreciated studies.

Disruption of white matter formation (myelination)

In a series of papers (Kabara, 1965; Kabara and Riegel, 1965; Kabara, 1975) which seems to have escaped the attention of contemporary practitioners, chemists at the University of Detroit examined the effects of methylphenidate upon cholesterol metabolism. Motivated purely by scientific curiosity arising from methylphenidate's chemical similarity to known cholesterol-lowering compounds, the investigators tested different concentrations of the stimulant in repeated studies of mice (age range: 7-9 weeks). In one such experiment, 90 adult mice were subjected to six days of intraperitoneal (i.e., intra-abdominal) injections of saline or methylphenidate (4 mg/kg or 20 mg/kg per day). At these dose levels, no differences in appetite or body weight were observed between the experimental subjects or controls. At the end of each treatment period, animals were sacrificed and tissue levels of cholesterol were examined in the liver, spleen, and brain. Although exposure to methylphenidate at both dose levels resulted in reductions of liver and spleen cholesterol, the most consistent and significant changes occurred within the brain (see Table 9.4).

Further experimental analyses suggested that this decrease in brain cholesterol (10-20 per cent in just six days) was due to the metabolic disruption of cholesterol production, rather than the stimulation of its breakdown. This discovery was all the more important when one

Table 9.4 Effect of methylphenidate upon brain levels of free cholesterol results = mg of cholesterol per gram of wet tissue

	Trial I	Trial II	Trial III
Control group	9.13	9.80	9.91
4 mg/kg	7.21	7.65	8.38
20 mg/kg	7.65	9.61	9.82

Source: Author's calculations from Kabara and Riegel (1965, p. 1928).

considers the fact that the brain must make all of its own cholesterol (none of the cholesterol from the peripheral bloodstream passes
through the capillary defence system, called the blood brain barrier, to
enter the tissue of the brain). Furthermore, the cholesterol, which the
brain creates, plays a key role in the construction and integrity of cell
membranes (Dietschy and Turley, 2004).

Certainly, objections can be made that these results are ultimately
irrelevant for human patients, due to the metabolic differences which
exist between species; the relatively high doses used in the animal procedure (humans typically consume doses of 0.5 to 1 mg/kg
twice a day); and the intraperitoneal route of administration. This
author is clearly mindful of the research documenting the doubling
of behavioural and chemical potency when other rodents have been
exposed to intraperitoneal rather than oral doses of methylphenidate
(Gerasimov *et al.*, 2000).

Nevertheless, it would be imprudent to dismiss the importance of
these studies off hand, without fully appreciating the relevance of disruptions in the levels of brain cholesterol. Because cholesterol is a
major building block in the synthesis of myelin (Vance *et al.*, 2005;
Dietschy and Turley, 2004), the Michigan studies are fully consistent
with the frequently repeated observations that methylphenidate does
nothing to reverse maturational delays in the white matter of ADHD
children.

In the early 1970s, a second group of researchers documented
metabolic disturbances associated with another stimulant. Curious
to know more about the family of compounds known as CADS –
an acronym for *cationic* (positively charged) *amphiphilic* (attracted
to water and fat molecules) *drugs* – scientists at the University of
Birmingham (Allan and Michell, 1975) explored the cellular effects
of a number of these agents. This included the stimulant drug,
amphetamine.

The research protocol involved the exposure of white blood cells
to various medications for a period of about four hours. Following the incubation with amphetamine, the research team observed an
increase in the synthesis of phosphatidylinositol (a kind of lipid used
in the construction of cell membranes). A parallel test suggested that
this effect was associated with a decrease in the synthesis of other
glycerolipids (fatty substances, such as phosphatidylcholine and phos-
phatidylethanolamine). These findings have important implications for
the process of neurodevelopment. To the extent that amphetamine
produces similar changes in the lipid composition of brain cells, it
is possible that this stimulant – like methylphenidate – perturbs the

balance of the most essential building blocks of myelin, inhibiting white matter whenever and wherever it is composed (Martinez and Mougan, 1998).

Lethal damage to grey matter

Although limited in number when compared to the plethora of investigations devoted to the neurotoxicity of street drugs, several research protocols have documented the capacity of prescription stimulants to inflict *lethal* damage upon the neurons of the brain.

In one key study, the cellular effects of methylphenidate were investigated in neonatal mice (postnatal day 5). Researchers in this experiment injected a single intraperitoneal dose of methylphenidate (0.5, 5, or 50 mg/kg) in several procedures designed to identify potential neuroprotective and neurotoxic effects of the drug (Husson *et al.*, 2004). Animals were sacrificed on day six of life, and the brains were then processed (TUNEL staining) and examined for cellular change. Results were significant for the observation that a single injection of methylphenidate, irrespective of dose, increased the rate of neural cell death in the grey matter (basal ganglia) as well as the white matter of the brain. Based upon these results, the researchers concluded that 'exposure to methylphenidate at early stages of brain development could have long-term detrimental effects.' (Husson *et al*, 2004:168)

A team of Brazilian neuroscientists (Martins *et al.*, 2006) explored the age-related effects of methylphenidate in a study of juvenile (25 days old) and adult (60 days old) rats. The experiment involved the administration of intraperitoneal injections of the stimulant (1, 2, or 10 mg/kg) over a period which ranged from one to twenty-eight days. At the end of the phase of drug treatment, tissue was analyzed for evidence of oxidative damage to brain protein and fat (lipid). To appreciate the impact of this experiment, a word of explanation may be informative.

Oxidative damage refers to the inevitable byproduct of cellular respiration. As aerobic organisms produce energy through the process of breathing, they simultaneously generate toxic substances known as 'reactive oxygen species.' Exogenous chemicals can also induce these compounds. When oxidative damage overwhelms a cell's defences, it leads to the disintegration of lipids and protein, ultimately resulting in tissue dysfunction and/or death.

Based upon comparisons to unmedicated controls, the Brazilian research team confirmed that methylphenidate was a cause of oxidative damage in multiple regions of the brain. For both age groups, non-statistically significant changes occurred with acute (one day) exposure to the psychostimulant. For young rats, chronic exposure at all doses resulted in statistically significant increases in both lipid peroxidation (multiple brain regions) and protein oxidation, the latter within the involuntary movement centre (striatum) and 'thinking' centres (cortex) of the brain. These findings are clinically important, because they provide experimental evidence of a crucial mechanism through which early exposure to a popular stimulant can cause grey (and white) matter decline – particularly, in the brain regions most associated with the symptoms of ADHD.

Although an abundant literature (Davidson *et al.*, 2001; Kita *et al.*, 2003; McCann *et al.*, 1998; Thompson *et al.*, 2004; Volkow *et al.*, 2001) documents the hazards of methamphetamine – a street drug *and* prescription drug associated with prolonged damage to neurons and glia – it is only recently that teams of investigators have focused attention upon the neurotoxicity of non-methylated, *prescription* amphetamine. For example, researchers at Washington University (Lotharius and O'Malley, 2001) exposed tissue cultures of dopamine neurons to a 10 uM concentration of amphetamine. In one procedure, midbrain cells were incubated with the stimulant for 4 to 24 hours and then examined for evidence of oxidative stress. Findings were remarkable for a 33 per cent increase in the oxidation of proteins within the first day of treatment. In a second procedure, cells were treated with amphetamine for a period of one to four days. This resulted in the significant but delayed appearance of damage to the dopamine neurons, characterized by degeneration of the nerve terminals (nerve endings) on the fourth day.

As with any *in vitro* (laboratory) experiment, it is important to relate the 10 uM concentration to the realities of clinical experience. Therapeutic doses of amphetamine in human patients (children and adults) typically lead to blood levels of 0.12-0.20 uM (Angrist *et al.*, 1987). Before dismissing the 10 uM study as irrelevant on the basis of inapplicable dosing, two facts should be appreciated. First, experiments in animals have shown that the brain levels of stimulants can exceed blood levels by a factor of 20 to 30 (Clausing *et al.*, 1995). This suggests that human brain cells could very well experience amphetamine exposures approaching 10 uM. Second, the lab experiment showed neuronal destruction after a limited exposure of just four days. In contrast, human patients are increasingly encouraged to consume their stimulants for a lifetime.

Endocrine disruption

The search for the missing link between stimulants and growth reduction has spanned decades as research teams have explored a variety of ideas. Many hypotheses have been advanced, but all of the following have had weaknesses associated with inconsistent findings in animals and humans (Aarskog *et al.*, 1977; Lurie and O'Quinn, 1991)), as summarized in Table 9.5 below.

One important area of research, which has been largely ignored, is the impact of prescription stimulants upon thyroid function. In 1980, scientists at the University of North Carolina (Greeley *et al.*, 1980) performed a series of experiments in which young rats (ranging in age from 5 to 31 days) were treated with methylphenidate for a period of 21 days (twice a day, subcutaneous injections at doses of 1, 3, 10, 35, or 100 mg/kg). Following a drug withdrawal period of 24 hours, blood samples were collected in order to examine the concentrations of thyroid hormones (T3, T4, and TSH).

Findings were remarkable for significantly lower levels of T3 and T4 in all of the medicated animals, regardless of gender, and

Table 9.5 Possible causes of stimulant-induced growth suppression

Hypothesis	Weakness
Malnutrition [protein, carbohydrate, fat deficiency]	Height suppression has occurred in many children despite normal weight and normal appetite
Growth hormone deficiency	Inconsistent findings; most studies have shown acute increases in growth hormone in response to stimulants, with normalization of GH over time
Somatomedin (IGF) deficiency	Inconsistent findings
Growth hormone receptor dysfunction	Not yet studied
Cortisol excess (too much glucocorticoid)	Unclear to what extent cortisol levels remain elevated with stimulant therapy; unclear if this would impair growth in childhood chronically

regardless of previous drug dose. Moreover, these changes were not related to a decline in food intake. Separate experiments revealed that the thyroid effects were reversible for most animals within 18 months of drug withdrawal. However, for males, an early exposure to higher doses of methylphenidate (35 mg/kg and above) had long lasting effects, preventing the maturational rise in TSH, which accompanies normal development.

Only one research team (Bereket *et al.*, 2005) has published a paper about the thyroid effects of methylphenidate in ADHD patients. Mindful of the flaws in methodology that had confounded previous growth studies, Turkish investigators conducted an investigation of prepubertal children (n = 42, age range: 6.5–10.3), who had never before received stimulant therapy. Fourteen children completed the full study, consisting of sixteen months of treatment and four assessments (every four months) of changes in growth (height, weight, and body mass index or BMI) and growth-related hormones (IGF-1, IGFBP-3, T3, T4, free T4, and TSH).

At baseline, none of the subjects displayed deficits in height or weight, relative to the reference population. All of them experienced height and weight reductions after the initiation of drug treatment. At baseline, none of the subjects displayed abnormal levels of somatomedin (IGF) or thyroid hormone. After a one-year period of drug treatment, the children displayed a mild increase in TSH, along with gradual but progressive declines in the levels of T3 (not statistically significant), and total and free T4 (statistically significant). Although these values remained within the normal reference range for most children, the trends (*11–18 per cent reduction over one year*) were concerning enough for this team of clinicians to advise the regular thyroid monitoring of like-medicated patients.

Investigations of other stimulants have replicated these findings of drug-induced thyroid dysfunction. In one such study (Budziszewska *et al.*, 1996), rats exposed to a two-week course of amphetamine incurred a reduction in serum levels of T4. In a study of non-ADHD humans (Valverde *et al.*, 1976), a one-week exposure to amphetamine (15 mg per day) resulted in significant reductions in the nocturnal patterns of growth and thyroid hormones.

While thyroid studies may seem trivial on the surface, their developmental significance must not be overlooked. Although physicians are trained to recognize thyroid abnormalities in terms of the impairment of adult metabolism, they may not realise the critical role that these hormones play in the development of the nervous system

(Konig & Moura, 2002; Santisteban & Bernal, 2005). In animal studies, reductions in thyroid hormone have been shown to impair the formation of myelin (Barradas *et al.*, 2001; Ferreira *et al.*, 2004); to impede the development of the cerebellum (Trentin *et al.*, 2003; Singh *et al.*, 2003); to inhibit neurogenesis in the hippocampus (a temporal lobe structure) (Montero-Pedrazuela *et al.*, 2006); and to disrupt energy production in the cells of the cortex and striatum (Martinez *et al.*, 2001).

Sleep disruption

One of the most common side effects of stimulants for patients of all ages is insomnia. In the Preschool ADHD Treatment Study (Wigal *et al.*, 2006) mentioned previously, 140 children between the ages of three and five were exposed to methylphenidate for a one-year period of treatment. Sleep disturbances were a significant problem for 30–50 per cent patients during drug initiation. For a full 20 per cent of the children, these problems *persisted* throughout the entire year.

In a study of school age children ranging in age from 6 to 8 (O'Brien *et al.*, 2003), experts in sleep medicine compared the nocturnal patterns of ADHD patients (47 referred to the specialty sleep clinic, 53 recruited from the general community) against 49 healthy controls. ADHD subjects and their families reported significantly more problems with nightmares, restless sleep, and initial insomnia. Compared to controls, they also experienced significant reductions in REM sleep (rapid eye movement sleep) and a significant increase in latency to first REM (i.e., the length of time prior to the onset of the first REM period at night). These disturbances were most severe among the subset of children with highest exposure to stimulant drugs (see Table 9.6).

Table 9.6 Sleep study in ADHD children vs. healthy controls

	ADHD speciality clinic	ADHD community sample	Healthy controls
% taking stimulants	72	51	0
% REM sleep	18	21	28

Source: O'Brien *et al.* (2003, pp. 239–40).

Other investigations have demonstrated even more clearly the relationship between stimulant therapies and sleep disruption. For example, an investigation of sleep changes (Valverde *et al.*, 1976) among obese adults exposed to a seven-day course of low dose amphetamine (15 mg) revealed significant reductions in the total amount of REM sleep: 97 minutes *before* amphetamine, 73 minutes *under the influence of* amphetamine.

A study of six healthy adult males (Nicholson *et al.*, 1980) tested the effects of the stimulant, pemoline (Cylert), when taken at therapeutic doses of 60 or 100 mg per day. Sleep studies revealed significant reductions in overall sleep duration, sleep efficiency (the proportion of time in bed that is spent in sleep), and the percentage of REM sleep.

Physicians are generally encouraged to instruct patients and parents to continue stimulant therapy, on the grounds that sleep disturbances are transient and trivial. However, these casual dismissals contradict the importance of sleep – particularly, REM sleep – upon neurodevelopment. Several facts are critical in this regard.

First, the proper function of the endocrine system depends upon the coordination of intricate feedback loops, which keep hormones and metabolism in balance. Because of the fact that many of these essential chemicals are released according to complex 24-hour cycles (circadian rhythms), some scientists have speculated (Lurie and O'Quinn, 1991) that the disruption of sleep by psychostimulants may upset the timing of growth processes in the developing child.

Second, research in animals has suggested a causal association between the reduction of REM sleep and neurodevelopment (Morrissey *et al.*, 2004). In a study of young rats exposed to clonidine (a drug which, like stimulants, reduces the amount of time spent in REM), investigators documented a statistically significant reduction in brain mass. This finding was associated with an abnormal increase in cells displaying the effects of programmed cell death (apoptosis). Based upon the age of the rats used in this study (postnatal days 7 to 14), the reader might reasonably conclude that REM sleep reduction impedes the process of synaptogenesis (the development of cell-cell connections).

Third, the investigations of long-time sleep researchers, such as J. Allan Hobson, have confirmed significant relationships between the process of REM sleep, learning, and memory (Hobson and Pace-Schott, 2002). While initial investigations focused upon the purpose of REM sleep as the most important stage of active dreaming (humans also experience dreaming during other stages of sleep), more recent research has demonstrated the cellular and functional consequences of disrupting this stage of nocturnal activity. For example, studies of young male rats deprived of REM sleep have revealed disruptions in the structural reorganization (plasticity) of the hippocampus. This finding helps explain the behavioural consequences of REM sleep dysregulation in humans, in whom the proper functioning of the hippocampus is required for the integration and consolidation of memory (Davis *et al.*, 2006; Rauchs *et al.*, 2004; Romcy-Pereira and Pavlides, 2004; Smith, 1996).

Chemical imprinting: The harmful re-wiring of the brain

The phenomenon of chemical imprinting (Andersen and Navalta, 2004; Insel, 2000) refers to the process by which exposures to environmental stimuli (such as psychostimulants) result in delayed, and in this case, harmful effects. Space constraints will limit the present discussion, but a few examples will hopefully stimulate the reader to seek out more research on this intriguing topic.

Within the ranks of American psychiatry, an ongoing controversy surrounds the subject of stimulant addiction. Based upon limited research in animals and horrifically flawed studies in humans, opinion leaders in the mental health field have promoted the early use of stimulant therapy as a means of preventing future cocaine or amphetamine dependence (Barkley, *et al.*, 2003; Biederman, 2003; Wilens *et al.*, 2003).

It is in the context of these claims that the most credible and comprehensive work in this area remains the Northern California Study on ADHD (Lambert and Hartsough, 1998; Lambert *et al.*, 2006). In that pivotal investigation, researchers followed the progress of 492 children longitudinally for a period of 28 years. Statistically significant associations were demonstrated between the early exposure to stimulant drug therapy, and future dependencies upon nicotine and/or cocaine, summarized in Table 9.7. The researchers also detected an association between the duration of childhood stimulant therapy and future addiction (see Table 9.8).

Even after controlling for the possible confounding factor of co-morbid behavioural difficulties, such as conduct disorder or oppositionality, the relationship between stimulant exposure in childhood and future stimulant addictions was maintained (Lambert *et al.*, 2006).

Table 9.7 Effect of ADHD and early exposure to stimulants

| | ADHD | | Stimulants | |
	No	Yes	No	Yes
% nicotine dependent	22	45	25	45
% cocaine dependent	11	23	12	24

Source: Lambert (2005, pp. 197–221).

Table 9.8 Intensity of early stimulant use and future addiction

	No stimulant	Stimulant for < 1 year	Stimulant for 1 year or more
% nicotine dependent	32	39	49
% cocaine dependent	15	18	27

Source: Lambert and Hartsough (1998, p. 540).

Early stimulant exposure in rodents has been linked not only to persistent changes in the neurotransmitter systems associated with mood and motivation (Bolanos *et al.*, 2003; Brandon *et al.*, 2001; Carlezon *et al.*, 2003; Moll *et al.*, 2001), but also to the systems associated with higher cognitive functions. Researchers in Canada and Michigan (Kolb *et al.*, 2003) have shown that stimulants (amphetamine, cocaine) limit the brain's capacity for future learning, by reducing the experience-dependent growth of neuronal dendrites.

Another team of scientists has made functionally analogous discoveries, (Lagace *et al.*, 2006) in their study on the long-term effects of methylphenidate (Ritalin™). After exposing juvenile rats (20 days old) to sixteen days of stimulant drug treatment (2 mg/kg intraperitoneal injections), the investigators euthanised the animals at different developmental stages. In a series of parallel experiments, one group of animals was tested for the amount of neurogenesis in the temporal lobe (day 85), and for the appearance and fate of these new cells as the rats matured (day 112). The researchers found that an *early exposure to methylphenidate impaired the survival of new neurons in the hippocampus of adults*. They concluded that early life exposure to methylphenidate can have enduring consequences – in this case, a decreased capacity for neuronal plasticity in a brain region which is critical for learning and memory.

Conclusion

The era of the psychostimulant marks a reprehensible period in the history of modern medicine. It is ironic that the field of paediatrics was born in the early 20th century (Brosco, 2001; Young, 1979), largely through the efforts of reformers and physicians, like Dr. Percy Boulton, who saw a link between the pace of child development and the emergence of disease:

> Arrest of growth, or loss of weight, precedes so many diseases that it may be looked upon as a danger signal, and if the 'caution' is noticed before the disease point is reached catastrophe may frequently be prevented. (Young, 1979: 230)

It is remarkable that Boulton's legacy has been reversed in less than a century –invalidated by the actions and attitudes of those clinicians who tell their patients that the toxicities of stimulants are only mild, limited, and fleeting.

Forty years of evidence have shown that stimulants are a prevalent source of developmental toxicity: disrupting the formation of cartilage, myelin (white matter), and neurons (grey matter); dysregulating endocrine functions; disturbing the sleep cycle; and destroying the brain's capacity to respond to future experiences with healthful re-wiring and new growth.

While sceptics may challenge the claim that stimulants are an unequivocal cause of brain damage in the children who consume them, they cannot dispute the fact that the drugs do nothing to reverse or normalise alleged delays in maturation, but may, in fact, preclude or postpone the development of self-control, abstract thought, and other forms of higher cognition.

It is time for the medical profession to repair this tragic and overly long chapter in its history.

Note

1. Z-score: – a statistical method which explains how far, and in what direction, a given data point deviates from the mean by expressing it in terms of standard deviation units. Z-scores 'standardize' values so that research findings from different populations can be more easily compared (Dawson and Trapp, 2004; Standard score, 2006).

References

Aarskog, D., Fevang, F. O., Klove, H., Stoa, K. F. and Thorsen, T. (1977) The effect of the stimulant drugs, dextroamphetamine and methylphenidate, on secretion of growth hormone in hyperactive children, *Journal of Pediatrics*, 90, 136–9.

Allan, D. and Michell, R. H. (1975) Enhanced synthesis de novo of phosphatidylinositol in lymphocytes treated with cationic amphiphilic drugs, *Biochemical Journal*, 148, 471–8.

Andersen, S. L. and Navalta, C. P. (2004) Altering the course of neurodevelopment: A framework for understanding the enduring effects of psychotropic drugs, *International Journal of Developmental Neuroscience*, 22, 423–40.

Angrist, B., Corwin, J., Bartlik, B. and Cooper, T. (1987) Early pharmacokinetics and clinical effects of oral D-Amphetamine in normal subjects, *Biological Psychiatry*, 22, 1357–68.

Ashtari, M., Kumra, S., Bhaskar, S. L., Clarke, T., Thaden, E., Cervellione, K. L., Rhinewine, J. *et al.* (2005) Attention-Deficit/Hyperactivity Disorder: A preliminary diffusion tensor imaging study, *Biological Psychiatry*, 57, 448–55.

Barkley, R. A., Fischer, M., Smallish, L. and Fletcher, K. (2003) Does the treatment of Attention-Deficit Hyperactivity Disorder with stimulants contribute to drug use/abuse? A 13-year prospective study, *Pediatrics*, 111, 97–109.

Barradas, P. C., Vieira, R. S. and DeFreitas, M. S. (2001) Selective effect of hypothyroidism on expression of myelin markers during development [Abstract], *Journal of Neuroscience Research*, 66(2), 254–61.

Bartzokis, G., Beckson, M., Lu, P. H., Edwards, N., Bridge, P. and Mintz, J. (2002) Brain maturation may be arrested in chronic cocaine addicts, *Biological Psychiatry* 51, 605–11.

Bartzokis, G., Beckson, M., Lu, P. H., Edwards, N., Rapoport, R., Wiseman, E. and Bridge, P. (2000) Age-related brain volume reductions in amphetamine and cocaine addicts and normal controls: Implications for addiction research, *Psychiatry Research: Neuroimaging*, 98, 93–102.

Bereket, A., Turan, S., Karaman, M. G., Haklar, G., Ozbay, F. and Yazgan, M. Y. (2005) Height, weight, IGF-1, IGFBP-3 and thyroid functions in prepubertal children with Attention Deficit Hyperactivity Disorder: Effect of methylphenidate treatment, *Hormone Research*, 63, 159–64.

Biederman, J. (2003) Pharmacotherapy for attention-deficit/hyperactivity disorder (ADHD) decreases the risk for substance abuse: Findings from a longitudinal follow-up of youths with and without ADHD [Abstract], *Journal of Clinical Psychiatry*, 64(Suppl.) (11), 3–8.

Biederman, J., Faraone, S. V., Monuteaux, M. C., Plunkett, E. A., Gifford, J. and Spencer, T. (2003) Growth deficits and attention deficit/hyperactivity disorder revisited: Impact of gender, development and treatment, *Pediatrics*, 111, 1010–16.

Boersma, B. and Wit, J. M. (1997) Catch-up growth, *Endocrine Reviews*, 18(5), 646–61.

Bolanos, C. A., Barrot, M., Berton, O., Wallace-Black, D. and Nestler, E. J. (2003) Methylphenidate treatment during pre- and periadolescence alters behavioral responses to emotional stimuli at adulthood, *Biological Psychiatry*, 54, 1317–29.

Brandon, C. L., Marinelli, M., Baker, L. K. and White, F. J. (2001) Enhanced reactivity and vulnerability to cocaine following methylphenidate treatment in adolescent rats, *Neuropsychopharmacology*, 25, 651–61.

Brosco, J. P. (2001) Weight Charts and well-child care: How the pediatrician became the expert in child health, *Archives of Pediatric and Adolescent Medicine*, 155, 1385–9.

Budziszewska, B., Jaworska-Feil, L. and Lason, W. (1996) The effect of repeated amphetamine and cocaine administration on adrenal, gonadal, and thyroid hormone levels in the rat plasma [Abstract], *Experimental and Clinical Endocrinology and Diabetes*, 104(4), 334–8.

Carlezon, W. A., Mague, S. D. and Andersen, S. L. (2003) Enduring behavioral effects of early exposure to methylphenidate in rats, *Biological Psychiatry*, 54, 1330–7.

Carmona, S., Vilarroya, O., Bielsa, A., Tremols, V., Soliva, J. C., Rovira, M., Tomas, J., Raheb, C., Gispert, J. D., Batlle, S. and Bulbena, A. (2005) Global and regional gray matter reductions in ADHD: A voxel-based morphometric study, *Neuroscience Letters*, 389, 88–93.

Castellanos, F. X., Lee, P. P., Sharp, W., Jeffries, N. O., Greenstein, D. K., Clasen, L. S., Blumenthal, J. D. *et al.* (2002) Developmental trajectories of brain volume abnormalities in children and adolescents with Attention-Deficit/Hyperactivity Disorder, *JAMA*, 288(14), 1740–8.

Charach, A., Figueroa, M., Chen, S., Ickowicz, A. and Schachar, R. (2006) Stimulant treatment over 5 years: Effects on growth, *Journal of the American Academy of Child and Adolescent Psychiatry*, 45(4), 415–21.

Clarke, C., Clarke, K., Muneyirci, J., Azmitia, E. and Whitaker-Azmitia, P. M. (1996) Prenatal cocaine delays astroglial maturation: immunodensitometry shows increased markers of immaturity (vimentin and GAP-43) and decreased proliferation and production of the growth factor S-100 [Abstract], *Brain Research. Developmental Brain Research*, 91(2), 268–73.

Clausing, P., Gough, B., Holson, R. R., Slikker, W., Jr. and Bowyer, J. F. (1995) Amphetamine levels in brain microdialysate, caudate/putamen, substantia nigra and plasma after dosage that produces either behavioral or neurotoxic effects [Abstract], *Journal of Pharmacology and Experimental Therapeutics*, 274(2), 614–21.

Courchesne, E., Chisum, H. J., Townsend, J., Cowles, A., Covington, J., Egaas, B., Harwood, M., Hinds, S. and Press, G. A. (2000) Normal brain development and aging: quantitative analysis at in vivo MR imaging in healthy volunteers, *Radiology*, 216, 672–82.

Davidson, C., Gow, A. J., Lee, T. H. and Ellinwood, E. H. (2001) Methamphetamine neurotoxicity: Necrotic and apoptotic mechanisms and relevance to human abuse and treatment, *Brain Research Reviews*, 36, 1–22.

Davis, C. J., Meighan, P. C., Taishi, P., Krueger, J. M., Harding, J. M. and Wright, J. W. (2006) REM sleep deprivation attenuates actin-binding protein cortactin: a link between sleep and hippocampal plasticity [Abstract], *Neuroscience Letters*, 400(3), 191–6.

Dawson, B. and Trapp, R. G. (2004) *Basic & Clinical Biostatistics*, 4th edn. New York: Lange Medical Books/McGraw-Hill.

Dickinson, L. C., Lee, J., Ringdahl, I. C., Schedewie, H. K., Kilgore, B. S. and Elders, M. J. (1979) Impaired growth in hyperkinetic children receiving pemoline, *The Journal of Pediatrics*, 94(4), 538–41.

Dietschy, J. M. and Turley, S. D. (2004) Thematic review series: Brain lipids. Cholesterol metabolism in the central nervous system during early development and in the mature animal, *Journal of Lipid Research*, 45, 1375–97.

Ferreira, A. A., Nazario, J. C., Pereira, M. J., Azevedo, N. L. and Barradas, P. C. (2004) Effects of experimental hypothyroidism on myelin sheath structural organization [Abstract], *Journal of Neurocytology* 33(2), 225–31.

Fields, R. D. (2005) Myelination: An overlooked mechanism of synaptic plasticity? [Abstract], *The Neuroscientist*, 11(6), 528–31.

Fisher, M. O., Nager, R. G. and Monaghan, P. (2006) Compensatory growth impairs adult cognitive performance, *PLoS Biology*, 4(8), 1462–6.

Fuster, J. M. (2002) Frontal lobe and cognitive development [Abstract], *Journal of Neurocytology*, 31(3–5), 373–85.

Gale, C. R., O'Callaghan, F. J., Godfrey, K. M., Law, C. M. and Martyn, C. N. (2004) Critical periods of brain growth and cognitive function in children, *Brain*, 127(2), 321–9.

Gerasimov, M. R., Franceschi, M., Volkow, N. D., Gifford, A., Gatley, S. J., Marsteller, D., Molina, P. E. and Dewey, S. L. (2000) Comparison between intraperitoneal and oral methylphenidate administration: A microdialysis and locomotor activity study, *Journal of Pharmacology and Experimental Therapeutics*, 295(1), 51–7.

Giedd, J. N., Blumenthal, J., Jeffries, N. O., Castellanos, F. X., Liu, H., Zijdenbos, A., Paus, T., Evans, A. C. and Rapoport, J. L. (1999) Brain development during childhood and adolescence: A longitudinal MRI study. *Nature Neuroscience*, 2(10), 861–3.

Gollub, R. L., Breiter, H. C., Kantor, H., Kennedy, D., Gastfriend, D., Mathew, R. T., Makris, N. *et al.* (1998) Cocaine decreases cortical cerebral blood flow but does not obscure regional activation in functional magnetic resonance imaging in human subjects [Abstract], *Journal of Cerebral Blood Flow and Metabolism*, 18(7), 724–34.

Greeley, George H. and Kizer, J. S. (1980) The effects of chronic methylphenidate treatment on growth and endocrine function in the developing rat, *Journal of Pharmacology and Experimental Therapeutics*, 215 (3), 545–51.

Greeley, G. H., Jahnke, G., Nicholson, G. F. and Kizer, J. S. (1980) Decreased serum 3,5,3'-triiodothyronine and thyroxine levels accompanying acute and chronic Ritalin treatment of developing rats, *Endocrinology*, 106, 898–904.

Hobson, J. A. and Pace-Schott, E. F. (2002) The cognitive neuroscience of sleep: Neuronal systems, consciousness, and learning, *Nature Reviews. Neuroscience*, 3(9), 679–93.

Husson, I., Mesples, B., Medja, F., Leroux, P., Kosofsky, B. and Gressens, P. (2004) Methylphenidate and MK-801, an N-methyl-D-aspartate receptor antagonist: Shared biological properties, *Neuroscience*, 125, 163–70.

Insel, T. R. (2000) *The Development of Brain and Behavior*, retrieved on 31 October 2006 at <http://www.acnp.org/G4/GN401000066/CH066.html>.

Kabara, J. J. and Riegel, C. A. (1965) Brain cholesterol IX: Effect of methylphenidate on the incorporation of specifically labeled glucose, *Biochemical Pharmacology*, 14, 1928–30.

Kabara, J. J. (1965) Brain cholesterol VIII: Effect of methylphenidate (Ritalin) on the Incorporation of specifically labeled acetate, *Proceedings of the Society for Experimental Biology and Medicine*, 118, 905–8.

Kabara, J. J. (1975) Brain cholesterol XVIII: Effect of methylphenidate (Ritalin) on [U-14C] glucose and [2-3H] acetate incorporation, *Proceedings of the Society for Experimental Biology and Medicine*, 150, 525–8.

Kaufman, M. J., Levin, J. M., Maas, L. C., Rose, S. L., Lukas, S. E., Mendelson, J. H., Cohen, B. M. and Renshaw, P. F. (1998) Cocaine decreases relative cerebral blood volume in humans: A dynamic susceptibility contrast magnetic resonance imaging study [Abstract], *Psychopharmacology*, 138(1), 76–81.

Kilgore, B. S., Dickinson, L. C., Burnett, C. R., Lee, J., Schedewie, H. K. and Elders, M. J. (1979) Alterations in cartilage metabolism by neurostimulant drugs, *The Journal of Pediatrics*, 94(4), 542–5.

Kita, T., Wagner, G. C. and Nakashima, T. (2003) Current research on methamphetamine-induced neurotoxicity: Animal models of monoamine disruption, *Journal of Pharmacological Sciences*, 92, 178–95.

Kolb, B., Gorny, G., Li, Y., Samaha, A. and Robinson, T. E. (2003) Amphetamine or cocaine limits the ability of later experience to promote structural plasticity in the neocortex and nucleus accumbens, *PNAS*, 100(18), 10523–8.

Konig, S. and Moura N. V. (2002) Thyroid hormone actions on neural cells [Abstract], *Cellular and Molecular Neurobiology*, 22(5–6), 517–44.

Lagace, D. C., Yee, J. K., Bolanos, C. A. and Eisch, A. J. (2006) Juvenile administration of methylphenidate attenuates adult hippocampal neurogenesis, *Biological Psychiatry*, 60 (10), 1121–30.

Lambert, N. M. (2005) Contribution of childhood ADHD, conduct problems and stimulant treatment to adolescent and adult tobacco and psychoactive substance abuse, *Ethical Human Psychology and Psychiatry*, 7 197–221.

Lambert, N. M. and Hartsough, C. S. (1998) Prospective study of tobacco smoking and substance dependencies among samples of ADHD and non-ADHD participants, *Journal of Learning Disabilities*, 31, 533–44.

Lambert, N. M., McLeod, M. and Schenk, S. (2006) Subjective responses to initial experience with cocaine: An exploration of the incentive-sensitization theory of drug abuse, *Addiction*, 101, 713–25.

Lisska, Megan C. and Rivkees, Scott A. (2003) Daily methylphenidate use slows the growth of children: A community based study, *Journal of Pediatric Endocrinology & Metabolism*, 16, 711–18.

Lotharius, J. and O'Malley, K. L. (2001) Role of mitochondrial dysfunction and dopamine-dependent oxidative stress in amphetamine-induced toxicity, *Annals of Neurology*, 49 (1), 79–89.

Lurie, S. and O'Quinn, A. (1991) Neuroendocrine responses to methylphenidate and d-amphetamine: Applications to Attention-Deficit Disorder, *Journal of Neuropsychiatry*, 3, 41–50.

Martinez, B., del Hoyo, P., Martin, M. A., Arenas, J., Perez-Castillo, A. and Santos, A. (2001) Thyroid hormone regulates oxidative phosphorylation in the cerebral cortex and striatum of neonatal rats [Abstract], *Journal of Neurochemistry*, 78(5), 1054–63.

Martinez, M. and Mougan, I. (1998) Fatty acid composition of human brain phospholipids during normal development, *Journal of Neurochemistry*, 71(6), 2528–33.

Martins, M. R., Reinke, A., Petronilho, F. C., Gomes, K. M., Dal-Pizzol, F., and Quevedo, J. (2006) Methylphenidate treatment induces oxidative stress in young rat brain, *Brain Research*, 1078(1), 189–97.

McCann, U. D., Wong, D. F., Yokoi, F., Villemagne, V., Dannals, R. F. and Ricaurte, G. A. (1998) Reduced striatal dopamine transporter density in abstinent methamphetamine and methcathinone users: Evidence from positron emission tomography studies with [11C]WIN-35, 428, *Journal of Neuroscience*, 18(20), 8417–22.

Moll, G. H., Hause, S., Ruther, E., Rothenberger, A. and Huether, G. (2001) Early methylphenidate administration to young rats causes a persistent reduction in the density of striatal dopamine transporters, *Journal of Child and Adolescent Psychopharmacology*, 11(1), 15–24.

Montero-Pedrazuela, A., Venero, C., Lavado-Autric, R., Fernandez-Lamo, I., Garcia-Vergudo, J. M., Bernal, J. and Guadano-Ferraz, A. (2006) Modulation of adult hippocampal neurogenesis by thyroid hormones: Implications for depressive-like behavior, *Molecular Psychiatry*, 11 (4), 361–71.

Mori, E., Hirono, N., Yamashita, H., Imamura, T., Ikejii, Y., Ikeda, M., Kitagaki, H. *et al.* (1997) Premorbid brain size as a determinant of reserve capacity against intellectual decline in Alzheimer's disease, *American Journal of Psychiatry*, 154(1), 18–24.

Morrissey, M. J., Duntley, S. P., Anch, A. M. and Nonneman, R. (2004) Active sleep and its role in the prevention of apoptosis in the developing brain [Abstract], *Medical Hypotheses*, 62(6), 876–9.

Mostofsky, S. H., Cooper, K. L., Kates, W. R., Denckla, M. B. and Kaufmann, W. E. (2002) Smaller prefrontal and premotor volumes in boys with Attention-Deficit/Hyperactivity Disorder, *Biological Psychiatry*, 52, 785–94.

MTA Cooperative Group (1999) A 14-Month randomized clinical trial of treatment strategies for attention-deficit/hyperactivity disorder, *Archives of General Psychiatry*, 56(12), 1073–86.

MTA Cooperative Group (2004) National Institute of Mental Health multimodal treatment study of ADHD follow-up: Changes in effectiveness and growth after the end of treatment, *Pediatrics*, 113 (4), 762–9.

Nagy, Z., Westerberg, H. and Klingberg, T. (2004) Maturation of white matter is associated with the development of cognitive functions during childhood [Abstract], *Journal of Cognitive Neuroscience*, 16, 1227–33.

Nicholson, A. N., Stone, B. M. and Jones, M. M. (1980) Wakefulness and reduced rapid eye movement sleep: Studies with prolintane and pemoline [Abstract], *British Journal of Clinical Pharmacology*, 10(5), 465–72.

O'Brien, M. L., Ivanenko, A., Crabtree, V. M., Holbrook, C. R., Bruner, J. L., Klaus, C. J. and Gozal, D. (2003) Sleep disturbances in children with Attention Deficit Hyperactivity Disorder, *Pediatric Research*, 54, 237–43.

Pizzi, W. J., Rode, E. C. and Barnhart, J. E. (1986) Methylphenidate and growth: Demonstration of a growth impairment and a growth-rebound phenomenon [Abstract], *Developmental Pharmacology and Therapeutics*, 9(5), 361–8.

Pizzi, W. J., Rose, E. C. and Barnhart, J. E. (1987) Differential effects of methylphenidate on the growth of neonatal and adolescent rats. *Neurotoxicology and Teratology*, 9, 107–11.

Poulton, A. (2005) Growth on stimulant medication; clarifying the confusion: A review, *Archives of Disease in Childhood*, 90, 801–6.

Poulton, A. (2006) Growth and sexual maturation in children and adolescents with attention deficit hyperactivity disorder, *Current Opinion in Pediatrics*, 18, 427–34.

Poulton, A. and Cowell, C. T. (2003) Slowing of growth in height and weight on stimulants: A characteristic pattern, *Journal of Paediatrics and Child Health*, 39, 180–5.

Rauchs, G., Bertran, F., Guillery-Girard, B., Desgranges, B., Kerrouche, N., Denise, P., Foret, J. and Eustache, F. (2004) Consolidation of strictly episodic memories mainly requires rapid eye movement sleep [Abstract], *Sleep*, 27(3), 395–401.

Rice, D. and Barone, S., Jr. (2000) Critical periods of vulnerability for the developing nervous system: Evidence from humans and animal models. *Environmental Health Perspectives*, 108 (Supplement 3), 511–33.

Romcy-Pereira, R. and Pavlides, C. (2004) Distinct modulatory effects of sleep on the maintenance of hippocampal and medial prefrontal cortex LTP [Abstract], *European Journal of Neuroscience*, 20(12), 3453–62.

Rushton, J. P. and Ankney, C. D. (1996) Brain size and cognitive ability: Correlations with age, sex, social class, arid race, *Psychonomic Bulletin & Review*, 3(1), 21–36.

Santisteban, P. and Bernal, J. (2005) Thyroid development and effect on the nervous system [Abstract], *Review of Endocrine and Metabolic Disorders*, 6(3), 217–28.

Singh, R., Upadhyay, G. and Godbole, M. M. (2003) Hypothyroidism alters mitochondrial morphology and induces release of apoptogenic proteins during rat cerebellar development [Abstract], *Journal of Endocrinology*, 176(3), 321–9.

Smith, C. (1996) Sleep states, memory processes and synaptic plasticity [Abstract], *Behavioural Brain Research*, 78(1), 49–56.

Sowell, E. R., Peterson, B. S., Thompson, P.M., Welcome, S. E., Henkenius, A. L. and Toga, A. W. (2003a) Mapping cortical changes across the human life span, *Nature Neuroscience*, 6(3), 309–15.

Sowell, E. R., Thompson, P. M., Welcome, S. E., Henkenius, A. L., Toga, A. W. and Peterson, B. S. (2003b) Cortical abnormalities in children and adolescents with attention-deficit hyperactivity disorder, *The Lancet*, 362, 1699–707.

Spencer, T. J., Biederman, J., Harding, M., O'Donnell, D., Faraone, S.V. and Wilens, T. E. (1996) Growth deficits in ADHD children revisited: Evidence for disorder-associated growth delays? *Journal of the American Academy of Child and Adolescent Psychiatry*, 35(11), 1460–9.

Standard score (2006) *Wikipedia* (December), retrieved on 18 January 2007 at <http://en.wikipedia.org/wiki/Standard_score>.

Strickland, T. L., Mena, I., Villanueva-Meyer, J., Miller, B. L., Cummings, J., Mehringer, C. M., Satz, P. and Myers, H. (1993) Cerebral perfusion and neuropsychological consequences of chronic cocaine use [Abstract], *Journal of Neuropsychiatry and Clinical Neuroscience*, 5, 419–27.

Swanson, J., Greenhill, L., Wigal, T., Kollins, S., Stehli, A., Davies, M. *et al.* (2006) Stimulant-related reductions of growth rates in the PATS, *Journal of the American Academy of Child and Adolescent Psychiatry*, 45(11), 1304–13.

Thompson, P. M., Hayashi, K. M., Simon, S. L., Geaga, J. A., Hong, M. S., Sui, Y., Lee, J. Y. *et al.* (2004) Structural abnormalities in the brains of human subjects who use methamphetamine, *Journal of Neuroscience*, 24(26), 6028–36.

Toga, A. W., Thompson, P. M. and Sowell, E.R. (2006) Mapping brain maturation, *Trends in Neuroscience*, 29(3), 148–59.

Travis, F. (1998) Cortical and cognitive development in 4th, 8th, and 12th grade students: The contribution of speed of processing and executive functioning to cognitive development [Abstract], *Biological Psychology*, 48(1), 37–56.

Trentin, A. G., De Aguiar, C. B., Garcez, R. C. and Alvarez-Silva, M. (2003) Thyroid hormone modulates the extracellular matrix organization and expression in cerebellar astrocytes: Effects on astrocyte adhesion [Abstract], *Glia*, 42(4), 359–69.

Uehling, B. S. (1969) Effects of chronic d-amphetamine sulfate administration during development in rats, *International Journal of Neuropharmacology*, 8, 43–8.

Valverde, C. R., Pastrana, L. S., Ruiz, J. A., Solis, H., Jurado, J. L., Sordo, C. M., Fernandez-Guardola, A. and Maisterrena, J. A. (1976) Neuroendocrine and electroencephalographic sleep changes due to acute amphetamine ingestion in human beings, *Neuroendocrinology*, 22, 57–71.

Vance, J. E., Hayashi, H. and Karten, B. (2005) Cholesterol homeostasis in neurons and glial cells [Abstract], *Seminars in Cell and Developmental Biology*, 16(2), 193–212.

Volkow, N. D., Chang, L, Wang, G. J., Fowler, J. S., Francheschi, D., Sedler, M. *et al.* (2001) Loss of dopamine transporters in methamphetamine abusers recovers with protracted abstinence, *Journal of Neuroscience*, 21(23), 9414–18.

Wheeler, T. L., Winsler, A., Chrosniak, L. and Smith, R. (2003) Behavioral and neurological dose effects of methylphenidate (MPH) in the male Long Evans hooded rat. Poster presented at the 33rd annual meeting of the Society for Neuroscience, New Orleans, LA, November, retrieved on 21 October 2006 at <http: //64.233.161.104/search?hl=en&lr=&q=cache%3AoMk9bVK2gIsJ%3A>, <www.gmu.edu%2Fdepartment> and <http://classweb.gmu.edu/awinsler/Students.html>.

Wigal, T., Greenhill, L., Chuang, S., McGough, J., Vitiello, B., Skrobala, A. *et al.* (2006) Safety and tolerability of methylphenidate in preschool children with ADHD, *Journal of the American Academy of Child and Adolescent Psychiatry*, 45(11), 1294–302.

Wilens, T., Faraone, S. V., Biederman, J. and Gunawardene, S. (2003) Does stimulant therapy of ADHD beget later substance abuse? Meta-analytic Review of the Literature, *Pediatrics*, 111, 179–85.

Young, J. A. (1979) Height, weight, and health: Anthropometric study of human growth in nineteenth-century American medicine, *Bulletin of the History of Medicine*, 53(2), 214–43.

Chapter 10

The Manipulation of Data and Attitudes about ADHD: A Study of Consumer Advertisements

Jonathan Leo and Jeffrey Lacasse

At this point in time, Direct-to-Consumer Advertising (DTCA) is only legal in the United States and New Zealand, but various commercial and political groups are actively seeking to legalize DTCA in Europe, Canada, and beyond (Priest, 2007). Recently, officials from the US White House have put pressure on the British government to allow DTCA (Boseley, 2006). As the medical establishments in the United Kingdom and Canada consider the potential ramifications of legalizing DTCA, it is valuable to consider the example of the United States, where such advertisements have been legal and widespread since 1997. In America, consumer advertisements are now ubiquitous and have become an integral part of popular culture. In many cases, the content of these advertisements may be taken as fact, despite a major disconnect between their slogans and the scientific literature (Lacasse and Leo, 2005; Lacasse and Leo, 2006a; Lacasse and Leo, 2006b).

In 1996, the pharmaceutical companies spent $791 million on consumer advertising, and by 2000 they were spending $35.1 billion (NIHCM Foundation, 2000). Paralleling this widespread increase of DTCA in America there has been a dramatic rise in the number of children diagnosed with ADHD and subsequently prescribed stimulant medication. Between 1994 and 1999, the production of Ritalin™ increased eight hundred percent, with ninety percent of it being consumed in the United States (See chapter ten by Hart for a more complete discussion of diagnostic rates). The purpose of this chapter is to examine the scientific evidence behind the statements made in psychostimulant advertisements, keeping in mind that patients look to their physicians to contextualize these advertisements, the scientific literature, and each patient's unique situation.

DTCA and the increased use of Ritalin™

A major goal of DTCA is to start a conversation, initiated by the patient and then elaborated on by the physician. According to one advertising executive, the goal is 'to drive patients to their doctor' (Loden and Schooler, 1998). Patients who have seen an advertisement for a disease are more likely to bring up any concerns about a potential symptom with their doctor. The proponents of DTCA point out that, from a public health perspective, this is beneficial because increased disease awareness in the general population results in more people being treated (Cutler, 2005). Implicit in this line of reasoning is that the consumer advertisements are accurate. If the advertisements are inaccurate, then the doctor-patient relationship is greatly complicated, as an explanation by a physician that differs from the information disseminated by the advertisements would be met with resistance and confusion by the patient.

The example of ADHD is particularly interesting to those following the proliferation of the consumer advertisements, for several reasons: ADHD has been the subject of considerable controversy over the years. It has no biological diagnostic markers; it has been theorized to be over-diagnosed in Western countries; and it can be treated by both psychosocial and pharmacological interventions. In addition, the most popular treatments for ADHD are Schedule II pharmaceuticals – psychostimulant drugs, such as methylphenidate or amphetamine, which carry both addictive properties and the risk of iatrogenic harm, and are largely prescribed to a vulnerable population – children – through proxy authorization and recommendation by their parents. In the early adoption of DTCA, adverts for such products were seen as unlikely, but have subsequently become commonplace in popular culture. There are now repeated advertising campaigns in mainstream magazines that promote psychostimulant treatment of children directly to parents. In addition, the emergence of the World Wide Web has provided a major venue for DTCA. Googling 'ADHD,' now inevitably links users to DTCA websites that promote psychostimulants.

Underlying any discussion of ADHD, and what every neuroscience researcher is aware of, is the understanding that the most straightforward experiment in all of neuroscience is the one seeking to determine if Ritalin™ works. Here, 'works' is defined as a short-term improvement in attention span. Whether the subjects are male or female, preschoolers or geriatrics, diagnosed with ADHD or not, given medication by a doctor or a friend, one point has been known for 75 years: stimulants improve anyone's and everyone's ability to pay attention.

As a case study in DTCA, we examined the presentation of several complex aspects in consumer advertisements about ADHD, such as neuroimaging, genetics, medication efficacy, and the chemical imbalance theory. For each topic presented in web-based or print advertisements, we looked at the evidence in the medical literature, and asked whether the advertisements accurately reflected the scientific literature. We focused on how practicing clinicians would have to explain to their patients – or patients' parents – that, contrary to the advertisements, scientists still have not answered these complex questions:

> *While the specific cause has not been confirmed, brain imaging research using a technique called magnetic resonance imaging (MRI) has shown that differences exist between the brains of children with and without ADHD* (Ritalinla.com).

Radiological images of the brain have become a powerful aid in the marketing of ADHD medications, as the images are believed to document the existence of a definable and visible neuropathological abnormality. The brain imaging pictures usually contrast a brightly coloured 'normal' brain to a slightly dimmer 'ADHD' brain (Rosack, 2004). However, the ADHD neuroimaging studies are plagued by a significant confounding variable. In the overwhelming majority of the ADHD imaging studies the ADHD children have had a prior history of medication use, making it extremely difficult to know if the reported differences between ADHD children and controls result from an idiopathic organic brain defect – as implied or stated in most studies' advertisements – or from brain changes resulting from prior drug use by the ADHD subjects (Giedd, Blumenthal, Molloy and Castellanos, 2001; Leo and Cohen, 2003).

For some scientists (National Institute of Mental Health, 2002), the issue of prior medication use was settled with the publication of a NIMH-sponsored study in 2002 (Castellanos *et al.*, 2002), which included a group of non-medicated ADHD children. The authors concluded that the brains of children with ADHD were three percent smaller than control brains. In addition, based on a comparison between the medicated and non-medicated ADHD children, the authors concluded that the medications were not responsible for the volume reductions. Yet, what could have been a simple comparison was confounded by the fact that, on average, the non-medicated ADHD subjects were two years younger than the control subjects. Prior to the publication of this study, a common justification by ADHD imaging researchers for using medicated ADHD subjects in their studies was that it was difficult to find non-medicated ADHD children. However, this does not explain why once a group of non-medicated ADHD children was identified, it suddenly became difficult to find age-appropriate controls.

In 2003, a second NIMH-sponsored study was published that also included medicated and non-medicated ADHD patients, yet, surprisingly, this study did not report on the comparison between these two groups; instead, the researchers combined the medicated and non-medicated children together into one ADHD group (Sowell *et al.*, 2003). Their justification for not reporting on the comparison between medicated and non-medicated ADHD children was the lack of uniformity between the subjects regarding medication -something which the first NIMH study never commented on. Since replication is an essential component of the scientific process, it is unclear why the comparison between the medicated and non-medicated ADHD children, which was considered so significant in the first NIMH study, was not deemed worthy of publication for the second NIMH study.

Leaving any specific criticism of the experimental design of these studies aside, there is a much broader problem with the brain imaging studies that makes interpretation of even well-controlled imaging studies more complex than what is portrayed in one-page advertisements, namely, differences do not necessarily equal disease. Even if a large number of children have a brain that is slightly 'different' than the average brain (and this group is getting larger every year), this fact does not necessarily lead to the conclusion that these children have a disease requiring medication. All behavioural traits fall onto a spectrum, and even if brain scans can eventually be used to identify which children belong at the ends of the spectrum, answers about how many children to medicate, whether it is three, five, or twelve percent of school-aged children, cannot be found in a radiological image.

For instance, Joseph Rey and Michael Sawyer, in *The British Journal of Psychiatry*, ask the question, 'Are Psychostimulant Drugs Being Used Appropriately to Treat Child and Adolescent Disorders?' (Rey and Sawyer, 2003, p. 284). They point out that the National Institute for Clinical Excellence (NICE) only recommends methylphenidate for children diagnosed with the severe hyperkinetic disorder and not for children with the inattentive or impulsive-hyperactive subtype, a guideline that only includes about one percent of the children in the community. Yet, the American Academy of Pediatrics casts a bigger net and states that even children with the inattentive or impulsive-hyperactive subtype should be given stimulant medication and/or behavioural therapy. Their net could potentially result in seventeen percent of the male children in the population being medicated.

In 2005, the *New York Times* interviewed several leaders in the field of ADHD imaging research who acknowledged the shortcomings of their field. According to the *Times*, 'imaging technology has not lived up to the hopes invested in it in the 1990s,' and, moreover, 'some experts say that the technology has been oversold as a psychiatric tool' (Carey, 2005).

Neurotransmitters

> *Research suggests an imbalance in the levels of dopamine and norepinephrine, two neurotransmitters (substances that may transmit messages in the brain), may account for many of the signs and symptoms of ADHD* (Adderall.com, 2006).

> *ADHD medications are thought to influence the balance of norepinephrine and dopamine in the brain, helping to improve functioning to more normal levels* (Concerta.net, 2008).

> *Studies show that the brains of children with ADHD may function differently than those of other children. These children may have an imbalance of chemicals in the brain that help to regulate behavior* (Ritalinla.com, 2008).

> *Attention Deficit Hyperactivity Disorder (ADHD) is a common medical condition...Studies have shown that the brains of people with ADHD may work differently, perhaps because of a chemical imbalance* (FocalinXR. com, 2008).

After reading these statements, the parents of a child with ADHD could hardly be faulted for requesting a 'Neurotransmitter Level Test,' leaving the doctor to explain the following: (1) the chemical imbalance theory is more 'metaphor' than scientific fact; (2) there is no valid test for neurotransmitter levels; (3) there are no scientific studies that have documented altered neurotransmitter levels in children diagnosed with ADHD; and (4) it is only through *indirect* evidence that the pharmaceutical companies can make these kinds of statements about chemical imbalances.

In addition, besides the lack of *direct* proof for chemical imbalances, there are significant findings, left unsaid in the advertisements, which contradict the theory. For instance, stimulants will help anyone pay attention, even children who have no diagnosis of ADHD (Rapoport *et al.*, 1978); and the same neurotransmitters, dopamine and norepinephrine, that are implicated in ADHD are implicated in numerous psychiatric conditions.

The issue of altered biochemistry or brain function in ADHD is complex and contested (see chapter four by Leo and Cohen). Consumers reading these advertisements, however, will have no inkling of this fact. They may also lack the skills to digest complex information on neurochemistry, but, in fact, these skills are not necessary to understand the bottom line on biochemistry and ADHD: All behaviour has its basis in neurochemistry, but despite impressive technological advancements and much research, claims of chemical imbalance in ADHD remain unconfirmed hypotheses. Will consumers reading these ads be under this impression?

> It is a medical condition linked to a chemical imbalance in the brain. It is officially recognized by leading medical experts and institutions, including the US Surgeon General, the American Psychiatric Association, and others (Strattera.com, 2007).

To add to the confusion, the Strattera™ website intersperses, or 'name drops,' amongst its description of chemical imbalances, the names of official organizations such as the Surgeon General and the American Psychiatric Association. While it is true that both these organizations claim that ADHD is a medical condition, to our knowledge, neither organization has ever provided direct evidence that ADHD is linked to a chemical imbalance or any other biological deficit.

Nature versus nurture

ADHD is a physical disorder caused by differences in how the child's brain works. Anxiety-producing factors, such as family conflicts or disruptions, can aggravate the disorder, but they do not cause it (Ritalinla.com, 2006).

The National Institute of Mental Health states that scientists are finding more and more evidence that ADHD does not stem from home environment, but from biological causes (Strattera.com, 2007).

Contrary to what is implied in these advertisements, the part played by genetics in ADHD – large or small – in no way rules out the possibility of the environment also playing a role. Even those scientists who believe that genes are extremely important will not go so far as to entirely discount the influence of the environment.

For many adherents to the genetic position, the greater concordance rate of ADHD in identical twins compared to non-identical twins is the strongest evidence in support of the genetic position, yet even these adherents acknowledge that this same data also points to an important role for *the environment*. In the words of ADHD genetic researchers Faraone and Biederman:

Most scientists who study the genetics of psychiatric disorders embrace the idea that these disorders are influenced by both genes and environmental factors. In fact the twin studies . . . provide the strongest evidence that environmental risk factors play a substantial role in the etiology of ADHD (Faraone and Biederman, 2000, p. 568).

Faraone and Biederman's explanation about the etiology of ADHD is clearly at odds with that put forth on Strattera™ website, which is in turn credited to the NIMH. Like many psychiatric genetic researchers, Faraone and Biederman are proponents of the diathesis-stress theory, which postulates that some children are born with a genetic predisposition to ADHD but that environmental triggers are necessary for the development of ADHD.

A recent paper in *Biological Psychiatry* highlights the fact that a person's childhood experience may interact to affect his or her risk of developing depression. According to Shelley Taylor, PhD, the lead researcher of the study, 'Genes are not destiny,' and, 'That means, among other things, that there is an important role that parents and even friends can play in providing protection against the risk of depression that stress can confer' (Taylor *et al.*, 2006; Hitti, 2006). As Shelley shows, contrary to the advertisements, scientists have not ruled out a role for the environment in the development of mental illnesses.

In advertisements for ADHD, the supposed genetic basis for ADHD justifies medical treatment. However, left unsaid in these same advertisements, is that a presumed genetic defect is in no way a prerequisite to prescribing stimulants. As of now, the medical community finds it entirely acceptable to prescribe medication for psychological stress brought on by environmental stressors. One need look no further than foster care programs, which medicate an inordinate number of children. Presumably, the common factor in these children is not their genetic makeup but their common environmental triggers. Although ADHD is considered a genetic defect, looking for a common gene in foster home children to explain their behaviour would seem to be a fruitless effort. Conversely, the results of a survey of environmental stressors in the children's lives would probably be very fruitful. The diagnosis and medication of children in foster homes is perhaps the best example of how, genes and biology aside, it is still an acceptable practice to medicate children whose behaviour is explained by the environment.

Several of the pharmaceutical companies' websites provide a page of questions for patients to print and take to the doctor, yet many of the questions are answered right on the website. On the Ritalinla.com website (http://www.ritalinla.com/info/treatment/ask-your-dr.jsp), the first question parents are to ask their doctor is, 'What are the benefits of Ritalin LA?' The answer provided on the website is, 'The ADHD medication Ritalin LA® (methylphenidate HCl) has been proven in studies to give children with ADHD important benefits such as:...' and the list goes on. Thus, parents arrive for a consultation with their doctor primed not only with a list of questions but also with the preprinted answers downloaded from the pharmaceutical company website. Doctors who give answers different from the script could very likely see their patients go down the street to another doctor.

Adderall™ campaign

In 2005, Shire Pharmaceuticals launched a widespread advertising campaign for their ADHD medication, Adderall XR™ (amphetamine). This campaign included advertisements in popular magazines and took place at a time when Adderall™ was skyrocketing in popularity. At the conclusion of the print advertising campaign, the following content was found on the AdderallXR.com website. These statements are covered in some detail here because they represent some of the most seductive claims put forth within psychostimulant advertising, and also because this particular campaign is one of the largest thus far. In this campaign, Adderall™ is promoted using the following phrases:

> '*A Trusted Solution for ADHD*' (Print campaign and AdderallXR. com).

There is little doubt that parenting a child diagnosed with ADHD can be exhausting, and most parents will naturally be looking for a 'solution.' However, the word 'solution' would seem to be an exaggeration – not just for Adderall™, but for any pharmacological intervention prescribed to children diagnosed with ADHD. Every scholarly source on ADHD that we are aware of recommends a holistic, multi-factorial approach, including educational interventions, behavioural techniques, family therapy to address long-standing conflicts, and so forth. The evidence-based treatment of ADHD, in fact, recommends using psychotimulant treatment as one modality among many in the integrative, combined treatment of ADHD. In fact, the Adderall™ prescribing information recommends this as well.

Combining the known necessity for multi-modal treatment of ADHD with the fact that many, if not most, children have residual symptoms even while being prescribed psychostimulants raises an important question: In light of these facts, can Adderall™ be accurately characterized as a 'solution' to ADHD? If parents believe these advertisements and approach a physician for this 'solution,' how will they react to a physician who is reluctant to prescribe psychostimulants in their particular case? How will they react to a physician who opines that Adderall™ is not a 'solution,' but simply one potential intervention that may or may not be as valuable as non-pharmacological approaches in a particular case?

> '*Schoolwork that Matches His Intelligence*' (Print campaign and AdderallXR.com).

Many children with ADHD struggle academically, and an improvement in this arena is welcomed by both parents and teachers alike. Psychostimulants are well known to improve concentration, and this effect is not dependent upon a diagnosis of ADHD, but takes place in 'normals' and among those who are above-average achievers in high-demand situations, for instance, among fighter pilots flying extended missions. The claim that Adderall™ will allow a child to complete assigned work at a rate that matches his or her intelligence is seductive, perhaps even more so, because many parents naturally believe that their children are quite intelligent.

However, the veracity of this statement is extremely questionable. There is scant evidence that long-term treatment with amphetamine results in a sustained improvement in global academic performance. A short-term study using a 'classroom analog' found that children who had taken Adderall™ did increase their production at completing math questions over a twelve-hour day, but it is highly questionable whether this one short-term experiment equates to the advertising claim made here. For instance, we have not seen any psychiatric research that establishes, for instance, that children on Adderall™ will manifest academic performance more highly correlated with their IQ than children who are administered a placebo. Such experiments are probably yet to be conducted. We have also not seen any research demonstrating that Adderall™ improves long-term academic performance, as measured by grades – curious, given that this outcome measure is easily obtained. As Furman discusses in chapter two of this book, there is good evidence that stimulant medications do not improve learning *per se*.

'Friends that ask him to join the group' (Print campaign and AdderallXR.com).

All parents want their children to have a happy and enjoyable social life, thus this advertising ploy will ring poignantly for most parents. However, the wording is particularly troubling, as the makers of Adderall™ are literally claiming that prescribing their medication will have predictable, positive effects on the social contacts of those children receiving treatment. We are not aware of any scientific evidence that this is, in fact, true, or any reason why this should be reasonably predicted. The psychology of social networks and child development would seem to suggest that there are a myriad of factors that might account for social relationships among children and that ADHD symptoms are but one facet of a multi-factorial system.

For instance, consider an adolescent child who formerly was impulsive, labeled as a 'weird kid,' and therefore was quite unpopular. Taking stimulants, she becomes less impulsive, but her reputation is already established, and although she is now far less impulsive, her social contacts do not respond to her differently now – she is not asked to 'join the group.' The advertising claim would seem to go unsubstantiated in this theoretical example. Or, consider the child who is popular among other children because he is extroverted and often makes wise-cracks in class; upon being prescribed stimulants, he becomes quiet and compliant, but his friends now consider him boring.

This second example is of interest, because Adderall™ is known to cause nervousness, emotional lability, and depression (FDA,2008). Obviously, these symptoms could be harmful to social adjustment. The FDA has raised concerns about the potential for psychostimulants to cause psychotic symptoms, aggression, and suicide. A link between chronic stimulant use and depression is well established. Thus, it seems that Adderall™ is being marketed using the phrase, 'Friends that ask him to join the group,' when, in fact, Adderall™ appears to have the potential to cause psychiatric symptoms that are potentially destructive to the process of social adjustment, at least in some children (FDA, 2008).

A similar claim is that Adderall™ will result in 'Family hour that lasts for hours.' This claim assumes that a very complex system, a family, ostensibly consisting of multiple members and their interactions and collective resentments, appreciations and biases, can expect that family time will be reliably extended by prescription of stimulants to one member, the child. It is subject to the same faulty logic brought up previously.

The Adderall™ webpage also provides a 'Doctor Discussion Guide,' which is a checklist that a parent can fill out online, click 'next,' and then immediately get a report to print and take to the doctor to start off the discussion about ADHD, and presumably about Adderall™. It is hard to imagine a doctor explaining anything about ADHD that does not fit the pharmaceutical companies' agenda, to a parent holding one of these preprinted checklists (Adderall.com).

Information asymmetry in mental health

Information asymmetry (or asymmetrical information) is an economic term referring to a situation wherein one party has more or higher-quality information than the other. The classic example, for which George Akerlof won the Nobel Prize in 2001, is the market for used cars, wherein sellers have intimate knowledge of their vehicles' reliability but buyers face significant uncertainty. This concept of information asymmetry also has applicability to the physician-patient relationship;

physicians have extensive training and knowledge in medicine, while most patients do not. For the manufacturers of psychostimulants and others involved in the 'ADD enterprise,' information asymmetry is a positive thing. It is in their financial interests for patients to be under the impression that ADHD is an uncontroversial, scientifically-established biologically-based genetic brain disease best treated with stimulants. As this analysis has demonstrated, this understanding represents a significant level of information asymmetry as compared to the overall scientific literature.

If DTCA were the only source of information about ADHD and psychostimulants, this would represent a very high rate of information asymmetry indeed. However, this is not the case. There are many other sources of information on these topics, among them two major institutions that may stand as a buffer to the consumer advertisements. These are (1) the press, serving a watchdog function for the public good, and (2) the academic medical journals, traditionally thought of as the guardians of evidence-based medicine. Taken together, these two institutions certainly have the potential to level the playing field and reduce information asymmetry of the type that is found within DTCA.

Academic medicine and DTCA

Whether it will be different in Britain remains to be seen, but in America, concurrent with the growth of consumer advertising has been a weakening of the wall between academic medicine and the pharmaceutical companies. According to Arnold Relman, a past editor of the *New England Journal of Medicine*, 'The academic institutions of this country are allowing themselves to be paid agents of the pharmaceutical industry. I think it's disgraceful' (cited in Moynihan, 2003, p. 1190). In a provocative essay in the *Public Library of Science Medicine*, Richard Smith, past editor of the *British Medical Journal*, boldly stated: 'Medical journals are an extension of the marketing arm of pharmaceutical companies' (Smith, 2005, p. 364). What Smith and Relman understand, and what the press has not focused on, is that the problem is not just with the companies but is also with scientific papers (Smith, 2006). The pharmaceutical companies make an easy target, but they have not operated alone.

Fortunately, their British counterparts may not show the same willingness to help the pharmaceutical companies. In general, the British medical journals have shown a greater willingness to publish papers written by scientists who take a critical view of the evidence base. Whether they can maintain this practice once the consumer advertisements become legal remains to be seen. Should the British press buckle under the pressure, the loss of its cautionary voice could have a negative impact on psychiatric science worldwide. Take the studies of SSRIs in children: While the American journals were publishing selective data, released by the pharmaceutical companies, about the use of SSRIs in children, in Britain, the *British Medical Journal* and *The Lancet,* both more open to non-industry views, published papers examining the unpublished data. It was these papers, published in the British journals, which provided the impetus for the FDA to step into the fray and look more closely at the original trials, and to eventually issue a black box warning for the SSRIs. Moreover, *The Lancet* editors characterized the studies as, 'Confusion, manipulation and institutional failure' (Editors, 2004, p. 1335). David Healy has gone so far as to suggest that these studies highlight the need for a new category of journal articles as the papers were conceived primarily as marketing projects and not scientific endeavors (Healy, 2003).

Much of the general public would be amazed to know that, though a university professor may be listed as an author on a scientific paper, it in no way guarantees that the professor actually wrote the paper. In some cases, scientific papers are written by a company representative, and the company then pays a professor for the use of his or her name on the author list. The practice is known as ghostwriting and is becoming more common in academic medicine. In 1998, the *Journal of the American Medical Association* (JAMA) published a survey documenting that eleven percent of the articles published in top-tier American journals had been ghostwritten (Flanagin *et al.*, 1998). In 2002, the *New York Times* published an article about the creation of a ghost-written article as part of the marketing campaign for a new long-acting version of Ritalin™ (Ritalin LA™), which acts for eight to nine hours, versus the competitor's twelve-hour version. According to the *Times*, the problem for Novartis, the manufacturer, was that it had no scientific evidence to back up claims that Ritalin LA™ was better. So Novartis hired Intramed, a medical education company, which in turn commissioned two university professors to write an article emphasizing the benefits of Ritalin™ LA. The two professors both agreed, and, according to the *Times*, in a tape-recorded conversation between the doctors and Novartis, one of the doctors said, 'I think we're quite clear on what you want the next manuscript to look like' (Petersen, 2002). To help with the article, Intramed also hired a ghostwriter, Linda Logberg, to write the first draft for the two doctors. Neither of the two doctors, Novartis, or Intramed saw any problem with the practice, however the ghostwriter saw the whole process as marketing masquerading as science. When the *Times* piece was published, the ghost-written article had not yet been published. The fate of the ghost-written article in question remains unknown, but a Pubmed search reveals that they were coauthors of a review published in 2003 on the pharmacotherapy of ADHD medications, with a focus on the long-acting versions of methylphenidate (Markowitz *et al.*, 2003).

In a recent interview, William Pelham provides insight into the interplay between the pharmaceutical companies, the medical journals, and academicians (Hearn, 2004). On the webpage of the ALZA Corporation, a subsidiary of McNeil Pharmaceuticals (*Concerta.net*), there are statements praising the benefits of Concerta, one being that ninety-six percent of the children taking the drug do not experience significant side effects (appetite, growth, and sleep). Pelham's study is cited as supporting evidence for this claim (Pelham *et al.*, 2001). However, in his interview, Pelham expressed dismay about the way his study was being characterized on the website, because his study was limited to children who had already used Concerta with no significant side effects – children who exhibited side effects would not have been placed in the study to begin with. Thus, the experimental design of the study included a pre-study phase to virtually guarantee that the children in the study would not exhibit side effects. Pelham expressed astonishment over the fact the FDA allowed ALZA to use his study to make its claims.

In addition, Pelham mentions that the company wanted him to delete a paragraph he wrote about the importance of behavioural therapy. In his words: 'The people at Alza clearly pushed me to delete a paragraph in the article where I was saying it was important to do combined treatments (medication and behavioral)', and 'It was intimidating to be one researcher and have all these people pushing me to change the text'.

For a follow-up paper, Pelham also mentions that the company did the data analysis and coordinated the writing of the paper. In his words, 'I insisted on seeing the analyses and having major inputs into the manuscript, and it was like pulling teeth to get wording and analyses changed. It was like a whitewash – a praise to Concerta' (Hearn, 2004).

The media and the pharmaceutical companies

Unknown, and unquantifiable, is the effect of DTCA on the interactions between the pharmaceutical companies and the press. In the
US, the pharmaceutical companies spend approximately $4 billion a
year on advertisements; in 2004, the combined DTCA revenue for the
New York Times, Time, and *Newsweek* was $123 million (Lieberman,
2005). Whether the press can maintain its objective status when it
comes to reporting on the pharmaceutical companies, at the same
time it is receiving large amounts of money from the companies, is
debatable. In 2003, *Time* published the article, 'Medicating Young
Minds,' about the increasing use of psychotropic medications for
young children (Kluger, 2003). The article had this somewhat surprising statement about the use of SSRIs in children: 'While an earlier
generation of antidepressants – tricyclics, such as Tofranil – didn't
work in kids, SSRIs do' (Kluger, 2003). That statement is surprising because, at the time it was made, the evidence base for using
SSRIs in children was marginal – at best. And it was certainly no
secret that it was marginal, as there were numerous scientists and
physicians pointing out the problems with the studies of SSRIs in children. Even officials at the FDA had acknowledged earlier in the year
that the evidence base for the use of these medications was slim and
the only medication to show superiority over placebo was Prozac. In
their words: 'for the 7 drugs evaluated in paediatric major depressive
disorder (MDD), data reviewed by FDA were adequate to establish
effectiveness in MDD for only one of these drugs, Prozac (fluoxetine)'
(FDA, 2003). How the reporters and, more importantly, the editors
at *Time* became so convinced about the effectiveness of the SSRIs in
children is unclear, but it was clearly *not* by reading the scientific literature. Take Prozac, which was the only one of the eight SSRIs that
the FDA approved for children. It was approved by the FDA for children in 2003, the same year the *Time* piece was published, on the
basis of just two controlled clinical trials. In the first study, Prozac
barely beat out the placebo, and in the second study, sixty-five percent
of the children in the Prozac study had a beneficial response, compared to fifty-three percent of the placebo patients, a difference that
was not statistically significant (see Leo, 2006, for a more extensive
discussion). In fact, just two months after *Time's* declaration that the
SSRIs work in children, the editors changed their minds and published
another article titled, 'Prescription for Suicide?' This second article was
much more circumspect about the effectiveness of the SSRIs in children

'most studies on effectiveness aren't really definitive. They don't prove one way or the other whether the drugs work significantly better than placebos' (Lemonick, 2004). As exemplified by the above example, it is too easy for the media, just as it is for the consumers, the journal editors, and physicians, to get caught up in the whole marketing blitz.

One of the more egregious practices, highlighting the influence the companies have over the press, is that television stations now present short clips, called video news releases, or VNRs for short, as if they were prepared by reporters when they were actually prepared by a corporation. The viewers believe they are watching an unbiased news presentation, when they are really watching an infomercial produced by a business. Instead of acting as a watchdog, the press is reduced to nothing more than a mouthpiece for the company. While not as egregious, another unsettling practice concerns reporters failing to maintain a critical viewpoint when hearing from 'health care experts.' As an example, take the recent three part series in the *New York Times* on children and mental health. Part three of the series focused on the issue of polypharmacy for children and correctly pointed out there is no solid evidence for giving multiple psychiatric medications to children. True, but hardly earthshaking, and few people will defend – at least publicly – the practice of giving multiple psychotropic drugs to children, some as young as twelve months old. Yet, while openly critical of polypharmacy for its lack of evidence, the *New York Times* gives its stamp of approval to the practice of giving single medications to children, although the evidence base appears to be no better than that for polypharmacy. 'Meager' best describes the strongest evidence the *New York Times* can scrape together: 'There is little doubt that some psychiatric medicines, taken by themselves, work well in children. For example, dozens of studies have shown that stimulants improve attentiveness.' Hardly a ringing endorsement for the practice. Can this well-known fact, that stimulants improve attention span, seriously be considered as valid evidence in support of using antipsychotics or antidepressants in three-year-olds? For that is the subject of the *New York Times* article in the first place. Hard to imagine – and it is even harder to imagine that the editors at the *Times* did not question their own flimsy evidence in making this statement.

Taking this train of thought a bit further, what about coffee and cocaine? They are also stimulants and improve attention span; do their effects also count as evidence in support of diagnosing and treating three-year-olds with psychiatric medications?

Given these examples, it is difficult to characterize the mainstream press as acting in an aggressive 'watchdog' role when it comes to pharmaceutical companies, children, and psychiatric medications.

The harmful effects of Ritalin™ turned upside down by the popular press

Imagine the following straightforward experiment, which has been performed numerous times with various drugs. Researchers administer a certain drug to young rats, and subsequently find that the drug has harmful long-term effects. If the drug in question is illicit, the results are usually held up as one more reason to refrain from using the drug. If the drug happens to be a prescription drug, most scientists would at least *suggest* the need for increased caution by the medical profession – especially if the drug's target market is young children.

Interestingly, William Carlezon and his colleagues at Harvard Medical School recently conducted the above experiment with Ritalin™ (Carlezon, Mague and Anderson, 2003), and, indeed, the researchers discovered that Ritalin™ had harmful long-term effects on the brain of developing rats. In their study, young rats exposed to Ritalin™ had an increased risk for depression later in adulthood. You would think that this would *suggest* that children diagnosed with ADHD and given Ritalin™ *might* be at risk. Instead, the popular press reported that the main message of the study was that children need an accurate diagnosis of ADHD.

Following the publication of the study, the American College of Neuropsychopharmacology (ACNP) published a press release (Lobliner, 2004), which declared that the study only has implications for 'normal' children and not for children diagnosed with ADHD. In fact, not only did the ACNP forgo the slightest suggestion that Ritalin™ *might* be harmful for 'ADHD' children, it went out of its way to explain that the results do not apply to 'ADHD' children. According to their logic, only if you have an *incorrect* diagnosis of 'ADHD' will Ritalin™ be harmful. The press release took data showing that Ritalin™ harms the brains of rats, and turned that data into the message that Ritalin™ will only harm children with an incorrect diagnosis.

The major flaw in the logic starts with the explanation that the rats in the study were not 'ADHD' rats, but were 'normal' rats. Labeling the *rats* as normal allowed the ACNP to assert that the findings only had implications for normal *children*. The ACNP established a dual role for Ritalin: On one hand, Ritalin™ is beneficial for children diagnosed with ADHD; yet, on the other hand, it is harmful to 'normal' children. When one considers that even drawing a line between 'ADHD' and 'normal' varies widely from one doctor's office to another, from one state to another, or from one country to another, the idea that there is some scientific reasoning involved in where to draw this line lacks credibility. If a committee ever developed a universal standard for ADHD, would Ritalin's™ apparent dual action – beneficial to some, but harmful to others – fall in line with the committee's decision?

A related question comes to mind: if Ritalin™ only produces harmful effects on the 'normal' brain, then whose definition of 'normal' will Ritalin™ follow? Many children in other parts of the world would not be given a diagnosis of ADHD in their own countries, but in America they would be easily labeled with ADHD. A correct diagnosis in America might not be the same as a correct diagnosis in their home country. Would Ritalin's™ effect on the brain follow their home countries' definition of ADHD or America's definition? As pointed out earlier in this paper, different medical organizations follow different criteria for the diagnosis of ADHD, which leads to dramatically different prescription rates.

As an example of the problem with the ACNP's logic, imagine these two scenarios. The parents of a young teenage boy are concerned about his grades and take the boy to a psychiatrist. After completing a short questionnaire, the boy is diagnosed with ADHD and given a prescription for Ritalin™. According to the ACNP, for this boy, the Ritalin™ will have a beneficial effect. Another boy, a classmate of the first boy, has a week of exams coming up and wants to improve his grades, so he decides to buy some Ritalin™ from the first boy. According to the ACNP, Ritalin™ will harm this boy. The idea that Ritalin™ is *not* harmful to the boy whose parent's filled out a short checklist, but is harmful to the boy who bypassed the checklist is problematic.

One month later, working from the original ACNP press release or one little changed from the original, the *Wall Street Journal* uncritically reported the ACNP's version of the study, 'This latest research has particular significance for healthy children who have been wrongly diagnosed and put on ADHD medication' (Parker-Pope, 2005). But the *Wall Street Journal* has missed the fact that there is no good reason to limit the significance of this study to *misdiagnosed* children. Indeed, this research has particular significance for *all children* taking Ritalin™, whether it was prescribed by a doctor or not. In the animal world there is no line between 'normal' and 'ADHD,' and there is no reason for the ACNP or the *Wall Street Journal* to draw one.

Misdiagnosed ADHD?

Some in the media have pejoratively referred to the practice of using a medication to improve performance in the classroom as 'academic doping.' What the press does not seem to understand is that 'academic doping' is fully supported by the medical community – as long as the medication is provided by a doctor. News organizations often present the controversy surrounding the increased use of Ritalin™ as if there were a clear boundary between the two situations – on the one side, Ritalin™ being used to *appropriately* treat a 'medical' illness, and on the other, Ritalin™ being used *inappropriately* to improve academic performance. A recent Reuters news report commented on the matter as follows:

Results of a survey of physicians suggest that parents often request a 'behavioural drug,' such as Ritalin™, with the goal of enhancing their child's academic performance *rather than treating an illness*. (Gale, 2006, Italics added).

Or take a recent editorial in the *Washington Post* titled, 'Millions Have Misused ADHD Stimulant Drugs, Study Says,' in which the author states, 'The statistics are striking because many young people recreationally using these drugs are seeking to boost academic and professional performance, doctors say' (Vendantam, 2006). In these examples, the assumption by the press is that using Ritalin™ to improve grades is a 'misuse' of the drug. Yet the practice of prescribing stimulants to improve academic performance is exactly why these medications are used in the first place, and the practice is fully sanctioned by the medical community. In fact, no official medical organization that supports the use of Ritalin™ has ever said that using Ritalin™ to improve academic performance is inappropriate.

According to Dr. Joseph Biederman, a leader in the child psychiatry profession, 'If a child is brilliant but is doing just OK in school, that child may need treatment, which would result in their performing brilliantly at school' (Gale, 2006). Sharing Biederman's view, as we have shown in this paper are the pharmaceutical companies who advertise improved academic performance as one of the features of stimulant medication. Consider the recent advertisement for Daytrana™, a Ritalin™ patch, manufactured by Shire, and applied to the hip in the morning: 'When you apply the Daytrana™ patch, you can help your child get ready for school, homework, and his entire day.'

Even the patient support groups condone the use of Ritalin™ for academic enhancement. Take the recent example of Johnny Holliday, a celebrity who is a spokesman for Children and Adults with ADHD (CHADD). In *Selling Sickness*, by Moynihan and Cassels, they report on the following interview with Holliday at a CHADD golf benefit:

Holliday said he was happy to help out with the event for free, because his daughter had once suffered with ADD, discovered in her case in eighth grade. 'I know the frustration she went through and her parents went through,' he told a reporter from the BMJ. As for the drugs, Holliday said, she had only taken her medication intermittently during school time, mainly to help with tests. 'It really did the job,' he said, before jumping back into his golf cart and adding with fatherly pride that she had just graduated from college with honors (Moynihan and Cassels, 2005, p. 63).

Holliday is not alone in his enthusiasm for the attention-enhancing aspect of stimulants, as a recent survey of physicians reported that two-thirds of primary care doctors recently reported receiving requests from parents to prescribe drugs with the goal of enhancing their child's academic performance (Gale, 2006).

In 1999, the editors of the journal, *Pediatrics,* elicited commentaries from several prominent physicians about the case of a teenage boy who had been taking Ritalin™ for several years. The editors saw the boy's scenario as an interesting case, worthy of commentary from a group of prominent child psychiatrists (Stein *et al.*, 2001; Cohen and Leo, 2002). Paradoxically, they have provided a much more interesting, albeit unintended case study. From a sociological point of view the subject of the case is not the boy, but is, instead, the doctors and journal editors, In other words, the behaviour of the adults is of much more interest than that of the boy. The case provides an excellent example of: (1) how there is little science involved in the diagnosis of ADHD; (2) how the medical community fully supports the use of stimulant medication as a performance enhancing drug; (3) how the same mindset that approves of using one psychotropic drug easily leads to the use of multiple medications; and (4) how the mainstream medical journals have given little attention to the ethical implications of controlling and altering children to meet the demands of our contemporary educational/cultural system.

The fifteen-year-old boy announced to his parents and his paediatrician that he wanted to stop taking his medication:

'I don't need it... I'm fine... I don't see why I should take it.' He purposefully did not take the medication for a few weeks and he said he could not tell the difference... However, his parents observed that his test results, when off the medication, were below his standard scores... They also noted that he was more distractible and less attentive when doing his homework during that time (Stein *et al.*, 2001, p. 974).

The most important variable in determining whether this boy should keep taking his medication was the parental satisfaction with the medication, and the subsequent commentaries all focused on how to convince the boy to continue taking his medication. The boy's wishes were not something to be listened to, but rather something to be managed, whether through dialogue or with another medication. Amazingly, as an example of polypharmaceuticals for children, one of the commentators even suggested that the boy's reluctance to keep taking his Ritalin™ suggested this was a sign that he needed another medication. Thus, the boy, who wants go off his one medication, would instead get two medications. None of the commentators in the *Pediatrics* article conjectured that the boy's wishes might be legitimate. More importantly, as a sign of how one sided the issue has become in the medical community, *the editors* did not give space to a single commentator who questioned the ethics of giving a medication to improve grades.

The ethical questions surrounding the use of Ritalin™ are becoming a larger issue, as once-medicated children are now reaching adulthood. According to a recent survey in the *LA Times*, a significant number of these adults are deciding to discontinue their medication (Healy, 2006b). The *Times* article quotes a twenty-seven-year-old woman who reflects back on the years she was medicated, 'It was kind of weirdly amazing... You get excited about monotonous work, honestly. Like, translating Spanish becomes totally fun... The thing is, it works. But why are we forcing people to be in that position that they should like something that they wouldn't ordinarily' (Healy, 2006a). In just three short sentences, this young woman goes right to the heart of the ethical dilemma of stimulant medication: Is it right to medicate people so that they do well in school? Yet nothing close to her straightforward insight can be found in the entire *Pediatrics* case study, which supposedly included the collective wisdom of an editorial staff, prominent physicians, and academic psychiatrists. The *Pediatrics* case demonstrates that all the talk of genetics, biology, and medicine simply provides a false air of legitimacy to what is nothing more than the disbursement of a performance-enhancing drug.

As often happens after statistics documenting the increasing use of stimulants for younger and younger children make the headlines, many of the opinion leaders in the psychiatry community state that there is a problem with 'over-prescribing' or 'misdiagnosis,' yet none of these leaders, or any of the major psychiatric organizations, have issued guidelines on how to identify this large group of 'misdiagnosed' children, nor have they clarified what they consider to be improper uses of prescribed stimulant medication (Johnson, 2006; Nakamura, 2002).

The dilemma for medical professionals who want to go beyond simply talking about misdiagnosed children and to actually move on to identifying these children is that, without an objective biological marker demarcating the line between the 'correctly' and 'incorrectly' diagnosed, the sole criterion for determining the appropriateness of stimulant treatment comes down to: are the adults in the child's life satisfied with the medication's effect? Presumably there are not many parents, unhappy with the medication's effects, who still continue to medicate their children. None of the medical professionals who talk about misdiagnosis have ever elaborated on how they plan to tell all these parents of misdiagnosed children that they should not be medicating their children, even though the medication is doing exactly what the advertisements say it should be doing.

Conclusion

In their advertisements, the pharmaceutical companies have intermingled non-controversial statements about the universal effect of stimulants on attention span, along with highly controversial statements about the speculative theory that up to twenty percent of the children in the US have an organic brain disease (NIHCM Foundation, 2005). As we have documented, the claims made in the consumer advertisements of ADHD medications are oversimplified, one-sided presentations of complex medical and social issues. The major difference between the advertisements and the medical literature is that the advertisements portray these issues as having clear, straightforward answers, while the medical literature is filled with ambiguity, conflicting results, and an ongoing debate. The advertising claims we have illustrated are controversial from a scientific standpoint, and at best, most of them should be explained as tentative hypotheses, not well established facts. However, the degree to which this advertising is shaping the public's perceptions of the issues should not be underestimated.

The full impact that the consumer advertisements have had on the diagnosis and treatment of ADHD requires further study, especially given that consumers may seek out information from other sources, such as the Internet. At present, it appears that information asymmetry is the norm within the ADHD field. There is a critical literature on ADHD, but it is rarely seen from major media outlets or in high-profile mainstream journal publications.

For those interested in providing consumers with well-balanced, scientifically-based information on ADHD, these consumer advertisements are troubling. We hypothesize that they are very effective at achieving their intended effect: guiding patients into the doctor's office and then guiding the conversation with the doctor. We assume that DTCA is an incredibly useful tool for pharmaceutical companies that manufacture psychostimulants. The net effect on the public, and the children who end up taking ADHD medications, is likely to be negative.

References

Adderall.com. (2006). Causes of ADHD. Retrieved January 12, 2007, from http://www.adderallxr.com/information/info-causes.asp

Boseley, S. (2006, November 14). Open up NHS to our drug firms, White House Demands. *The Guardian*. Available at: http://www.guardian.co.uk/usa/story/0,,1947279,00.html.

Carey, B. (2005, October 18). Can brain scans see depression? *The New York Times*.

Carlezon, W. A., Mague, S. D., and Anderson, S. L. (2003). Enduring behavioral effects of early exposure to methylphenidate in rats. *Biological Psychiatry*, 54, 1330–7.

Cohen, D., and Leo, J. (2002). A boy who stops taking stimulants for 'ADHD': Commentaries on a *Pediatrics* case study. *Ethical Human Sciences and Services*, 4(4), 189–209.

Concerta.net. (2008). Retrieved January 20, 2008, from http://www.concerta.net/concerta/pages/about-treatment.jsp

Cutler, D. (2005). *Your money or your life: Strong medicine for America's health care system*. USA: Oxford University Press.

Editors. (2004). Depressing research. *The Lancet*, 363, 1335.

Faraone, S., & Biederman, J. (2000). Nature, nurture, and attention deficit hyperactivity disorder. *Developmental Review, 20*, 568–81.

FDA (2003). Reports of suicidality in pediatric patients being treated with antidepressant medications for major depressive disorder (MDD). October 27. Available at: http://www.fda.gov/cder/drug/advisory/mdd.htm

FDA (2008) Adderall Label. August 15. Available at: http://www.fda.gov/cder/foi/label/2004/021303s005lbl.pdf

Fumento, M. (2003). Trick Question: A liberal hoax turns out to be true. *The New Republic* (March 17, 2003).

Gale, K. (2006). Ritalin requests often deemed inappropriate [Electronic Version]. *Medscape*. Retrieved November 9, 2006 from http://www.medscape.com/viewarticle/544602.

Giedd, J. N., Blumenthal, J., Molloy, E., and Castellanos, F. X. (2001). Brain imaging of attention deficit/hyperactivity disorder. *Annals of the New York Academy of Sciences*, 931, 33–49.

Healy, D. (2003) *Let them eat prozac.* Toronto, Canada: James Lorimar and Company.

Healy, M. (2006a, December 18). The ritalin kids grow up: In their own words. *LA Times*. Available at: http://www.latimes.com/features/health/la-he-adhdleadin18dec18,0,6714796.story?coll=la-home-health.

Healy, M. (2006b, December 18). The ritalin kids grow up: Many of the ADD generation say no to meds. *LA Times*. Available at: http://www.latimes.com/features/health/la-he-adhd18dec18,0,7025025.story?coll=la-home-health.

Hearn, K. (2004). Here, kidiee, kiddie *Alternet.com.* Available at:http://www.alternet.org/drugreporter/20594.

Javers, E. (2006, January 13). A columnist backed by Monsanto. *Business Week Online*. Available at: http://www.businessweek.com/bwdaily/dnflash/jan2006/nf20060113_2851_db035.htm.

Johnson, L. (2006). Study: ADHD drugs send thousands to ERs [Electronic Version]. *ABC News*. Retrieved September 9, 2006 from http://www.usatoday.com/news/health/2006-05-24-adhd-drugs_x.htm.

Kluger, J. (2003). Medicating young minds. *Time Magazine*. December 8, 162 (22). Available at: http://www.time.com/time/magazine/article/0,9171,1006034,00. html.

Lacasse, J. R., and Leo, J. (2005). Serotonin and depression: A disconnect between the advertisements and the scientific literature. *Public Library of Science Medicine*, 2(12), e392.

Lacasse, J. R., and Leo, J. (2006a). Authors' Reply. *Public Library of Science Medicine, 3*(2).

Lacasse, J. R., and Leo, J. (2006b). Questionable advertising of psychotropic medications and disease mongering. *Public Library of Science Medicine*, 3(7), e321.

Lemonick, M. (2004). Prescription for suicide. *Time Magazine*. February 9, Available at: http://www.time.com/time/magazine/printout/0,8816,993276,00.html.

Leo, J. (2006) The SSRI trials in children: Disturbing implications for academic medicine. *Ethical Human Psychology and Psychiatry*, 8, 29–41.

Leo, J., and Cohen, D. (2003). Broken brains or flawed studies? A critical review of ADHD neuroimaging studies. *The Journal of Mind and Behavior,* 24, 29–56.

Lieberman, T. (2005). Bitter Pill. *Columbia Journalism Review,* Available at: *http://www.cjr.org/issues/2005/4/lieberman.asp.*

Lobliner, J. (2004). New study shows early ritalin may cause long-term effects on the brain. *EurekAlert.* Available at: http://www.medicalnewstoday.com/medicalnews.php?newsid=17691

Loden, D., and Schooler, C. (1998). Making DTC advertising work harder. *Medical Marketing and Media,* 33(4), 38–45.

Markowitz, J. S., Straughn, A. B., and Patrick, K. S. (2003) Advances in the pharmacotherapy of attention-deficit disorder: Focus on the methylphenidate formulations. *Pharmacotherapy,* Oct 1281–99.

Moynihan, R. (2003) Who pays for the pizza? Redefining the relationship between doctors and drug companies. 1: Entanglement. BMJ, 326 (7400) 1189–92.

Moynihan, R., and Cassels, A. (2005). *Selling sickness: How the world's biggest pharmaceutical companies are turning us all into patients.* New York: Nation Books.

Nakamura, R. (2002). Attention deficit hyperactivity disorder: Are children being overmedicated? [Electronic Version]. *Government Reform United States House of Representatives.* Available at: http://www.eurekalert.org/staticrel.php?view=adhd.

NIHCM Foundation. (2000). Prescription drugs and mass media advertising, 2000.

NIHCM Foundation. (2005, February 2005). Children's mental health: An overview and key considerations for health system stakeholders. Available at: http://www.nihcm.org/finalweb/CMHReport-FINAL.pdf

NIMH. (2002). Brain shrinkage in ADHD not caused by medications. Available at: http://www.nimh.nih.gov/events/pradhdmri.cfm

Parker-Pope. (2005). Studies linking ritalin and depression highlight the risk of overdiagnosing ADHD. *The Wall Street Journal.*

Pelham, W. E., Gnagy, E. M., Burrows-Maclean, L., Williams, A., Fabiano, G. A., Morrisey, S. M., et al. (2001). Once-a-day Concerta methylphenidate versus three-times-daily methylphenidate in laboratory and natural settings. *Pediatrics,* 107(6), E105.

Petersen, M. (2002, November 22). Madison Avenue plays growing role in drug research. *New York Times.*

Priest, A. (2007). CanWest set to challenge ban on DTCA. *Canadian Medical Association Journal,* 176(1), 19–20.

Rapoport, J. L., Buchsbaum, M. S., Zahn, T. P., Weingartner, H., Ludlow, C., and Mikkelsen, E. J. (1978). Dextroamphetamine: Cognitive and behavioral effects in normal prepubertal boys. *Science,* 199(4328), 560–3.

Rey, J. M., and Sawyer, M. G. (2003). Are psychostimulants being used appropriately to treat child and adolescent disorders? *British Journal of Psychiatry*, 182, 284–6.

RitalinLA.com. (2006). Myths about ADHD. Retrieved October 17, 2005, from http://www.ritalinla.com/info/about/myths-about-adhd.jsp

Rosack, J. (2004). Brain scans reveal physiology of ADHD, *Psychiatric Times*, 39(1), 26.

Smith, R. (2005) Medical journals are an extension of the marketing arm of pharmaceutical companies. *PLoS Medicine*, Available at: http://medicine.plosjournals.org/archive/1549-1676/2/5/pdf/10.1371_journal.pmed.0020138-S.pdf

Smith, R. (2006). Lapses at the *New England Journal of Medicine. J R Soc Med*, 99(8), 380–2.

Sowell, E. R., Thompson, P. M., Welcome, S. E., Henkenius, A. L., Toga, A. W., and Peterson, B. S. (2003). Cortical abnormalities in children and adolescents with attention-deficit hyperactivity disorder. *The Lancet*, 362, 1699–707.

Stein, M.T., Shafer, M.A., Elliott, G.R., and Levine, S. (2001) Challenging case: Adolescence. An adolescent who abruptly stops taking his medication for Attention Deficit Hyperactivity Disorder. *Pediatrics*, 107, 974–8.

Strattera.com. (2007). ADHD fact and fiction. Retrieved January 12, 2007, from http://www.strattera.com/1_3_childhood_adhd/1_3_1_2_adhd_fact.jsp

Taylor, S. E., Way, B. M., Welch, W. T., Hilmert, C. J., Lehman, B. J., and Eisenberger, N. I. (2006). Early family environment, current adversity, the serotonin transporter promoter polymorphism, and depressive symptomatology. *Biological Psychiatry*, 60(7), 671–6.

Vendantam, S. (2006, February 25). Millions have misused ADHD stimulant drugs, Study says. *Washington Post*. Available at: http://www.washingtonpost.com/wp-dyn/content/article/2006/02/24/AR2006022401773_pf.html.

Chapter 11

The Deficiencies of Drug Treatment Research: The Case of Strattera™

David Cohen, Shannon Hughes and
David J. Jacobs

By the start of the 21st century, a certain naiveté about the validity of findings from drug industry funded clinical trials seemed to have dissipated from the fields of psychiatry and psychopharmacology. Indeed, only at his or her own risk and peril, and that of his or her patients, would a clinician choose to accept as valid the latest positive findings from the latest clinical trial about the latest 'promising' drug. Even among mainstream observers, there occurred a growing realization that the drug industry had penetrated every nook and cranny of the enterprise of testing drugs for human consumption, and, with the sole aim of increasing market shares for its products and profits for its shareholders, had passed off countless infomercials as scientific studies attesting to the safety and efficacy of these products. A flood of studies, media investigations, actions by regulatory bodies, and leaks from judicial cases documented how the industry had bought off or co-opted presumably impartial academic researchers, journal editors, peer-reviewers, journalists, state health administrators, and federal regulating agencies. Editorials appearing in the most prominent medical journals lamented that the entire clinical trial enterprise might be characterized by deception and manipulation, such that the boundary between marketing and scientific activities had been virtually eliminated.

This chapter explores the extent to which the new critical awareness, as well as parallel regulatory requirements, may have impacted the initial clinical trials of Strattera™ (atomoxetine), a drug manufactured by Eli Lilly & Company and approved for marketing by the United States Food and Drug Administration (FDA) for the treatment of ADHD in children and adults in November 2002.

Within nine months of its launch in January 2003, 2.15 million prescriptions had been written for Strattera™, and the drug took 16 per cent of the ADHD drug market versus methylphenidate's and amphetamine's share of 24 per cent and 22 per cent, respectively. This 'fastest ever growth for an ADHD medication' (Eli Lilly & Company, 2003) brought $370 million in sales its first year, when those who prescribed knew, by definition, virtually nothing about it beside what its sponsor had publicized.

The chapter identifies concerns voiced by critics over the past decade about deficits in the evaluation of new drugs, and examines, using published journal articles and unpublished data from the FDA, the extent to which clinical trials for Strattera™ met these concerns. In particular, it focuses on what data available by the time of its launch in early 2003 revealed about Strattera's™ *psychoactive* effects and *adverse* effects. This chapter constitutes an effort to deconstruct what officially passes as expert knowledge on the effects of popular psychiatric drugs, using Strattera™ as an example.

Such an exploration is warranted for several reasons. First, Strattera™ was billed as the first 'non-stimulant' drug approved for the treatment of ADHD. Since the first reported use of Benzedrine on children with 'minimal brain dysfunction' in 1937, prototypical stimulants such as methylphenidate (e.g., Ritalin™) and amphetamines (e.g., Dexedrine™, Adderall™) remained the mainstay of drug treatment for children labeled as ADHD. However, because of their euphoric and performance-enhancing effects that led to habitual use by millions of people and sensational use by members of deviant subcultures, governments tightly controlled the use of stimulants (i.e., Schedule II substances under the United Nations' 1971 Convention on Psychotropic Drugs) in many parts of the world. That stimulants labelled as 'dangerous' by one federal agency, the Drug Enforcement Administration, were approved for prescription to basically normal children by another government agency perpetually rankled proponents of the drug treatment of ADHD. The arrival of an effective 'non stimulant' that would remove the stigma of abuse and diversion and eliminate federal controls applied to Schedule II drugs would be a significant achievement by its manufacturer. This would also allow for the easier promotion of the drug for 'adult ADD,' for which Strattera™ was simultaneously marketed immediately upon its approval. Strattera's™ promotional materials hinted at this vast untapped market: '60% of children carry their disorder into adulthood. Experts estimate 4% of adults in the US, more than 8 million people, have ADHD and most of them are undiagnosed' (Eli Lilly, 2003).

Second, Strattera™ was the first 'new chemical entity' (NCE) since Cylert (pemoline, approved in 1975, removed from the market in 2003) that the FDA approved for the treatment of ADHD. All other medications were amphetamines or methylphenidate or extended-release formulations of such (such as Concerta™ and Ritalin LA™). They were able to support their applications to the FDA on the original applications that led to the original approvals of the amphetamines and methylphenidate following the 1962 Kefauver-Harris amendments to the Federal Food, Drug, and Cosmetic Act of 1938. For an NCE, more extensive preclinical and clinical data would be required for submission to the FDA.

Third, confirming the adage that only when a new psychiatric drug arrives, do mainstream authors begin to openly criticize existing drugs, the arrival of Strattera™ coincided with unusually frank expressions of dissatisfaction with stimulant medications. Biederman, perhaps the leading proponent of stimulant treatment in America, and a paid consultant and investigator for Eli Lilly, wrote in the introduction to a Strattera™ clinical trial that 'there are significant limitations to treatment with psychostimulants, which are not effective or well-tolerated in approximately 30 per cent of school-age children with ADHD. Adverse effects such as insomnia, decreased appetite, and irritability may lead to discontinuation or dosage limitations. The lack of adequate full-day treatment often results in recurrence of impairing symptoms at home and in the community' (Biederman et al., 2002, p. 2). Similarly, pharmacy professors Caballero and Nahata (2003) noted in a review of Strattera™ studies that '~30% of patients may not respond to [stimulants], and others may not be able to tolerate them because of adverse effects such as nausea, vomiting, and insomnia' (p. 3066). Therefore, the extent to which Strattera™ actually offers a more benign adverse effect profile over stimulants needs to be determined.

Finally, the FDA Modernization Act passed by the United States Congress in 1997, and the FDA's 'Pediatric Rule' of 1998 required new paediatrics assessments in clinical trials for drugs that would be marketed for children. These and other regulations published by the

FDA at the end of the 1990s that addressed the design and conduct of paediatrics clinical trials of psychoactive drugs, might have created, at least superficially, a 'rigorous' regulatory climate for the evaluation of Strattera™, which arrived on the scene amidst widespread controversy over the psychotropic medicating of America's children (Zito *et al.*, 2000). Atomoxetine is 'one of the first NCEs developed under the stringent new FDA pediatric regulations and guidelines,' reassuringly wrote two Eli Lilly employees (Allen and Michelson, 2002, p. 48). Similarly, Wernicke and Kratochvil, investigators in several Eli Lilly funded-studies of atomoxetine, emphasized that 'In comparison with other drugs that have been studied for the treatment of ADHD, atomoxetine has been subjected to an unusually rigorous investigation of its safety, tolerability, and efficacy in children and adolescents with ADHD' (2002, p. 54).

The production of clinical trials of Strattera™

Over the past decade, a converging series of critiques focusing on clinical trials of psychotropic drugs identified several worrying issues (Cohen, 2005). Analysts concluded that sponsors were inappropriately involved in the design and execution of studies, investigators and journals were caught in conflicts of interests, and published results of trials tended to distort or conceal negative findings and emphasize positive findings.

For example, by the time of its market launch in January 2003, 11 articles reporting on Phase II and III studies of Strattera™ were available in the published literature. All these studies were funded by Lilly, with additional support to investigators by the National Institute of Mental Health in two studies. In several studies, the authors were Lilly employees. A cursory review of the more than 50 clinical trials of atomoxetine indexed in the Medline database as of this writing (early 2007) also shows that the vast majority are funded by Lilly. Several reviews of these studies, as well as commentaries on the treatment of ADHD with non-stimulants that appeared since the approval of Strattera™, are also authored by Lilly employees or with full or partial funding from Lilly. Other noticeable patterns within the more than 300 publications on Strattera™ include re-analyses of previously published studies, analyses of sub-samples of subjects from larger previously published studies, additions of a single outcome measure (e.g., a quality of life variable) to previously published articles resulting in newer publications, and other strategies. As a result, it may look to the uninitiated observer that a vast number of scientific publications from several teams in several countries focus on atomoxetine. Presumably, this is designed to increase confidence that atomoxetine has been well studied and thus that its effects are well known.

Some authors, however, suggest precisely the opposite: that in fact the psychological alterations that psychotropic drugs produce and are expected to produce in those who ingest them remain largely unknown, (1) because of the avoidance by ideologically and commercially compromised researchers to study psychiatric drugs as *psychoactive* drugs, and (2) because of the refusal, in the conventional randomized controlled trials (Phase III studies) that form the basis for FDA approval of new drugs, to study *adverse effects* seriously (Jacobs and Cohen, 1999; Cohen and Jacobs, 2007).

What is known about Strattera's™ psychoactive effects?

Strattera™ or atomoxetine (formerly known as tomoxetine) is classified as a 'selective norepinephrine uptake inhibitor' (Bezchlybnik-Butler and Jeffries, 2005). This suggests that one of its initial and notable measured effects in neurotransmission is to block the return of norepinephrine or noradrenaline (NE) back to the nerve cell for recycling, once NE has been released into a synaptic cleft for transmission to other nerve cells. This has the short-term result of increasing the concentrations of NE floating in the synapse. Standard descriptions emphasize that 'Atomoxetine is a highly specific inhibitor of the presynaptic norepinephrine transporter with minimal affinity for other neurotransmitter receptors or transporters' (Allen and Michelson, 2003, p. 46). This recalls the countless 'scientific' descriptions first made about Prozac and serotonin starting in the late 1980s, when that first 'selective serotonin reuptake inhibitor' (SSRI) was being promoted as clean, safe, 'specific' and 'selective.' (Later evaluations of SSRI neuropharmacology showed that focusing on an initial 'selective' action merely distracted researchers from observing subsequent cascades of transient and long-lasting neurochemical changes involving other neurotransmitters.)

In an early study by Lilly Laboratories (Zerbe *et al.*, 1985), atomoxetine's inhibition of NE uptake was taken to 'suggest that [it] may be effective in the treatment of endogenous depression' (p. 139), on the model of desipramine, a well-known NE uptake inhibitor. The title of that publication identified the drug as a 'potential antidepressant.' According to released FDA documents described ahead, Lilly

launched several clinical trials to market atomoxetine as an antidepressant and as a treatment for urinary incontinence. These trials were
halted and their findings remain unpublished, and only a few hints
about them are discussed in the FDA documents. Later, once Lilly
decided to seek approval for the ADHD indication, authors asserted
that the 'pathophysiology of ADHD' seemed 'to involve the interaction of norepinephrine, epinephrine, and dopamine in modulation of
attention and impulsivity' (Biederman *et al.*, 2002, p. 1).

It is important in this respect to note that a drug is not used as
treatment in a clinical trial because of its (largely unknown) effects on
the central nervous system. Rather, it is used because it has reliably
produced distinct psycho-behavioural states – such as agitation, sedation, catalepsy – in earlier animal (preclinical) and normal
human (Phase I) studies leading to the open trials (Phase II) and randomized controlled trials (Phase III) on diagnosed patients. If that is the
case, 'The overriding question thus becomes: What psychosocial alterations and medical consequences (neurological and others) does the
regular use of a centrally active drug bring about short and long-term?'
(Cohen and Jacobs, 2007).

To answer such a question necessitates ascertaining the drug's psychosocial effects on 'normal' volunteers prior to testing the drug
with psychiatrically diagnosed individuals, because multiple co-present
personal difficulties (the 'psychiatric disorder') confound the determination of these effects. For example, does a drug that seems to reduce
depressive symptoms have specific 'antidepressant' properties or non-
specific 'emotional numbing' properties (Moncrieff and Cohen, 2006)?
Either could produce changes in individuals that would be rated as
'improvement' (Jacobs and Cohen, 1999). Randomized controlled trials are simply not designed to allow observers to make a distinction
between, say, 'improved mood' while on a drug as a return to normal from a depressed state or as a sign of drug-induced frontal lobe
damage (Hoehn-Saric *et al.* 1990).

Unfortunately, the necessity to document the drug's neurological and
psychosocial effects on normal volunteers prior to its investigatory
clinical use is minimally recognized at best. Phase I studies conducted
by pharmaceutical companies and submitted to the FDA as part of
the drug approval package seem to have a shadowy existence in terms
of how and why they are conducted, how data are collected, coded,
and interpreted, what is actually reported to the FDA, and who has
access to the original data (Healy, 2004). Phase I studies appear to
be conceived and conducted as toxicology studies (and sometimes as

'abuse liability' studies), not as *human psychoactive drug investigations* – for which no established study method exists. As a result, Phase I studies seem to shun discovering just what psychological states might be experienced by those who will take a psychoactive drug.

The case of Strattera™ illustrates this well. As of this writing, only two Phase I studies have been published. The report from the first (Zerbe *et al.*, 1985), conducted on 11 male volunteers, describes its aim as 'to investigate the clinical pharmacology of tomoxetine in humans and to define its safety and mechanism of action' (p. 139). Subjects were alternatively given placebo and single doses of atomoxetine in varying amounts. The authors state that 'Adverse experiences were monitored by close clinical evaluation and periodic completion of a standard questionnaire' (p. 140), but provide no description of the questionnaire. One brief table lists the following (mostly physical) effects reported only on atomoxetine: decreased appetite, headache, palpitations, sleeplessness, cough, indigestion, dry mouth, diarrhea, orthostatic hypotension, nervousness, funny taste, weakness, and difficulty focusing. In accord with then-ongoing efforts by Lilly to market antidepressants, the article concludes 'According to prevailing theories that increased NE within the central nervous system are effective in treating depression, tomoxetine should be a clinically effective antidepressant at these doses… [F]urther clinical trials to investigate the efficacy of tomoxetine in the treatment of depression are warranted' (p. 143).

The second published Phase I trial (Heil *et al.*, 2002), conducted in March 2000, was undertaken for a different purpose altogether: to rule out that atomoxetine produces stimulant effects. The FDA was undertaking Strattera's™ review and sought assurances that its 'abuse liability' was low. Fourteen 'light drug users' completed, in six experimental sessions, receiving placebo, atomoxetine, and methyphenidate in a double-blind, Latin square design. This time, 'subjective measures' were included, but they consisted of a 49-item true-false questionnaire 'containing empirically-derived drug sensitive scales' measuring stimulant, dysphoric/psychomimetic, euphoric, and sedative effects. Heil *et al.* concluded: 'Across the doses and time frame examined and with the instruments tested, atomoxetine does not engender pleasurable subjective drug effects, suggesting that it is unlikely that atomoxetine will have abuse liability' (2002, p. 154).

The FDA's internal review of this study (FDA, 2002d) found much to criticize, including the use of subjects without any significant experience with stimulants and the apparent reporting of various stimulant and dysphoric effects as if due to methylphenidate administration when individual case records showed the effects followed atomoxetine administration. Moreover, the FDA reviewers stated, 'As a known drug of abuse with a Schedule II designation, methylphenidate would be expected to significantly differentiate from placebo on subjective measures in order to validate the study design' – which it failed to do. These points are not raised here to confirm the correctness of the FDA's approach, but to contrast how carefully the FDA reviewed 'abuse potential' of atomoxetine and how carelessly, as we discuss ahead, it reviewed the trials' assessment of behavioural or psychological adverse effects.

In sum, rather than inform observers about the likely or possible psychological effects or alterations that atomoxetine might have on users – who will be expected to remain on the drug for months or years – these two Phase I reports merely managed to communicate that atomoxetine might produce various annoying physical effects and was not pleasant to take.

How should Phase I studies attempting to properly assess psychosocial effects proceed? Cohen and Jacobs (2007) suggest that, in addition to using normal volunteers, 'other informants who know the subject well and can observe the subject in his/her natural environment should also contribute information. The consequences of drug discontinuation, also from multiple informant perspectives, must be investigated. Finally, subjects' accounts once definitely off the drug (e.g., several months after the last dose) must be compared to their accounts under the influence.' These authors further believe that 'Without such information from undiagnosed normal volunteers, diagnosed persons have no realistic basis on which to decide to be treated or not with the drug.'

Selective presentation and publication of adverse effect data in trials of Strattera™

As mentioned, by the time Strattera™ was brought to market in early 2003, 11 publications reporting on eight Phase II and III trials conducted from 1984 to 2002, in Canada and the United States, and funded by Eli Lilly (two were co-funded by the NIMH), could be located in the Medline database. As Table 11.1 shows, on average, each study lasted 7.6 weeks (range: 6–12 weeks). They reported on a total of 1,584 subjects, of which 943 (including 641 children and adolescents) were exposed to atomoxetine.

Table 11.1 Published trials of atomoxetine as of FDA approval, November 2002

Authors, published report	n ATMX[+] Placebo	n placebo	Age (years)	Length (weeks)	Design	No. of efficacy measures	Adverse Effect measure
Kratochvil et al. (2001)	Analysis of one site's results from Kratochvil (2002)						BBAEQ-M[++] and 'spontaneous open-ended questioning'
Spencer et al. (2001)	30 /–	–	7–14	11	open-label, no control	5	'spontaneous reports from parent or child'
Kratochvil et al. (2002)	184/44	44	7–15	10	open-label, MPH[+++] comparison	4	'open-ended questions'
Spencer et al. (2002)*	129/124	124; MPH = 38	7–13	9	double-blind, RCT[++++]	3	'unsolicited adverse events'

Table 11.1 (Continued)

Authors, published report	n ATMX[+] Placebo	n placebo	Age (years)	Length (weeks)	Design	No. of efficacy measures	Adverse Effect measure
Michelson et al. (2001)	213/84	84	8–18	8	RCT, dose-response	5	'open-ended questioning'
Michelson et al. (2002)	85/85	85	6–16	6	double-blind, RCT	5	'open-ended questioning'
Biederman et al. (2002)	Subset-analysis of girls in Spencer (2002) study						
Michelson et al. (2003)*	270/266	266	adult	10	double-blind, RCT	7	'open-ended questioning'
Spencer et al. (1998)	22	–	20–59	6	double-blind, crossover	5	none
Chouinard (1984)	10	–	40–56	6	open-label	5	none
Chouinard (1985)	6-week follow-up of Chouinard (1984) study						

+ Atomoxetine.
++ Barkley Behavior and Adverse Effects Questionnaire – Modified.
+++ Methylphenidate.
++++ Randomized controlled trial.

In early 2003, FDA also released on its website many of the documents comprising its own internal evaluation of the clinical trials for Strattera™ submitted to it by the sponsor for approval for the treatment of ADHD (FDA New Drug Application 21-411). These documents contain a wealth of material about Strattera™, including a detailed review (referred to as 'FDA review'), dated July 2002, of four of the eight trials mentioned above. These are the main efficacy and safety data considered by the FDA when evaluating Strattera™ for market approval (Although the FDA describes '6 short-term, placebo-controlled trials,' four of these are in fact two duplicated studies occurring simultaneously in different sites [Michelson *et al.*, 2003; Spencer *et al.*, 2002], with their reports containing results from all sites.) The FDA adds that 'efficacy data were collected in 4 open-label trials, however, these data are difficult to interpret and were not reviewed with regard to efficacy' (p. 4).

One must note that although atomoxetine was approved, and is marketed and promoted, to treat a 'chronic' condition, the only studies reviewed by the FDA were short-term studies. In an unusual move, the FDA stated that 'the issue of longer-term efficacy will need to be addressed in the future' (FDA, 2002a, p. 9). One must note further that the FDA explicitly rejected results from 'a year long, placebo controlled relapse prevention study, [which] had negative results and was not reviewed, because the study did not support any of the claims which the sponsor (Eli Lilly) has requested' (FDA, 2002b, p. 3). Few details about this longer-term study are provided in the FDA review, making it difficult to compare it to recently published reports of a longer-term study of atomoxetine which do *not* mention any negative results (e.g., Newcorn *et al.*, 2006; Hazell *et al.*, 2006).

According to the FDA review, data from another 1,274 or 1,324 atomoxetine exposed subjects in ten different studies were available in a 'historical' data set from the previously-mentioned abandoned programs by Eli Lilly examining the efficacy of the drug for urinary incontinence and for major depression. The FDA review provided some summary statistics about these ten studies, including rates of serious adverse effects reported by the sponsor, but to our knowledge only one small open study has been published (Chouinard *et al.*, 1984, 1985). These ten trials may be of particular importance as off-label prescribing for Strattera™ has, predictably, increased since its approval. For example, without benefit of data on abandoned trials of atomoxetine for depression, it is difficult to make sense of recent case reports suggesting that atomoxetine be used in drug augmentation strategies to treat depression (e.g., Carpenter *et al*, 2005).

The 'measurement' of efficacy and safety in published studies of Strattera™

Jacobs and Cohen (1999) and Cohen and Jacobs (2007) make several points related to the inability of conventional clinical trials to provide a true picture of a drug's adverse effects. They suggest that ascertaining harm from treatment takes a distinctly subordinate position to the goal of establishing superiority of a tested drug to placebo. This is because, first, trials typically use structured, pre-established scales that limit open-ended exploration of effects; second, investigators and subjects are strangers, and meet for a few minutes once every week or two during which ratings of subjects are made and during which the subjects' spontaneous speech opportunities are quite limited, further narrowing the range of comments bearing on drug-induced experiences; and third, that only data gathered while subjects are undergoing treatment is considered relevant, despite the importance of retrospective, post-treatment data in properly interpreting a psychoactive drug experience. Overall, then, Cohen and Jacobs conclude that the subject's voice in a conventional clinical trial is essentially muted and replaced by the investigator's voice and ratings, and thus that outcome measures amount only to 'standby' measures of the true outcomes of interest.

Part of this critique involves the recognition that ascertaining 'efficacy' of a psychiatric drug is less important than ascertaining its 'safety.' Once on the market, a drug is prescribed for many indications besides its officially approved one, to different individuals than those on whom it was tested, for much longer periods than the initial trials, and concomitant to many other drugs. All these conditions increase its potential for causing harm. Thus, the drug's subjectively undesirable effects and unambiguously harmful effects should be investigated with care, rigor, and ingenuity – or at least equal to the effort expended to ascertain 'therapeutic' effects. How does this critique apply to the Strattera™ trials available at the time that physicians rushed to prescribe it?

As Table 11.1 shows, five of eight published studies included only investigator-rated measures for efficacy and safety. Three also included self-rated measures, but none were used as primary outcomes. Moreover, the primary efficacy measure for all the paediatrics studies was the ADHDRS-IV-Parent: Inv, a modified version of the ADHDRS-IV-Parent scale, an 18-item scale with which parents directly assess the severity of each of the 18 DSM-IV diagnostic criteria. The modification consisted in 'having the *investigator* score the ADHDRS-IV-Parent: Inv based on interviews with parents *about their children's* behavior at weekly visits' (FDA, 2002b, p.11, italics added).

Judging from the published reports, the procedures used to elicit subjects' descriptions of adverse effects and to rate them directly challenge the assertions cited earlier that Strattera™ was subjected to 'unusually rigorous investigation of its safety and tolerability.' In nine published reports, measurement of adverse effects was elicited only via 'self-report' (one study), 'spontaneous reports from parent or child' (one study), 'unsolicited adverse event reports' (two studies), and 'open-ended questions' (four studies). One study did not report on how measurements of adverse effects were collected.

One published report mentioned, in addition to 'spontaneous open-ended questioning,' the use of a rating scale, the Barkley Behavior and Adverse Effects Questionnaire–Modified (BBAEQ-M), to gather adverse effects information from the 10 subjects in the study. The BBAEQ-M was originally constructed to assess effects of stimulant drugs and modified for use in the atomoxetine trial. Compared to the original scale, the BBAEQ-M contains five additional items (low energy, talking too much/non-stop talking, heart racing/pounding, dry mouth, and constipation) and modifications of three existing items (insomnia, irritability and anxiousness). Like the major ADHD scale used as an efficacy measure, the BBAEQ-M was, according to a clinician in the trials, administered interview-style by a physician or nurse to the child's parent: 'It could be a self-administered scale, however, then you run across the problem of people reading the item differently and responding differently (doing it interview style helps to 'standardize' it)' (B. Vaughan, personal email communication, November, 20, 2003, parentheses in original).

It is important to note here that the FDA review states clearly that the BBAEQ-M was used in two studies, and implies that it was used in most or all other studies. Since the FDA review does not provide the BBAEQ-M ratings for each study, one cannot tell which – FDA review or published articles – is most reliable. If the FDA review correctly summarizes the procedures, then one must wonder why data from the only adverse effect rating scale of an entire clinical trial program for a new chemical entity is not provided in the published article, or in the FDA review. On the other hand, if the published version is to be trusted, then the assessment of behavioural adverse effects appears derisory.

Overall, how does the assessment of 'efficacy' compare to the assessment of 'safety' in the published trials? To answer this question, we counted the number of rating scales used to measure therapeutic and adverse effects, and the number of words in each published article describing the methods of evaluation. The results strongly suggest that – at least in published reports – the assessment of adverse or side effects was basically a *distraction* from the task of showing Strattera's™ superiority to placebo to treat 'ADHD.' The average number of ADHD scales per study was 4.8 (range 3–7), while the BBAEQ-M was used in a single study. The average number of words per article describing methods of assessment of the primary therapeutic outcome (reduction of ADHD-like behaviour) was 211 (range: 61–394), while for adverse effects it was a mere 21 (range: 0–35).

Criteria or cut-off points for actually reporting or listing observed adverse effects in the published reports also varied from study to study and were considerably less systematic than for reporting the therapeutic outcomes. Three studies reported no particular criteria. Two studies reported what they termed the 'most frequent' and 'most common' adverse effects, without any definition. One study stated: 'there were no serious adverse effects, except for....' One study reported adverse events 'occurring in >10% of treatment group' and another three studies that included those undesirable effects 'reported in at least 5% of patients in any treatment group.' Finally, one study listed an adverse effect if it was 'reported in at least 5% of patients in any treatment group and statistically significantly more frequent than placebo.' In sum, no consistency or uniformity in criteria, procedures, style, or even language was observed among the 11 reports of clinical trials.

Serious adverse events in the published reports vs. the FDA review

Altogether, the 11 published reports of eight studies of atomoxetine show a serious adverse event (SAE) rate of 0.7 percent. SAEs, as defined by the FDA, refer to events resulting in hospitalization, serious disability, or death (no deaths were reported to have occurred). The FDA review, however, reports a 2.1 percent SAE rate from ADHD studies and a whopping 7 percent SAE rate from the historical studies on incontinence and major depression (see Table 11.2) – which may be why these trials were abandoned.

Table 11.2 Different accounts of number of subjects and serious adverse effect rates in atomoxetine clinical trials

	FDA review of 16 July 2002		Published as of December 2003 (% FDA review)
	No. of subjects in clinical trials		
	ADHD[+]	Abandoned programmes: MDD[++] urinary incontinence	
Atomoxetine	2337	1274 or 1324	952 (26%)
Placebo	585	710	595 (46%)
Methylphenidate	82	–	44 (54%)
	Percentage of serious adverse effects		
	2.1%	6.98% or 6.72%	0.7% (20.6%)

[+] Attention Deficit Hyperactivity Disorder.
[++] Major Depressive Disorder.

The FDA review further lists 'the SAEs that were reported for more than one atomoxetine subject' through November 15, 2001: appendicitis ($n = 9$), depression (5), accidental injury (5), burns (3), hostility (2), urinary tract infection (2), convulsions (2) and overdose (2). This totals 30 instances of a SAE in which multiple subjects are affected (FDA, 2002c, p. 24). An additional 32 SAEs are reported as of a November 2001 cutoff date and another 37 cases reported from the cutoff through July 31, 2002. The identified 30 multiple SAEs occur across eight studies, of which only two were published at the time of Strattera's™ introduction to the market. The six unpublished studies contain 8, 7, 4, 3, 2 and 2 SAEs, respectively. Of note, the FDA identified three SAEs in the trial published as Michelson *et al.* (2001) and one SAE in the trial published as Michelson *et al* (2003). However, neither publication mentions the occurrence of any serious adverse events. This instance of publication bias illustrates why the stated knowledge about psychotropic drugs from credentialed experts must be treated with caution and scepticism.

The exclusion of post-treatment ratings

The FDA review includes detailed schematic descriptions of the sponsor-provided protocol for every clinical trial of Strattera™ included in the approval package submitted to the FDA. Every protocol includes a planned discontinuation of the medication and a specific post-treatment assessment phase, usually lasting up to four weeks and including a minimum of four planned ratings. Unfortunately, neither the FDA review nor any of the 11 published reports included any data from these discontinuation periods, nor was there any indication that the FDA took any interest in these data.

Summary: efficacy and safety

Overall, traditional self-report instruments were modified for clinician interviewing and clinician rating, creating an obvious barrier against hearing the patient's voice to determine important outcomes or simply to contribute to 'what is known' about Strattera's™ effects. In essence, then, what Strattera™ was being tested for by Eli Lilly during the mid-to-late 1990s – anti-ADHD-like behaviour – became its 'main effect,' while its *genuine* main effects, that is, the alterations in feeling, thinking, and behaving that a psychoactive drug would be *expected to induce in people regardless of why it is used*, remain essentially unknown.

Furthermore, in most studies adverse events appeared to have been 'observed' only if they were first 'spontaneously' reported or expressed by the participant or by his or her parent, if they were recognized as worthy of recognition as a 'drug effect' by the investigator, if they were actually recorded by the investigator, if they were then coded or classified as an adverse effect, if they were reported to the sponsor, and if they were reported to the FDA (and if they were then chosen for inclusion in a 'scientific' report of the trial submitted for publication).

Naturally, this has been for decades the usual, conventional method with which sponsors have assessed and reported behavioural adverse effects, and the usual, conventional method with which the FDA has approved new drug applications. Thus, even as trials testing a 'new chemical entity' within an 'unusually stringent' regulatory climate, the

Strattera™ clinical trials simply are not worthy of distinction from countless other clinical psychopharmacotherapy trials whose validity has been decisively challenged.

To be or not to be a 'non-stimulant'

Strattera™ is everywhere called a 'non-stimulant', the semantic equivalent of calling a beverage 'non-water'. If it does not have stimulant effects, what effects does it have? The previous section has argued that no data was gathered in the Strattera™ clinical trials to bear on this question. Some data on adverse effects, however, might suggest an outline of Strattera's™ adverse effect profile.

As discussed, in the early 1980s Lilly explored atomoxetine as a treatment for depression. The first two reports of clinical use of atomoxetine are by Chouinard and colleagues (1984, 1985), on a small open trial with ten adults. The descriptions indicate that the drug was having typical stimulating effects: Chouinard *et al.* (1985) wrote that atomoxetine produced a 'marked mood-elevating effect' within a mere two days (p. 76); that 'All [10] patients were prescribed chloral hydrate for insomnia, five of whom still needed it at Day 84'; and finally that '[despite] a significant reduction in anxiety scores ... the patients remained particularly sensitive to outside stresses' (pp. 75–6). Abrupt mood-elevation, long-lasting insomnia countered with sedatives, and irritability – also known as mania – constitute a characteristic form of behavioural toxicity of stimulants (Also in 1985, Chouinard published one case report of mania involving atomoxetine, probably one of the ten subjects described in the previous studies).

In 2003, only one published study included a comparison of atomoxetine (n = 184) with methylphenidate (n = 40), and the authors fortunately listed the adverse effects rated in the two study groups (Kratochvil *et al.*, 2002). As shown in Table 11.2, we extracted from the list the main types of adverse effects of stimulants according to Bezchlibnyk-Butler and Jeffries (2005) for atomoxetine and methylphenidate, and listed them side by side. Limitations of the data and sample sizes aside, Table 11.3 suggests that atomoxetine's adverse effect profile is a stimulant adverse effect profile, an even stronger one than methylphenidate's.

These preliminary data do not establish anything definitive, except perhaps to remind us that attributions of properties (or lack of properties) to drugs are not the properties themselves.

Table 11.3 Adverse effects in the only study comparing atomoxetine with a stimulant when Strattera was launched

Body system	Effects	% Atomoxetine (n = 184)	% Methylphenidate (n = 40)
Central nervous	Nervousness, insomnia, hyperkinesia	39.8	26.5
	Headache	31	32.5
	Depression	2.7	5
Gastro-intestinal	Abdominal pain	43	7
	Anorexia	19	15
	Vomiting/nausea	22.3	5
	Diarrhea	7.1	2.5
Allergic	Rhinitis, pharyngitis	24	27.5

Conclusion

The diagnosis of ADHD will continue to be applied to millions of children, and millions of them will continue for the foreseeable future to receive drugs to treat their 'disorder' (Cohen, 2007). New drugs for ADHD will continue to be introduced as the European and Asian markets continue to open up to stimulants, and data from future trials will be submitted to the FDA and journals and be considered part of the scientific literature.

The problem with discrepancies between published and non-published versions of clinical trial data, and with business-as-usual ways of evaluating psychoactive drugs for human consumption, is that preventable harm occurs, yet when it does its causes become very difficult to establish. A recent retrospective case review by Henderson and Hartman (2004) of 153 atomoxetine-treated individuals found that no less than 51 (33 per cent) manifested either 'extreme irritability, aggression, mania, or hypomania induction.' Many of them were receiving either additional antipsychotics, anticonvulsants, or other drugs, and it is difficult to know which single drug or combination may have contributed to this outcome. The wide discrepancy between this rate and the rate that can be estimated from the published trials and the FDA review does not mean that case reports are methodologically inferior forms of investigation. It means rather that clinical trials leave the clinician completely unprepared for the reality of the complex and unpredictable effects of psychoactive drugs, and that more careful, ingenious, and creative ways to assess drug effects must be implemented promptly.

References

Allen, A. J., and Michelson, D. (2002). Drug development process for a product with a primary pediatrics indication. *Journal of Clinical Psychiatry*, 63(Suppl 12), 44–9.

Bezchlybnik-Butler, K. Z. and Jeffries, J. J. (2005) *Clinical handbook of psychotropic drugs* (15th rev. edn.). Ashland, OH: Hogrefe and Huber.

Biederman, J., Heiligenstein, J. H., Faries, D. E., Galil, N., Dittman, R., Emslie, G. J., Kratochvil, C. J., Laws, H. F., Schuh, K. J., and the Atomoxetine ADHD Study Group. (2002). Efficacy of atomoxetine versus placebo in school-age girls with attention-deficit/hyperactivity disorder. *Pediatrics*, 11(6). Retrieved 15 September 2003 from http://www.pediatrics.org/cgi/content/full/110/6/e75

Caballero, J., and Nahata, M. C. (2003). Atomoxetine hydrochloride for the treatment of attention-deficit/hyperactivity disorder. *Clinical Therapeutics*, 25(12), 3065–3083.

Carpenter L.L., Milosavljevic N., Schecter J.M., Tyrka A.R., and Price L.H. (2005). Augmentation with open-label atomoxetine for partial or nonresponse to antidepressants. *Journal of Clinical Psychiatry*, 66(10), 1234–38.

Chouinard, G., Annable, L., and Bradwejn, J. (1984). An early phase II clinical trial of tomoxetine (LY139603) in the treatment of newly admitted depressed patients. *Psychopharmacology*, 83, 126–8.

Chouinard, G., Annable, L., Bradwejn, J., Labonte, A., Jones, B., Mercier, P., *et al.* (1985). An early phase II clinical trial with followup of tomoxetine (LY139603) in the treatment of newly admitted depressed patients. *Psychopharmacology Bulletin*, 21(1), 73–6.

Cohen, D. (2007 March 15). What may be learned from the USA? Directions to support 'ADHD' children without medication. National ADHD Conference, School of Education, University of Edinburgh, Scotland.

Cohen, D. (2005). Clinical psychopharmacology trials: Gold standard or fool's gold? In S. A. Kirk (ed.), *Mental health and the social environment: Critical perspectives*. New York: Columbia University Press.

Cohen, D., and Jacobs, D. J. (2007). Randomized controlled trials of antidepressants: Clinically and scientifically irrelevant. *Debates in Neuroscience*.

Eli Lilly & Company (2003, July 23). *Strattera posts fastest launch ever for a new ADHD medicine*. Indianapolis: Eli Lilly & Company.

Eli Lilly & Company. (2004). *Eli Lilly & Company 2003 annual report, notice of annual meeting, and proxy statement.* Indianapolis: Eli Lilly & Company.

Food and Drug Administration. (2002d, July 31). Center for Drug Evaluation and Research. Abuse liability assessment of NDA 21–411.

Food and Drug Administration. (2002a, July 25). Center for Drug Evaluation and Research. Application Number 21-411. Administrative Documents (P2).

Food and Drug Administration. (2002b, July 1). Center for Drug Evaluation and Research. Application Number 21-411. Medical Review (P2).

Food and Drug Administration. (2002c, July 16). Center for Drug Evaluation and Research. Application Number 21-411. Medical Review (P3).

Hazell, P., Zhang, S., Wolanczyk, T., Barton, J., Johnson, M., Zuddas, A., Danckaerts, M., Ladikos, A., Benn, D., Yoran-Hegesh, R., Zeiner, P., and Michelson, D. (2006). Comorbid oppositional defiant disorder and the risk of relapse during 9 months of atomoxetine treatment for attention-deficit/hyperactivity disorder. *European Child and Adolescent Psychiatry,* 15(2), 105–10.

Healy, D. (2004). *Let them eat Prozac: the unhealthy relationship between the pharmaceutical industry and depression.* New York: New York University Press.

Heil, S. H., Holmes, H. W., Bickel, W. K., Higgins, S. T., Badger, G. J., Laws, H. F., and Faries, D. E. (2002). Comparison of the subjective, physiological, and psychomotor effects of atomoxetine and methylphenidate in light drug users. *Drug and Alcohol Dependence, 67,* 149–56.

Henderson, T. A., and Hartman, K. (2004). Aggression, mania, and hypomania induction associated with atomoxetine. *Pediatrics,* 114(3), 895–6.

Hoehn-Saric, R., Lipsey, J. R., and McLeod, D. A. (1990). Apathy and indifference in patients on fluvoxamine and fluoxetine. *Journal of Clinical Psychopharmacology,* 10, 343–5.

Jacobs, D. J., and Cohen, D. (1999). What is really known about the psychological alterations produced by psychiatric drugs? *Journal of International Risk and Safety in Medicine, 12,* 37–47.

Kratochvil, C., Bohac, D., Harrington, M., Baker, N., May, D., and Burke, W. (2001). An open-label trial of atomoxetine in pediatric attention deficit hyperactivity disorder. *Journal of Child and Adolescent Psychopharmacology,* 11, 167–70.

Kratochvil, C., Heiligenstein, J., Dittman, R., Spencer, T., Biederman, J., Wernicke, J., *et al.* (2002). Atomoxetine and methylphenidate treatment in children with ADHD: A prospective, randomized, open- label trial. *Journal of the American Academy of Child and Adolescent Psychiatry,* 41, 776–84.

Michelson, D., Faries, D., Wernicke, J., Kelsey, D., Kendrick, K., Sallee, F. R., *et al.* (2001). Atomoxetine in the treatment of children and adolescents with attention-deficit/hyperactivity disorder: A randomized, placebo-controlled, dose-response study. *Pediatrics, 108, 5*. Retrieved September 15, 2003, from http://www.pediatrics.org/cgi/content/full/108/5/e83

Michelson, D., Allen, A., Busner, J., Casat, C., Dunn, D., Kratochvil, C., *et al.* (2002). Once-daily atomoxetine treatment for children and adolescents with attention deficit hyperactivity disorder: A randomized, placebo-controlled study. *American Journal of Psychiatry*, 159, 1896–901.

Michelson, D., Adler, L., Spencer, T., Reimherr, F., West, S., Allen, A., *et al.* (2003). Atomoxetine in adults with ADHD: Two randomized, placebo-controlled studies. *Biological Psychiatry*, 53, 112–20.

Moncrieff, J., and Cohen, D. (2006). Do antidepressants cure or create abnormal brain states? *PLoS Medicine*, 3(7), e240.

Newcorn, J. H., Michelson, D., Kratochvil, C. J., Allen, A. J., Ruff, D. D., Moore, R. J., and Atomoxetine Low-dose Study Group. (2006). Low-dose atomoxetine for maintenance treatment of attention-deficit/hyperactivity disorder. *Pediatrics*, 118(6), e1701–6.

Spencer, T., Biederman, J., Wilens, T., Prince, J., Hatch, M., Jones, J., *et al.* (1998). Effectiveness and tolerability of atomoxetine in adults with attention deficit hyperactivity disorder. *American Journal of Psychiatry*, 155, 693–5.

Spencer, T., Biderman, J., Heiligenstein, J., Wilens, T., Faries, D., Prince, J., *et al.* (2001). An open-label, dose-ranging study of atomoxetine in children with attention deficit hyperactivity disorder. *Journal of Child and Adolescent Psychopharmacology*, 11, 251–65.

Spencer, T., Heiligenstein, J., Biederman, J., Faries, D., Kratochvil, C., Conners, C. K., *et al.* (2002). Results from 2 proof-of-concept, placebo-controlled studies of atomoxetine in children with attention-deficit/hyperactivity disorder. *Journal of Clinical Psychiatry*, 63, 1140–7.

Wernicke, J., and Kratochvil, C. (2002). Safety profile of atomoxetine in the treatment of children and adolescents with ADHD. *Journal of Clinical Psychiatry*, 63(Suppl 12), 50–5.

Zerbe, R. L., Rowe, H., Enas, Gregory, G. G., Wong, D., Farid, N., and Lemberger, L. (1985). Clinical pharmacology of tomoxetine, a potential antidepressant. *Journal of Pharmacology and Experimental Therapeutics*, 232(1), 139–43.

Zito, J. M., Safer, D. J., Dosreis, S., Gardner, J. F., Boles, J. and Lynch, F. (2000) Trends in prescribing of psychotropic medication in pre-schoolers. *Journal of the American Medical Association*, 283, 1025–30.

Chapter 12

The Role of Diet and Nutrition in ADHD

Basant K. Puri

It is clear from this book thus far that there are serious problems with the conventional pharmacological treatments currently available for ADHD. This applies to both the older stimulant medications and the recently introduced non-stimulant treatment. Therefore there is a need to re-think ADHD treatments. In this chapter I shall begin by outlining some of the adverse side-effects of conventional treatments, and then consider two important aspects of dietary and nutritional approaches, namely the role of removing artificial additives from the diet of hyperactive individuals, and the evidence in favour of the therapeutic use of fatty acid supplementation.

Conventional pharmacological treatments

In the United Kingdom, at the time of writing the following three conventional pharmacological treatments are available for ADHD: dexamfetamine (dexamphetamine) sulphate, methylphenidate hydrochloride, and atomoxetine. The first two of these are older stimulant treatments, and the third a more recently introduced non-stimulant one.

Stimulant medications

Dexamfetamine sulphate is available worldwide under several trade names, such as: Dexedrine in the United Kingdom; Adderall, Desoxyn, Desoxyn Gradumet, Dexedrine, Dexedrine Spansule and DextroStat in the United States of America; and Dexedrine and Dexedrine Spansule in Canada. The history of the use of dexamfetamine (amphetamines) has been detailed elsewhere (Puri, 2005). In summary, it was found by chance, in the 1930s by Dr Charles Bradley that amfetamine sulphate (Benzedrine), when given to children as a treatment for headaches resulting from the invasive neuroimaging procedure of pneumoencephalography, led to an improvement in attention and hyperactivity in children with ADHD symptomatology (Bradley, 1937). Later research studies went on to associate the action of amphetamines with dopaminergic neurotransmission, although the underlying cause and effect remain obscure (Puri, 2005).

Dexamfetamine is contra-indicated in the following conditions: cardiovascular disease – including moderate to severe high blood pressure; excitable states or states of agitation; hyperthyroidism; a history of alcohol abuse or illicit drug use; glaucoma; pregnancy; and breast-feeding. Dexamfetamine may adversely affect the patient's ability to carry out skilled tasks, so that it is probably better for adults to avoid driving while taking this stimulant medication. Alcohol may interact with this stimulant and should therefore probably be avoided (by adult patients). The more common side-effects associated with dexamfetamine include (Puri, 2005): insomnia – this is one reason why some drug addicts take amphetamines in the first place, as 'uppers' that will keep them awake; restlessness; irritability; excitability; nervousness; night terrors; euphoria – again, this is a reason why amphetamines are abused, for the 'high' that can be experienced with their use; tremor; dizziness; headache; convulsions – if there is a history of epilepsy and seizures occur, then the dexamfetamine treatment should be discontinued; addiction (to amphetamines); psychosis – the effects can be almost indistinguishable from the some types of schizophrenia, at least initially; anorexia; gastro-intestinal problems; retarded growth in children – because of this side-effect, the child's growth progress needs to be regularly monitored by the prescribing doctor; dry mouth; sweating; an increased heart rate (tachycardia); the pain of angina; palpitations; increased blood pressure – patients taking dexamfetamine should have their blood pressure monitored regularly; visual problems; cardiomyopathy, in which the muscle of the heart becomes inflamed and no longer works as efficiently as before, may occur after long-term use of this stimulant medication. Furthermore, dexamfetamine can provoke the occurrence of the following movement disorders in those who have a predisposition to them: choreoathetoid movements – the writhing, 'dancing' movements of the limbs seen in Huntington's chorea (Huntington's disease), for example; tics; and Tourette syndrome.

Methylphenidate has been mentioned several times already in this book. It is available worldwide. In the United Kingdom, it can be prescribed under the trade names Ritalin™ and the slow-release preparation Concerta XL™. It is a compound which was synthesized in 1944, since when its worldwide sales have been enormous.

As with dexamfetamine, methylphenidate is contra-indicated in the following conditions: cardiovascular disease – including moderate to severe high blood pressure; excitable states or states of agitation; hyperthyroidism; a history of alcohol abuse or illicit drug use; glaucoma; pregnancy; and breast-feeding. Methylphenidate may adversely affect the patient's ability to carry out skilled tasks, so that it is probably better for adults to avoid driving while taking this stimulant medication. Alcohol may interact with this stimulant and should therefore probably be avoided (by adult patients). The most common side-effects associated with methylphenidate include (Puri, 2005): insomnia and other sleep disturbances; depression; confusion; restlessness; irritability; excitability; nervousness; night terrors; euphoria; tremor; skin rash; itching; urticaria – hives or nettle rash; dizziness; headache; pyrexia; convulsions – if there is a history of epilepsy and seizures occur, then the methylphenidate treatment should be discontinued; addiction (to methylphenidate); psychosis – as with dexamfetamine sulphate treatment, the effects can be almost indistinguishable from the some types of schizophrenia, at least initially; arthralgia; anorexia; alopecia; gastro-intestinal problems; retarded growth in children – because of this side-effect, the child's growth progress should be regularly monitored by the prescribing doctor; dry mouth; sweating; exfoliative dermatitis, in which there is a reddening scaly inflammation of much, if not all, of the skin – it can be fatal; erythema multiforme, which is an allergic reaction of the skin and/or mucous membranes (such as the lips) – severe cases require treatment in hospital (in the case of very severe cases, in an intensive care unit or burns unit); an increased heart rate (tachycardia); the pain of angina; palpitations; hypertension – patients taking methylphenidate should have their blood pressure monitored regularly; visual problems; cardiomyopathy – see under dexamfetamine above; thrombocytopenic purpura, in which the body's immune system attacks its own blood platelets; thrombocytopenia, in which there is a reduction in the number of platelets in the blood; leucopenia, in which there is a reduction in the number of white blood cells circulating in the bloodstream;

and urinary problems. As with dexamfetamine, methylphenidate can provoke the occurrence of the following movement disorders in those who have a predisposition to them: choreoathetoid movements; tics; and Tourette syndrome. Rare side-effects of methylphenidate include: hepatic damage; muscle cramps; and cerebral arteritis.

Non-stimulant medication

The non-stimulant non-amphetamine-derivative medication atomoxetine has become available for the treatment of ADHD during this decade, being marketed by Eli Lilly and Company as Strattera™. It selectively inhibits the reuptake of noradrenaline (norepinephrine).

A serious side-effect of atomoxetine is the risk of hepatic damage. Other side-effects include (Puri, 2005): anorexia; dry mouth; nausea; vomiting; abdominal pain; constipation; dyspepsia; flatulence; palpitations; tachycardia; increased blood pressure; postural hypotension; hot flushes; sleep disturbance; dizziness; headache; fatigue; lethargy; depression; anxiety; tremor; rigors; urinary retention; inflammation of the prostate gland; sexual problems (in adult patients); menstrual disturbances (in menstruating female patients); mydriasis; conjunctivitis; dermatitis; pruritus; skin rashes; sweating. Less common side-effects are cold hands and cold feet.

Discussion

It can be seen that the main conventional treatments currently in use for ADHD have a wide range of adverse side-effects, some of which are very serious. An alternative treatment approach is therefore needed. Two such approaches, both essentially relating to diet and nutrition, are now described.

Removal of artificial additives from the diet

Published studies

The first report linking hyperactivity in children to artificial food flavourings and colourings was published in 1975 (Feingold, 1975). In due course, this idea gave rise to elimination diets for ADHD, the most famous of which is probably the Feingold Diet, from which are eliminated artificial food colourings, artificial flavourings, natural salicylates, and certain preservatives. Furthermore, chronic administration of food colourings appears to affect dopaminergic pathways in the developing rat (Shaywitz et al., 1979). A meta-analysis of the effect of the Feingold Diet on childhood hyperactivity published in 1983 showed a statistically non-significant improvement associated with this diet (Kavale and Forness, 1983).

Recently, Schab and Trinh (2004) published a meta-analysis of 15 double-blind placebo-controlled trials evaluating the effects of artificial food colourings on childhood behaviour which met their primary inclusion criteria. The subjects studied by the trials had to be less than 18 years of age. The diagnostic criteria chosen for the children encompassed a spectrum of illness variously labelled as minimal brain dysfunction, hyperkinesis, hyperkinetic reaction, hyperactivity, attention deficit disorder and ADHD. The trials had to employ an intervention which could isolate the effects of artificial food colourings. This constituted challenging hyperactive children with such substances or placebo or by submitting children to blinded diets which either did or did not contain artificial food colourings. With one exception, all the trials which were entered into the meta-analysis were randomized; in the case of the exception the order of treatment was fixed beforehand. The overall result of this meta-analysis was that the effect size was 0.283 (with a 95 per cent confidence interval of 0.079 to 0.488), corresponding to a change of a little more than one standard deviation. The authors pointed out that, assuming a normal distribution of response to artificial food colourings, 'this change represents a shift from the 50th to the 61st percentile of hyperactivity for the average hyperactive child in the population of trials' (Schab and Trinh, 2004, p. 427). They concluded that their meta-analysis supported the hypothesis that artificial food colourings promote hyperactivity in hyperactive children, as measured on behavioural rating scales.

Also in 2004, Bateman and colleagues published a large double-blind placebo-controlled trial in which a general population sample of preschool children were challenged with artificial food colourings and benzoate preservatives. This study appeared too late to be included in the Schab and Trinh (2004) meta-analysis described above. In their study, Bateman *et al.* (2004) screened almost two thousand three-year-olds for the presence of hyperactivity, and most had skin prick tests to identify atopy to *Dermatophagoides pteronyssinus*, grass pollen, feline allergens, cows' milk, eggs and peanuts, with atopy being defined as one or more reactions with an average wheal diameter of at least 2 mm in the presence of a positive histamine control and negative saline control. The hyperactivity and non-hyperactivity groups were each further dichotomized into those who were and those who were not atopic on the basis of these skin tests. Following baseline assessment, the children were placed on a diet which eliminated artificial colourings and benzoate preservatives for a period of one week. During the subsequent three-week within-subject double-blind crossover study the children received, in random order, periods of dietary challenge with a drink containing 20 mg daily of artificial colourings plus 45 mg daily sodium benzoate (active period), or a placebo mixture (placebo period), supplementary to their diet. The children's behaviour was assessed by a rater blind to dietary status, using observations during a period of free play and the 'bear and dragon' task, a delay-aversion 'hiding stickers' task and 'draw-a-line slowly and walk-a-line slowly' task, and by parental ratings of behavioural changes based on the Weiss-Werry-Peters Activity Scale. The researchers found a significant reduction in hyperactive behaviour during the withdrawal phase. They also found a significantly greater increase in hyperactive behaviour during the active period compared with the placebo period, based on parental reports, without a significant effect of the presence or absence of either hyperactivity or atopy. No significant differences were found based on the objective testing in the clinic. The authors concluded that: 'There is a general adverse effect of artificial food colouring and benzoate preservatives on the behaviour of 3 year old children which is detectable by parents but not by a simple clinic assessment. Subgroups are not made more vulnerable to this effect by their prior levels of hyperactivity or by atopy' (Bateman et al., 2004, p. 506).

Discussion

In summary, there is evidence to support the benefits, in terms of effects on hyperactive behaviour, of the removal of artificial additives from the diet of children.

Fatty acid supplementation

The fatty acid model

The fatty acid model of ADHD was published by Richardson and I in 2000, and proposed that 'at least some features of ADHD may reflect an underlying abnormality of fatty acid metabolism...a functional deficiency of certain long-chain polyunsaturated fatty acids could contribute to many of the features associated with this condition' (Richardson and Puri, 2000, p. 79). This fatty acid model can help account for many of the features of ADHD, including: the higher

ratio of boys to girls; the association with minor physical abnormalities; sleep problems; the association with allergies and related health
problems such as upper respiratory tract infections, skin disorders and
asthma; the association with somatic symptoms such as headaches,
stomach-aches, susceptibility to infections and general malaise without
an obvious cause; emotional and mood disorders; and the association
with specific learning or language difficulties, such as dyslexia.

Long-chain polyunsaturated fatty acids

The omega-3 and omega-6 long-chain polyunsaturated fatty acids play
important roles in the structural integrity of cell membranes, not only
those which surround living cells, but also those which are associated
with many intracellular organelles, such as those of the mitochondria,
the nucleus and lysosomes. This occurs because certain long-chain
polyunsaturated fatty acids, particularly arachidonic acid (an omega-
6 fatty acid) and docosahexaenoic acid (DHA) (an omega-3 fatty
acid) can form part of the phospholipid molecule (at the Sn2 position); in turn, the phospholipid molecules make up the cell membrane
bilayer. Abnormal phospholipid molecules in cell membranes, caused
for example by a deficiency of long-chain polyunsaturated fatty acids
or by the inappropriate use by the body of manufactured trans-fatty
acids (which occur abundantly in the modern diets of many children),
lead in turn to a reduction in cell membrane flexibility and a decrease
in the degrees of freedom of membrane proteins.

Three of these long-chain polyunsaturated fatty acids are also vitally
important as the precursors of eicosanoids such as prostaglandins,
thromboxanes and leukotrienes. They are the omega-6 long-chain
polyunsaturated fatty acids dihomo-γ-linolenic acid and arachidonic
acid, and the omega-3 long-chain polyunsaturated fatty acid eicosapentaenoic acid, or EPA for short.

In principle, given that children tend to have a good intake of the
precursor short-chain omega-6 and omega-3 fatty acids linoleic acid
and alpha-linolenic acid, respectively, and given that living mammalian
cells contain a set of enzymes to allow the conversion of these
short-chain fatty acids into all the biologically important long-chain
polyunsaturated fatty acids, a deficiency of the latter should not arise.
(Indeed, there is evidence that the modern Western diet may contain
far too high a level of linoleic acid.) In practice, however, deficiencies of key omega-6 and omega-3 long-chain polyunsaturated fatty
acids do commonly occur. A key reason for this appears to be the
susceptibility of the first enzyme, which acts on both linoleic acid

and alpha-linolenic acid, to many factors which tend to be prevalent. This enzyme is delta-6-desaturase, and factors which inhibit its action include the stress hormone cortisol, viral infections, a functional deficiency of key micronutrients (which may be caused by a relatively high intake of 'junk food' and refined carbohydrate-based products) and caffeine. The effects of such inhibition would be expected to include many of the features associated with ADHD, hence the fatty acid model of Richardson and Puri mentioned above. A prediction of this model is that dietary supplementation with certain omega-6 and omega-3 long-chain polyunsaturated fatty acids should be beneficial in respect of ADHD symptomatology. A good dietary source of omega-6 fatty acids is evening primrose oil. This is a rich source of the omega-6 fatty acid gamma-linolenic acid, which in turn can be converted by the body's cells into dihomo-γ-linolenic acid and thence arachidonic acid. By giving gamma-linolenic acid, inhibition of delta-6-desaturase is by-passed on the omega-6 front. On the omega-3 side, an excellent source of eicosapentaenoic acid is pure eicosapentaenoic acid itself. This in turn gives rise to the EPA-derived eicosanoids and to DHA. Note that there are good theoretical reasons why DHA itself should not be administered in supplement form. DHA, a 22-carbon long-chain polyunsaturated fatty acid containing six double-bonds per molecule, is particularly susceptible to lipid peroxidation. While this is not a problem with most dietary forms of DHA, in which the DHA is usually in the presence of factors which inhibit peroxidation, this may unfortunately not be the case with respect to DHA supplements. In turn, beta-aldehydes result from such peroxidation. They, in turn, act as powerful free radicals, which may damage cell membranes and even DNA.

Published studies
We shall begin by looking at randomized double-blind placebo-controlled trials of evening primrose oil alone in hyperactivity in children. The first such study was that of Aman et al. (1987), involving 31 children selected for marked inattention and overactivity in a crossover study. As might be expected from the foregoing discussion, taking evening primrose oil was associated with a significant increase in dihomo-γ-linolenic acid levels. Evening primrose oil supplementation was also associated with significant changes in two performance tasks and with significant improvement in parental ratings on the subscales designated as Attention Problem and Motor Excess of the Revised Behaviour Problem Checklist. However, a variety of eight

other psychomotor performance tests and two standardized teacher rating scales failed to indicate treatment effects. With the experiment-wise probability level set to 0.05, just 2 out of 42 variables showed treatment effects. The authors concluded that supplementation with evening primrose oil alone produced minimal or no improvements in hyperactive children selected without regard to baseline fatty acid levels. It should be noted, however, that each child only received the evening primrose oil for only four weeks, which is likely to be too short a period over which to notice significant changes. The second randomized double-blind placebo-controlled trial of evening prim-rose oil was from Ohio State University (Arnold *et al.*, 1989). In this study evening primrose oil was compared with placebo and also with *d*-amphetamine. It took the form of a Latin-square double-crossover study, with random assignment to sequence, in which 18 boys with ADHD received one month each of evening primrose oil, placebo and *d*-amphetamine. Teachers' ratings showed a trend of evening primrose oil effect between placebo and *d*-amphetamine. This trend reached a significant level of p less than 0.05 only on the Conners' Hyperactiv-ity Factor. The authors concluded that their study had not established evening primrose oil as an effective treatment for ADHD, although the caveat regarding length of treatment mentioned with regard to the previous evening primrose oil study clearly applies again here. (In our paper describing the fatty acid model, Richardson and Puri [2000] mentioned that long-chain polyunsaturated fatty acid levels in the brain might take up to three months to recover from a chronic defi-ciency state and that this should therefore be regarded as an essential consideration in the design of treatment studies.)

Considering next the use of just DHA alone, there has been one such randomized double-blind placebo-controlled trial, namely that of Voigt *et al.* (2001). In this study, from the Mayo Clinic in Rochester, Minnesota and the Baylor College of Medicine in Houston, Texas, 63 children with ADHD, who were all receiving effective maintenance therapy with conventional stimulant medication, were randomized to receive either 345 mg DHA or a placebo daily for four months. The DHA group did not fare better than the placebo group. In fact, taking pure DHA daily was associated with a significant *worsening* on two important components of the Test of Variables of Attention (TOVA). Errors of omission, a TOVA component that reflects inatten-tion, increased significantly in the DHA group but not in the placebo group, and errors of commission, a TOVA component that reflects impulsivity, decreased significantly in the placebo group but not in the DHA group.

In 2004, a Japanese study was published which involved the use of high DHA and low EPA (and no evening primrose oil) (Hirayama *et al.*, 2004). The long-chain polyunsaturated fatty acid supplementations were administered using fortified foods. Twenty children with ADHD received supplementation with 514 mg DHA plus 100 mg EPA daily through this means, for two months, while a comparison group of 20 ADHD children received the same extra foods but not fortified with omega-3 long-chain polyunsaturated fatty acids. As with the previous DHA study, in this high DHA study the active group did not show any improvement in ADHD and actually showed a *worsening* in some symptoms. As the authors stated, 'visual short-term memory and errors of commission (continuous performance) significantly improved in the control group compared with the changes over time in the DHA group' (Hirayama *et al.*, 2004, p. 467).

There have been several studies using EPA, DHA and gamma-linolenic acid (from evening primrose oil). In the Purdue University study, 50 children with ADHD-like symptoms were randomized to receive either an omega-3 and omega-6 long-chain polyunsaturated fatty acid supplement or an olive oil placebo for four months (Stevens *et al.*, 2003). The active group received the following fatty acid doses daily: 96 mg gamma-linolenic acid, 40 mg arachidonic acid, 80 mg EPA and 480 mg DHA. Only 2 out of 16 outcome measures showed a significant improvement associated with the active group, namely conduct problems (parental ratings) and attention symptoms (teacher ratings). In another American study published in the same year, Harding *et al.* (2003) compared methylphenidate with dietary supplementation. Ten children with ADHD received between 5 mg and 15 mg methylphenidate two to three times daily for four weeks, not having received it before the onset of the study. A comparison group of another ten children with ADHD received several nutritional supplements daily, including 1000 mg salmon oil, providing 180 mg EPA and 120 mg DHA, and 200 mg borage oil, providing 45 mg gamma-linolenic acid. Subjects in both groups showed significant gains in the Full Scale Response Control Quotient and the Full Scale Attention Control Quotient of the Intermediate Visual and Auditory/Continuous Performance Test. Their improvements in the four sub-quotients of the Intermediate Visual and Auditory/Continuous Performance Test, namely the Auditory Response Control Quotient, Visual Response

Control Quotient, Auditory Attention Quotient and Visual Attention Quotient, were also significant and essentially the same in both groups. A randomized double-blind placebo-controlled trial using a higher ratio of EPA to DHA, together with evening primrose oil, was that of Richardson and Puri (2002). In this study, 41 children with learning difficulties, mainly dyslexia, were recruited who also suffered from ADHD symptoms. Twenty-two of them received the following fatty acid supplementation daily: 864 mg linoleic acid, 96 mg gamma-linolenic acid, 42 mg arachidonic acid, 186 mg EPA and 480 mg DHA. The comparison group received olive oil (which, in retrospect, was a poor choice as olive oil may itself have beneficial actions – see Puri and Richardson, 2000). None of the children received stimulant medication during the course of this study. While being matched for symptoms at baseline, after three months the fatty acid group showed significant improvements, compared with the placebo group, on the following scales from the Conners' Parent Rating Scale (CRPS-L): Anxious-Shy, Cognitive Problems, Psychosomatic, Conners' Restless-Impulsive, Conners' Emotional Lability, Conners' Global Total, DSM Inattention, DSM Hyperactive-Impulsive, DSM Global Total. Finally, Richardson and Montgomery (2005) published the main findings from the large Oxford-Durham study in which 110 children who were not receiving any medication were randomized to receive either fatty acid supplementation or a placebo (olive oil). All the children had a DSM-IV-TR diagnosis of developmental coordination disorder and they all suffered from ADHD symptoms. The active group received the following daily doses of fatty acids for three months: 60 mg gamma-linolenic acid (from evening primrose oil), 558 mg EPA and 174 mg DHA. Again, while both the active and placebo groups were matched in terms of symptomatology at baseline, after three months the fatty acid group showed significant improvements, compared with the placebo group, on the following 12 (out of 13) scales of the Conners' Teacher Rating Scale (Revised: Long Form): Anxious-Shy, Oppositional, Cognitive Problems, Hyperactivity, Social Problems, Conners' ADHD Index, Conners' Restless-Impulsive, Conners' Emotional Lability, Conners' Global Total, DSM Inattention, DSM Hyperactive-Impulsive, DSM Global Total. There were also significant increases in the active group in auditory short-term memory.

Discussion
In summary, as the ratio of EPA to DHA increases, so the results from trials of omega-3 fatty acids become better. At one extreme, using

a ratio of zero (that is, with no EPA and just DHA in the supplementation) the fatty acid group actually fares worse than the placebo group. The omega-6 long-chain polyunsaturated fatty acid gamma-linolenic acid is also very important, and evening primrose oil is a good source of this. Therefore, an ideal supplement to use in ADHD is a combination of ultra-pure EPA (with no DHA present) and evening primrose oil.

Conclusions

While there are several adverse side-effects from conventional pharmacotherapy for ADHD, there appears to be good evidence in support of the alternative use of fatty acids and of removing artificial colourings from the diet. Based on the evidence detailed in this chapter, an ideal treatment would be to remove all artificial colourings and other additives from the diet, in combination with supplementation with ultra-pure EPA (with no DHA present) and evening primrose oil.

References

Aman, M. G., Mitchell, E. A. and Turbott, S. H. (1987) The effects of essential fatty acid supplementation by Efamol in hyperactive children, *Journal of Abnormal Child Psychology*, 15, 75–90.

Arnold, L. E., Kleykamp, D., Votolato, N. A., Taylor, W. A., Kontras, S. B. and Tobin, K. (1989) Gamma-linolenic acid for attention-deficit hyperactivity disorder: Placebo-controlled comparison to D-amphetamine, *Biological Psychiatry*, 25, 222–8.

Bateman, B., Warner, J. O., Hutchinson, E., Dean, T., Rowlandson, P., Grant, C., Grundy, J., Fitzgerald, C. and Stevenson, J. (2004) The effects of a double blind, placebo controlled, artificial food colourings and benzoate preservative challenge on hyperactivity in a general population sample of preschool children, *Archives of Disease in Childhood*, 89, 506–11.

Bradley, C. (1937) The behavior of children receiving Benzedrine, *American Journal of Psychiatry*, 94, 577–85.

Feingold, B. F. (1975) Hyperkinesis and learning disabilities linked to artificial food flavors and colors, *American Journal of Nursing*, 75, 797–803.

Harding, K. L., Judah, R. D. and Gant, C. E. (2003) Outcome-based comparison of Ritalin® versus food-supplement treated children with AD/HD, *Alternative Medicine Review*, 8, 319–30.

Hirayama, S., Hamazaki, T. and Terasawa, K. (2004) Effect of docosahexaenoic acid-containing food administration on symptoms of attention-deficit/hyperactivity disorder: A placebo-controlled double-blind study, *European Journal of Clinical Nutrition*, 58, 467–73.

Kavale, K. A. and Forness, S. R. (1983) Hyperactivity and diet treatment: A meta-analysis of the Feingold hypothesis, *Journal of Learning Disabilities*, 16, 324–30.

Puri, B. K. (2005) *Attention-Deficit Hyperactivity Disorder*. London: Hammersmith Press.

Puri, B. K. and Richardson, A. J. (2000) The effects of olive oil on ω3 fatty acids and mood disorder, *Archives of General Psychiatry*, 57, 715.

Richardson, A. J. and Montgomery, P. (2005) The Oxford-Durham study: A randomized, controlled trial of dietary supplementation with fatty acids in children with developmental coordination disorder, *Pediatrics*, 115, 1360–6.

Richardson, A. J. and Puri, B. K. (2000) The potential role of fatty acids in attention-deficit/hyperactivity disorder, *Prostaglandins, Leukotrienes and Essential Fatty Acids*, 63, 79–87.

Richardson, A. J. and Puri, B. K. (2002) A randomized double-blind, placebo-controlled study of the effects of supplementation with highly unsaturated fatty acids on ADHD-related symptoms in children with specific learning difficulties, *Progress in Neuropsychopharmacology and Biological Psychiatry*, 26, 233–9.

Schab, D. W. and Trinh, N.-H. T. (2004) Do artificial food colors promote hyperactivity in children with hyperactive syndromes? A meta-analysis of double-blind placebo-controlled trials, *Journal of Developmental and Behavioral Pediatrics*, 25, 423–34.

Shaywitz, B. A., Goldenring, J. R. and Wool, R. S. (1979) Effects of chronic administration of food colorings on activity levels and cognitive performance in developing rat pups treated with 6-hydroxydopamine, *Neurobehavioral Toxicology*, 1, 41–7.

Stevens, L. J., Zhang, W., Peck, L., Kuczek, T., Grevstad, N., Mahon, A., Zentall, S. S., Arnold, L. E. and Burgess, J. R. (2003) EFA supplementation in children with inattention, hyperactivity, and other disruptive behaviors, *Lipids*, 38, 1007–21.

Voigt, R. G., Llorente, A. M., Jensen, C. L., Fraley, J. K., Berretta, M. C. and Heird, W. C. (2001) A randomized, double-blind, placebo-controlled trial of docosahexaenoic acid supplementation in children with attention-deficit/hyperactivity disorder, *Journal of Pediatrics*, 139, 189–96.

Part IV

Alternative Paradigms for ADHD

Chapter 13

Mind Magic

Jon Jureidini

Introduction

ADHD represents a conceptual advance on hyperactivity and minimal brain dysfunction by formulating behaviour problems in terms
of deficits of attention and other executive functions (Barkley, 2001).
But brain functioning is more complex than the ADHD conceptualisa-
tion would have us believe. This chapter sets out how the concept of
self-regulation helps to make better sense of children's behaviour problems. I argue that the behaviourally disturbed child is compromised in
his capacity to use his imagination to deal with his predicament. He
therefore signals his need for outside help with self-regulation through
displays of affect, and/or seemingly dysfunctional behaviours.

According to the approach to behaviour disorders in children that
might be characterized as the DSM approach, the emphasis is on listing
symptoms rather than listening to what families might be able to tell us
about themselves (American Psychiatric Association, 2000). If enough
symptoms on the ADHD list can be ticked, a diagnosis is made, as long
as functional impairment, pervasiveness and persistence are present.
Once made, a DSM diagnosis is stable – the condition can remit or go
away but there is little scope to look for a better explanation for the
list of symptoms. Rather, diagnoses tend to accumulate, so that failure
to respond to ADHD treatment often leads to additional diagnoses like
oppositional defiant disorder, conduct disorder and anxiety disorder.

DSM is biased to attribute symptoms to inattention. For example, the symptom 'often has difficulty sustaining attention in tasks
or play activities' falls under Inattention, even though there are other
common reasons for failure to complete tasks (for example, not understanding what is required). It would be more desirable to group

the DSM symptoms with less presupposition about their causes, for example:

- overactive and noisy (all six symptoms listed under the heading of Hyperactivity);
- clumsy with cues ('often does not seem to listen when spoken to directly'; 'is often forgetful in daily activities', 'is often easily distracted by extraneous stimuli', all symptoms listed under Impulsivity); and
- avoids or fails to complete tasks (most symptoms under Inattention).

Ambiguities about definition and threshold remain, as they always will when a syndrome is characterized by a pattern of behaviours rather than pathognomic signs or symptoms. But at least we purge the DSM criteria of unjustified inferences about the specifics of the underlying cognitive dysfunction. This chapter takes the position that the symptoms of ADHD and the dysfunction that accompanies them constitute a final common pathway for multiple possible sources of distress and disturbance. That the behavioural pattern exists is not disputed; the symptoms can be readily and reliably identified and have been the subject of thousands of published papers. But reliability does not confer validity, and what is disputed is that 'ADHD' offers an adequate explanation for most children presenting with these symptoms.

An alternative approach – behaviour disorders as manifestations of dysregulation

The prevailing view is that the cognitive dysfunction underlying all or most of the symptoms of ADHD is a failure of those executive functions responsible for inhibiting a dominant response to perform a subdominant one (Barkley, 2001). This is sometimes described as a failure in self-regulation. It is important to distinguish my use of the term 'self-regulation' from that of Barkley, who refers to a range of inhibitory executive functions involved in focussed attention and delayed gratification, for which 'self-control' might be a better label. My approach has more in common with that of Fonagy and colleagues who highlight the role of interpersonal relationships, regulation of arousal and mentalization (in my terms, imagination) in maintaining cognitive and emotional integrity (Fonagy *et al.*, 2002). Self-regulation is performed both by the self directly and by using others in *relationships*. Just as parents and other adults must take responsibility for ensuring an infant is warm, well-fed and safe, a child is dependent on others to help manage arousal in a changing environment. Telling and being told stories, being held (physically and emotionally) and the parental capacity to reflect, all contribute to self-regulation. Moderate *arousal* in a supportive context enhances function and future adaptation. Repeated or overwhelming over-arousal damages the brain in a way that undermines the capacity to manage arousal. This affective dysregulation often manifests as increasing impulsivity, aggression and reduced cognitive efficiency (Fonagy *et al.*, 2002). But intense physical activity and displays of distress or anger can all serve self-regulation. These behaviours are not necessarily manifestations of failed function, but may represent attempts by the individual to achieve regulation in the face of some dysregulating influence (usually some source of unmanageable arousal). They are therefore, in the first instance, adaptive and communicative.

Most often, children's problematic behaviour is conceptualised as either simply naughty or as being symptomatic of ADHD or some other disorder. Children whom clinicians see with behavioural problems are at varying stages in the process of developing the capacity to regulate their arousal. They will be experiencing family and broader environments that will be more or less self-regulating. Exploring the impact of a broader range of cognitive and environmental factors on self-regulation offers a more meaningful understanding of apparently unproductive behaviour than does ADHD. It might also offer a way of thinking about the use of medication in dealing with children's behaviour, not as a specific treatment for a mental illness, but as a temporary strategy to dampen arousal or to increase opportunities to experience the self–environment relationship differently and more positively.

What resources are required to self-regulate?

Adults don't usually think of themselves as magicians: can you hypnotize yourself, read minds, time travel? Unless you have autism, you do more of this than you might think. All of these are magical skills, in that they call on imagination to change things in the real world. Children need to be magicians at times, and as adults (parents, teachers, clinicians) we need to be able to use our imagination to change their worlds for them. *Hypnosis* is a special example of the capacity to focus the attention on one set of stimuli and avoid attending to others that are potentially more engaging. Concentrating on a video game does not test this important kind of attention because by their nature video games capture attention. The demands of the classroom are different. Often what is on offer from the teacher is less potentially stimulating than things that are happening around the room, out of the window or in the child's head. We assume it is in the child's best interests to attend to the prescribed task; this is not always so. As Jensen *et al.* (1997) have argued, the special cognitive state required to focus attention on one set of stimuli is opposed by any need to scan the environment for danger or opportunity (response-readiness). Only when we can be confident of our physical and social safety, or that no unique opportunity will unexpectedly present itself, does it make sense for us to sacrifice response-readiness for focused attention. Ideally the classroom is just such a setting, but this is not always the case.

Children's optimal capacity for focussed attention limits but does not determine how they will perform in any given situation. If a child seems unable to sustain attention for more than a few minutes, that may reflect incapacity. It may also mean that some other factor is making him perform below his capacity for focussed attention, or heightening his response-readiness. A child with learning difficulties will attend better in the classroom if the teacher understands her difficulties and if she is secure at home. She will be less well regulated if she is hungry, forgets her glasses or is being bullied. So a primary deficit in attention is but one explanation for a child not completing tasks or responding to cues. Amongst the other internal factors that can contribute to similar patterns of behaviour is deficient *mindreading*. It helps social functioning to be able to predict and understand others' behaviours in terms of their thoughts and feelings (Theory of Mind). A complete failure to do so will result in an inability to engage with others, as is the case for severely autistic individuals. Autistic children may be unworried by their mindreading failure, but children with lesser degrees of difficulty with mindreading do become hyper-aroused as a consequence of their inability to make sense of other peoples' behaviour. This in turn leads to task non-completion, unresponsiveness to social cues, and overactivity. For example:

Nine-year-old Freddie asks a question in class. Kylie interrupts as the teacher is beginning to answer. The teacher sounds irritated when she answers Freddie. Freddie, failing to guess that the teacher's irritation is explained by Kylie's interruption, experiences the teacher as irritated with him. If the teacher is able to correctly mindread Freddie's distress, she can take corrective action to reassure him.

Mental *time travel* is the capacity to call on memories of previous experiences and to anticipate the future in the service of dealing with current demands and distress. As adults we often have difficulty empathizing with how readily children become 'lost in the moment'. They may, at least temporarily, become incapable of seeing that things will change with time. Thus, the seemingly undemanding expectation that a child should be able to see out the last five minutes to the end of class may not be realistic for a distraught ten-year-old. The teacher will need to scaffold the child's capacity to see into the future. On the other hand, a child might be involuntarily propelled into some other time. A vivid traumatic memory might intrude, and be difficult to put aside in the interests of participation in whatever is going on in class. Or it may be overarousing in a way that cannot be managed mentally, but instead results in (hyper)activity.

A fourth form of mind magic is the capacity to *tell stories*. Telling stories, even factual recounts, is an active, imaginative process that requires the bringing together of memories, feeling and knowledge. It helps us both to make sense of and to manage the arousal associated with ordinary, potentially distressing experiences, thereby enhancing social and academic function. Children need to be able to organize their experience into meaningful (coherent and cohesive) reportable episodes – to see that things have a beginning, middle and an end. We begin to learn to tell stories from earliest infancy. Just as he will later develop the ability to parse speech into meaningful segments even though the cues for this are not available in the gaps/spacing in ordinary speech, the four-month-old can abstract episodes with narrative structure. The fundamental shape of narrative is attractive to her, and she favours the crescendo–peak–decrescendo shape of tension build-up and release that characterizes the peek-a-boo game over other interpersonal interactions (Rochat *et al.*, 1999). We know that infants at this age can grasp agency and causal relationships, and it seems that they can further pick out, from all the input received from internal and external environments, those things that belong together, and to recognize the beginning and end of episodes that have such structure. But the need for parental scaffolding persists throughout the pre-school years and beyond for linguistic narratives (Nelson, 2000). Complex emotionally laden experiences are more likely to overwhelm a child who does not have a resilient capacity to organize these events into stories. In the simple example described above, Freddie's ability to make sense of his experience and of subsequent similar experiences will be enhanced if he can tell himself a story about his teacher's interaction with himself and Kylie. His capacity to do so might be enhanced if his teacher tells him the story of what just happened.

It is obvious that none of these aspects of mind magic is free standing. The greater the capacity for self-hypnosis, the more effective will be the ability to create coherent cohesive stories, a task that would in turn be made more difficult by an incapacity to mindread other peoples emotional responses. Remember also that the capacity for any of these cognitive skills/mind magic will be different according to the emotional circumstances. What a child *can* do does not predict what they *will* do, especially under pressure. Children may be able to use their imaginations to self-regulate when under no emotional pressure but lose their capacity to do so when distressed. Whenever children become compromised in their capacity to read minds, they rely on our capacity as adults to understand their distress and help compensate for their difficulties.

Given the importance of imagination to children's cognitive and emotional development, it is vital to understand how adults might facilitate or stifle the development of imagination in early childhood. It is our duty as parents, carers, educators and therapists to respond to children's communication. To do so facilitates all development, including better behaviour management. Children develop mind magic out of the capacity of those around them to do it for them. They learn to read their own and other minds by having their minds read to them by others (Vygotsky, 1966).

Adult help comes in two forms:

(1) The capacity of the adult to make the child feel sufficiently safe to function, while at the same time supporting their need to explore and develop mastery. In infancy this factor is manifest in the parents' capacity to provide a secure base. As the child grows older and its circle of adult support widens other adults contribute, for example, child-care workers and teachers. Ongoing attachment experiences determine the secure-base behaviour that allows the child to make good choices about how to respond to ambiguous circumstances that may carry danger or opportunity. This in turn will contribute to the development of the child's own capacity for self-regulation (Meins *et al.*, 2002).

(2) The capacity of the adult to assist directly with mind magic for the child, for example, scaffolding narrative, helping to focus attention, reading and interpreting the child's thoughts and feelings and providing a temporal perspective when the child is caught in the moment.

A child's development corresponds with an increasing capacity to hold herself together without adult help, but even adults are not independent self-regulators, and under pressure, seek or elicit regulating responses from others. For example, if we are fortunate, an irrational outburst of impatience after a frustrating day at work will elicit a hug, a gin or a timely challenge, all of which potentially help us to recover our capacity to regulate ourselves. Regulation of others is not only from adult to child; for example, an infant's apparent over-activity might have the effect of enlivening a depressed parent (Stern, 1985). Although children are more likely than adults to act rather than think, self-regulation through action remains an option in adult life. For example, on hearing the distressing sound of a crying baby from an adjacent hotel room, we might attempt to manage our increasing arousal by distracting ourselves from the sound through focusing on something else (cognitive strategy). We might also act by leaving the room (action). In different circumstances different action and thinking strategies will have different costs and benefits.

Behaviour should be understood, before it is managed

Children who present with behaviour problems are often prone to unregulated displays of affect, in particular angry outbursts or tantrums. It is common for others to respond to such angry behaviours in an antagonistic way. Such antagonistic responses might result from an understandable misreading of the angry communication. Anger not only stakes territory or challenges authority, to which the appropriate response is fight, submission or flight. Angry behaviour can also be a signal to a potential caregiver that things are not right and require correction. No-one should think that the angry cry of a hungry baby is a signal to leave the baby alone. Too often angry or aggressive displays by children are received as 'go-away' anger rather than 'help-me' anger, to which the appropriate response is protective and/or regulatory behaviours from potential caregivers. Children are often clumsy in their perception, expression and understanding of their own feelings. It is not uncommon for a child who might be expected to be experiencing fear or sadness to behave in an apparently angry fashion. It is our responsibility as adults to do better at reading the child's affective state and to recognise that anger may signal the need for increased comfort and reassurance rather than combat.

Because behavioural symptoms need not be manifestations of failed cognitive functions, but can be active attempts to achieve regulation in the face of unmanageable arousal, we might question the common clinical response of trying to eliminate 'bad' behaviour, either with medication or behaviour modification. What then is the place of behaviour modification in responding to dysregulated children? All animals are constantly responding to rewards and punishments (or, in more sophisticated animals, the *possibility* of rewards and punishments). Unfortunately, the most obvious behaviours and contingencies are not always the most important ones, and more covert rewards and punishments are operating below our awareness. Adding external systematized rewards or punishments will be effective only to the extent that it achieves sufficient status in the existing mental economy, especially by resonating with and amplifying existing reward/punishment systems. Behavioural programmes will be more useful when the target behaviour is read in its emotional, cognitive, and environmental context (such as the quality of the child's relationship with teachers).

Behavioural interventions mainly work by increasing motivation. Interventions are more effective when the child feels a sense of mastery from the achievement of success. Increased motivation often breeds success through extra *effort* being invested in overcoming difficulties, so that interventions will be less successful if effort is already being expended at high levels. We have only so much effort available to us; a child who is pre-occupied with managing his distress about his father's violence towards his mother is unlikely to be able to expend much extra effort on academic pursuits, no matter how well designed the behaviour modification programme. Behavioural interventions will also be less successful if the child is fearful of the task. Children *can* be persuaded by sufficient rewards and punishments to undertake feared tasks, but unless such situations are properly managed, increased exposure to fear will increase anxiety and increase avoidance.

Once a child has learnt by association that a given situation is dangerous, he will avoid that situation. But avoiding something scary has the potential to make a child *more* scared the next time he is threatened with exposure to it; the more he avoids a feared situation, the worse it gets. On the other hand, by staying in the feared situation until the fear has subsided a child may learn that it is not so dangerous. Fear/avoidance can generalize to affect other areas that are not a direct source of anxiety. For example, a child with a specific learning disability can come to experience all academic tasks as anxiety provoking even though his particular difficulties may only be in a circumscribed area. The cue for generalization could be the task similarity (solving a problem) or environmental (pen and paper, the room, the teacher).

Conceptualizing a piece of behaviour as meaningless or the manifestation of some psychiatric or medical disorder will lead us towards a conditioning approach. We do better to seek the cause of a child's fear or avoidance. If there are good grounds for this fear, we will want to change the circumstances. If not, we will want to help the child to become less sensitive to his fear through gradual exposure to the feared situation, whether the signal for anxiety is a conditioned stimulus (the classroom for a child with learning disability), or whether the fear is unconditioned (the pain associated with grief can elicit avoidance without any conditioning). Sometimes specific desensitization programmes are needed, but often the recognition of fear and avoidance is enough:

> *A bright boy with a previously undiagnosed receptive language disorder was intermittently behaving badly in class. It was established that his problem behaviour tended to be triggered when the teacher gave instructions to the class. Once it was recognized that he had language difficulties, it could be seen that his earliest problems arose when his teacher gave complex verbal instructions. He had learnt that the negative arousal associated with the humiliation of feeling stupid when he could not understand her could be lessened by playing the fool. That had now become his first response to any scenario that reminded him of situations in which he had felt foolish. Once the teacher understood his predicament she was able to read his mind more readily and modify her responses to him. His behaviour changed without his being placed on any programme.*

Thoughtful strategies

When a child presents with some combination of overactivity, failure to complete tasks and social unresponsiveness, the first question should not be 'Does this child have ADHD?' Rather it should be 'What is this child's predicament?' (Taylor, 1979). The task is to listen rather than to list, to trawl the history for *clues* rather than *symptoms*. Assume that the behaviours represent an attempt to self-regulate (hold it together) in the face of some inner or outer threat, or as a way of avoiding that threat.

Thoughtful questions to ask when faced with troublesome behaviour include:

(1) Is the child physically or cognitively compromised?
(2) Is the child distracted by events in the environment or inner worries?

(3) Is the behaviour having the effect of allowing the child to avoid some feared event or challenge?

In most cases the answer to these questions will identify a clear focus for intervention, through some combination of:

(1) scaffold the child's capacity for mind magic
(2) altering the environment to make it less dysregulating
(3) providing a structured, graded programme to achieve gradual mastery over fears.

Conclusion

Self-regulation is a more complex concept than executive function. It also offers a more productive way of understanding problematic behaviour as both a communication of the child's emotional state and a fall-back coping strategy to manage over-arousal when imagination fails. The child who behaves badly or expresses unregulated feelings is telling us that things are not right in his life and or that his capacity to use imagination to manage his arousal has been exceeded. If this behaviour is problematic for others we know that, at least temporarily, those around him have not been able to scaffold his imagination and contain his feelings. A clinician will be most useful to the child and his family when she uses her own imagination to help make sense of why this particular child presents with this pattern of behaviour at this time.

References

American Psychiatric Association (2000) *Diagnostic and Statistical Manual – Text Revision* (DSM-IV-TR™, 2000). American Psychiatric Association.

Barkley, R. A. (2001) The executive functions and self-regulation: an evolutionary neuropsychological perspective, *Neuropsychology Review*, 11, 1–29

Fonagy, P., Target, M., Gergely, G. and Jurist, E. J. (2002) *Affect Regulation, Mentalization and the Development of the Self*. New York: Other Press.

Jensen, P. S., Mrazek, D., Knapp, P. K., Steinberg, L., Pfeffer, C., Schowalter, J. and Shapiro, T. (1997) Evolution and revolution in child psychiatry: ADHD as a disorder of adaptation, *Journal of the American Academy of Child and Adolescent Psychiatry*, 36, 1672–9.

Meins, E., Fernyhough, C., Wainwright, R., Das Gupta, M., Fradley, E. and Tuckey, M. (2002) Maternal mind-mindedness and attachment security as predictors of theory of mind understanding, *Child Development*, 73, 1715–26.

Nelson, K. (2000) Memory and belief in development, in D. L. Schacter and E. Scarry (eds), *Memory, Brain and Belief*. Cambridge, MA: Harvard University Press.

Rochat, P., Querido, J.G. and Striano, T. (1999) Emerging sensitivity to the timing and structure of protoconversation in early infancy, *Developmental Psychology*, 35, 950–7.

Stern, D. (1985) *The Interpersonal World of the Infant: A View from Psychoanalysis and Developmental Psychology*. New York, Basic Books.

Taylor, D. (1979) The components of sickness: Diseases, illnesses, and predicaments, *The Lancet*, 2, 1008–10.

Vygotsky, L. (1966/1976) Play and its role in the mental development of the child, *Soviet Psychology*, 12, 62–76. (Reprinted in English in *Play: Its Role in Development and Evolution*, ed. J. Bruner, A. Jolly and K. Sylva. New York: Penguin.)

Chapter 14

ADHD and Other Sins of Our Children[1]

Simon Sobo

Introduction

A case is made that the symptoms of ADHD describe children when they cannot connect to imposed expectations. In the classroom, they don't feel part of the group. Unlike the other students, they aren't trying to do what the teacher is directing them to do. They are out of the flow. Even if they began the morning with good intentions, once boredom and restlessness take hold, all bets are off. Those who fear the consequences of making a disturbance drift off into daydreams, or look around the classroom for almost anything that might entertain them. Those with more spark can't sit still and they make a lot of noise.

Bored, trapped children have always acted this way. The challenge of how to motivate children so they don't feel subjugated when an activity is not about them and when the expectations of others are the agenda, has challenged educators and parents for as long as children have been forced to go to school. A variety of factors can contribute to difficulty concentrating, not least of which is the fact that getting any child motivated to learn, work, and be responsible is always a challenge. Enormous outpourings of parental time and energy are expended on children trying to inspire, cajole, threaten, lecture, or bribe them to buy in. The message is universal. They must stop dilly dallying, gain self control, act with consideration for others, and like it or not, do tasks demanded of them. In America, every generation has a new philosophy of child rearing that advocates different strategies. Books, newspapers, and magazines are filled with good advice, which is a sure indication there are no simple solutions.

In the past, it was assumed that the successful development of the capacity to learn how to work begins very early, with good habits inculcated as soon as possible, and later reminders repeated as necessary. Shaming the child, inducing a fear of punishment, many of today's no-nos were never proudly proclaimed, but whether acknowledged or not, they were assumed to be an unfortunate necessity, indeed, often a crucial part of the mix – spare the rod, spoil the child. The trick was how to instil proper fear without breaking a child's spirit. It was not unlike turning a wild bronco into a proud steed. How do you transform an easily frustrated little package of misdirected energy into a young gentleman or lady, bringing pride to his or her parents and teachers, and self-satisfaction from a job well done?

How do you prepare children to keep a cool head when a task is challenging, or competition is keen? How much guilt is useful before it backfires or is received as 'blah-blah blah'? Encouragement is essential but it can deteriorate into empty cheerleading, or worse, false happy talk that is thinly disguised nagging.

Keeping a step ahead of children is the first rule for both parents and teachers, but it isn't always easy. Harnessing a force of nature is never a sure thing. When children dominate they can return to their natural state – frenetic entropy that can be observed in schoolyards whenever they are playing a game without rules. Two or three generations ago, completely unsentimental views of children's natural tendencies were commonplace, and acted on. For instance, grammar school students were asked to sit with their hands clasped on the desk straight in front of them. 'Attention!!!!' sergeants in the army scream at their young recruits. Good first- and second-grade teachers usually had a certain firm tone that the students understood to mean 'no more fooling around'. Here and there, even in the past, inspiring teachers could go easy on the rules and didn't need a commanding voice. However, the average teacher policed the classroom for any signs of noise or movement. If needed, a sharp comment from them could snap a student out of his reveries. Evidence for the necessity of discipline was easy to find. In the event that a teacher stepped out of the classroom, chaos erupted like a volcano.

Connecting to a child at home, so that he or she 'listens', precedes the greater challenges in the classroom. If parents fail to accomplish this at home the problems will only get worse at school. There are numerous ways this can go amuck, particularly in modern times. It was once understood that children need a safe nest when learning to fly. Fathers and mothers used to stay together in loveless marriages, not always because the family, *per se*, was sacred, but because divorce was considered too disruptive for the children. That is no longer the case. Unfortunately, marital discord in an intact family can be just as undermining. In some homes, the tensions at home are so overpowering that there is little energy left for school's requirements.

The difficulties are not always on the surface, and the results can be complicated. Withdrawn depressed parents, broken by circumstance, can convey a helplessness that plays havoc with a child's ability to feel mastery and concentration when meeting school's challenges. Drugs, alcohol, incest, physical abuse, a long list of horrendous home environments, can make school requirements irrelevant. Severe chronic physical illnesses in a family member can do the same thing. But the opposite can also occur. Occasionally, school becomes a haven, the one place where the child finds purpose.

Poorly functioning day-care centres can get a child off to a terrible start, especially if child-care workers come and go, or children are moved from one centre to another. Some parents desperately search for the right place, hoping to approximate a stable underpinning that will foster the bonding that will be so crucial when effort is called for. In some families overwhelming pressures to excel can be brought to bear on a student. Repeatedly being a disappointment to one or both parents can hurt deeply enough so that tuning out can bring relief from the anxiety and pain of trying and failing. On more than one occasion I have seen a situation when one of the two children is the star, and the other, almost by necessity has given up.

The problems can also be less dramatic. Parents know the appearance of a distracted child. The moment they start to lecture, one look at the child and they know he, or she, has gone to another place and time. Some loving mothers have great difficulty being forceful enough to get their children in line. It is not unusual to find ADHD children who misbehave with their mothers, ignoring all admonitions, but do not behave this way with their father. They wouldn't dare. It can also go the other way with fathers as the sugar daddy and mothers as the successful taskmaster. Some children, particularly in divorce situations (where parental guilt may be enormous) can wrap their parents around their pinkie. Then there is of course the 'baby of the family.' Standards get less and less with each child until finally the baby is overindulged, expecting to be given rather than asked to perform. The consequences become clear over time.

Obviously, there are many ways that children can become a casualty of unsuccessful parenting. ADHD is only one of the by products.

Because the impairment is similar, regardless of what caused it, we may question whether it is appropriate to paint with broad brush strokes, to label the problem as a single 'illness'. There are arguments for and against. But one unfortunate result of the illness model as an explanation for these kids is that doctors (or 'experts' as they call themselves) have stepped forward with a simple 'cure'. No surprises here. If all you have is a hammer every problem becomes a nail. By assigning a diagnosis, and supplying a sciency explanation for the phenomenon, the problem reduces to what doctors do. They give drugs.

We cannot entirely dismiss this approach. A small number of those labelled with ADHD may have something physically wrong with their brains. An example, at the extreme, is mentally retarded or brain-damaged children, who, for obvious reasons, have great difficulties sitting still for hours at a time and staying on task. Historically, neurologists believed that a minimal brain dysfunction was the culprit. They looked for minor neurological defects that might bolster their argument. It is not unreasonable to expect that some children, today labelled ADHD, may have a still undetectable genetic or biological problem, yet don't have clear-cut neurological symptoms. But, ADHD has become a major social phenomenon, a catch-all for most distracted children not paying attention in school, or doing as expected. It has long since expanded beyond neurologists and the idea of 'minimal brain dysfunction'. Millions upon millions of children are now routinely labelled with ADHD. Indeed, by the time a doctor gets involved, a child's teacher has probably made the diagnosis and knows the cure.

This would all be fine if solid research supported the argument that ADHD is a biological illness. But the evidence is sparse or ridiculously exaggerated. Not that there haven't been thousands upon thousands of articles seeming to confirm that ADHD is biological. However, the fact is that the cause is still unknown (Horton, 2004; National Institutes of Health, 1998). Moreover, for an illness whose aetiology is repeatedly and confidently claimed to be biological, there is not a single biological test that can be used to determine whether or not a child has ADHD. Nothing in the urine, the blood, the spinal fluid, no X rays or CAT scans or MRI (see Chapters 1, 2, and 3). Poppycock flourishes when we need answers to a problem, but don't have them. It is a tool of aggressive salesmen. Expert doctors trump the opinions of ordinary physicians who don't have time to give long and complex thought to all of their patients' problems.

One striking bit of evidence against the argument that ADHD results from a biologically caused deficit in the ability to pay attention, is the simple fact that most of these children have no difficulty keeping their attention focused on activities that are fun. Many can sit for hours with video games that require extraordinary focus. I evaluated a student who told me his mind completely fogged over when he had to read something for school. Without his medicine he could go over a page a hundred times and absorb nothing. 'Really?' I asked, 'You aren't able to read anything?' 'Well,' he told me, 'there is one exception.' He was totally into mountain biking. Each month his mountain biking magazine arrived and he devoured that without medicine.

The medical cure for ADHD patients' inability to confront drudgery is stimulants, which have a long history of working pretty well for this purpose. Most of the drugs work similarly to cocaine. In the nineteenth century cocaine was the most popular miracle drug in the world, regularly used and extolled by the likes of President McKinley, Queen Victoria, Pope Leo XIII, Thomas Edison, Robert Lewis Stevenson, Ibsen, Anatole France and a host of other renowned members of society.[2] Sigmund Freud wrote the following about it, 'You perceive an increase of self-control and possess more vitality and capacity for work.'[3] According to the Sears, Roebuck and Co. Consumers' Guide (1900), their extraordinary Peruvian Wine of Coca 'sustains and refreshes both the body and brain... It may be taken at any time with perfect safety... it has been effectually proven that in the same space of time more than double the amount of work could be undergone when Peruvian Wine of Coca was used, and positively no fatigue experienced.'

After he read this article, my son, who was then at Yale, told me that one afternoon he was complaining about the work he had before him, two finals and three papers that were due. His schoolmate piped in, 'I got some Ritalin™, want it?' The daughter of a friend said the same thing was going on at McGill. They are not alone. Here are some headlines from the *New York Times*:[4]

'Latest Campus High: Illicit use of Prescription Medication, Experts and Students Say.'

'Ritalin™ makes repetitive, boring tasks like cleaning your room seem fun' said Josh Koenig a 20 year old drama major from NYU.

'Katherinen Plyshevsky, 21, a junior from New Milford NJ majoring in marketing at NYU said she used Ritalin™ obtained from a friend with ADHD to get through her midterms 'It was actually fun to do the work,' she said.

Freud realized he had made a big mistake advocating the use of cocaine when he witnessed the horrible effects it was having on some of his friends. The downside of this miracle drug was also well described by Robert Lewis Stevenson, who wrote Dr. Jekyll and Mr. Hyde during seven days and nights while he was high on cocaine. For many years, Stephen King wrote all of his novels while high on stimulants. He has said that the Kathy Bates character in his 'Misery' (a nurse who has literally imprisoned him) represented that habit.

Besides ADHD diagnosed adolescents, and their friends, who sometimes borrow their meds when they have to do chores that they dread, stimulants ('greenies'), according to David Wells (Wells *et al*, 2003), and more recently Mike Schmidt (2006), have long been part of the professional athletes' equipment, helping them to step up to the plate with confidence. It changes their state of mind from a passive, reactive, position to a take-charge, proactive stance. Or as one basketball player put it, 'Give me the ball. I can make the shot.' This taking charge, 'I can do it' feeling, when approaching tasks, is a key element in most people's perception of whether they are up to a challenge, and whether it is 'work' or pleasurable.

The use of medication should not be dismissed out of hand. From a strictly practical standpoint, stimulants are very often helpful. But the propaganda surrounding their use, generated by 'experts', lacks intellectual integrity. Considering the controversial nature of this issue, who pays for experts' work, should ordinarily disqualify them from claiming to speak objectively. Billions upon billions of dollars are at stake for drug companies, depending on whether or not ADHD is proven to be biological. Are those sufficient motives for their paid experts to, not only lose proper scientific caution, but also become aggressive about selling a point of view that profits their sponsors? The former editor of the New England Journal of Medicine (NEJM), Marcia Angell, wrote an editorial entitled, 'Is Academic Medicine for Sale?' (Angell, 2000). She followed this with an impassioned book, 'The Truth about the Drug Companies: How They Deceive Us and What to Do about It' (Angell, 2004). The editor of the British equivalent of the NEJM, *The Lancet*, wrote in the *New York Review of Books*, 'Journals have devolved into information laundering operations for the pharmaceutical industry' (Horton, 2004).

Despite these criticisms, 'experts' continue to churn out article after article placing pressure on non-experts to follow their 'guidelines.' The effect is, unfortunately, that most doctors, at least in the United States, follow these guidelines unthinkingly, given that they are written by professors who hold prestigious positions in many of the finest universities in the United States. Medical practitioners, like everyone else, are very busy and must go on faith for many of their decisions. In addition, we cannot ignore groupthink, which has a way of determining acceptable and unacceptable points of view.

There is also a problem with the DSM IV paradigm (Sobo, 2001).[5] DSM IV was meant to define and categorize clusters of symptoms in a clear-cut way. While that has its merits, it has also encouraged an illusion that these clusters are like 'strept' throat, a disease that can be cured with a drug like penicillin. There we understand the cause and the cure is a rational response to it. Despite the public's general impression, and the assured pronouncements of the experts, we do not possess that kind of understanding in psychiatry in general and ADHD in particular. Modest, tentative formulations would be far more appropriate.

In good part, this chapter is a description of my upbringing and how we were motivated by our parents to forsake our more natural ADHD tendencies and do well in school. It describes a far from perfect environment, but one, nevertheless, that was culturally coherent. Purpose was clearly defined, a quality in far shorter supply in our more chaotic modern existence. It is much harder for parents to create this today, lacking a cultural milieu which fosters it. I believe my memories (and speculations!!) may be helpful as a contrast to current very different perspectives about how parents approach their children. One thing is clear. The problems that ADHD imply will not go away with a change in diet, tough love, soft love or any other bit of magic, even the magic offered by those claiming to speak in the name of science. I believe that bad science, science totally lacking science's clarity about what is known and not known, is worse than sensible, if imprecise, literary speculations and reasoning.

A memory

Fifty-three years ago. I'm ten years old and I am trying to listen to a sermon in the synagogue. The rabbi has a firm, sweet, modulated voice, commanding, wise, a radio voice they used to call it. The problem is I can't listen. He fades right out. At best, I'm good for two or three words, maybe a sentence but after that I'm gone. I've been stuck in the same seat for what feels like hours. I stayed with the rabbi for the first five minutes but now it is ten minutes after he lost me.

Very lightly my feet begin to tap on the floor. The sound is barely audible. A worshipper across the aisle, a man in his 50s, glares at me. Only silence is allowed in the synagogue. I stop tapping. I sit still. But not long after that I move around in my seat. At most, the only sound I am making is from the wool of my jacket rubbing against itself. It doesn't matter. The man's anger goes up another notch. I sit absolutely still. But within a minute or two, unconsciously I stretch my fingers and crack one of my knuckles. This brings a look that could kill. He is joined by his wife who views me with utter disgust. They seem to have found a mission for the morning. Educate me in the ways of God. The first communication:

Or else!

It has never occurred to me to find out what 'or else' might actually be. My parents wisely left that to my imagination, a far more effective tool than actual punishment. So I take their disapproving stares seriously. I try harder to listen to the rabbi, this time as hard as anyone could try to listen to another person.

I have no better luck. A few sentences and I'm gone again. I finger a cuticle on my thumb, rub it, and start to pick at it. I nip at a tiny piece of the cuticle, which winds up tearing in the process. It smarts. It oozes cherry red. I suck on my finger, than take it out to see if blood is forming. It isn't, but I suck the finger again, just to be sure. The rabbi's voice becomes passionate. He may be nearing his finale. Suddenly I can listen without difficulty.

I'm wrong. The rabbi is shameless. He is fond of mini crescendos, playing in the foothills before taking a shot at the lofty heights of the majestic.

Only a false ending is the one thing I cannot put up with. He won't fool me again. I'm really gone. The person across the aisle glares at me more than he has all morning. What am I doing now? I have been 1000 % silent and still. I have bothered no one.

There is no choice. I take on the expression of several of the most pious listeners in my row. Devotion emanates from them and by osmosis soon my expression resembles theirs. He has won. I have joined the others.

But, my furtive eyes reveal the truth. They dart around the room.

High up the stained-glass windows portray Moses holding the Ten Commandments menacingly above his head. He looks stern, just like the man across the aisle. However, the windows are very beautiful. Moses' deep blue robe glows lit up by the sun. His eyes have a luminescent intensity that shoots straight out at the congregation – straight at me. A serpentine black line twists and turns, wiggles its way across the window. On to the next panel, then the next, 'til the line comes to an end. I find another line and follow it but that soon grows old. A hair is growing out of a mole on the back of the neck of the person in front of me. It's gross but it's kind of interesting. Until, it isn't interesting. It's just gross. I'm beginning to run out of ways to make the time go faster.

In a prison, rules are a very serious business. In the synagogue they are taken more seriously then any other place I know. Actually, it is worse than prison. The silence rule doesn't apply there. Here it is total. The only exception is when you pray.

No talking unless you are talking to God.

Rule two. You cannot get up and go somewhere else when you feel like it. Like it or not you must remain in your seat, stand when you are told to stand, sit back down when they tell you to be seated. And I have described how when you are seated you can't move around, which is torture. I like to move around. So do all my friends.

Being dressed up isn't helping the cause either; I'm beginning to sweat. My starched collar is too tight around my neck. If I could open my collar that would definitely help. That isn't allowed. This is God's house – his rules. The only time I saw an open collar was when Mr. Gordon had a heart attack. The sick are allowed to do all kinds of things that everyone else cannot do. God is fair. He allows this. But I have no excuse, so the collar is to stay buttoned and tight. Rule 3. Rule 4, 5, 6; in addition to no noise, no whining, no questions. Unnumbered rule but the most important one; synagogue is a sacred place so act accordingly.

> I whisper to my mother,
> 'What time is it?'
> She puts her fingers to her lips.
> I persist.
> She mouths the words.
> '10 AM.'
> 'Ten?' I whisper back.
> 'Shhh'
> She turns back to the rabbi.

Two hours 'til the services will be over. I look around for something else to do but I can't find anything. I keep looking around. The man in front of me adjusts his skull cap. He's wearing a watch. 10:02. Ten-o-two! Jeez. Only two minutes have passed.

I saw this movie on TV. The hero is alone in a dungeon. He's not been outside his cell in twelve years. The only sound he hears is a drop of water every five or ten seconds. At times the hero (maybe it was Errol Flynn) studies each drop as it forms on the ceiling, exuding out of mildewed stones into a fully formed droplet. Drip. The process is repeated...Drip. Everyday the same, the same, the same. I estimate the drips in a minute: eight on average, times 60 minutes, times 24 hours, times 365 days. Over 4 million in a year, around 50 million over 12 years.

Drip.

Camera on a mouse positioned safely against the dungeon's wall, slowly moving forward, sniffing, looking, and listening for danger, eyes shooting pictures in every direction, whiskers acting like feelers as he moves forward. Our hero is delighted to have company. For Errol Flynn almost anything different would be like finding a pot of gold. Two hours is like two years when you're 10 years old. Anything other than the sermon, or the hairy mole, the stained glass windows, or the wood grain of the seats in front of me. Anything not old would be gold.

It wasn't always boring at the synagogue. Sometimes it was fun. We'd invent games. For example, every time we got to the Shmonah Esrai, a very long prayer which is read silently, we raced each other to see who'd finish first. No cheating. You had to read every word. At one point you have to bow, knees first, then your chest parallels the floor, then down goes your head, then up comes your head back to the standing position. Some of the pious danced their bow, some bowed in a courtly manner. Others just did it business like. We would go so fast that we looked like we were part of a choppy Charlie Chaplin film. We zipped through the prayer 'til finally, at the end, we were like race horses coming down the stretch. Mark won last time but this time I was going to beat him. I finished. My head popped up to look around at the others. Yes! I won! They were still at it. It was like finishing an exam early, triumphantly bringing it to the teacher, trying not to look show-offy, but sneaking a look at the other students still nervously scratching out answers with their pencils.

The adults in the congregation also sought victory in the Shmonah Esrai. Lips moving silently, the faithful reverently bent their knees. Down again, up again, they swayed to a familiar rhythm brought from Eastern Europe many years before. These were modern men dressed to the nines, white on white shirts, gold cufflinks and tie-pins, hair in place, Vitalis carefully applied.

They were visiting an earlier time and place. A soft echoing moan, almost a melody could be discerned. They prayed, chanting as their fathers had chanted, and as their grandfathers and their great grandfathers had chanted. Dovened in exactly the same way, the same voice, the same beat, the hum – in this process the voices of father and grandfather were returned to their sons. The dead visit us in recognizable physical characteristics, the same eyes, the same lips, the same smile – my father and youngest son both lift their right eyebrow in response to a quip. Prayer was the most sacred place to meet. Their children's imitation reincarnated the departed. Father and son, father and grandson were together again, together in obedience, together in their sway.

It wasn't just family. It was tribe. Every Shabbis the same ancient words were repeated, exactly the same way, with the exact same rhythm, repeated as they had been repeated for five hundred, perhaps a thousand years. The next generation would also do it that way, and the next generation and the next, each part of a chain, doing their part to keep it going, make it continue exactly the same forever.

It was a glimpse of eternity. The inspired were transported. The scattered, fleeting impressions of daily life dissolved. The noise of everyday life can easily engulf the unwary. If only during this prayer, everyday troubles were left behind. It was like the inevitable insight at a funeral when the noisy, aggravating, unjust pursuits of the real world become illusion, placed in perspective as the nonsense they are in the larger scheme of things.

But the sermons, any sermon, even the best sermon, within 10 or 15 minutes I usually had had enough. I had no manoeuvring room. I was trapped.

It reminded me of the study periods in the auditorium at school. Like assistant principals all over New York City at the time, Mr Burke was hired muscle. He stood in front of the auditorium making sure we understood that he was going to nail us if we were anything other than serious. We needed to be reminded every day that standing behind our women teachers was power, real power. It gave bite to their bark. Mr Burke watched us very closely. You didn't want to go to his office. Stories of his punishments had been repeated many times among the students. One look and you knew they were true. The tight wrinkles across his forehead told you. So did his barely disguised clenched fists. Daring you. Daring you to make trouble.

Sermons were uncomfortable even without Mr Burke backing up the rabbi. At school you didn't have to question if you were bad or good. It didn't matter. The rules were clear so you knew how to stay out of trouble. But a sermon? You might walk in feeling fine but in those days a skilful rabbi could make you rethink just what kind of person you really are. He could make you wonder about all the ways that you didn't live up to your ideals. Or he could create new ideals that you hadn't even thought of before. He could lure you into promising yourself, and more importantly, God, that you will try harder to be better. That's a dangerous combination. It asks the ultimate question, whether deep down you are really good.

For the first 13 years of my life I believed that at every moment I was watched by God. And not just what I did; he knew my every thought. Telling my children about this, we all agree it was almost surreal. An omniscient, omnipotent, omnipresent being monitoring me (and everyone else). It now seems absolutely wild – back then it was absolutely true. You never really questioned it. God's presence was a fact of life. With God as judge you perpetually prepared for your trial. So being good was the only way to go, and when not good, sincere remorse was necessary.

On and on the rabbi's voice continued. It was like being stuck in a car, crowded together for a long trip. Remember this was 50 years ago, before there were sports utility vehicles (SUVs), before Sony Walkmans or Gameboys, before car air-conditioners, back then going on a trip could be more of a trap than a trip. It would go on forever. 'Mom are we there yet?' When was the rabbi going to realize enough was enough?

I wasn't the only one in this predicament. All the children at synagogue had been ordered to sit still. Mark's mother had him sitting on his hands hoping that would stop them from flapping around, or making spit balls. Allen's hands were held tightly together, out in front of him, where his mother could see them. Mark tried to stare straight ahead. He tried his best to listen. But his eyes were like mine. They darted here and there in search of action, hoping to catch someone else's eyes also darting around, and the two of you could share a brief moment of rebellion, which we did. But, it was just that split second...

The rest of the time it was prison. Prison is a bleak place. It means you've finally lost. Total capitulation, the fight's over. They get to call all the shots, unless you want to escalate it from being behind bars to being put in shackles. Anything to break the monotony, any stimulation at all might have done the trick. It might restore the balance more to my liking – a joke whispered to my sister, a noogie in the arm of my brother, getting up and walking around, tapping my feet, making a funny face at Mark...Anything!

Now it seems like it would have been easy to regain some form of control. Then I gave no serious thought to mounting a protest. The icy stares of my mother could put a quick end to even a peep, to any and all shenanigans, not to mention the fear that God himself might be offended and then I'd be in real trouble.

We were taught to be good

The ability to sit still and quietly apply oneself for extended times to unwelcome tasks does not come naturally to human beings, especially children. It is a virtue and, despite claims to the contrary, virtues do not blossom without careful care. For although there may or may not be excesses of worthiness in us, planted there by our genes, by nature, long-lasting virtues only flourish when they are cultivated.

Our parents get the first crack at building our character, at teaching us what is expected. Who can forget Pinocchio's long nose as punishment for his lying, or his father's broken heart when he cut out of school and went to the pleasure palace? The three little pigs and the wolf who blew their house down – what a fine hero the diligent pig was, the one who didn't play all the time and planned for the future. His neat little brick home saved the day. And my friend the choo-choo train that kept saying, 'I think I can. I think I can' and just kept climbing and climbing until over the hill he cried out, 'I thought I could. I thought I could' – I can still hear the happy rhythm of my mother's voice as she proclaimed the choo-choo's victory.

But other methods are needed. In the 1940s and 50s and even the early 60s parents did not think of themselves as their children's friends. That awaited adulthood, and maybe even then, a parent was still a parent, the voice of the right way to do things. This was an era before psychobabble. No one cared about making children feel guilty. It was a parent's job to do exactly that. They had to prepare their little ones for the future. Like an untrained pet dog, children could easily become obnoxious. Innocent play could become annoyingly noisy, and there was the grabbing, and squabbling about who was entitled to what, and whose turn it was, and who hit whom first.

This era was well distanced from Jean Dubuffet, and Jackson Pollack and later the aptly named counter-culture and all those who extolled the natural, the child, letting go, creativity, Zen, spontaneity, as a superior state of consciousness. On the contrary, in Queens, where I grew up, letting go wasn't a real choice. No one doubted that parents were in charge, or that they had things basically right. They had a mission. They had to civilize us. We were like wild broncos. Our parents had to calm us down, jump on our backs and hold on 'til we became comfortably ready to follow their directions. Little by little parents tried to teach their wunderkind how to not act like a child, how to forgo the pursuit of pleasure and pay attention to what was expected. Preparing their children for 'life' was how parents showed their real love, not with loads of candy and gifts and hugs, but by doing what was needed to keep their children on task. Parents did not give a second thought about whether they were cool. They knew they were party poopers. They knew nothing of quality time. The essence of parental identity consisted of doing whatever had to be done, bribing, cajoling, threatening, whatever it took to remind their charges not to stray too far from the chosen path.

Yes, hugs and kisses, fun, and parties, were part of the mix. That mix varied from home to home. But special occasions were just that, occasions. Christmas (Hanukah for us) and your birthday added up to two occasions a year. Reward was never a given, never assumed. Unconditional love would have been considered a goofball notion in the 50s. Instilling virtue was at the very core of child rearing and education. It was not considered an easy goal to accomplish otherwise the lessons would not have been so incessant. No opportunities were wasted at school. Spelling, penmanship, grammar lessons took every opportunity to educate the child 'The early bird gets the worm', 'a stitch in time saves nine' – over and over, encapsulated wisdom was hammered home, until these truths became reflex, until they were on an entirely different plane than a good idea, or a word to the wise, until they became eternal truth. In the generation before mine, when misbehaviour occurred, a student might have to write one of these sayings a hundred times on the blackboard as punishment for his or her misdeed.

The linchpin of this system of values was God. In ways that were not necessarily thought out, he made the laws. Psychologically a lot is accomplished when this occurs. You are offered a deal. Obey me and you have a protector, a leader mightier than all other forces. It goes further. He is all knowing and all good. He is just. Putting the rule maker on a sanctified plane transforms fear of authority into respect. The obedient feel righteous, 'saved', perhaps, at times, in a state of grace. Those who follow God share in his exalted idealized state, or will when they are rewarded in Heaven.

Freud agreed that character building derives from a war but, as an atheist, he gave it a different spin. Children's natural inclinations and parents' intentions for them are on a collision course. The price paid for locking up the pleasure-seeking self isn't trivial. He argued that the basic cause of neurotic misery, of all kinds of crippling inhibitions has to do with the things that animals do freely and openly but that human beings must control. Although we rise above our animal bodily drives, our bodily imperatives, our oral, anal, and genital urges have to be regularly satisfied. He thought the drives utilizing these parts of the body were of great importance in stirring up conflicts. He derived their energy from sexuality. I don't think he was correct about this, but the basic point remains. Animals screw and eat and defecate openly. When, they come across a stranger the first thing they want to do is smell its asshole and genitals.

Society demands that we be civilized, that we learn the right way to satisfy ourselves. Animals know nothing of euphemisms, or anxiety. Their fear is fear. It fits the occasion, and then it is gone. They do not have to hide their sexual secrets and longings. They do not have to try to be better. They sleep when they want to and without difficulty. They are unaware of anything being asked of them. Like a counter-culture mantra, they simply are. They know how to be. In Queens, the worst thing in the world was to be like an animal.

My parents, particularly my mother, used the tried and true as her main weapon to keep us focused. Her willingness to sacrifice, her distilled virtue never seemed put on. Centuries of practice had perfected her identity, her embrace, her hold on us. It was hopeless to resist. She inspired us. She reached a deep place that clarified our direction. She was part of an army of millions, subtle and not so subtle Jewish American Sarah Bernhardts, her theatre arguably most effective when she believed in it, when we became her dream. It was done quietly, no nagging, nothing other than praise, but when you did her proud she was enthralled. Disappointing her dreams for my future would be like sticking a dagger in her heart.

The Jewish guilt schtick soon enough became good for a laugh on Broadway, and many a psychoanalytic session was spent trying to rid the soul of the cloying imprisonment of maternal martyrdom and expectations from us that would make it all worthwhile. However, there are many variations. Catholics of my generation told me about the nuns at school smacking their fingers with rulers when they stepped out of line. That kind of crime and punishment created different complications. And there were many other ways of getting the message across. But whatever the particulars of child rearing that each culture used, and there were many, each knew that character building was a never-ending struggle against children's natural tendencies. Victory against temptation could never be assumed. Learning how to subdue and transform the natural, the beast, our heart of darkness, finding a way to ignore Satan, required effort. To return to Freud's perspective – murder, stealing, lying, unallowable sexuality, sins of every variety make up the stuff of our entertainment in films, books, theatre, and newspapers. Freud understood the reason. *Side by side with virtues our psyche demands a steady supply of vice.*

In the old country, values were perceived as permanent endowments, rooted by years and years of belonging to a community. Our modern hallowed qualities, originality, creativity, individualism, self-expression were the very opposite of desirable. Too much freedom was the surest way to a fool's paradise, to mind games in the service of chicanery. Tolerance was a desirable virtue. But a relativistic moral perspective was no perspective at all. Everyone in the community knew the rules. In the old country you knew where a person came from. You knew his parents, his aunts and uncles and grandparents. Any one of them had the right, the duty to protect the family's name. You were part of a greater whole. Individuals' behaviour reflected not only on themselves but on the rest of their family, perhaps for generations to come. A person who wanted too much fun was going to get into trouble. He was the kind of person who would hang out on street corners or at the local pool hall. Parents worried that their children could turn into someone like that. In Freudian language, the Pleasure Principle had to mature into the Reality Principle. 'Yes' had to be met with a lot of 'no's. Ulysses, James Joyce's or any other variety, was not a hero. He was a lost soul away from his family. 'Yes yes yes yes' meant adventures had gotten out of control.

Times change. It may take a village to raise a child but there are no longer villages. Our jets and jeeps bring us to far-off places where the soil under the feet is sacred, where families have remained in that exact place for hundreds, perhaps thousands of years. It is not our soil. Nothing is. Even in our own land, we are wanderers. The average American moves 12 times in a lifetime. *You Can't Go Home Again* was written by an American. In many parts of the world people never leave home.

Today's children

The kids sent to psychiatrists today are less likely to be tangled up by inhibitions. It's more often the opposite. A lot of children are sent to psychiatrists because of their lack of inhibitions. They have problems controlling their impulses. It is not unusual for such children, when they get into trouble, to be devoid of fear (as in 'Uh-oh wait 'til my parents find out'). Nor do they necessarily lose their bluster when a trip to the principal's office is threatened. Many are not rattled at all. ADHD kids are known for their bravura. Some say they do this to make up for their poor self-image. Some say this bravura is exactly the problem. They haven't learned that in certain situations being reined in is the only way to get where you have to be. Sometimes, in America, if the principal has spoken too harshly to a child, or physically grabbed him to bring him under control, parents are ready to sue.

Following the successful inculcation of 1960s (all you need is love, nature is good) beliefs, generating fear became an unacceptable motivator in the modern educational lexicon. Children were recast as basically good, as lovers of learning when properly inspired. This meant no more Mr. Burkes teaching with their countenance 'obey or you will be in deep doo-doo.' It was said that using fear threatens a child's self-esteem. I assume that deep inside, some of the kids now brought to a principal's office know they are screwing up, and their 'self-esteem' isn't the greatest. But, then, self-esteem is very different from what it once was.

During my childhood feeling good about yourself was connected to staying out of trouble. And this was connected to the larger picture. Ultimately, you would be endowed with self-esteem by being obedient to God's rules, kind of stick with what you are supposed to do and you'll be okay. You will be protected by God. You will go to heaven. He will be on your side because he knows you are good – something like that. In my 20s in Berkeley it was said that we must find God in ourselves. Everyone was a God if he or she found the inner voice. Not so in the 1950s. It was being on the same page as the rules. God was the perfect one. Not us. We lived under the cloud of original sin, guilty until our virtue might prove us innocent.

Operating within a context where God's will must be done, used to give parents backbone. It made nuanced strategies superfluous. Whether to guide children to the right path through 'time-outs' or 'you're grounded' or by 'showing you mean business' might or might not be effective for a given child, but overall it was less important than the socially agreed upon absoluteness of the moral order. There was no need for child rearing 'experts' in magazines, on TV, in newspaper columns, in best-selling books to educate parents about the latest and ever-changing certainties of 'scientific' child rearing (with the implied threat that anything else was child abuse). In the old system what parents did with their children was a natural outgrowth of the larger purpose. Moral purpose shaped and encompassed all behaviour. Although I am now an atheist, I suspect that it was the critical ingredient that kept me from having ADHD.

For those no longer involved with a living God who listened and watched, and judged, renewal could no longer come from being more observant. Historically, the most brilliant Jewish thinkers, day in and day out, studied the Torah, believing it contained God's wishes and commandments. The Bar Mitzvah was a key moment in life, because from that time forward the child will be treated as an adult, meaning morally responsible for behaviour. Modern thinkers went for the jugular. Seeking to be free of guilt, they attacked most guilt as 'neurotic'. The intricate web of family relationships, the silent and complicated, the implicit sticky emotions that cause so much angst and misery were described as 'symbiotic', 'enmeshed', 'judgemental'. It was not just intellectuals. Bar Mitzvah celebrations turned into almost Dionysian feasts.

I recall those years now as I write this, but as recently as a month or two ago my former life ruled by God would have seemed to have happened so long before that it is almost as if it were centuries rather than decades ago. It is almost as if it weren't me but another person who lived within God's domain. I suppose that means that as much as I might like to sentimentalize my Jewish heritage in bagels and lox and black and white cookies, if I met my grandparents for the first time they would seem peculiar to me. I suppose it also means that some Muslims' view of us as infidels would not seem strange to my grandparents. They would agree that our popular culture has become bizarre, especially the prominence of sexuality, but also the completely looser, less strictly defined ideas of proper religious practice.

I don't want my explanations for ADHD to be dismissed as self-righteousness. Perhaps at 63, I have become a fuddy-duddy – the kind of old-fashioned, out-of-it kind of person that in my 20s I swore I would never become. Be that as it may, I am arguing that much of the behaviour in our children that we label ADHD can be explained by the historically unprecedented ability of so many members of our society to gear their lives towards the fulfilment of pleasure, by a deterioration in our moral fibre, by a pervasive need for immediate gratification, immediate sensation, less talk more action, bam, bam, bam MTV. Our editors despise words formulated in the passive tense; despise characters who yield their will-power, who settle into routines in which they are absorbed into a conventional sensibility. Unlike the religious people of my youth who, above all, valued convention, who knew that the way to nirvana was dissolving 'me' in the larger permanence of the group's rituals, in contemporary culture rituals represent ossification. They 'say' nothing. Forever is *de facto* not a good thing. It is not American. It is against progress. We profess to want characters that stand out, that want change and bring change, that make a statement, that are unique. America insists on verbs, insists that we keep things moving. Our news is delivered in sound bites. We don't like talking heads at the movies. We discard old ideas as old-fashioned. We need to get on with it quickly, smartly zip along our charged-up path ahead.

Sin and ADHD

The medical view of kids with ADHD is that it is a biological illness unrelated to child rearing. ADHD kids are born with it. Parents haven't done anything wrong. They are innocent of all charges that would have been levelled against them in the past for raising wild kids. By law we have banned religion in our schools. And we have marginalized religious preoccupations in our understanding of behaviour. It has become improper for professionals to classify what is going on with a kid in moral terms. A public school teacher who carried on about God would be out of a job. When a kid is in trouble, teachers do not think of contacting the family's clergyman. They think doctor.

I appreciate the esteem granted to my profession. The ideal doctor is trained to be dispassionate, to use a scientific point of view to get at the truth. The rules of science, the discipline of science, allow us to arrive at cold hard facts whatever the implications. In our modern liberal concept of reality we will settle for nothing less. Doctors and all professionals must leave moral spin out of formulations about cause and effect. We pay good money to reap the benefit of this way of looking at things.

But, while religion has no place in classifying an illness, what if we are not talking about an illness? We get so used to approaching issues in a modern way that it never occurs to us to step back and question the assumptions behind our viewpoints. Let us start with this. Who made doctors experts on child rearing? It is a relatively new concept. Doctors were once assigned the role of treating illnesses, not providing a perspective about misbehaving children. When did we make them all-knowing about child rearing? Was Dr Spock's book that good? Okay, Freud talked about the importance of childhood experiences but few people accept Freud today. Just how far have we come with our scientific knowledge about how the brain works? If we can scientifically explain ADHD then the discussion is over and doctors should replace moral pedagogues as the best way to approach wild kids. But, if we don't have the scientific knowledge, then what?

I am not an anti-science, anti-technology person who wants 'holistic' or alternative care for patients because science is inherently anti-human. Quite the opposite, I would be thrilled if the treatment of psychiatric patients could be reduced to the application of well-researched and confirmed scientific findings, which in turn would lead to logical and well-thought out treatment. I would relish writing prescriptions that are as effective, as antibiotics are for strept throat. When scientific methods lead to the understanding of a phenomenon there is nothing like it in getting the job done. Antibiotics, which we take so for granted, are truly miraculous, as is the polio vaccine, cholesterol-reducing agents, and many other life-saving medicines. We rightly appreciate firemen as heroes because they put their own life on the line. But, if we want to talk about heroes who have literally saved ten, perhaps hundreds of millions of lives, we cannot ignore scientists as our true miracle workers. Indeed, all reported miracles performed on earth by Jehovah or Jesus pale when compared with what our scientists have been able to accomplish. Never mind walking on water. They have allowed human beings to fly from here to Texas. They have taken some of us to the moon. Good or bad, science is clearly the most effective way to understand reality and effect change.

The other chapters in this book make it pretty clear that the science simply isn't there.[6]

Summary

1. It has always been known that it's difficult to get children to do what you want them to do rather than what they want to do. When children are forced to sit quietly in situations that fail to engage them they daydream or become fidgety, and disruptive.
2. Our culture has changed radically, from one in which moral concerns were at the centre of experience, to a more pleasure oriented, stimulus-bound existence. Being bad was always exciting for young people. Temptation is not new. But since the counter-culture smashed the rules, being bad has been particularly good. When this sensibility predominates it is easy to get bored and distracted when work rather than fun is the agenda.
3. Like everyone else I swing back and forth on the issue of independence, pleasure and vice versus virtue. I stand accused of rooting for

the sinners in movies like Chocolat and Footloose where religion is
rightly seen as the enemy of pleasure and self-expression. Moreover,
I am in awe of people like Michael Flatley, the man with the 'Feet of
Flames' and creator of River Dance, winner at 17 of the all-Ireland
flute championship, once a golden glove competitor, who, growing
up in Chicago, was an ADHD-diagnosed Irish charmer. He paid no
attention in class and still is not willing to pay his dues to those
with authority. I am in awe of many other diagnosed and undiagnosed people with ADHD who are talented and living free. I am
not in awe of people who will make a mess of their lives because
they never learned how to do comfortably things that they don't
like doing. This chapter jumps back and forth arguing both for and
against discipline.

4. Children with a variety of physical defects in their brain have trouble concentrating on tasks, learning the rules that are supposed to
   govern their behaviour, and behaving in the way expected of children with a normal capacity to synthesize, integrate, and act with
   self-control when confronted by rules and tasks. Children with
   nothing physically wrong may have the same problem. The vast
   majority of the millions of children diagnosed with ADHD have
   not yet been shown to have anything physically wrong with their
   brains.

5. Beyond the specifics of claims and counterclaims about biological
   causality, I am itching for a debate in which doctors, patients and
   society might properly address not only the use of stimulants, but
   what their widespread use implies about increasingly common difficulties parents seem to be having raising children to be motivated
   and focused on work when it is required of them. It is a challenge
   for every parent. It always has been. The question is whether we
   are doing worse than we used to do or, whether we have simply
   reached a point of affluence when pleasure seeking can be safely
   pursued without jeopardizing our children's lives and livelihoods.

6. Throughout the chapter I take a trip down memory lane. I think
   it is a valid way to get perspective, not only on one's own childhood, but, also on the problems kids face today. It is useful if
   done honestly. When revisited in recollection our lives offer vast
   new opportunities for discovery. The past is the ground on which
   we stand; the foundation, the basis for what we do now and all
   the 'now's to come. Parents should regularly try to understand
   what went on in their own childhood. They should learn most of
   what they have to know from their own parents, sifting through,

rejecting, accepting, and maintaining the dialogue. It is a decent antidote to the points of view of experts, who wave their scientific 'findings' indiscriminately and often without a solid basis in fact.

The web address of the full version of 'ADHD and Other Sins of Our Children' is http://www.geocities.com/ss06470/ADHD.html

Notes

1. This chapter is a shortened version; the web address of the full version of 'ADHD and Other Sins of Our Children' is http://www.geocities.com/ss06470/ADHD.html
2. See 'History and uses of the Coca leaf' http://www2.truman.edu/~marc/webpages/andean2k/cocaine/history.html
3. The Life and Work of Sigmund Freud, Volume I (1856–1900) (New York: Basic Books, 1953), p. 82–3.
4. 'Latest Campus High: Illicit use of Prescription Medication, Experts and Students Say:' NY Times Page B8 3/24/00.
5. See Sobo, Simon 'A Reevaluation of the Relationship between Psychiatric Diagnosis and Chemical Imbalances' http://www.geocities.com/ss06470/index.htm
6. The internet version of this article also pursues the science in some detail. The web address of the full version of 'ADHD and Other Sins of Our Children' is http://www.geocities.com/ss06470/ADHD.htm

References

Angell, M. (2000) Is academic medicine for sale? *New England Journal of Medicine*, 342, 1516–18.

Angell, M. (2004) *The Truth about Drug Companies*. New York: Random House.

Horton, R. (2004) The dawn of McScience, *New York Review of Books, 51*, 7–9. See also Mental Health: A report of the Surgeon General, available at http://www.surgeongeneral.gov/library/mentalhealth/chapter3/sec4.html>.

National Institutes of Health (1998) Diagnosis and Treatment of Attention Deficit Hyperactivity Disorder National Institutes of Health Consensus Development Conference Statement, 16–18 November.

Schmidt, M. (2006) *Clearing the Bases*. New York: HarperCollins.

Sobo, S. (2001) *A Re-evaluation of the Relationship between Psychiatric Diagnosis and Chemical Imbalances*, available at <http://www.geocities.com/ss06470/index.htm>.

Wells, D. and Kreski, C. (2003) *Perfect I'm Not: Boomer on Beer, Brawls, Backaches, and Baseball*. New York: William Morrow.

Chapter 15

Canaries in the Coal Mine

Chris Mercogliano

We all know about the proverbial canary in the coal mine. Miners carried the caged yellow songbirds down into the shafts with them because canaries are especially sensitive to methane and carbon monoxide. If they stopped singing, the miners knew there was cause for concern. Swaying indicated the air was really getting bad. Then, if a bird fell over dead, it meant that an explosion was imminent and it was time to get the hell out of there.

The world's struggling children, whether they are labelled ADD, ODD, OCD, or whatever abbreviated nametag society elects to pin on their behavioural selves, are the new millennium's canaries in the coal mine. If indeed such kids *are* suffering from actual deficits, or traumas, or other forms of distress, and not just reacting against environments that are unsuited to their real physical, emotional, and social needs, then it is imperative that we begin to see their so-called symptoms as distress signals – *not* as evidence of some sort of neurological pathology. It is time for us to tune into those messages, to move beyond the ADHD paradigm and examine in the broadest terms what their agitation, difficulty in focusing and processing, impulsiveness, over-aggressiveness, or depression are trying to tell us about the condition of their lives.

Inner wildness

The crux of their SOS is this: childhood itself is in trouble. The relentless forces of modernity are pressing in from all sides, slowly but surely squeezing out the novelty, the independence, the adventure, the wonder, the innocence, the physicality, the solitude – the juice, if you will – from the lives of all of today's children, labelled or otherwise.

Of greatest concern is the alarming impact of the changes on the luminescent spark that animates the young, serves as the source of their uniqueness and creativity, and supplies the energy and the impetus for them to become whom they are intended to become. I have chosen to call this spark 'inner wildness'.

Why 'inner wildness?' 'Inner' denotes its approximate location, which is deep beneath the human surface, out of reach of the conscious mind. 'Wildness' defies description by these linear symbols we call words, but attempts to describe an elusive essence that strives mightily to resist the control of others. The term also invokes the urgent and parallel importance of preserving the earth's outer wildness, the wildlife and wild places without which existence would become a barren exercise.

The idea emerged while I was in the middle of writing a book about how the unusual school where I have worked since 1973 assists students with behavioural and cognitive difficulties without resorting to the use of bio-psychiatric labels or drugs. I had been researching the question of why there was suddenly an epidemic of children – primarily boys – whom mainstream scientists and medical professionals claim to be suffering from a chemical imbalance in their brains, most likely genetic in origin. In evolutionary terms, how could as many as 10 million kids have come down with a new disease virtually overnight? The idea defied reason. After carefully sifting through the voluminous ADHD literature, it made even less sense to me.

A clue arrived in the mail when a dear friend, who has spent the better part of her 40-year career as a special-education teacher on Native American reservations in Minnesota and New Mexico, sent me an essay she had come across in the *New York Times*. Rosalie is equally dubious about the idea that kids who can't sit still in class and concentrate on academic tasks, or who refuse to do as they are told, have a medical disorder. The article, 'A Strange Malady Called Boyhood', written by Pulitzer Prize-winning science writer Natalie Angier (1994), suggested that there has been a subtle but relentless shift in our culture's definition of what constitutes a 'normal' boy. The nineteenth-century Tom Sawyer/Huck Finn archetype – brash, wilful, naughty, rambunctious, aggressive, always dirty – is no longer acceptable. Today, parents, teachers, psychologists, and paediatricians alike increasingly view the temperamental and behavioural distance between such boys and an ever narrower definition of normality as evidence of pathology. Such boys, they feel, are sick enough to require medication.

And the powerful psychotropic drugs with which we then 'treat' them enforce society's new definition all the way down to the biochemical level.

The free school's experience

Angier's ideas resonated with my experience at the Albany Free School, a non-coercive, democratic, inner-city school for 65 students ages 2 through 14, where we permit Sawyeresque behaviour in children as long as it doesn't violate the rights and sensibilities of others. Here, we eschew assigning labels to kids who don't fit in or measure up. We say that a child who is constantly on the move is *highly* active, which is a descriptive term, not *hyper*active, which is a prescriptive one. Since the school is always buzzing with noise and activity, highly active kids don't really stand out, and are not considered to have or to be a problem. Moreover, we've noticed that when highly active children can run, and jump, and climb, and yell, and dance, and dig holes in the sandbox, and hammer ten-penny nails into two-by-fours in the wood shop to their hearts' content, they gradually settle down and develop the ability to modulate their energy level. The trouble begins when you suppress their need to move and do.

Similarly, we say that kids with minds like hummingbirds, who aren't yet inclined to spend long stretches reading, writing and figuring, are flighty, or easily distracted, not that they have attention deficit disorder. The interesting thing about these children is that, given the chance to pay attention to what *they* want to pay attention to, they will often spend hours at a time working on a drawing, or a birdhouse, or a new skateboard move. When it is *their* choice, they will devour good books and stories and keep asking for more. But if you try to force them when the desire and excitement are missing – that is when the trouble begins.

Meanwhile, the redefinition of childhood norms urged me to reflect on my own boyhood, which straddled the second half of the 1950s and the first half of the 60s. I began making comparisons between my youth and that of my father and grandfather, and that of today's children, now two generations hence. I noted the striking changes in the fundamental nature of play, of school, of work, of electronic media and their impact on childhood, and finally of adolescence – all changes that impact on girls just as much as boys, though sometimes in different ways.

Adult control

Across this broad spectrum, one change in particular began to stand out as a sort of common denominator: today, virtually every arena of a child's life is subject to some form of adult mediation, supervision, or control. Kids go from before-school programmes to school, from school to after-school programmes, and from there to a host of extracurricular lessons and organized sports. Even the youth peer culture into which young people retreat to gain a sense of independence has become a commercial product created and promoted by adults – profit-hungry professionals interested only in exploiting an increasingly lucrative market, not in the inner well-being of the younger generation. As the CEO of MTV put it when asked how he regarded the huge influence his television empire has on children: 'We don't just influence them – we own them' (Nader, 1996, p. ix).

Suddenly it occurred to me that we are witnessing not only the taming of Mark Twain's wild boys, but the systematic domestication of childhood itself.

The birthing process

A pattern of domestication is established even as we draw our first breath, and it repeats itself at every stage throughout childhood. The problem begins at birth. In the name of risk management, current obstetrical practices have turned what was once a natural, you might say 'wild', process into a carefully scripted medical procedure. The technological interventions that are part and parcel of the modern hospital birth often cause serious breaks in the all-important mother–infant bond, which nature intends to occur immediately following emergence from the womb. Research shows that the skin and eye contact that take place between mother and newborn when the baby is held at the left breast, close to the mother's heartbeat, is essential to the complete awakening of the brain centres that will accomplish the rapid-fire developmental steps that lie ahead (Pearce, 1992, pp. 110–11).

At the same time, according to child-development expert and author Joseph Chilton Pearce (1992), the uninterrupted connection between mother and newborn activates a corresponding set of 'birth intelligences' inside the mother. This instinctive form of knowing, which cannot be taught, enables her to communicate intuitively with the baby and respond confidently to its signals.

Right after today's typical birth, however, the baby is taken away from the mother and attended to by the delivery-room nurse, with numerous additional separations soon to follow over the course of the hospital stay. To make matters worse, more than 85 per cent of American women are anesthetized during labour and nearly 25 per cent deliver by Caesarean section, a figure that is still rising (www.Childbirth.org/section/SFAQ.html 1998). Studies indicate that infants are depressed for as much as a week by maternal birth drugs, and that the coming in of the mother's milk is delayed by 24–36 hours (Brazelton, 1989). The result of this domestication is that the overwhelming majority of today's babies are being denied the instinctive, developmentally active beginning that was once their birthright, effectively sowing seeds of passivity that can last throughout their childhoods.

As the child grows

Meanwhile, the same kind of cautious over-management that governs childbirth has steadily crept into contemporary childrearing. Hyperconcern for their children's safety and development is causing mothers and fathers to monitor their kids' activities and whereabouts far more stringently than my mom ever did. Fearful that their children will be left behind once they start school, many parents also focus on formal learning at ever earlier stages of growth. Or parent substitutes – nannies, day-care providers, preschool teachers – are doing so in their stead. Oftentimes both occur.

As children grow older, there is the above-mentioned proliferation of extracurricular programmes and lessons. Solitude and reflection are lost in the constant shuffle from place to place and structured activity to structured activity. The evolution of play reveals a similar trend.

A vivid example, which I think serves as a metaphor for what is happening to all areas of childhood leisure and recreation, is the change that has taken place in swimming. In my grandfather's day, children swam – usually unsupervised – in lakes, rivers, creeks, and old abandoned quarries. When my father was a child, public pools began to appear, providing children with two options: they could walk to the nearby pool, or, given the time and a serviceable bicycle, they could choose the wilder of the two venues. Fast forward to my childhood: a high fence has been built around the quarry to keep out youthful swimmers. 'No Swimming' signs have been posted along the riverbanks because the current is sometimes strong enough to endanger the inexperienced. But all is not lost. The pool has two diving boards, one a scary height above the water, which is deep enough to make it an exhilarating challenge to swim all the way down and touch the bottom. Yes, lifeguards are on hand to make certain that no one drowns; however, there remains at least a measure of daring and adventure. Now let's examine today's swimming pools. Diving boards have disappeared from a great many of them, and the majority of newly constructed pools no longer even have deep ends – they are a uniform three-and-a-half feet in depth, with white lines to create individual swimming lanes. If children are lucky, a permissive lifeguard might still let them jump into the water.

Meanwhile, our compulsory, factory-style, standards-driven model of education has become perhaps the largest single agent of childhood domestication. As I have already noted, students who are too untamed – and very little inner wildness is fast becoming too much – are quickly subdued and brought back into the herd by means of bio-psychiatric labels and drugs. The demands of high-stakes testing have forced schools to eliminate nearly every vestige of physicality, imagination, and creativity from the curriculum; more than ever, classrooms are becoming places where kids spend their days like cloned sheep, grazing passively in a pasture of uniform right answers.

And so it goes with children's access to meaningful work. When I was a child, even as young as five, there were numerous opportunities to earn money. My first attempts to establish a regular income involved pulling my wagon around the neighbourhood in search of two-cent-deposit bottles. In a good week I brought in as much as five bucks, not a bad pay-check for a kindergartener in 1959. Most importantly, that money was entirely mine to save or spend as I saw fit.

On hot summer days my young pals and I would set up a lemonade stand on the corner, an easier and even more lucrative enterprise than bottle collecting. Then, as soon as I was strong enough to wield a garden spade or a snow shovel, pull a leaf rake, and operate a lawn mower, I graduated to a set of seasonal businesses that kept me flush with cash year-round. By the time I was seven I had my own bank account, and I can still remember the delight of watching my personal capital increase from the tens to the hundreds of dollars as I approached my teenage years.

Today, only on rare occasions do I see little kids hawking lemonade. Likewise, seldom can young entrepreneurs be found cutting their neighbours' grass or raking their leaves anymore. With the base of our economy having morphed from industry to service, child workers have largely been displaced by adult-operated franchises that perform household and landscape tasks on a subscription basis. Schoolwork has become the primary, and for some the only, job of childhood, displacing even household chores. Almost all of the children I know depend on their parents for money, which very often comes with strings attached – yet another blow to the sense of autonomy that feeds a young person's emerging sense of self.

Electronic media

Then there is the proliferating onrush of electronic media that profoundly dominate the life of every child in America, regardless of geography, race, or social class. According to media researcher Emory Woodard (2000, p. 3), 98 per cent of American homes own at least one television, with the average in homes with children (aged 2–17) now at nearly three sets per household. Virtually half of all American kids (47 per cent) have a TV in their bedroom, and that figure increases sharply with the age of the child. An overwhelming majority (78 per cent) has basic cable, and 31 per cent have premium cable. Sixty-eight per cent have video-game equipment, and that figure is rising steadily. More than 90 percent of homes with children have at least one personal computer and 75 percent of those computers have online access, another number that is climbing fast. The bottom line: the average American child spends over four-and-a-half hours a day *sitting in front of some kind of screen.* And perhaps the most shocking finding of all: that figure was up *nearly 10 per cent* from the previous year, 1999.

Another survey of media use by communications researcher Donald Roberts (2000), in which he measured the overall media exposure of young people aged 8–17 (including the extra hours added when they use more than one medium at a time, e.g. checking e-mail while listening to music), found that the average child is exposed to nearly eight hours of media daily. The rate varied somewhat by race, with African-American youth reporting ten hours, Hispanic youth nine hours, and whites seven hours every day. As for socioeconomic variation, the rate of exposure to TV, videos, radio, and video games was inversely related to the income level of the respondents, whereas there was a positive correlation between income and computer use.

Communications researcher Frank Bocca (2000) then took a projective glance into the future, noting that youth born into the television generation will spend the equivalent of seven years of their lives watching television. But what about members of the so-called 'Internet generation' – those born after 1993? The computer, Bocca says, has reached the status of 'meta-medium' because of the way in which it potentially combines televisions, books, magazines, newspapers, typewriters, radios, and game consoles in a single interface. Based on current estimates of the time young people spend with these various media, his guess is that an average member of the internet generation might spend as much as *20 years* at a computer during his or her lifetime. At this point, so early in the computer era, with cyberspace expanding so rapidly – the size of the internet has approximately doubled every year since 1990 – the long-term effects of this new trend are anyone's guess.

All of this is not to say electronic media are inherently harmful to children. As toys and as tools, they have tremendous potential to foster the wonder, discovery, autonomy, and creativity that fuel inner wildness. However, as Canadian scholar and social critic Marshall McLuhan (1994) warned at the inception of the Technological/Information Age in the 1960s, these powerful new forms of technology can be double-edged swords at every turn.

It was McLuhan who uttered the iconic and oft-repeated statement, 'The medium is the message', by which he meant that it is the process, not the content of technology that affects and alters culture. Moreover, we tend to become so entranced by how much easier and faster a new form of technology enables us to do things that we fail to notice its power to control us without our awareness. For example, he wrote, it doesn't matter whether a machine is turning out corn flakes or Cadillacs. The medium of mechanization and mass production carries the message of restructuring human work and association. We are so pleased by the ease and comfort of travelling in an automobile that we fail to recognize the fragmenting and dehumanizing effects of the manufacturing process on the people who produced it, and beyond that on the environmental havoc wreaked by a car-based society.

Likewise with children and electronic media. While, again, modern entertainment and information technologies provide kids with unprecedented interfaces with the world around them, with them seemingly at the controls, recent research is beginning to tell a different story.

Let's begin with TV, the first electronic medium to begin reshaping children's lives. There is mounting evidence that constant exposure to violent and heavily sexualized imagery is profoundly modifying the behaviour of young people, seldom for the better. For instance, according to paediatrician Victor Strasburger and social scientist Edward Donnerstein (1999), who conducted a comprehensive review of all of the relevant studies over the past 20 years, violence on television, in videos, and in movies absolutely leads to aggressive behaviour by child and teenage viewers. How could it not, they concluded, given that young people annually view an estimated 10,000 acts of violence, and, in addition, 22.4 percent of the music videos they watch portray overt violence, with 80 percent of those featuring highly attractive role models as the aggressors.

Strasburger and Donnerstein are quick to point out that media violence is hardly the sole cause of violent behaviour. Poverty, racism, inadequate parenting, and the dissolution of the family may all have more impact. However, the use of violence to achieve goals or settle conflicts is learned behaviour, and such learning, they say, occurs in social contexts such as the family and peer groups – with television functioning as a 'super peer' in this respect.

Moreover, on a broader cultural level, media violence can not only encourage antisocial behaviour, but it can also increase a young person's perception that the world is a mean and dangerous place. In light of the fact that many parents already perceive the world to be unsafe and keep their kids on tight leashes as a result, this media-generated effect on the next generation of mothers and fathers has huge implications for the future of inner wildness.

Next we must consider the impact of the advertising industry that in so many ways controls the television medium. According to Susan Linn (2004), a professor of psychiatry at Harvard Medical School and author of *Consuming Kids: The Hostile Takeover of Childhood*, the fact that children influence $600 billion in annual spending has not been lost on corporate America. She estimates that the combined budget for advertisements aimed at kids is more than $15 billion a year – two-and-a-half times the 1992 figure. Regarding highly addictive substances like alcohol and tobacco, Linn (2004) is quick to point out how important it is to those industries to get to kids early. For instance, she says, research shows that people who start drinking before the age of 15 are 4 times more likely to develop an alcohol dependency than those who don't start until they're 21. Moreover, lifetime alcohol abuse is the highest among individuals who take their first drink between the ages of 11 and 14, and the industry depends on alcoholics for a large share of its profits. Together, underage and adult problem drinkers account for nearly half of all alcohol sales. Tobacco companies, likewise, are well aware of the research showing that the younger kids are when they start, the more likely it is they will become regular smokers and the less likely they will ever successfully quit. If a young person can reach the age of 20 without taking a puff, Linn notes, he or she has almost no likelihood of ever starting, as 90 percent of all smokers pick up the habit before they turn 18 – the legal age for buying cigarettes.

A report by the journal *Pediatrics* Committee on Communications, (1995) cites the example of the infamous Joe Camel billboard and magazine campaign, for which the Camel Cigarette Company ad men created a new logo featuring a friendly, slouchy old camel with a cigarette jutting out of his mouth. Surveys revealed that one third of all three-year-olds and nearly all kids over the age of six could recognize the logo – in fact, Old Joe was as familiar to them as Mickey Mouse – and that the ad campaign was actually more effective among children and adolescents than adults. Not coincidentally, Camel's share of the underage cigarette market equalled $476 million in annual sales – one third of all cigarette sales to minors.

On the extremely sensitive and complex issue of sex and sexuality, so integral to an adolescent and young adult's sense of well-being and autonomy, the media have virtually nothing constructive to say. Teenagers annually view nearly 15,000 sexual references, innuendoes, and jokes, of which only 170 deal with birth control, abstinence, sexually transmitted diseases or pregnancy. Prime-time television's so-called 'family hour', from 8 pm to 9 pm, contains more than eight sexual incidents per hour – four times as many as in 1976 – with nearly one third of family-hour shows containing sexual references.

According to Linn (2004), sex has always been a favourite tool of advertisers, but now it is also being used to sell the very media offerings that attract the young viewers that sponsors want to reach. Ads for TV programmes, movies, and music highlight sexual content just as they highlight violence, and the messages aren't just about sexual behaviour itself. Equally important, they are about what it means to be male and female, what attracts us to each other, and how males and females treat one another.

The increased sexualization of the media is taking its toll. Studies cited by Linn (2004) showed that one third of 10- and 11-year-olds surveyed reported that the pressure on them to have sex is a big problem, and that girls in the early stages of puberty are especially vulnerable to media messages regarding sex. Additionally, the younger a girl is when she has intercourse for the first time, the more likely she is to feel that it was unwanted. Furthermore, in a national survey of sexually active young people, 81 per cent of 12- to 14-year-old boys and girls said they wished they had waited until they were older.

The chronic passivity and inactivity that electronic media engender are already having another clear-cut and equally alarming effect: childhood obesity. According to physiologist Carol Torgan (2002), the number of significantly overweight kids has reached epidemic levels, with the number doubling in the last two to three decades. Currently one child in five is fat, and that figure is still rising too. The increase is in both children and adolescents, and in all age, race, and gender groups.

Moreover, obese children are now turning up with diseases like type-2 diabetes that used to occur only in adults. They also tend to remain overweight as adults, continuing to put them at greater risk for heart disease, high blood pressure and stroke. But perhaps the most devastating effect of all to an overweight child is the most immediate one: social stigmatization. Children who are teased and excluded because of their physical appearance are very likely to suffer right away from low self-esteem and depression.

An in-depth discussion of the highly complex relationship between children and electronic media is beyond the scope of this chapter. My primary concern here is with their potential to suppress inner wildness, and with the question of whether the media represent yet another form of control over children's minds, bodies, and spirits. When it's time to decide how to handle the conflicts of daily life, and whether and when to experiment with alcohol, drugs, or sex, are young people actually making their own choices? I am deeply concerned that the answer is increasingly becoming 'No.'

Arrested adulthood

Finally we arrive in the shifting sands of adolescence and early adulthood, where we encounter perhaps the most glaring signs that the domestication of childhood is already beginning to weigh heavily on young people. A rapidly increasing number of adolescents, according to a recent study by the University of Pennsylvania's Network on Transitions to Adulthood (Settersten and Furstenberg, 2005), are experiencing significant delays and difficulties in becoming full-fledged adults. Researchers have discovered that the average age at which young people reach the traditional markers of adulthood – finding a career, achieving financial independence, forming their own household, starting a family – has taken a sudden statistical leap upward, with many people not achieving them all until well after age 30. Such a striking change has led Canadian sociologist James Côté (2000, p. 180) to coin the term 'arrested adulthood' to describe this extended period of transitional limbo, a state into which some individuals appear to be settling permanently.

Journalist Alexandra Robbins and web-site administrator Abby Wilner (2001), both in their 'twentysomethings', as they refer to their transitional decade, found so many of their peers unable to establish fulfilling adult lives that they decided to write *Quarterlife Crisis*. The authors based their insights on a combination of their own life experience and interviews with more than one hundred fellow 'twentysomethings'. Their conclusion:

> So while the midlife crisis revolves around a doomed sense of stagnancy, of a life set on pause while the rest of the world rattles on, the quarterlife crisis is a response to overwhelming instability, constant change, too many choices, and a panicked sense of helplessness. Just as the monotony of a lifestyle stuck in idle can drive a person to question himself intently, so, too, can the uncertainty of a life thrust into chaos. The transition from childhood to adulthood – from school to the world beyond – comes as a jolt for which many of today's twentysomethings simply are not prepared. The resulting overwhelming senses of helplessness and cluelessness, of indecision and apprehension, make up the real and common experience we call the quarterlife crisis.

Robbins and Wilner's research reveals a disturbingly high rate of mental and emotional disorders among twenty-somethings, including addiction, anxiety, depression, and many other kinds of problems, and their book is an urgent call for a far more comprehensive understanding of why so many young people are getting stuck and what can be done to help set them free to seek their unique destinies.

Part of the problem, according to Côté – and here he is joined by historian of childhood Stephen Mintz (2004) – is that many of those struggling to gain their footing in modern adulthood face a multitude of contradictions. On the one hand they are more fully integrated into the consumer economy than ever before, but on the other hand they are more segregated in their peer culture, with very little contact with adults other than their parents, teachers, and coaches. There is more space inside their homes, but less space outside. Technological progress continues to make life easier, while at the same time it removes many of the mental and physical challenges that stimulate children's ability

394   CANARIES IN THE COAL MINE

to think at the complex levels needed to succeed in the adult world that awaits them. And the biggest change of all is that young people are maturing sexually and psychologically at an ever earlier age, with many facing adult choices much sooner than previous generations did – and yet our society isolates and infantilizes them, and offers very few positive ways for them to express their hard-won maturity. We give them, in other words, a maddening double message: grow up fast, but you really don't need to grow up at all.

Room for hope

Thankfully, agree Côté and Mintz, there is an upside to the radical social and cultural upheaval confronting today's children. Their lives will be longer and healthier, and in most cases more materially prosperous than those of their predecessors. They will have greater choices, including the choice to devote themselves to childrearing. Because of the relaxing of traditional religious, cultural, and social barriers and taboos that has taken place over the past 50 years – as well as the reduction in racial and gender inequity – a majority of the younger generation will enjoy far more personal freedom and face far fewer external restrictions than generations past. The playing field, so to speak, will be more level and more open than ever before in human history.

At the base of the current situation lies a monumental paradox, however. Young people can take advantage of the current open-ended nature of adulthood only if they have as much self-knowledge as they have knowledge of the world, and if they are assertive, playful, creative, and, persistent – all of which are attributes of inner wildness. Yet, so many of our extant institutions are steering them in the opposite direction, towards passivity, conformity, ambivalence, and a lack of determination.

Fortunately the demise of inner wildness is anything but a foregone conclusion. There is plenty that those of us who choose to involve ourselves in the lives of children can do to preserve and enhance their uniqueness, spontaneity, and natural exuberance.

On the microcosmic level, simple acts like getting kids out into nature – even if the only option is a city park – and turning off the boob tube, putting away the videos no matter how educational they may be, and instead reading exciting, engaging stories to children are instant sources of nourishment for their inner wildness. Fairy tales are especially good because embedded in them, according to child psychiatrist Bruno Bettelheim (1976) and Jungian analyst Marie-Louise von Franz (1970), are rich, archetypal symbols and themes that enable children to integrate rather than suppress the turbulent dimensions of their personalities.

The good news is that undomesticated activities are generally elemental. They involve doing less, not more. They don't depend upon expensive, hard-to-access resources. If parents and other key adult figures in kids' lives are willing to relax their control and trust children to author their own experience, it is absolutely possible to restore the novelty, the independence, the adventure, the wonder, the innocence, the physicality, the solitude – the juice – to childhood. The domestication of childhood, in other words, is quite reversible.

On the macrocosmic level, school districts can band together to resist the current onslaught of federally mandated testing, which is punishing teachers and administrators as well as students. As of this writing, a number of states are taking steps to free themselves from having to implement the No Child Left Behind Act (NCLB), with Utah taking the lead when its legislature voted in 2005 to abandon NCLB entirely and return to its own standards and other means of accountability. Opponents argue that the testing is excessive and will force schools to cut other important programmes in order to fund the tests.

Also, concerned parents, teachers, and activists can contribute to the national explosion of educational alternatives reminiscent of the 1960s and 70s, resulting in hundreds of new, innovative schools, both public and private, in the last decade alone. Some parents decide to teach their children themselves: according to the National Home Education Research Institute (www.nheri.org, 2007), as many as 2 million households – and 7 percent more each year – are opting not to turn their kids over to a monolithic educational system that often has little regard for their children's inner well-being.

This diverse set of options reflects a wide array of approaches to teaching and learning, but taken as a whole they share a common commitment to fostering originality, individuality, and autonomy. They recognize that children need to be on their own often enough to become fluent in responsible decision-making, while at the same time they need nurturing relationships with adults who serve as mentors and role models, not taskmasters. They need real knowledge and experience and the chance to learn from their own mistakes, not constant immunization from risk. To quote Stephen Mintz (2004, p. 383), they need 'challenging alternatives to the world of malls, music lessons, instant messages, and play dates', and real opportunities to explore where their place in the adult world might one day lie.

Conclusion

I will leave it to others in this volume to unpack the complex physiological and psychological details that make up the ADHD debate. My
purpose here has been to view the issue through a broader lens, and in
so doing attempt to locate the sources of the difficulty – to the extent
that children have real and not merely perceived problems – outside of
the child where they rightly belong.

Indeed, the young people bearing the panoply of bio-psychiatric
labels are modern society's canaries in the coal mine, a human warning
signal for what is in store for more and more children if we don't soon
start pumping oxygen into the increasingly dead socio-cultural air they
are forced to breathe every day of their lives. These kids aren't sick,
as the medical establishment would have us believe; rather they are
exhibiting signs of distress and unmet core needs. Their inner wildness
is being stifled and it is affecting every level of their being.

The right response to their signal is not to classify and drug them. It
is to reclaim childhood, as developmental psychologist Bill Crain urges
in his recent book by that title, and to restore it to its rightful place as
a preserve in which kids can grow slowly, and if need be, fitfully into
their authentic selves.

This article is adapted from Chris Mercogliano's book, *In Defense
of Childhood: Protecting Kids' Inner Wildness* (Beacon Press, 2007).

References

Angier, N. (1994) A strange malady called boyhood, *New York Times* 24 July.
Bettelheim, B. (1976) *The Uses of Enchantment*. New York: Knopf.
Bocca, F. (2000) New media technology and youth: Trends in the evolution of
    new media, *Journal of Adolescent Health*, 27S.
Brazelton, B. (1989) *Infants and Mothers*. New York: Dell.
Committee on Communications (1995) Children, adolescents, and advertising,
    Pediatrics, 95, 2.
Côté, J. (2000) *Arrested Adulthood*. New York: New York University Press.
Linn, S. (2004) *Consuming Kids: The Hostile Takeover of Childhood*. New
    York: The New Press.
McLuhan, M. (1994) *Understanding Media: The Extensions of Man*. Cam-
    bridge, MA: MIT Press.
Mintz, F. (2004) *Huck's Raft: A History of American Childhood*. Cambridge,
    MA: Harvard University Press.
Nader, R. (1996) *Children First: A Parent's Guide to Fighting Corporate
    Predators*. Washington, DC: Corporate Accountability Research Group.
National Home Education Research Institute (<www.nheri.org>).

Pearce, J. (1992) *Evolution's End: Claiming the potential of our intelligence*. New York: HarperCollins.

Postman, N. (1982) *The Disappearance of Childhood*. New York: Delacorte Press.

Robbins, A. and Wilner, A. (2001) *Quarterlife Crisis: The Unique Challenges of Life in Your Twenties*. New York: Tarcher/Putnam.

Roberts, D. (2000) Media and youth: Access, exposure, and privatization, *Journal of Adolescent Health*, 27S.

Settersten, R. and Furstenberg, F. (2005) *On the Frontier of Adulthood: Theory, Research, and Public Policy*. Chicago: University of Chicago Press.

Strasburger, V. and Donnerstein, E. (1999) Children, adolescents, and the media: Issues and solutions, *Pediatrics* (January), 103.

Torgan, C. (2002) Childhood obesity on the rise, National Institutes of Health, *Word on health* <www.nih.gov/news/WordonHealth/jun2002/childhood-obesity.htm>.

Von Franz, M. L. (1970) *The Interpretation of Fairy Tales*. New York: Springer.

Woodard, E. (2000) *Media in the Home 2000*. University of Pennsylvania: Annenberg Public Policy Report.

Chapter 16

'Good' Science, Expectations, Villains, and Hope[1]

Thom Hartmann

Train up a child in the way he should go: and when he is old, he will not depart from it.

(Proverbs 22:6)

At a recent national conference on ADHD, one speaker suggested 'good science' argues that ADHD is entirely a pathological condition, a genetic illness, and that there is no value whatsoever in a person 'having ADHD'.

Anybody who may seek to offer hope to ADHD children or parents was accused of telling 'Just So stories'. The speaker suggested that ADHD is purely a genetic defect, the neo-Darwinist theory being that sometimes genetic problems are simply 'weaknesses in the evolution', and that 'qualities of ADHD place individuals at the lower tail of an adaptive bell curve'. If you have the 'defect' of ADHD you're doomed to struggle and most likely fail.

Let's say (as a 'Just So' story) that we identified 200 cars as they came off the assembly line, each having transmission gears made of an inferior metal. All the rest of the cars made that year had good gears, but these 200 are weak and marginally defective. Nonetheless, we let the car company sell them in the open marketplace, and get a list of all the people who bought them. Two, five, ten, and fifteen years later we do an outcome follow-up, contacting the cars' owners and asking them how things are. As you can predict, there would be a higher incidence of transmission failure among those cars than among the rest of the cars manufactured that year.

This is the predicating assumption of so-called 'outcome studies'. They assume that people are like cars – or any other inanimate object – and subject only to their own internal weakness or strengths.

But it's a fantasy.

Dozens of studies over the years – and common sense – have demonstrated the accuracy of Bandura's 1986 Social Cognition theory. That theory suggests that there is not just one thing (like a weakened brain or weak inhibition) that determines a person's outcomes as they go through life: there are at least three. They include the personal factors, such as intelligence and neurology; the influence of others, particularly in social, school, and family contexts; and the ability of self-reflection. This last – self-reflection – is perhaps the most important of all, because it determines the filter through which a child or adult views and experiences everything they see, hear, and feel in their lives. It creates a self-fulfilling feedback loop between the social and the biological factors, which will tend to amplify whatever self-belief is held.

Cars don't think and they don't interact socially: their outcome is purely a result of how well they're made, used, and maintained. They don't create internal expectations about themselves, and then try to prove the accuracy of those expectations by testing them against the world. They don't listen to what others tell them about who and what they are. If we told 200 cars with normal transmissions that they would have transmission failure soon, it wouldn't affect their performance: they're not listening.

But with people, such suggestions become a self-fulfilling loop. If I believe I'm not capable of asking Suzie to the school dance, I won't do it. Standing alone at the dance, I watch her with somebody else and the certainty of my belief is reinforced. I was right: there's the proof. So the next time I think of asking somebody out, I'm even more reluctant or frightened or certain that I'll fail. Everybody has experienced this in his or her life in one area or another (and no car ever has). As Henry Ford said, 'Whether you believe you can, or you believe you can't, you're absolutely right.'

So we take a group of children and tell them that they have a brain disorder, and we tell their parents that they're more likely to fail. We track down their teachers and tell them these children are genetically most likely to be the problem children in the classrooms. And then, lo and behold, they fail at a higher rate than 'normal' children. How astounding!

In fact, studies done on quite 'normal' children have demonstrated that children will almost always strive to meet the expectations of their parents, teachers, and peers . . . for better or for worse.

Imagine if we were to design a study where 200 perfectly normal children were told in early grade school that they had a brain disorder. They were informed that they were potential problems, with a higher-than-normal risk of drug abuse, behaviour problems, and school failure. Their teachers could see on their academic transcripts that they suffered from a disability. And their parents were informed that these children were facing a very difficult future. Additionally, to really bring the case home, the children are each given two to three sugar pills a day, although we tell them they're taking a psychoactive drug that will 'balance their brain'.

They took these pills, and carried this label of being defective, and saw a doctor monthly, for five or ten or twenty years. Careful records were kept of whenever they acted out or failed, and both parents and teachers were regularly questioned about such behaviours.

What do you think the outcome would be?

Of course, we'll never know . . . because to do such a study would be criminal. We'd be accused of child abuse, of warping the futures of a group of otherwise perfectly normal children. And the charges would be accurate.

Yet if this were something we'd be reluctant to do to our most resilient and 'normal' children, then why would we ever consider it a good idea to inflict on those we think may be most at risk?

In many ways, the debate that's shaping up around ADHD resembles the classic Victorian notion that all social problems are the result of a single cause: the villain. The Victorian 'villain story' was always told in four parts: a social problem is seen; a villain is identified as being responsible for the problem; the villain is rehabilitated; the social problem is solved.

But in today's world, the child whose learning style doesn't match the teaching style of our public schools has been identified as the villain.

Lower standards and expectations are set for him, proving to him the truth of his label. And over and over again he can't conform to the factory-like atmosphere of the school, demonstrating to him and everybody else that the label was correct in the first place.

I firmly believe – and all of my experience tells me – that it is time for us to set aside these stories of sickness and villainy. It's time for us to look at the structure and nature of our schools. It is time for us to tell the rogue elements within the research community who seek to absolutely and utterly stigmatize our children with the 'no hope, no value' label of ADHD that we are not interested in our children being the villains in their dramas any more.

It is time for us to give our children back their humanity and their hope.

ADHD: disorder or difference?[2]

The 'Hunter in a Farmer's World' metaphor was first used in the original 1993 version of *Attention Deficit Disorder: A Different Perception* (Hartmann, 1993) to characterize the life situations in which those with ADHD often found themselves.

Those who still portray ADHD/ADD as a disease now popularly use the metaphor to refer to subsequent Thom Hartmann books, many of which address the ongoing wounding of our children. *Attention Deficit Disorder: A Different Perception* has recently been called a 'Just So Story,' 'mind candy', and 'unreputable' by the editor and owner of a privately published subscription newsletter (Barkley, 2000a; Goldstein and Barkley, 1998). The editorialist's surprisingly harsh front-page commentary is in response to a book that was foremost a story told by a father Thom Hartmann (Hartmann, 1999) who wanted to find an alternative to what he considered an emotionally destructive story told to his son about the way his son's brain functioned! Although initially flattered by all the recent attention Dr Barkley has shown the earliest version of the Hunter/Farmer hypothesis, we find it tragic, self-serving, and blatantly unscientific that he would present it only in part, and that the part he'd choose was significantly misrepresented.

Attention Deficit Disorder: A Different Perception provided a more feasible (and substantially more accurate) reinterpretation of the widespread fable used by those who wish to depict ADHD persons as 'deficient' and 'disordered'. In subsequent Thom Hartmann books and articles, more attention was directed towards building the skills and self-esteem of ADHD children and adults. These efforts have been widely embraced by many, but aggressively opposed by those in the ADHD circuit who responded to our call to keep ADHD children's egos intact with, for example, Barkley's Marie Antoinette-like retort, 'If feeling good is the clinical goal, then why not just give them heroin?' (Barkley, 2000a) In contrast to such unfortunate and derisive rhetoric, the Hunter/Farmer hypothesis maintains that self-esteem is not a drug used to pacify but a sword that can be used to fight off the evils of despondency and self-hatred, and to provide hope for ADHD children.

The Hunter/Farmer hypothesis presumes that, irrelevant of where one is placed on the ADHD continuum, one not only has weakness to be compensated for, but also ADHD-related strengths that we must nurture. Contrarily, Barkley and those who consider ADHD to have no value whatsoever promote an absolute acceptance of the 'disorder' perspective and a total reliance on compensatory or defensive strategies, offering 'authoritative' advice about how to 'take charge' of such children (Barkley, 1995). Their disorder perspective assumes that there is one, single, superior (non-ADHD) way of behaving and being in the world, in all times and cultures, and that all other humans not so endowed are defective, lack creativity and have reduced intelligence.

Barkley's recommendation that ADHDers be authoritatively controlled and taught to avoid pursuing new opportunities for themselves (stimulation-seeking/risk-taking), however, is like telling an entrepreneur to quit looking for new market and business opportunities, an inventor to stop trying to see how things work (or how they could work better), or a hockey player to stop trying to score goals! Some ADHDers might be able to find contentment under the scourge of such defeatist (and possibly self-fulfilling) prophecies, but not without giving up many of their lives' hopes, aspirations, and goals along the way. The debate concerning whether ADHD is a disorder or a difference has considerable implications, not only for ADHD research, but also for those adults and children along the ADHD continuum who deserve more than a life spent only meeting the minimum threshold of their real potential.

Like the perpetually duelling Smothers Brothers, with their constant refrain of, 'Mom always liked you best', the world of ADHD research and speculation often seems to devolve into acrimony around whose theory is most or least supportable (or which brother is superior: the ADHD one or the over-focused one). Unfortunately, in this process one of the early casualities has been accuracy. Because of Barkley's newsletters' wide circulation, it seemed important to provide a rebuttal, and to correct at least a few of his mischaracterizations of the genesis, reasoning, and details of the Hunter/Farmer metaphor.

In two recent issues of his for-profit newsletter, Barkley has editorialized that the Hunter/Farmer metaphor was 'laughable' and 'inconsistent with evolutionary theory' since, according to his (mis)interpretation of the Hunter/Farmer metaphor, he says it states that hunters have evolved into farmers rapidly over the past 10,000 years since the agricultural revolution. We are, however, more apt to agree with those who state that, biologically, humanity has evolved very little since our hunting and gathering days (Pinker, 1997), or that existing differences between populations are likely due either to founders' effects (genetic differences among founding families, many of whom were immigrants) or to the differential 'pruning' effects of nature, pestilence, culture, and rivalry (Nesse and Williams, 1995).

We have always suggested that the 'Hunter gene' and the 'Farmer gene' have been with us since the earliest dawn of the human race: neither 'evolved' from the other (indeed, this spectrum of behavior is seen within species across the animal kingdom, from dogs and cats to chimps and the great apes). There has always been a need, in all societies, for the 'adventurous explorer' and for the 'careful bookkeeper', whether it be hunting and then skinning animals, or planting crops and entertaining the planters. The core of the hunter/farmer hypothesis, in short form, is that in hunting/gathering societies those persons with the 'hunting gene' are rewarded and have an increased probability of procreation, and among agricultural and post-agricultural/industrial societies (such as today) the 'farming gene' is celebrated and increases the social and procreative advancement of farmers.

All theories on human development, regardless of content, fall into two categories: those, such as the Hunter/Farmer hypothesis, that take the difference perspective and those, such as the executive functions model, that take the disorder perspective. The perspective one decides to incorporate into one's model or hypothesis has enormous implications concerning how one treats individuals and how one interprets their behaviour.

For example, no one will argue that hunters do not exhibit extreme difficulty in reciting nonsense syllables in correct sequence, or that they do not have poor rote memories. The disorder perspective attempts to 'cure' such deviancy by encouraging (or forcing) ADHD children to work harder on sequence and rote.

Alternatively, the difference perspective assumes that different people may need to utilize different techniques to achieve the same goals. The difference perspective presumes that there are different ways of remembering, and different ways of processing and organizing input. As an example, researchers indicate that, in contrast to the excellent rote memories possessed by Farmers, intelligent Hunters not only boast, but are also able to take advantage of their 'superior' incidental memories (Ceci and Tishman, 1984; Shaw and Brown, 1991). In other words, since Hunters are predisposed to scan their environments, they are more apt to record and then later utilize background information. Conversely, Farmers are more likely to think in terms of an object devoid of context.

The limit in scope of the disorder perspective is both its major asset and its greatest liability. It's easily grasped and propagates readily because it neatly compartmentalizes a complex range of variables, and appeals to the latent moralist in our culture and in each of us.

On the other hand, it ignores the fact that both people and environments are complex and variable, largely disregards the effects of context on performance, and overlooks evidence that human weaknesses in one environment often turn out to be powerful or even vital and adaptive assets in another (Ceci, 1996; Hartmann, 2000; Nesse and Williams, 1995; Shaw and Brown, 1991). For example, rather than questioning the desirability of the 'brick' factory-style school house with it's large class sizes and homogeneous instruction methods, the disorder perspective places blame for failure squarely on to the child (Reid *et al.*, 1993). Not surprisingly, the disorder perspective sees adaptation and disorder as two distinct categories, rather than two aspects of a single phenomenon (Barkley, 2000a).

What is an adaptation and is ADHD one?

An adaptation, according to Barkley, is something that appears in hindsight to have been 'designed for some purpose' or to solve 'particular problems'. The human thumb is commonly considered such an adaptation, although the real adaptation may be the human creativity that allowed us to find a use or two for this oddly positioned finger. Other inventions, such as handcuffs or the inside of jars, could be used to 'prove' that the thumb may also be maladaptive in certain circumstances. Which view of the human thumb is right? Probably all three. The thumb debate is but a small example of the importance of avoiding absolute statements in an evolutionary context. Likewise, Barkley has described the type of absentmindedness often experienced by persons with ADD/ADHD as proof of a mental 'deficit', whereas other scientists view it as one of the 'side consequences of a generally adaptive architecture that sometimes gets us into trouble' (Schacter, 1999). As you can see, a disorder may not be the opposite of an adaptation, but its complement.

The topics of evolution and adaptation were also explored extensively by Pinker (1997) in a book that can best be described as an intelligent elaboration of Dawkin's selfish gene theory. Nonetheless,

Barkley's use of Pinker's work to discredit adaptation in the Hunter/Farmer hypothesis is inappropriate since Pinker indicates that at least one cornerstone of the Executive Functions model, delay of gratification, may be maladaptive. Pinker proposes that not only is going for the quick reward more adaptive, but that risk-taking, another common hallmark of ADHD, is also more adaptive in the long run. In other words, defining disorder and adaptation as absolute opposites is a fallacy that's not supported by most evolutionary theorists and researchers.

In 1997 when Barkley first presented a variation on Strang and Rourke's 1983 Executive Functions model to explain ADHD, he chose to incorporate into his model the existing body of literature of brain function, and to emphasize the similarity between symptoms of pseudopsychopathy (right frontal lobe damage) and ADHD. The right-frontal-lobe brain damaged individual has been shown to experience increases in motor activity, talkativeness, and a lack of tact and restraint (Kolb and Whishaw, 1990), symptoms commonly associated with ADHD. Animals with frontal-lobe damage cannot adapt to new situations or environments, while humans with such lesions similarly experience extreme difficulties in situations requiring problem solving and unique solutions. Because he assumes ADHD to be synonymous with this type of brain damage, Barkley (1997) concluded, rather incorrectly, that persons with ADHD are also less capable of creative thought, and stated this hypothesis concerning ADHD and creativity explicitly in several of his writings.

If brain damage research had been used to build the Hunter/Farmer hypothesis, *Attention Deficit Disorder: A Different Perception* might have explored the difficulties associated with being a right-frontal-lobe-damaged individual in a world taken over by people with left-frontal-lobe-damage. Described in non-disorder (difference) terms, left-frontal-lobe-damaged 'farmers' could be seen as objective (rather than indifferent), exerting emotional self-control (rather than showing little overt emotion), able to show enough self-regulation to remain silent (rather than showing little or no verbal output), and speaking only when spoken to (rather than failure to initiate conversations). However, this silly analogy was never used in *Attention Deficit Disorder: A Different Perception* or any subsequent Thom Hartmann book or article for that matter, because Hunters are not right-frontal-lobe brain-damaged persons, and Farmers are not left-frontal-lobe brain-damaged persons: each are, instead, two end-points on a continuum of human variability.

To understand the role of brain pathology research in validating the Executive Functions model, we need first to determine what the Executive Functions model would look like without reference to brain damage. The Executive Functions model would still compare the more liberal and flamboyant ADHDers unfavourably to the more conservative and restrained 'statistical norm'. Americas 'brick' factory-like schoolhouses would still be seen as the epitome of human civilization and accomplishment. And, like Phillip Rushton (Di Cresce, 2000), the Executive Functions model would still see a negative correlation between IQ and promiscuity. In summary, we would still have an ethnocentric (almost Aryan) commentary of genetic endowment differences.

Without these highly questionable (and, in the opinion of these authors, outright flawed) ideological underpinnings, however, what remains of the Executive Functions model is simply a theory of individual variation. The Executive Functions model tends to focus on post-base-line variation in human response to environmental stimulation while ignoring important differences in how such stimulation may initially be experienced by the individual. We agree that after controlling for base-line differences between Hunters and Farmers, there may be important executive function differences among Hunters and among Farmers. Additionally, these 'executive function' differences may turn out to be one among the many variables that help determine whether ADHD will produce an entrepreneurial success or a chronic criminal.

As the Hunter/Farmer hypothesis predicts, there are base-line differences in the ways individual Hunters and Farmers each experience and cope with depression, boredom, frustration, and joy. However, these base-line differences do not fully explain why one Hunter (or Farmer for that matter) may or may not experience depression at a dysfunctional level. Instead, the Hunter/Farmer hypothesis suggests that it's the driving need or hunger for aliveness which animates most ADHD/ADD behaviours, and executive function is only a small (but significant) variable that determines how this need or hunger is satisfied (through socially adaptive means, such as a high-stimulation job in an emergency room, or socially maladaptive means like becoming a bar-room brawler).

Seen in this light, Barkley's so-called executive system may be nothing more than a fight-or-flight response mechanism, acting like a rubber band that exerts its influence at both ends of the ADHD continuum. Evidence which indicates that having a 'happy temperament' as an infant is associated with improved prognosis for Hunters while some environmental factors, such as having experienced abuse, are associated with negative life chances (Grizenko and Pawliuk,1994), lends support to the prospect that the Executive Function model is a theory of within-Hunter variation rather than of Hunter/Farmer differences. To recapitulate, if one were to divide the population into groups based on individual differences in tolerance of (or desire for) novelty, the individuals in each group would still vary in both their tolerance of and their exposure to adversity or stress. Theoretically, those in each group whose threshold for stress has been exceeded may exhibit many of the cognitive difficulties associated with the so-called executive functions.

Researching ADHD adaptation and self-esteem

The myopic nature of the disorder perspective leads to narrow and incomplete answers. Previously, disorder perspective researchers seemed to believe that everything we needed to know about ADHD we could gain through a better understanding of the workings of methylphenidate. Now, Barkley (2000a) writes that we should only ask the purpose of the Executive Function system rather than consider whether there are also adaptive functions associated with ADHD-like behaviours. Although knowing a little bit more concerning methylphenidate, such as its effects during pregnancy, or concerning the function of executive control processes may provide some benefit, neither is an adequate replacement for a better understanding of humanity and its complexity throughout the ADHD continuum.

Some self-proclaimed empiricists appear to have difficulty with what they consider murky constructs, such as self-esteem, which are associated with subjective emotions. In contrast to the so-called ambiguousness of self-esteem, these 'empiricists' appear more comfortable with the presumably more precise language used in the DSM-IV definition of ADHD, such as 'often', 'excessively', and 'extraneous'. Other researchers, however, are less predisposed to automatically dismiss clinical observations and case studies, and more apt to report trends and to design research studies so as to settle theoretical disagreements and uncover a wider range of truths. It is to these other researchers that we will now turn.

According to longitudinal ADHD research, a positive self-esteem is associated with resiliency, autonomy, and a sense of humour

(Hechtman, 1991), all factors that are known to boost the immune system and improve one's general physical well-being in a wide range of studies. Conversely, low self-esteem is associated with the feelings of helplessness stemming from a belief that personal failure is due to unchangeable factors such as inherent inability or inferior intellect (Brooks, 1994).

Considering these associations between self-esteem and how one's life turns out, one should not be surprised that, when asked, many ADHD individuals indicate that what was most helpful to them while growing up was having an adult who believed in them (Hechtman, 1991), or that ADHD children who have a good relationship with their grandparents fare better (Grizenko and Pawliuk,1994). Whether they be parents, teachers, or clinicians, adults wield a great deal of influence over the self-concepts and performance of those children with whom they are entrusted. Often the single most significant variable in a child's life that will determine his or her success was the presence of an adult who believed in and supported the child.

Rosenthal and Jacobson were the first to show that experimental manipulation of teacher expectations may influence student outcome. The researchers informed teachers that the performance of randomly picked students was going to improve dramatically. These 'spurter' effects were more pronounced in first and second graders and in students of whom teachers traditionally held lower expectations, such as minority students (Boocock, 1980). The question left unanswered by Rosenthal and Jacobson's research is how specifically teacher expectation led to changes in student grades.

Elementary school teacher Jane Elliot proposed that a teacher's expectations influence student performance through their influence on teacher behaviour. She dramatically illustrated the power of self-concept by using eye colour differences to explain the concept of discrimination to her students. She found that her students actually performed better at their assignments on the day when their eye colour was deemed superior and worse on the day when their eye colour was considered inferior (Boocock, 1980).

Researchers Becker, Place, Tenzer and Frueh (1991) also found an association between teacher's impressions of and behaviour towards various students when they exposed teachers to one of three taped conversations between a female librarian and a young girl. The second and third tapes were identical to the control tape, except that in one tape the child interrupted the adult, and in the other the child engaged in three acts of tangency. For example, when the librarian suggested

French food as a possible topic, the girl in the tangency condition started talking about how she lost her tooth after biting into an apple.

As expected, teachers' perceptions of both student ability and the likeliness that the student would receive their help were lower in both the interruption and tangency condition than in the control condition. Not surprisingly, teachers described the child in the interruption condition as a 'poor listener', and the same child in the tangency condition as having 'poor attention' or being a 'dumb blond'. More needs to be known concerning the effects of these attitudes on teacher and student performance.

A more detailed look into the impact of self-esteem on both hunters and farmers may also benefit greatly from the body of research on priming and relational schemas (scripts).

Priming is a scientific term denoting any experimental or naturally occurring manipulation which makes some memories or information more readily accessible than other information (Baldwin, 1992). A priming stimulus can be anything – a word, a picture, an instruction, a facial expression, or even an emotion. For example, what Weiss (1992) refers to as 'flooding' and what Hallowell and Ratey (1994) refer to as 'hyperfocusing on the negative' may just be the effects of priming combined with the interconnection of emotion and memory retrieval. Since ADHD questionnaires tend to focus on the negative aspects of ADHD, it is possible that the act of filling these questionnaires out immediately prior to task performance can call forth (prime) negative memories and emotions in ADHD participants that may influence task performance. The potential for priming to bias research results has not previously been explored in ADHD research. The failure of ADHD researchers to reduce the occurrence of this type of bias when designing studies is one of the ways in which many of the existing studies of ADHD and its outcomes are potentially flawed and altogether at odds with accepted scientific models.

In summary, we find the work of those who attempt to position ADD/ADHD entirely as a pathology, 'a failure of evolution', or a character trait of 'no value whatsoever', to be more rooted in thinly veiled pseudo-morality and eugenics than in science. Vast bodies of literature – as well as common sense and the positive personal experiences of millions with ADHD – are conveniently ignored, overlooked, or dismissed. In Barkley's words, we find contempt and a reductionist, mechanistic world-view that allows only for pathology and non-pathology.

By obsessively focusing on negatives and refusing to acknowledge any evidence of value in ADHD, anywhere, anytime, under any circumstances, the increasingly small circle of 'pure pathology' advocates are bringing only pain, power-based relationships (between parents told to 'take charge' of their ADHD children, as well as between professionals and their clients), and the most massive labelling, segregation, and ostracizing seen in our public schools since the early days of 'separate but equal' education among the races.

There are those who are more concerned about the appearance of being a 'good' parent or 'good' teacher who may take comfort in the pronouncement that their children were 'born with this problem' and that 'you should neither assign blame to yourself nor accept it from others' (Barkley, 1995). Such fatalistic pronouncements serve only to release parents, teachers and researchers from their responsibility and guilt concerning their children's failures (Reid *et al.*, 1993). The wounding wreaked on millions of children by their being told they are brain-deficient and have a mental disorder, however, is largely ignored by the pathology proponents, as is the agony endured by other parents who read in Barkley's newsletter that their children's condition, 'rather than representing an adapted evolved set of valuable qualities, reflects weaknesses in the evolution'.

It is time we set aside this one-dimensional 'villain story', which focuses solely on 'the burden of ADHD to affected individuals, to their families, and to society' (Barkley, 2000b), and on how ADHD is a 'deficiency in functioning' which makes one 'less capable' (Barkley, 2000a). Science doesn't support the absolute pathology model, common sense doesn't support it, and certainly any sincere hope for therapeutic outcomes and healthy children doesn't support it. It's time to stop the wounding, the finger pointing, and the critical, condescending tone used to refer to and address those with ADHD and their advocates. It's time to walk away from the doomsayers and look to the light of a new day and world where all children are valued for their unique gifts.

Notes

1. Reprinted with permission and thanks from http://www.thomhartmann.com/outcome.shtml
2. Reprinted with permission and thanks from http://www.thomhartmann.com/disorder_or_difference.shtml, written with VaudreeLavallee.

References

Baldwin, M. (1992) Relational schemas and the processing of social information, *Psychological Bulletin*, 112, 461–84.

Barkley, R. (1995) *Taking Charge of ADHD: The Complete Authoritative Guide for Parents. Become an Empowered Parent – A World-Renowned Expert Tells You How to Help Your Child and Yourself!* New York: Guilford Press.

Barkley, R. (1997) Behavioral inhibition, sustained attention, and executive functions: Constructing a unifying theory of ADHD, *Psychological Bulletin*, 121, 65–94.

Barkley, R. (2000a) More on evolution, hunting, and ADHD., *The ADHD Report*, 8(2), 1–7.

Barkley, R. (2000b) Genetics of childhood disorders: XVII. ADHD, part 1: The executive functions and ADHD, *Journal of the American Academy of Child and Adolescent Psychiatry*, 39, 477–84.

Becker, J. A., Place, K. S., Tenzer S. and Frueh, C. (1991) Teachers' impressions of children varying in pragmatic skills, *Journal of Applied Developmental Psychology*, 12, 397–412.

Boocock, S. (1980) *Sociology of Education: An Introduction, Second Edition.* New York: University Press of America.

Brooks, R. (1994) Children at risk: Fostering resilience and hope, *American Journal of Orthopsychiatry*, 64, 545–53.

Ceci, S. (1996) *On Intelligence: A Bioecological Treatise on Intellectual Development.* Cambridge, MA: Harvard University Press.

Ceci, S. and Tishman, J. (1984) Hyperactivity and incidental memory: evidence for attentional diffusion, *Child Development*, 55, 2192–203.

Di Cresce, G. (2000) Rushton's racial link to IQ rapped – Prof. dismissed as crank, *The Winnipeg Sun* (3 February), p. 4.

Goldstein, S. and Barkley, R. (1998) ADHD, hunting, and evolution: 'just so' stories, *The ADHD Report*, 6(5), 1–4.

Grizenko, N. and Pawliuk, N. (1994) Risk and protective factors for disruptive behavior disorders in children, *American Journal of Orthopsychiatry*, 64, 534–40.

Hallowell, E. and Ratey, J. (1994) *Driven to Distraction: Recognizing and Coping with Attention Deficit Disorder from Childhood through Adulthood.* New York: Pantheon Books.

Hartmann, T. (1993) *Attention Deficit Disorder: A Different Perception.* Nevada City, CA: Underwood Books.

Hartmann, T. (1999) Whose disorder is disordered by ADHD, *Tikkun*, July/August, 17–21.

Hartmann, T. (2000) *Thom Hartmann's Complete Guide to ADHD.* Nevada City, CA: Underwood Books.

Hechtman, L. (1991) Resilience and vulnerability in long term outcome of attention deficit disorder, *Canadian Journal of Psychiatry*, 36, 415–21.

Kolb, B. and Whishaw, I. (1990) The frontal lobes, in *Fundamentals of Human Neuropsychology*, 3rd edn. New York: W. H. Freeman.

Nesse, R. and Williams, G. (1995) *Why We Get Sick: The New Science of Darwinian Medicine*. New York: Vintage Books.

Pinker, S. (1997) *How the Mind Works*. New York: Norton.

Reid, R., Maag, J. and Vasa, S. (1993) Attention deficit disorder as a disability category: A critique, *Exceptional Children*, 60, 198–214.

Schacter, D. (1999) The seven sins of memory – Insights from psychology and cognitive neuroscience, *American Psychologist*, 54, 182–203.

Shaw, G. and Brown, G. (1991) Laterality, implicite memory and attention disorder, *Educational Studies*, 17, 15–23.

Weiss, L. (1992) *Attention Deficit Disorder in Adults – Practical Help for Sufferers and their Spouses*. Dallas: Taylor Publishing Company.

Index

Printed and bound by CPI Group (UK) Ltd, Croydon, CR0 4YY